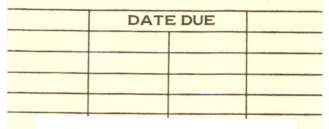

	DATE DUE		

DEFY THE DARKNESS

A TALE of COURAGE
in the SHADOW of MENGELE

JOE ROSENBLUM
WITH DAVID KOHN

Foreword by David A. Hackett

PRAEGER

Westport, Connecticut
London

Library of Congress Cataloging-in-Publication Data

Rosenblum, Joe, 1925–
    Defy the darkness : a tale of courage in the shadow of Mengele / Joe Rosenblum with
David Kohn ; foreword by David A. Hackett.
        p.   cm.
    Includes bibliographical references (p.   ) and index.
    ISBN 0–275–96862–6 (alk. paper)
    1. Rosenblum, Joe, 1925–   2. Jews—Persecutions—Poland—Miñdzyrzec Podlaski.   3.
Holocaust, Jewish (1939–1945)—Poland—Miñdzyrzec Podlaski—Personal narratives.   4.
Mengele, Josef, 1911–   5. Jews—Poland—Miñdzyrzec Podlaski—Biography.   6. Miñdzyrzec
Podlaski (Poland)—Biography.   I. Kohn, David, 1944–   II. Title.
DS135.P63 R66987   2001
940.54'05'092—dc21
[B]   00–027734

British Library Cataloguing in Publication Data is available.

Library of Congress Catalog Card Number: 00–027734
ISBN: 0–275–96862–6

First published in 2001

Praeger Publishers, 88 Post Road West, Westport, CT 06881
An imprint of Greenwood Publishing Group, Inc.
www.praeger.com

Printed in the United States of America

The paper used in this book complies with the
Permanent Paper Standard issued by the National
Information Standards Organization (Z39.48–1984).

10 9 8 7 6 5 4 3 2

Contents

Foreword

As a historian, I have read and heard many stories by survivors of the Holocaust, but Joe Rosenblum's memoir, *Defy the Darkness: A Tale of Courage in the Shadow of Mengele*, stands out as one of the most remarkable. It is not only a convincingly portrayed history of the time, but it is also a gripping story, filled with suspense and numerous brushes with death. Thanks to Joe Rosenblum's own strength of character, his sharp memory and eye for detail, and the writing skills of his co-author, David Kohn, we have a book that captures this terrible time of suffering for the Jews of Europe in a dramatic historical and personal narrative. It is a book that most readers will scarcely be able to put down once they have begun.

The author was a boy of only 14 when German troops invaded Poland in September 1939. His native city, Miedzyrzec, was located in eastern Poland, near what would soon become the Soviet border. It was a town of 16,000 people, a thriving commercial center, with a population that was 75 percent Jewish. He was born Icek, the oldest son and one of six children of Samuel and Mindl Rosenblum. (When he came to America after the war, he changed his given name to Joe.) Somehow young Joe managed to survive three and a half years under the grimmest possible conditions in the crowded Jewish ghetto created in Miedzyrzec by German occupation forces. Then he survived two more years in the terrible Nazi concentration camps of Majdanek, Auschwitz-Birkenau, and

Dachau, before making a final death march with prisoners from Dachau. He was liberated by U.S. forces on May 1, 1945.

Despite the loss of most of his family, it is clear from the text that Joe Rosenblum is not a bitter man. His innate optimism and faith in humanity seems to have not only survived the Holocaust, but also to have been strengthened by the suffering he went through between 1939 and 1945. He remains grateful for the help given him by a Polish Gentile family, the Zbanskis, who hid him on their farm for three summers in the early part of the war. He learned that even the cruelest prisoner *Kapos* and Nazi camp officers still had a human side that could be appealed to in a way that would enhance his chances of survival. In more than one case, his conduct toward others would make the critical difference between life and death.

Rosenblum's story clearly counters one of the persistent stereotypes about the Holocaust—the lack of resistance of Jewish victims, who are sometimes characterized as walking toward their deaths in the gas chambers like sheep to the slaughter. While there is some truth to that image, particularly in regard to the final stages of the process of mechanized killing in mass extermination camps like Auschwitz, the stereotype distorts what is really a far more complex story. The author's account shows us that there was much resistance in many different forms, at least where there was still hope for a favorable outcome. During the period of the ghetto in Miedzyrzec, young Joe smuggled himself in and out of the fenced perimeter to bring food to his family and tore wooden planks out of abandoned factories at night for firewood. One of the more dramatic incidents in his story is the surprise raid on the headquarters of the hated Jewish police in Miedzyrzec, conducted by armed men from the Warsaw Jewish underground shortly before the Ghetto Uprising. For several months, the author joined a band of Russian partisans hiding in the forest and participated in raids they conducted on Polish police stations. Later he risked his life as a member of the corpse-carrying detail (*Leichenkommando*), smuggling messages to far-flung parts of the camp for the Auschwitz underground, and assisted in what eventually became the revolt of the *Sonderkommando* that led to a mass escape and the destruction of Crematorium III at Birkenau (October 7, 1944). Though he was sleeping in another part of the camp at the time, he heard and felt the blast when the crematorium was blown up and he saw the SS guards running toward the section where the revolt occurred.

But how did the author manage to stay alive against such formidable odds, the reader may ask? There are probably a number of factors that help to explain his survival, but nearly every survivor of the Holocaust speaks of "luck" as the primary factor. Perhaps there is an element of "survivor's guilt" in the designation of luck or chance as a factor—the feeling of "why me?" that the individual who is still alive has when so many friends and family members are dead. At times chance had a pure randomness to it, such as being in one place and not another when a roundup or a mass killing took place, or being late or early when some such action was about to take place. On one occasion, Joe was smuggling food to the lumberyard where his brother worked, only to witness German guards in the act of killing 37 boys, including his brother, with machine guns. Another such incident in his life was the discovery of a fifty-dollar bill in a trash bin at Auschwitz that he was able to trade for food and assignment to a better work detail.

But, at other times, I believe that incidents attributed to "luck" were more likely manifestations of elements deeply rooted in personal character. At stake is the distinctive ability that some individuals have to break through interpersonal barriers and relate to strangers, even enemies, in a way that gives them an interest in that person's survival. I am convinced from reading the manuscript that Joe Rosenblum is one of those unique individuals who can reach out and relate to others in that distinctive way. That special skill may help to explain some of the more unusual incidents in his story.

Perhaps the most astonishing incident in this book is the occasion where the author's life is saved through surgery performed by Dr. Josef Mengele, the Nazi camp doctor at Auschwitz, who was dubbed by many survivors as the "Angel of Death." Mengele later became infamous as the doctor who pointed left and right with his baton as newly arriving prisoners at Auschwitz were selected for extermination. (He was also the doctor who conducted cruel medical experiments on dwarfs and twins in the highly secret Block 10 in the main Auschwitz camp, which Rosenblum never saw.) But is it possible that he could be the doctor who saved the life of an ordinary Jewish prisoner with a potentially fatal infection? I think under the special circumstances described above, the answer is definitely yes. Robert Jay Lifton, author of the book *The Nazi Doctors*, argues that many of these Nazi medical men had a bifurcated personality that allowed them to be coldly unemotional in their professional duties in the concentration camps, but able to retain seemingly normal personal lives, outside and alongside their official functions. I know from my own research that some of the camp doctors at Buchenwald, particularly Dr. Erwin Ding-Schuler and Dr. Waldemar Hoven, developed close personal relationships with prisoner *Kapos* and hospital personnel which led to saving the lives of a few individual prisoners. At the same time, they continued to coldly perform their professional functions in a mechanical way, leading to the deaths of many thousands of other prisoners. Although I know less about Dr. Mengele, I think it is quite likely that he was capable of acting in a similar fashion, one that resulted in saving the life of the author of this book.

Rosenblum quickly learned at Auschwitz that there were several keys to survival in a concentration camp. One of them was to maintain his personal appearance, despite the considerable difficulties of doing so under the circumstances. It meant hunting for discarded razor blades and scraps of soap, washing himself daily in ice-cold water, and securing better clothing and shoes when the opportunity presented itself. Rosenblum wrote that if you kept yourself clean, you looked better and you improved your chances of being assigned to a better work detail. It was also a matter of expressing and maintaining a sense of hope. Those prisoners who lost all hope, who lost all interest in their appearance, were called by the other prisoners "Muslims" (*Muselmänner*). They were the ones who were marked for death in one form or another, as their fellow prisoners could tell from the blank looks of despair in their faces.

Another key to survival for concentration camp prisoners was to develop close personal ties with other prisoners, though this, too, was difficult under the watchful eyes of SS guards and prisoner foremen. In his book *The Survivors*, Terrence des Pres has convincingly shown that the social environment of the concentration camp was not based solely on the "law of the jungle," man against man, but it was one where relationships with others were vital to survival. For Joe, still a young man in his teens, it meant finding mentors whose help could be enlisted to improve his chances of survival. First he encountered Max, an influential prisoner who befriended him and eventually brought him into contact with the camp's underground resistance. Later, he met a prisoner doctor who worked in Mengele's clinic, a man whom many of the prisoners appropriately knew simply by the name of "Father." Friendships with other prisoners such as Hymie and Nuftul, though often cut short by tragedy, helped men like the author survive the hardest of times. At other times, Joe was a mentor himself, as for example with a younger man named Hana, whose life he saved in Auschwitz, and whom he encountered again in a subcamp near Munich at the end of the war. Everywhere he eagerly sought out his *landsmen*, compatriots from his hometown and region, hoping for bits of news about friends and relatives.

A third key to survival was the ability to maintain hope in the face of the constant threat of death and the dehumanizing conditions of the concentration camp. In one of the earliest and most famous accounts by a concentration camp survivor, *Man's Search for Meaning* by the Viennese psychiatrist Victor E. Frankl, the author argues that only those prisoners who had a sense of hope, who had something to live for, were able to survive. He wrote: "The prisoner who had lost faith in the future—his future—was doomed." Frankl developed a complex theory called "logotherapy" to explain it, by which he meant faith in a religious or philosophical system of beliefs. For Joe Rosenblum, the answer was much simpler: hope was maintained by his own personal dream. Often he dreamed that, like his successful uncle Yudel, after the war he would own his own business, with people working for him. "I will have a bristle factory, a home, a wife and children, a truck," he wrote. It was this simple but recurring dream that allowed him to maintain a sense of hope, a vision of his own personal future, when many others around him fell into despair.

Finally, it took personal courage to survive, to endure the frequent hardships and beatings. Rosenblum showed that courage time and again, when he smuggled himself in and out of the ghetto on his visits to the Zbanski farm, and when he escaped to the forest to join the Russian partisans. After arriving at Majdanek concentration camp, he had to fight off a gang of prisoners who were trying to steal the potato peelings he was smuggling back to share with the men of his barracks. At Auschwitz, he eventually joined the underground movement, knowing well the risks it involved. It also took tremendous physical courage to undergo an operation to remove his severely infected tonsils, performed by a prisoner doctor using a sharpened butter knife, without the aid of anesthetics.

But as Terrence des Pres reminds us in *The Survivor*, physical courage and acts of resistance are not the only forms of resistance, especially in the concentration camps. Survival itself was an act of resistance, when seen in the context of a system designed to produce death as its outcome. To defy death, by whatever means possible, was at the same time to defy the enemy. To keep one's morale high, to exhibit hope, when the system was designed to crush that hope, was to resist morally, if not physically. The author and thousands of others like him did both of those things. For their courage in facing these extreme situations, the survivors of the Holocaust deserve the admiration of us who live in more comfortable times.

By emphasizing hope and courage in analyzing the Holocaust, there is the danger, as noted scholar Lawrence Langer warns, of trivializing and misinterpreting the nature of the event. There was of course the enormous dark side of the Holocaust that far outweighed the relatively few points of light that helped maintain a sense of optimism. Rosenblum's account speaks eloquently of the extremes of hunger and cold which attacked the body at its most elemental level. His all-consuming hunger forced him to eat moldy food, garbage, bark, even worms, insects, and live frogs. For most of us, such hunger is almost inconceivable, but not meeting the most basic needs of the body also meant certain death. And then there was the cold—the freezing winds that blew through the undernourished and thinly clad prisoners forced to work all day in subfreezing temperatures. The winter of 1944–45 was one of the coldest in decades. By then, Rosenblum was in a work detail clearing bomb damage in the Munich railyards. But as anyone who has visited the Bavarian capital in the winter knows, the wind blowing from the Alps is bone-chilling, even for one wearing a thick parka.

Most important of all, the reader must remember that an entire world, the world Joe Rosenblum knew as a boy, was destroyed by World War II and the Holocaust. His family was gone—father, mother, sisters, brothers, uncles, aunts, and numerous cousins. His native city of Miedzyrzec would never be the same again. Its houses and buildings were destroyed, as was nearly all of its Jewish population. A city that once had an imposing stone synagogue, built around 1800 to hold 3,000 worshipers, had almost no Jews at all after the war. Miedzyrzec suffered the same fate as the Lithuanian town pictured in the Tower of

Life exhibit at the U.S. Holocaust Memorial Museum—an entire community had been annihilated.

Miedzyrzec, although not as well known as some sites of the Holocaust, developed a certain notoriety in World War II. It became one of the Nazi ghettos that served as collecting points for Jews from various parts of Europe, before they were finally rounded up and transported to extermination camps. The town figures prominently in Christopher Browning's *Ordinary Men: Police Battalion 101 and the Final Solution in Poland*, because that unit was stationed in the area in 1942 and 1943. A half-dozen photographs in the book depict the deportation of the Jewish population of Miedzyrzec, possibly including images of the very transport Joe Rosenblum was on. There were no less than seven deportation actions conducted with great brutality between September 1942 and July 1943, ending in the total liquidation of the Jewish population of the town. According to Browning, the German soldiers stationed there, finding it difficult to pronounce the town's Polish name, called it *Menschenschreck*, or "human horror." Daniel Goldhagen's *Hitler's Willing Executioners* also discusses, somewhat more briefly, the role of Police Battalion 101's activities as part of the final solution in Miedzyrzec.

Joe Rosenblum visited his hometown briefly in the summer of 1945 only to find that virtually none of his friends and relatives had survived. He returned to Munich determined to find a way to make his future in the United States, where he had an uncle in Detroit. Once in America, he started life over again as a house painter, eventually running his own successful contracting company. Here the dreams he held onto in the dark days of the concentration camp were gradually realized.

In reading Joe Rosenblum's book, we encounter once again the human face of the Holocaust that lies behind the almost incomprehensible statistic of six million Jews killed, along with millions of other victims. Perhaps as we read the plain prose of an ordinary man, we realize that, like all survivors, Joe was not so "ordinary" after all. It took tremendous character and strength of will to survive the darkness intact, to retain a sense of faith in humanity and hope for the future. This remarkable book captures that spirit, and the act of writing it is perhaps Joe Rosenblum's greatest legacy to our generation. At a time when the number of suvivors is rapidly dwindling, it is vital that we record and collect their experiences. We are all in his debt for once again drawing upon that faith and courage—this time to tell us his story.

—David A. Hackett

Acknowledgments

Although writing is a solitary art, writers do not produce a book alone. We are no exception. We have many people who have helped us along the way. Our friend, Mark Schwartz, gave us encouragement and support throughout the project. Our agents, Brenda Feigen and Joanne Parrent, were there to help us negotiate the winding roads of the publishing world. Our editor, Heather Staines, was most helpful with her comments, her wise words, and her insights. Dr. David Hackett was far more thorough and insightful than we ever expected.

We also want to say thanks to the people who have been part of our lives: We want to express our indebtedness to the memories of Joe's parents, brothers, sisters and other relatives, who were lost to the ravages of the Holocaust. Among the living, we especially want to thank the Zbanski family, whose towering courage in concealing Joe's identity allowed his family to live for several more years and permitted him to survive. We also thank Kazamiera and Stanislaw Kukuryka and the other Zbanski descendants for their unfailing love and hospitality.

We would be remiss if we did not thank our wives, Mary Sue Donohue and Elke Rosenblum, for enduring with a smile the loss of hundreds of hours of companionship as we toiled on this book.

In addition, Joe and David would like to thank each other for being there throughout the long, painful times, and for each other's unflinching desire to

_____

make the writing of Joe's life during the German years produce a book in which we both can take pride.

Finally, we want to express our admiration of and tears for the millions of souls of many nationalities and ethnicities whose lives were cruelly ripped from them during this dark hour of history.

PUBLISHER'S NOTE

At the author's request, he is referred to as *Joe* throughout the book. His given name was *Icek*, but he americanized his name to *Joe*. He now thinks of himself as Joe, and that's how his name is presented in the story.

PART I

THE SHADOWS SPREAD

Chapter 1

Mother's Trees Stand Naked

My mother's fruit trees told us the life we knew was crumbling. For three weeks in September 1939, my mother and I stood for hours on a hilltop overlooking her miles of orchards: apples, plums, pears, and many other fruits, a green blanket with riotous reds, purples, and yellows stitched in.

My mother and I, along with my brothers and sisters, stood and watched swarms of desperate arms strip the trees of their fruit—and with them, our newly won comforts and our hope. We could see the fruit being smashed, carried away, or consumed. Eventually, most of my family would suffer the same fate.

At first, just a few people appeared in bunches of twos and threes. They pulled down the branches with grasping hands or shook the limbs, and bushels of fruit fell to the ground. Then they carried away the fruit in bags, in their clothes, or in anything else they could find.

Soon the refugees came in clusters of ten and twenty. Then hundreds. We could see the tree branches become increasingly bare, splotched with zigzag white spots. We could see where branches were broken and bent, while the people scrambled like a ragged ant army over the barbed wire. We could see their faces, white and frantic.

They didn't stay long. If the branches were low enough, the people would just bend a few and pull off the fruit while their hands shook and trembled. They kept their suitcases and bags of belongings close, afraid their possessions might be stolen by people who'd already taken their fill.

As the lower branches turned naked, the interlopers started climbing my mother's trees, gingerly shinnying out on limbs so they could shake or lower the branches for their friends and family.

My mother, Mindl Rosenblum, was a strong woman, in both body and character, fiercely proud of every tree she owned. Even so, she didn't try to stop any of the trespassers. Instead, every day she wore an elegant dress, as though she were attending a society event. She actually was attending the end of our society. The Germans had just crashed through the Polish army lines. That fact meant the Germans were coming, and we all knew what that meant, or thought we did.

During these few weeks, my mother mostly endured the wrecking of her orchards in silence, dressed every day in one of her long, splendid dresses, with shoes in matching colors, her hair piled high on her head in an elaborate style. Several times she had told us she wanted income from the orchards to pay for sending my brother Hymie and me to foreign medical schools. For the two months before the bombing, my mother had packed fruit, while all three of her trucks were busily speeding to Warsaw and back around the clock.

Now, every once in a while, she would look at me with her large brown eyes turned sad, and say "Life is all over. All of the years we worked, all the things we hoped for, they're gone. It's the end of our future, the end of the orchard, the end of the money. We lived a good life these past couple of years. Now, God knows what's going to happen."

Because of my rich uncle, Yudel, we all had a pretty good idea that what would happen was going to be disastrous.

We lived in Miedzyrzec, located about forty miles from the Russian border, near Brest-Litovsk. It is also southeast of Warsaw and north of Lublin, thirty-five miles from the Russian border and seventy miles from Treblinka. Yudel was a very modern man. As early as 1935, he had a radio and a telephone. In Poland, only a few people in any city of our size had either luxury. Yudel had both. He didn't look as though he were rich. He was five feet, eight inches, and was built like a barrel. He looked more like a wrestler.

He made his money from pig bristles, which were used for paintbrushes, clothing brushes, combs, and brushes for polishing shoes. He was so illiterate he couldn't sign his own name, but he had been all over the world. He had forty-five people working for him, plus a few relatives. He created the idea of building slaughterhouses in small Chinese villages.

Farmers there traditionally would go to another town and pay to have their hogs butchered. Yudel did the butchering for free, but with the understanding that all the bristles from the hogs would belong to him. Then he'd ship the bristles to his factory in our town, where they would be treated, then sent to factories which made them into various kinds of brushes. He had customers in the United States, France, and England. I myself worked in Yudel's bristle factory after school. Yudel also owned a wholesale egg business which shipped thousands of eggs a year to England and even to Germany.

When my father, Samuel, and I went to visit Yudel on Saturdays, we would admire his tabletop radio, the only one in town. It held both fascination and menace. We always went to Yudel's house after attending synagogue on Saturday. It was a family tradition—first celebrate the Sabbath, then attend a gathering at Yudel's. My father, brothers, and I would dress up in our finest clothing. Sometimes my mother would go, too, elegant in high-heeled shoes and calf-length dresses trimmed in lace and made of silk. Usually, the dress was either bright purple or deep red. For the occasion, she always prepared fish and pastries, which she carried in sparkling clean glass containers.

Though not many of the women in the family attended these affairs, nobody doubted my mother's right to be there. As Yudel's little sister Mindl, she knew at least as much about politics and business as any man in the room. She also was universally respected for her skill and knowledge, both of which had made her orchard enterprise bloom. Meanwhile, my sisters, Sara, Fay, and Rachel, were visiting some of their girlfriends or attending a science club or political meeting instead.

Politics, business, the comings and goings of the relatives, all were the staples of our Saturday conversations. Sometimes my father would tell his World War I stories, most of which we'd all heard countless times before.

We all were on our best behavior. We would talk, sip tea, munch cookies, and say hello to my father's cousins and brothers who lived in the city as well. Yudel's daughters, Sara, Rachel, Shana, and Liche; his sons, Hymie and Morris; and his wife, Mate, would stay dressed in their best synagogue garb and serve us food on silver platters. We would sit in Yudel's deep-cushioned chairs and marvel at the thick, polished wood of his furniture.

My brothers Hymie and Benny would run around the room, or tug at the ears of Yudel's Saint Bernard dog, who suffered through my brothers' rough-housing with a far better nature than I would have.

Hymie Kronhartz often was there. He was the son of Sarah, my mother's sister. Hymie Kronhartz was tall, with sculpted good looks. He was well respected in our town and in our family. He had graduated from a university, now lived on the main street in our town, and was a master photographer and portrait painter. He had a studio visited by the wealthiest people in town, who wanted their likeness captured by his skilled hands and eyes.

All of us would pause when Yudel turned on the radio. I myself was fascinated by it, both as an object and as a source of news. I was passionate about talking politics, and I loved listening to Yudel's radio. It constantly amazed me that Yudel could just turn a knob on a box and voices would come pouring out, especially that of Adolph Hitler.

I had been hearing Hitler's speeches on that radio since 1935. Although I was now fourteen, I had been reading for several years, so I knew about Hitler's grabbing one country after another. And I knew Hitler's voice. Every time he would snatch another country, we would hear another speech about why it was necessary.

We also had movie theaters in our town, so we all had seen newsreels about the Kristallnacht in November 1938, when in one night the Nazis attacked thousands of Jews and destroyed centuries-old ghettos all over Germany and Austria. All of us in the family watched and listened to those reports and trembled. We knew if Hitler ever made it to our Poland, he would do even worse to us.

We were right, though the awaiting ugliness was beyond what anyone could have imagined. How could we? I knew from my father, Samuel, and others that during World War I, the Germans had treated Polish Jews as brothers. We had no way of knowing the stabbing hatred in their hearts this time.

I particularly remember hearing Hitler's speech justifying his annexation of Czechoslovakia in March of that year. He had already sent troops to occupy the Rhineland and annexed Austria. I could feel Yudel's tea go sour in my stomach as I listened to Hitler's ranting.

The bad times are closing in on us, I thought. *We have had our homes, our businesses, our lives here. We have been citizens of this town for hundreds of years. Our whole family has lived a peaceful life. Still, we have no place to run, no place to go, no place where we are welcome.*

All of us had hoped England and France would put a stop to Hitler's devouring other countries. By this time, we were reading about *Der Fuehrer* and the Nazis every day in the press. And, of course, there were his radio speeches.

We had been living a comfortable life. There wasn't a trace of anti-Semitism in our city, but I still knew a lot about Hitler. I had learned by reading, but listening to his speeches was actually more educational. I heard the menace in his voice. I heard the hatred drench his words. He frightened me.

We were all terrified after hearing that speech about Czechoslovakia. My family talked long and hard. We knew Poland was near the top of Hitler's list, and our feeling that England and France wouldn't stop him made everyone's voice shake.

We also had some Jews living in our city who had lived under Hitler. The year before, Hitler had stripped German Jews whose parents were both Polish Jews of their property and shipped them back to our country. These people survived here by peddling perfumes and shoes. They told people what happened to them, and how Hitler was whipping up hatred against our people.

Our family had lived very well during the last five years. Our city, which was on the road between Berlin and Moscow, was Miedzyrzec, meaning "surrounded by rivers," as indeed it was. Our city was both one of the richest in Poland and almost exclusively Jewish. We thought of both facts as our good fortune. They may have been our greatest calamity.

Miedzyrzec was bursting with prosperity. We had about sixteen thousand people living there, of whom only four thousand were not Jewish. We had pharmacies, universities, a hospital, movies, and a theater. We had religious schools to which Jews from all over Europe came to study.

The city was filled with factories. The largest industry was making bristles for countries worldwide. There were dozens of such factories, of which Uncle Yudel's was only one. We had a leather tannery and factories making fertilizer and farm equipment. We had twenty bakeries and just as many butcher shops. We had a fire department with the newest trucks.

Aside from being prosperous and largely Jewish, my city had committed another sin in German eyes. We knew what the Germans were doing to our people in Germany, and we despised them for it. In 1935 and 1936, Germans sent trucks full of their glassware to our city. They made good glassware, but if it was German-made, we wouldn't touch it. I can just imagine how our attitude must have eaten away, like dripping acid, on the Nazis' pride.

Whatever the reasons, we could see trouble coming. By listening to Yudel's radio and reading the newspapers, we knew Hitler wanted to take over Danzig, one of our most important ports. We knew when the Polish government refused him. We also knew when the Germans took that refusal as an excuse to declare war. After all, Hitler had a much bigger army.

Every unmarried man in Poland who was in good physical shape and over age eighteen was being drafted. My father was still with us. He wasn't drafted because he had already served in the army and was married. I was four years too young, so I was allowed to stay home. In fact, none of my immediate family was drafted. The closest the draft struck was when the son of our next-door neighbor had to go, as did hundreds of others. Our city seemed emptier now. Most of the men were gone, and the women and children had to do the work men would have done. My mother, however, already was laboring in her orchards. The whole family was extremely proud of what she had accomplished since she had bought one small orchard four years before.

In 1935, after bearing six children, she had told my father, Samuel Rosenblum, it was her turn to start a business. My father didn't mind. We needed the money. All of us children volunteered to do our share. My sister Sara became a seamstress and ran the house. Fay, the oldest, worked in an underwear factory. Rachel,

Hymie, Benny, and I went to school. Meanwhile, my mother set out to build an orchard empire.

She was succeeding. My mother had an almost magical ability to calculate during the winter how much fruit each tree would bear come summer. As a girl, she had worked during the summer with her parents in many orchards. Her parents had never owned them, but she had inherited the experience of peering at the buds, knowing what fruits would bloom and when. That first year she had a six-acre apple farm. She had six times that acreage three years later.

In 1938, the year before we were standing on that hill together, she had bought the orchard we were standing in. At five hundred acres, it was one of Poland's largest. It was in an ideal location, on the main highway between Berlin and Moscow.

Buying the orchard was difficult, but accomplishing it was a tribute to my mother's character and skills. The orchard was owned by a sharp-tongued old woman whose sons and daughters didn't want the business. Several people wanted to pay her large sums, but the woman trusted only my mother to treat the property with the respect and appreciation it deserved.

My mother had a charm about her everyone liked. She had grown up among Polish Gentiles, spoke Polish fluently, and was very smart. As Yudel's sister, she had learned much about politics and business matters. She was smart enough to get the vast financing she needed to buy the orchard by finding two silent partners.

Most people had confidence in my mother and her integrity after meeting her only once. Her trademark was her elegant way of dressing. No matter what the occasion, unless she was working in the fields, she would wear high heels and a stylish dress. She was five feet, three inches, and had rich black hair. She needed no jewelry to be attractive, though she had plenty: The way she dressed, spoke, and carried herself were striking enough on their own. When she worked in the orchards, however, she dressed plainly for the hard, sweaty work ahead.

Now, as the German bombers blackened the sky over my mother's orchards and the refugees ripped the fruit from her trees, all of her hard work and our family's new prosperity began crashing down around us. The war between Poland and Germany had started that summer of 1939, and German bombs were raining down on our little city. The bombardments lasted for more than two weeks. Clumps of planes came at us from all directions. At times, we almost felt surrounded from the air.

Our city was on the highway connecting Germany and Russia, and tens of thousands of people were running east toward the Russian border to hide from the bombs and strafing. The roads were clogged with people on foot, in cars, on bicycles, with small bags or suitcases strapped with rope to every conceivable section of their vehicles and themselves.

Polish military jeeps and trucks, many containing soldiers with parts of their body wrapped in bandages, were on the road to Russia too. The Germans knew they could catch those military vehicles on the highway, and that highway ran right through my city. From the moment the sun peeped over the horizon until its last stray rays winked out at night, the Germans bombed us.

The first bombing run was a bitter taste of what was to come. The planes came in like a pack of wild animals, exploding factories and highways. They bombed the city's largest synagogue, which could hold over three thousand worshipers.

My father, Sara, and I hadn't dared to stay in our house. During the first week of bombing, we leaped from ditch to ditch as we saw buildings we had known all our life splintered into tiny pieces. Anything that moved was raked with machine-gun fire.

People all around us were gunned down as they were running or huddling in the ditches. I had never seen death before. Now, I saw people with bullet holes in their heads, arms and legs blown off, pieces of people, some still dripping blood, flung in every direction. I was numb and in shock. A few times I was so fearful I urinated in my pants.

I saw the creases in my father's face deepen during that week. He was frightened for Sara and me. After six days of bombing, my father packed some of our belongings in a paper sack. Then he looked at us sternly, trying hard not to let the worry show.

"I'm afraid if we are all in one place most of our family will be killed," he told us.

He sent Rachel and Benjamin to my mother's orchard. Her quarters were in an old barn which held a few beds, a small stove, and some pots and pans. The living was a little primitive, but a lot safer. Nobody was bombing my mother's trees.

Hymie and Fay were already there. Father took Rachel and me with him to hide in a nearby town with some relatives. That town was surrounded by trees and away from the highway, so he thought it would be relatively safe from the bombing. He was wrong. The bombing so dismembered the buildings around us my father sent Rachel and me to our mother's orchard the next day.

"Go and be with your mother in the orchard. It's safer there. Even the Germans wouldn't bomb an orchard," he said.

Rachel and I walked to my mother's groves, about ten miles from our city. Every mile or so, we had to take headlong leaps into a ditch to avoid the deadly splatter of machine-gun fire. All I had with me were a couple of shirts and a few pants when we arrived that night.

Even though the Germans were mercilessly bombing our city, we continued to be aware of what was happening in the war only because the old woman who had owned the orchard was still living there. One condition of the orchard's sale to my mother was that the seller could stay until the mortgage was paid. Mother, my brothers and sisters, and I gathered in her house.

The woman, like Yudel, had both a radio and a telephone. We huddled at night around her radio and listened to scattered news reports. The old lady's house had just one floor, but it had a rich green garden and a couple of servants. She'd give us milk, chickens, and other food to cook in the small cottage my mother used during harvest.

According to the radio reports, the Germans didn't spare a single city. The accounts were sketchy. A newscaster would be on the air for a few minutes, then run for cover as the German bombers rained destruction.

The people who were looting my mother's orchards would stop and talk with her, struck by the elegantly dressed lady who silently watched them rip fruit from trees she owned.

The people were on bicycles, on motorcycles, and on foot. They even were in cars, along with horses and buggies. They clotted the highway. Mother sometimes would take delicate steps toward them. The people were all from cities close to the German border, because Krakow and Lodz were about 150 miles from my mother's orchard. The refugees would tell her what was happening and how close the Germans were. Then they would continue east.

We were so confused. We knew bombs were thick in the air above our own city and all the others. We knew buildings were in flames and people were in hiding. We knew about it, but we didn't see it. Even so, we began to understand what to expect. The refugees also would tell my mother that when the Germans reached a city, they would root out the Jews and shoot them. My mother only nodded in acknowledgment.

Four weeks after the war started, on September 27, we heard a dull voice announce on the radio that the Polish army had surrendered to the Germans. By that time, my father had joined us, but the orchard had been stripped. Every bit of fruit had been plucked off the branches and off the ground, even the rotten pieces. The orchard was gone. There was nothing to do but go back. We hated to leave the old woman. She told us that most of her relatives had already gone to Romania, then to England. What she didn't say was that the relatives were rich enough to afford to leave. We never did find out what happened to her.

Some people from our city who were doing a little bit of business in a nearby town stopped in the orchard. They told us our house hadn't been touched. A few minutes later, after they left, my mother told us we were to return to our city. Her eyes filled with tears. I had never seen her like this.

"It's all over for us," she said. "This is the beginning of our end. We have to return and try to go on with life—if we can."

She was almost clenching her teeth, and I could see by the white line around her jaw that she was trying hard to look more poised than she felt. My father looked tired and small.

When we returned to our city a few days after the bombing, life was very different. The same day we returned, the Russians set up a small command post. A gloom had settled over the people. All the stores now had dirty padlocks and chains across them; no lights flickered inside.

We saw that many houses and buildings had been destroyed, not by bombs, but by flames which ate entire blocks. Scorched wood, twisted metal, and the flotsam of everyday life such as pots, pans, and dolls, were scattered everywhere. Bombs had blown sturdy homes into rickety structures held up by a beam or two.

We rounded a corner and saw our house. Amazingly, it was still intact. Not even a scorch mark. Yudel lived several blocks away. His house had not been touched, either. But across the street from his back door was the town's Jewish hospital, which now was a stinking heap. The sooty ashes stood in stark contrast to the white of the bandages, linen, and medicine labels, which lay in soggy piles.

The city was without medical care. Some of us had no home. We were all without food, because all shipments into the city had stopped. Still, the Russians were starting to get organized. They stayed for only eight days. They had made an agreement with the Germans to pull back across the Bug River, about thirty-five miles away from our city. When the Russians knew they were to depart, they sent a truck with a raspy public address system throughout our neighborhoods.

"People, we are moving out. If you want to escape the Germans, now is your only chance," the tinny, disembodied voice in the truck announced. "You have a chance to get away from the Germans. We can save you. We will have trains here to take you to Russia. If the Germans come, you might die."

They kept their word. For several days, coal trains belching sooty gray smoke came and went around the clock. They stopped in our city and many others near their border.

About three thousand people from our city took the Russians up on their offer. The people who left and the people who stayed were largely split along generations. The people who were young enough not to have much to lose, who didn't own a house, furniture, or other creature comforts but were old enough to find work, were the ones who chose to leave.

Sara wanted to go. I heard my mother and father discussing in our kitchen whether they should leave, too. They were from an older generation, and they remembered how kindly the Germans had treated them during World War I. My father many times had told me a story about when he and several other Jews from our town were being taken by German ship to another Polish city so they could work. The ship was carrying food as well as vodka. One of the Jews sneaked into a corner and, when nobody was looking, got conspicuously drunk. The

Germans started hollering at the stuporous Jew: "How could you not include your Jewish brothers?" they yelled. "How could you be so selfish that you kept the vodka to yourself?"

While my mother and father were talking in the kitchen, my father reminded my mother of this same story again.

"How could the Germans be so bad? They treated us like brothers during the war. Besides, we have this house you've just redone. Look at all our electrical appliances, that deep couch, the white tile floors, the large wooden kitchen table and chairs. Thank God, the bombing didn't destroy a single dish or chair. Why should we leave this place, when we have so much here?"

I shuddered when I heard this. I had read and heard far too much to believe the Germans would be gentle with Jews this time around.

My mother, however, loved the house. She had inherited it—it actually was one unit in a four-plex structure—two years before. She had bought new furniture, including a wooden couch, some chairs, mirrors, and other pieces. My mother had filled the whole house from the bare walls during 1937–38. She also had inherited the warehouse next door.

My father had a job working for the Polish government, delivering cigarettes from government warehouses to small shops. Though that job was gone, he still had plenty of goods in my mother's warehouse behind the four-plex, where he stored his cigarettes and numerous other products, which he sold wholesale. Piled high inside the building were glassware, pots and pans, and leather.

Ultimately, my father thought we owned too much to leave, and my mother wasn't hard to convince. They had a house which had been newly fixed up; the family had nice clothes, nice furniture, a good life. In addition, my brother Benny was only five years old, far too young, my parents thought, to be uprooted. To avoid the Germans, we would have had to abandon everything to flee to a strange country, and they didn't see the sense of it.

Yudel felt the same way as my father, though one of his sons and a daughter did leave on the trains. My sister Sara also wanted to go. My mother agreed, but only on one condition.

"I'm not going to let you leave as a girl alone. You have to get married first," she told Sara. Fay also wanted to flee, but she was only seventeen, though she did have a fiancé, a furrier named Hymie Firman, who was leaving for Russia. My mother refused Fay, a fact that played on her conscience until the day she died, gasping for breath in a cattle car.

When the Germans came in October, it was as though our old lives had stopped, and a new and darker life was beginning. Hundreds of German jeeps swarmed in, along with thousands of foot soldiers. They lost no time in throwing Jews out of their homes. Within three days I saw a dozen evictions.

They all followed a pattern. The Germans marched into a house, declared they were taking it over, and gave the occupants fifteen minutes to get out. I saw men, women, children, dressed in nightgowns, underwear, or sometimes nothing at all.

They were running from the cruel jeers of the Germans, who yelled out such things as "Run, Jewish dogs, run," and other taunts my parents would be embarrassed I had heard. The Germans made particular fun of the women. As each ran from what had been her home, her body was poked and grabbed by leering soldiers.

The frightened residents grabbed whatever they could. A jacket, a pillow, maybe some pots and pans. They didn't know themselves where they were going to go. If they were lucky, they could find shelter with friends or relatives in lower classes, whose homes the Germans wouldn't confiscate because the location or construction was undesirable.

Sometimes the soldiers beat people. They used a cane, a strap, two-by-fours, closet poles, whatever was available.

Every day there were more evictions as the ugly green German military vehicles and swastika flags lined the city. In the most disgusting eviction I saw, German soldiers threw into the street a bed containing a paralyzed, elderly man whimpering in fear. His children immediately picked up the bed and took him away. They carried him to our area, where he was taken in by some friends.

One of the men who lived in our city had been perhaps the richest man in Poland. He had been in the fur trade and had a palace near our house. He, wisely, had fled. The Germans moved into the building with knots of tanks, trucks, and artillery, and made it their headquarters. Later, toward the end of 1942, they would take people to the courtyard there and shoot them.

We weren't worried about eviction. The Germans wanted to take over the homes of the rich people: doctors and lawyers, places with nice furniture. They wanted homes which had cars and were located on the main streets, near restaurants, hotels, the fire department, and city hall. Our city also had a huge open-air marketplace, which the Germans now used to park supplies and trucks.

Where I lived was quite different. The streets were short, narrow, and entirely made of cobblestone. Cars and trucks would have a very hard time maneuvering. In addition, our home wasn't fancy enough to draw the Germans' attention.

Meanwhile, it was clear that if Sara were to leave soon, the wedding to Gerald Isenberg had to be arranged. My parents put together a _minyan_, a gathering of ten men, in our living room. My mother was always an excellent baker. In addition, every year she had made wine from some of the fruits in her orchards. As a result, we had a few loaves of _challah_, a tasty Jewish bread, along with some apple, strawberry, and cherry wine, for the wedding feast.

Still, the ceremony had an undertone of sadness. The sound of the groom shattering the traditional wine glass sounded to me like the breaking of bones.

Three days later, I drove Sara and her husband to the riverbank in my father's horse and buggy. My father had paid someone to take the pair across the Bug River to Russia by boat.

On the way there, my sister and I talked. We both had a sense that the family's life was going to get a lot worse very shortly.

"God knows what will happen to our people," Sara said to me.

When we arrived at the riverbank, I gave Sara a big hug and a kiss on the cheek. As she and her husband were being rowed across the river, I almost cried. I wondered whether I would see her again.

Oh, God, I want to go with her, I thought to myself. *I want to go, but I wish I were a lot older. I'm only fourteen. Who would give me a job? Who would keep me safe?*

There was no answer, of course. So I made clucking sounds at the horse, who turned around and took me home.

Soon the food shortages began gnawing in every stomach. Of the twenty bakeries in town, only one was allowed to remain open. Thousands of people lined up at 1:00 A.M. to be there when the bakery opened at 6:00. Fortunately, my brother Hymie and I were short, and we wiggled past a lot of people when they weren't looking. After five or six hours, we would reach the front of the line, where we received a slice of bread apiece. We took our prizes home underneath our coats, so nobody would steal them. Our father would slice each piece into smaller pieces, just so we could all live for another day.

Sometimes we would reach the window where the bread was being given out and the baker would say, "I'm so sorry. We have nothing left," and we would cry inside.

For six months, we were able to supplement this meager diet by using the goods my father had stored in my mother's warehouse to trade with farmers who came to barter food for goods.

The farmers didn't have much to trade because the Germans were confiscating much of the crops. We would trade clothing for food. My mother also had gold pieces, jewelry, fancy clothes, fur jackets.

My father would trade his cigarettes, cases of soap, pots and pans, candles, glassware. He also had tillers for the farmers' tractors. In return, my parents would receive mostly potatoes and flour for my mother to bake bread, as well as American dollars. Polish currency was worthless. We knew that soon the farmers wouldn't come anymore and the warehouse would be empty.

I had wanted to see my mother's jewelry, to see what was happening to her store of treasures. However, that was a sight forbidden to me, and I would never have thought of disobeying my parents.

Despite the alarming signs, we had two reasons to be hopeful. One was the memory my parents and others of their generation had of the Germans' being good to us during the last war. The other reason was my first cousin, Hymie Kronhartz, the talented artist with his own studio, where he fashioned oil paintings and took photographs. He lived in a rich part of town. While everybody else was being evicted, Hymie was left alone.

When the German generals and the colonels and the captains all moved into confiscated homes, they were Hymie's neighbors. Hymie was given a green arm band with a small Jewish star in the middle of it, and a special passport. Only one Jew in each city had these special privileges, and he was the one in ours.

The reason the Germans gave him such indulgences was that they wanted Hymie to make flattering portraits of them. The Gestapo and SS men wanted their likenesses looking fierce and proud, so they could send the photographs and paintings back to relatives and friends in Germany. Hymie could make them look the way they wanted to look to people in the Fatherland.

We weren't allowed to go to Hymie's house—it was, after all, in the German part of town. He, however, was allowed to go anyplace, and he often visited Yudel, who in turn told us that Hymie still was doing well, as were his three children, brother, and wife, who all lived with him. We also heard news about him from other people. Hymie was a popular man, and people took note of him.

When I heard Hymie was well, I was glad. The fact that he had privileges didn't change our living conditions one bit, but the knowledge heartened us all.

At least there is a little light, I thought. *Maybe this means they will let some of us survive.*

Each of my parents repeatedly said the same thing. We still couldn't imagine what the Germans actually were going to do to us. As it turns out, our ignorance gave us some peace we would never have had if we'd known the truth of what was to come.

Chapter 2

Signs
of
Danger

Them Nazis began hammering at us much sooner than my parents could possibly have imagined, smothering our lives with regulation after regulation, telling us what we had to do, and how and when we had to do it.

We had to wear patches above the left pocket on our shirts. The patches displayed a yellow Star of David, a six-pointed star which symbolized our religion. We had always thought of it as an emblem of pride. The Nazis wanted to make it a badge of shame.

If a German spoke to a Jewish man, the Jew had to take off his hat. We could no longer walk on the sidewalk. Only the Polish and German Gentiles could walk there. The Nazi method of enforcement was direct and brutal. If we refused to take off our hat or dared to walk on the sidewalk, Germans would beat us with their fists, with sticks, with a cane, with anything.

We were good people, used to obeying the rules of our religion and our city and country out of pride. Now, we obeyed because we had no choice. Whatever they did to us, we had to accept it meekly and quietly. If we didn't, then the treatment would get worse. At least, that's what we believed. Nobody dared to criticize the Germans openly.

We couldn't even criticize them in private, except to our closest friends. The

Germans had spies everywhere. However, because this was a closely knit community, we knew who the spies were, and we made sure we told them nothing incriminating.

Soon drunken Nazi soldiers and SS showed up on our streets, and when they did, they would beat us. We had always prided ourselves on our clean and safe streets. Now we had nowhere else to walk but the streets, and they were full of danger.

A lot of people who had gone to Russia were dribbling back into our city, dejected and scared. Winter in Russia was bone-chilling, and they had nowhere to live. At least here they had a home, no matter how humble.

But the people with the best homes were in some danger, too. The Germans had evicted only some of the rich people. Those remaining had a lot of goods stashed away. Many times I saw Germans pull up to a rich person's house in a cart. I could hear the screams and yells as they beat the Jews, mostly the men, and then came out with their arms full of fine furs, clothing, as well as gold and silver objects of all sorts.

One time I saw a horse-drawn cart pull up to the house of some people I knew well. The people in the cart were laborers. Many of them, with few places to find honest work, were helping the Germans loot Jewish homes as a way to make a living. The SS and Polish police walked around a corner on foot, then banged on the door. When it opened, the SS yelled, "We know you've got bristle."

It didn't take much intelligence to figure that out. The man had owned a bristle factory.

"We want the product. We know you have it," the SS screamed.

The fact they had bristle was so obvious the family would have been killed if they'd lied. So the father took the Nazis to the back of the house where his warehouse was. The laborers tramped through the house, loaded up on bristle, and took it away. If the family had denied having bristle they would have been beaten to death and the Germans would have found it anyway. I didn't stay around to watch the rest.

After the Nazis left, I saw the family's son on the street.

"They cleaned us out. They took our jewelry, our bristles, the silk and flannel we had for special clothing, everything," he said mournfully.

Our family wasn't spared. Those few of us who had radios or telephones had to turn them in. The Germans confiscated Yudel's.

"They just came and pulled them out of the wall, no questions asked," Yudel told me. "All they said was that if I didn't like it, the alternative was a bullet."

There was no escaping into anonymity, no hoping the Germans wouldn't know who we were or where we lived. We had to carry a passport which showed our nationality and age, but no photograph.

In addition, we had to register immediately with the Jewish Registry. In every city there was a Jewish agency which controlled Jewish affairs. In our city, there was one already in existence. It was the Jewish Council, which had been there for hundreds of years. The council's duties covered a wide spectrum of our lives, ranging from working on voluntary donations for various causes, to helping the poor, as well as choosing the rabbi and assistant rabbi for the city. It also supported the Jewish schools, hospitals, fire department, and orchestra. It collected taxes on each household. Because our town was so heavily Jewish, the Council essentially was the city government.

As a result, the Jews in our city had already registered with the council. The registry had on file our name, birthday, age, family members, and address. Now the Nazis were perverting the council's registry to their benefit. In addition, any new German regulation would be posted by the council.

The Germans were particularly interested in all Jews ages fourteen through sixty, because these were the ones who could work. The council members chose who would be picked as slave labor for the various jobs Germans assigned to us.

The council consisted of eight members, each of whom had inherited the job, one his father, grandfather, and great-grandfather had held too. The Germans, however, added a member: Lazar. Lazar was about six feet tall, with thick arms, prominent cheekbones, movie star looks, and a deep voice.

Often he would dress in a nice suit jacket and tie. He was beardless. The Germans had forced Jews with beards to shave them off, but men his age didn't wear beards anyway.

Lazar was a peculiar man. He was brilliant. His sisters and brothers were nice people who worked hard, gave to various charities, and were generally admired. Lazar had married before the war, but his parents refused to give him anything. They told him to build up his fortune on his own.

Lazar had decided he would indeed make his own fortune, and he was in a hurry to do it. Supposedly Lazar was a furrier by trade, working in a factory making coats. In fact, he had ten to fifteen men working for him who would break into shops and warehouses, then steal furs, pelts, bristles, and anything else of value. They would either sell their booty on the black market or ransom it back to its original owner. Lazar also ran a protection racket, making sure the police didn't bother people who were running a business without a license.

He suited the Germans' purpose perfectly. They had sought him out to make him head of the Jewish Council because he was the local underworld king, a strong man with a strong mind. But if Lazar hadn't done the job, somebody else would have. He was basically a messenger for the Gestapo, who made sure they had the work force they required.

People still respected Lazar because he couldn't have stopped the Gestapo. People also were afraid of Lazar, and that's a quality the Germans admired.

Lazar was particularly useful to the Gestapo, two of whom had been assigned to our city to liquidate Jews. Heinrich and Dietrich were their names. They were there because in December our city had been declared a ghetto, a dumping ground for Jews from all over Europe. We didn't know this fact at the time, but we found out soon enough.

We learned very quickly the difference between the SS and the Gestapo, at least in our city. The SS hunted down partisans and people who were prominent in politics. They were the ones who closed up the businesses and were in charge of shipping out of the city anything the Third Reich might have needed. The Gestapo were in charge of beatings and killings.

Heinrich and Dietrich would roam the streets all day. Together and separately, they would whip Jews with a short-handled riding whip whose braided leather lashes were laced with wire. The whips hung from their thick black belts, the handles sitting right next to their Lugers. They were their own law. If they didn't like you, if they'd had a bad day and wanted to take it out on you, there was nothing you could do.

Lazar would tell them whatever they wanted to know: who had a lot of money, who worked in the government, who was politically active. He would pinpoint who was part of the intelligentsia: teachers, doctors, lawyers, rich manufacturers, politicians. In short, anybody who was wealthy or prominent. To the Germans, these people were particularly suspect. Lazar also would tell who belonged to Zionist or Communist organizations. I knew about what he was doing because news traveled very fast.

The minute the Germans came in, beating became a sport. Almost immediately, some of them satisfied their blood lust by hitting us. At first, the men from the regular army, the Wehrmacht, didn't do beatings. Later, however, even these relatively decent men turned to attacking us. As time went on, more and more of the Germans would beat us, until there were very few who restrained themselves.

There were ample opportunities for hitting and kicking us. Many people were forced to work for the Germans, cleaning the buildings the Germans lived and worked in, chopping wood, that kind of thing. In order to approach many of the buildings, the Jews had to walk on the sidewalk. There was no other way to get indoors. But because we were forbidden to walk there, the Germans would use that as an excuse to start hitting us with their fists, with belts, with anything they wanted to.

It happened to me several times. When the Germans saw that Jewish star patch, their faces narrowed, their fists knotted, and they would just jump on us and start flailing away.

"Juden, Juden, Juden. Pigs. Scum," they would yell. Then they would start kicking us with their heavy boots. Those boots, if they hit the right spot, could break bones. To fight back was to risk worse punishment, so people just curled up in a ball, waiting for the Germans to get tired.

We were safest in our own area. Where my family lived wasn't near the main street or any important buildings, so the Germans weren't much interested in us. Whenever we went to the main street, though, we were in danger. Most of the shops there still had the pockmarked boards that had been nailed over them during the bombing. Yudel's egg and bristle businesses were shut down. The few businesses that were open had been taken over by Christians.

If a woman were wearing a Jewish star, the Nazis would insult her in the same way as they would a man. But they didn't rape the women, nor did they beat them. Not at first. For some reason, they wanted to show what they considered a good face. That pose lasted for a few weeks, but the mask quickly fell off. Then they treated women the same, beating, kicking, spitting on them as much as the men. They'd kick the face, the groin, wherever their arrogance led them to.

We could not even have our homes to ourselves. The Jewish Council soon told us Jews were being transported to our city from the western half of Poland, and we would have to take in one family apiece. We found out only when a member of the Jewish Council came to our house and announced we would be taking in a Jewish family from another city. The family was right behind him at our doorstep. All they had were a couple of small suitcases, a couple of bundles of underwear, and a small pot.

"You must take in these people. Make the best of it," he said.

We're in for a very long ride, I thought.

The family was pitiful. They had no friends or relatives here. The little boy and girl huddled together in a corner. The father looked at us soulfully and said, "Please do what you can for us. We didn't ask to be here."

"We'll do the best we can," my father replied.

"Don't worry about us," their father said. "We'll make it as long as we have a roof over our head. We're not going to make your life miserable."

It was a very tight squeeze. Our home was only somewhere between 450 and 600 square feet. That first night both families ate together. We felt sorry for them. Our situation was pitiful, but at least we knew the neighbors and were living on our own street. They knew nobody. We had a dinner of potatoes and bread and Father said a little prayer: "Thanks to God, that we have what we do have."

Our new family, whose name I don't remember, had two parents and two children. The husband was middle-aged, perhaps forty-five. The wife was in her forties, with long black hair. The children, a boy and girl, were ages seven and eight.

The man and woman were always apologetic about being there. They were aware the Jewish culture requires seeing to the well-being of guests, but it wasn't as though we had invited them to move in. They knew this was going to be a bad time. We already had five children and my parents there. Now we had four more people.

Our part of the four-plex had two bedrooms, one for our parents and one for the children. We gave the new family one of the bedrooms. In the kitchen, there was a stationary bench which seated four people. It had a finished top which covered up a bed. At night, we removed the top, and that's where my brother Hymie and I slept. My parents slept in their bedroom with my youngest brother, Benny. Fay and Rachel were sleeping together on a pullout couch in the living room. Fortunately we had plenty of blankets, enough even to share with the new family.

I do give the father credit. He went from door to door begging for a month. After that, he would work for farmers at night, chopping wood, cleaning stables. He'd get a few potatoes and carrots for a night's work. He also went out at night to the old factories and ripped wood off them, then made money by carrying wood to the people who needed it. The mother stayed with the kids in their bedroom or took them outside to play.

Hymie Firman, Fay's fiancé, had built a kitchen in our breezeway so we could cook in comfort during the summer. That kitchen was where the new family now cooked.

The two families lived in the same house but had very separate lives. We would bid each other good morning, then go on with our individual existences. We all admired the family for being as self-sufficient as they were.

The Germans began to strangle our city slowly. How we were to find food and clothing and heat our homes in the biting cold of winter—which sometimes fell to as low as twenty degrees below zero—those problems were ours, not theirs.

After a few weeks, I overheard my parents talking.

"The end is near," my mother told my father. "We just don't know when it's going to happen. Someday, maybe someday very soon, we will all be dead."

Still, they tried hard not to let us know how they felt. Instead, they took us into their confidence as to what they were going to do to keep us fed.

"We've got to start trading our valuables. We can either cry and feel sorry for ourselves or do something," my father told us. "The best thing we can do is try to gather enough food to keep ourselves going."

So we went to work. I volunteered to clean the Germans' stables and feed their well-muscled horses, which they used for carrying weapons and food. The soldiers who tended to the horses were middle-aged transport workers, too old to do any real fighting.

I would wash down the stables until everything shined and was in order. When I fed a horse, I made sure no bit of oat stayed on the floor for long. It was second nature to me. We were very clean people in our own home. Our house was immaculate, and all the children learned to do their part to keep it that way. In addition, my father at one time had owned horses, which, of course, the Germans had taken away. I had cleaned my father's horses and stable, so I just did the same for the Germans.

Whatever job I did, I had to do it 100 percent, no matter whom I was working for. My first time in the German stables, I washed down their horses with a bucket of water and a big comb. By the time the Germans returned, every horse was glistening.

"Danke schön, danke schön," they said over and over and over.

They walked around their horses, admiring how clean they looked. Some of them even gave me pieces of stale bread and some soup. When I cleaned their wagons, I got the same reaction. They patted me on the head and gave me more soup and stale bread, much of which I took home.

"There's a lesson here," I told Hymie. "Our parents may be very clean people, but the Germans worship cleanliness." It was a lesson which was later to help save my life again and again.

Hymie, who along with me was too young to be on the Germans' list for potential slave labor, also was doing odd jobs for the German army. They also would give him old bread, soup, whatever they had left over. Sometimes the food he and I took home was all we had to eat in the house.

Most of the rest of my family was forced into slave labor. The Jewish Council assigned my sisters to be maids for some of the three hundred German officers stationed there. My sisters kept the places clean and the ovens warm. At least the officers didn't attempt to molest them sexually.

My father was sent to work unloading boxcars on a train which moved between the borders of Russia and Germany. The train stations were about thirty-five miles apart. The Germans would send goods to Russia, largely leather, dishes, trucks, and cars. The Russians would send back cotton bales, wheat, and oil. Every night my father came home he looked a little older, his face more sunken, his shoulders more stooped. Lines appeared in his face, and his hair started graying. He was thirty-eight years old, but he looked ten years older.

The Germans were beating him constantly. I knew only because our father told us. "There's a lot of beatings and they want us to work harder even when we don't have the energy. I go there only with a couple of pieces of bread and a little water. I don't have the strength," he would weakly whisper to me.

We kept hearing rumors of people in other towns being rounded up and shipped off to unknown places, but it wasn't happening to us. We heard about these incidents because the Jews who had been uprooted from elsewhere told us. Those people, who were in their forties, would tell us about their children, teenaged and up, who had been shipped off to work camps; the younger children stayed with parents.

"When are they going to start doing this to us? Why are they shipping people here, instead of shipping us somewhere else?" I asked my parents. They didn't know. Nobody in the city did.

We were too busy worrying about staying alive to think about those questions for long. The food shortages created a black market. Many of us had kept valuables hidden: jewelry, gold pieces, even a few American dollars. At night, my parents and others would walk about four miles out of town to barter with the farmers for food, mostly bread and potatoes. Meat and eggs were luxuries nobody could find or afford. Anyone caught traveling outside the city was beaten, so people had to be careful when they went.

Then the snow came, one of the worst snows anyone had ever seen. It fell in cascades, blown by a wind whose chill cut right through to the bone. The snow was piled twelve feet high, paralyzing the city. The only way anything moved was by horse. The farmers used horse-drawn wagons to get to town; snow blocked people from reaching them.

Every part of the city was white because there was no way to clean off so much snow. Any sidewalk or road that was shoveled out was coated again by the next day. The snow was to fall for three or more months.

The Germans were desperate to keep the roadways clear for their military vehicles. They wanted to deliver food and materiel to the army, which by then was spread out all the way to the Russian border. They hit upon an obvious solution: use the Jews.

There were perhaps fifty cities between us and the German border. Every city and town had to contribute people to the snow-clearing effort. Many, including my father, were forced to shovel snow off highways. I was still free of the Jewish Council because I was just turning fourteen, and I hadn't registered yet. Not being on the register meant not being assigned jobs or targeted for whatever evil the Germans had in mind. Under the circumstances, I was privileged, and my parents were glad I had yet to be caught up in the Nazi tentacles.

Still, I saw my father come home exhausted, sometimes bloody from a beating, sometimes not. He was a now ragged man, burned out from the beatings and hard labor. I was the oldest boy. To me, my decision was clear.

When my father went to work early one morning, I looked at my mother and sisters and said, "I don't know how much longer Father is going to last the way he's going. I can't stand watching this. I'm the oldest boy. I will take over for him."

My mother started crying and hugged me.

"You're so young, and they're beating people," she wailed.

"He's my father. I'm younger. It's my duty," I said, pulling away from her embrace. She turned away so I couldn't see her weeping, but her shoulders heaved and bobbed and I could hear her sniffling and blowing her nose. I felt bad, worse than she did, but I had to do this.

The next day when my father dragged himself home from work, I confronted him.

"Father, I'm taking over for you. I haven't been registered yet, so the Germans don't even know I exist. You've burned out."

My father looked at me, sadness and relief crowding his face. I saw puddles of moisture forming at the corners of his eyes. He was not an emotional person, but this gesture clearly moved him.

"You want to do it? Go ahead. But it's not going to be easy."

"I'm ready for it."

I got up at 3:00 A.M. and walked in the bone-chilling night air to the designated place. My mother gave me a piece of bread and water in a glass bottle I put in my pocket. We had to be there at 7:00. The snow was so high we had to crawl on it like monkeys.

About eighty of us were packed like herrings into a single truck. When we arrived, we were told we each had to shovel off twenty feet of highway down to the ground. The problem was that snow continued to fall, so we couldn't get the job done no matter how hard we shoveled.

We didn't get a lunch break. We just nibbled on whatever we had brought while we kept shoveling. Soon after I arrived, I saw my first real beating. The guy next to me was too slow for the guards, so they walked up to him and started whipping him on his face and back.

"You're not moving fast enough. Faster, faster, faster," the guard yelled at him. I was shocked, but that feeling soon wore off. Every day was to become like that, and I took my share of beatings. We were finally allowed to quit about 6:00 P.M.

I worked at clearing snow all winter. We were constantly wet. Many people caught colds, which soon seeped into their lungs and became pneumonia. The weather was constantly below zero. Many of us died. It was no surprise. I wore what most people wore: a thin jacket and pants, plus an old sweater. My shoes were always wet from melting snow.

We worked seven days a week with little to eat. My mother would continue to give me a small container of warm water and a slice of bread. It was all the family could spare.

When I took over for him, my father did not sit around the house. He tried to do his part. He had a gun, a small pistol left over from his job delivering government cigarettes. The cigarettes were quite valuable, so the government had issued him a gun to protect himself. Hymie and I knew about the gun because we'd found where he'd hidden it in the attic rafters.

Every once in a while, Hymie and I would go up to the attic, pull down the gun, and look it over, feeling its heaviness in our palms, pretending to shoot it. We had never fired it, of course. Father would have beaten us into mush. Now he took the gun with him when he again went out at night.

I heard my father talking to my mother. "Whatever we have, we have to sell it for food," he said. "Without food we die. The farmers will trade for anything because with all the Jewish stores shut down, there's hardly anything they can buy."

When he plunged into the darkness, he had valuable cargo for bartering. Yudel had many expensive goods he'd bought from the profits of his egg and bristle businesses. Even though they'd been shut down, they had made Yudel a good living, so he had gold pieces and dollars. Polish money was worthless. Yudel also had dozens of shoes, pants, underwear, tablecloths, and sheets. Sometimes we even traded our winter clothes.

My father often would share our food with other families. Seeing people go hungry tore at his heart. He did the same for the family living with us. Their father was working hard just to feed his family, but sometimes they had nothing.

"How could I let them go hungry under my own roof?" my father would ask me. I admired his attitude, and I understood sharing food was one way to express that we were still human beings, not animals. It is a belief I've carried through-out my life.

Neighbors found out about my father's forays to the farmers' homes and gave him some of their own clothing to trade. My father would put the gun in his large black winter coat and load up what Yudel gave him as well as clothing and boots, plus pots and pans from my mother's warehouse.

Usually, he would stuff it all into a three-foot-high sack, then wrap the sack around his neck like a scarf. He crawled through the snow in winter and swam a shallow river during the summer. When he returned a few hours later, the sack would have some food, such as stale bread, potatoes, carrots, whatever the farmers had to trade. Usually, the food was enough to last us for about five days. Each of us got a piece of bread every day, and whatever was left we had for dinner. We all were looking more gaunt, and our clothing started to flop around our dwindling bodies.

The Germans made the Jewish police station from a nearby converted synagogue, intentionally desecrating our religious institutions. Our lives were further complicated by traitors among us. Within the first few months of their occupation, the Germans formed a Jewish police squad. The ones who joined were in their late teens and early twenties. They all were from rich homes, so they were accepted because their parents had enough money to bribe the Germans. I knew the families because Yudel had introduced me to them. They were all sons of manufacturers, people whose businesses had made leather soles, bristles, carriages.

Being a Jewish policeman was a good deal for people without a conscience. They got extra food and they could move around the city a lot more freely than the rest of us. I was never approached for the job, and my father never would have let me do it. He wouldn't have hurt a buzzing fly on the wall.

"The traitors. They're not going to help our agony. They're making it worse for us for their own selfish reasons. Those bastards," he muttered. He hardly ever swore in front of us. This time he was angry.

Still, I hadn't seen any Jewish policemen. Then one day I turned a corner and saw a half dozen of them walking smartly, patrolling our street. They had a hat and uniform similar to those of the Polish police, with two differences: The Jewish police had to wear a Star of David on their cap, and they didn't carry any weapons, just a rubber truncheon.

It's not enough we have the Germans on our backs. Now we've got our own people sucking up to the Germans. They're going to turn us in, spy on us, beat us, make our lives even more miserable. These traitors think the Germans are going to be grateful and save them. They're wrong, I thought.

The Jewish police turned out to be worse than I imagined. Lazar was in charge of them as well, and he made sure they did the Germans' bidding. In fact, the Jewish police later became spies for the Germans, turning in many people who were going into hiding.

For now, they were just patrolling. Sometimes they would accompany us to our work sites. To show their loyalty to the Germans, they would beat us harder than the Germans did.

I was stunned that some of our own people would turn on us. I knew their parents had English pounds, dollars, gold, and lots of material goods and connections to carry them through the war. Poor people didn't stand a chance, and these traitors were living proof. Even so, they still had the nerve to live among us as neighbors.

Soon, the Germans had restricted the number of wells we could use. There was no such thing as running water in our town, so wells were our only source. Now, we could use only two, though there were nearly a dozen in the whole city. Of the two, one was right outside the Jewish police station. We soon heard stories of the Jewish police grabbing people who went to that well and forcing them into slave labor. Now, nobody would go there for water.

The second well was way in the rear of our city, about a quarter of a mile to the south of our house. The hours weren't restricted. We would go there after 9:00 P.M., when the Germans stopped patrolling.

Meanwhile, a lot of young Christians in their late teens to perhaps late twenties were being taken away, forced to work in German farms and factories. The soldiers wouldn't take many Jews. We were not trustworthy enough to work on their assembly lines. Instead, Jewish boys were working on roads and highways.

A few people were doing well. Some farmers always had extra food, even though the Germans required them to contribute 25 percent of their crop to the war effort. Germans went out to each farm and counted what was there and told the farmer how much to donate. In every village there was someone who was responsible for delivering what the farmers were forced to give.

There was a live animal depot in each town, where each farmer had to surrender however many cattle, pigs, or horses he had been commanded to relinquish. During the winter, most of them still could come into town easily using a horse-drawn sled.

Some farmers still had plenty of food because they hid part of their crop and sold it on the black market. However, if the Germans caught us trading with the farmers, they would stomp and beat us. Getting wood was just as perilous. We found old factories the Germans had shut down. The factories were made of wood, and we ripped off the boards and carried them home to burn in our new stove. When my mother had remodeled our home, she had installed modern kitchens. We had two, one in the breezeway, where we cooked during summer, and the other, a coal-burner, in the kitchen.

It was ironic that we were taking such primitive measures to feed such a modern appliance, but we had no way to get coal. The factories I picked to plunder were the ones closest to our home, the nearest was five blocks away. I kept going back to that one, which had made sheepskin pelts for leather jackets worn by the Polish air force.

The factory was all wood, from the doors to the walls. Even the windows were boarded up with wooden planks. I searched for the oldest wood I could find, because those pieces were aged and weak, and thus easier to yank out of the structure.

I would wait until about midnight. By that time the Germans had gone to bed and the Polish police would have taken over. I would sneak over to the sheepskin factory and use a hatchet to chop out the nails so I could pull off the boards. The winds were howling and ice was hanging off the roofs; the temperature froze my bones. But after twenty minutes, I would have enough wood to last two or three days.

This foraging was treacherous because there was no way to remove the planks without making noise. Getting caught was dangerous. Our curfew was 8:00 P.M. at the latest, and when the police spotted anyone out after that time they would shoot to kill. A couple of times I came close to death. On each occasion, I heard the crack of rifle fire and a pinging sound as bullets ricocheted off something metallic, or a "plunk" as a bullet buried itself in the wood near my head. When I heard those sounds, I picked up the hatchet and whatever wood I had and ran, bent over, so I'd be hard to see.

We had one consolation. Even the Germans were having a miserable life in this monster of all winters. That didn't stop them from harassing us, of course. Germans often made unannounced searches of our homes. They'd just burst in. If you didn't answer them correctly, they'd punch you in the nose or hit you over the head.

Jewish manufacturers who had warehouses were particularly vulnerable. The Germans either forced them to go to their warehouses and bring back goods or went to the warehouse themselves and took whatever they wanted.

Yudel was smart. He hid some stuff in his warehouse, but he also hid a lot of valuable things in less obvious places, such as under his house, or in the factory basement, where he'd had a false wall installed. There he stashed finished bristles, clothing, and lots of other goods.

The Jewish police knew my father had cooking utensils and harness liner material, which was pig bristle waste, in his warehouse. They soon demanded he turn over all that material to them. It was midafternoon when our door hit the wall with a loud "thwack." They had kicked it in, then rushed into our living room.

"We want all your pots and pans and harness liner. Now, dammit, or we'll shoot you and your children," they screamed.

My father had no choice. They took everything they wanted. We even had to deliver some of it to their warehouses. They took most of what we had, but they were picky, leaving behind broken and second-class merchandise. My parents couldn't say anything. We all were too stunned and scared.

Our situation was typical. When the Jewish police came to call, they always knew what they were looking for. If you had a way to hide it, you did. If you didn't, you had to cough it up. Soon after that visit, my father built a double wall where we could hide our boots, jackets, coats, and my mother's elegant dresses. The Germans always wanted coffee beans, fur, leather, leather soles, fancy women's clothing—they particularly liked fox and mink fur—shoe soles, things like that.

Despite our precautions, the Jewish police came to our house a couple of times and carted away new clothes, coats, furs, a half dozen pairs of my father's new shoes. The Jewish police lived among us. They knew what we had and where we had it. If they hadn't known, a snitch likely had told them.

When they came into our house, they'd say, "Give it up. If you don't, the Germans will come here and you'll regret it. Better to give it to someone like us than have them come to call."

Every time they said that, I wanted to cut out the tongues of these traitors, but I kept quiet. I had to. One time the Polish police and the Germans came. They knew my mother and father had valuables.

"You've got to obey the law," one German soldier said to my father, jabbing his finger into my father's chest. "Give up all your gold and silver, or your life will be hell."

The Germans often subjected us to speeches when they first barged into our homes. They'd tell us to give up our valuables, scream at us how the Jews were responsible for the war, how the American Jews were supporting the war and it was all our fault.

The German leading the group did the same thing this time. Then my father went to the bedroom and returned with his gold watch; my mother offered a pair of heirloom earrings.

"OK, take these," Father said. "That's all we've got."

The Germans couldn't prove otherwise, so they all left. Actually, my parents were hiding the rest of their valuables in a waterproof sack under the floor.

After the intruders left, my mother turned to my father and said, "They want to slowly eliminate us. We will all be dead soon. It's just a matter of when."

We knew when a neighbor was beaten because neighbors still talked to each other. We knew much worse was happening elsewhere. The Jews who were uprooted from other cities and dropped into our homes would recount shootings, or beatings that continued until the victims screamed their last scream.

We also learned what was going on from the Germans themselves. When we had to work for the Germans, we sometimes got to see their newspapers, which we stole and sneaked home. Most of us spoke and read German because we spoke Yiddish, which is a first cousin to German. We knew and understood what the stories said, and that meant we knew what Hitler was doing to Jews.

The winter went on like a curse. The roads still were choked with snow and the Germans couldn't move their vehicles. All winter we cleaned off snow; the next day the roads would be covered again.

Even so, the Germans were still pouring more Jews into our city. Teenagers and people in their twenties and even thirties were being shipped off to factories as slave labor. The old, middle-aged, very young, the sick and crippled, were taken to us. The Germans knew the one thing we had in abundance was lots of empty factories, warehouses, and synagogues.

We knew Jews were being evicted from their homes elsewhere. We could see the factories filling up, and we saw more and more people going door to door begging for food. We knew people slept on the floors of these buildings with no food, running water, or heat. We knew people in these buildings were shivering, covering up their faces and heads with only the clothes they had with them for warmth.

Many died. There was no heat in those buildings, and the corpses were cast out in front of the doorway, mostly children and old people, hundreds of them. The grave diggers had a small, two-wheeled pushcart on which they loaded eight or ten corpses and took them to the graveyard to be dumped in mass graves. Then they'd go back for more. Most of the corpses were frozen solid.

I tried foraging for food when I came home from work. We were all vultures, looking for something to break up so we could keep warm. One day I followed the grave diggers from the factories and the synagogues to the cemetery. Over and over again, I saw the mass graves, the piles of arms and legs and death-grinning heads, their eyes open in a kind of wide-eyed amazement that they had died such a terrible death. Dead from starvation or freezing to death. I threw up.

We saw many of the dispossessed at our door. The parents would send their young children, because they knew people had more compassion for kids. With them they'd have a little plate, which they held out while looking at us with pitiful eyes.

"Please, please, give us whatever food you can spare. We're starving," they'd say, with big round eyes and runny noses. We would give them a little crust of bread, a small piece of potato. The children came all day and night.

The family living in our house was no exception. They sent both children out to beg, even after the husband had gone to work helping the farmers. I didn't resent their being in our house. It could have happened to us. They were our brothers and sisters. They belonged to this country. They just wanted a happy home, a job, and a chance to raise their children. These children didn't fight or whine. I even gave them some of my old shoes, shirts, and some blankets.

"We have everything; you have nothing," I told them. "Hitler took away all of our freedoms. And so it is with you."

Our people had always kept to themselves, had always been proud of being good neighbors. But when people are starving, they're bound to steal. We had piled potatoes and carrots under some straw, but the supply kept dwindling. We knew neighbors were stealing food from us, but my father only shrugged his shoulders.

"It's no shame to steal when you're starving. People need to survive," he said.

There was a Jewish hospital in a now-abandoned synagogue. It was staffed by volunteer Jewish doctors, who did the best they could. However, the hospital had no medicine. People were dying by the hundreds. Because Yudel's house was right across from the hospital, I saw what went on there far more than I cared to.

Then one day, as the snow was melting in small rivers around the city and the sun began to feel warm again, a sign appeared in the town square. The sign said: "All young people gather in the square in a week to report for job assignments. Whoever does not show up and is caught will be shot."

We didn't know the meaning of the sign, but we knew it could not be good.

Chapter 3

The
Christian
Disguise

A few nights after the menacing sign appeared in the town square, we heard a knock on our door. Germans would have just barged in, so it had to be someone else. My father opened the door a sliver, and outside there was a Jewish neighbor who owned a mill and lived with his sister across the street. My father ushered him into our kitchen, where my mother and I already were sitting.

He looked at me and my blond hair and blue eyes very closely. Then he slowly turned toward my father.

"Joe is well behaved, clean, and neat. With the color of his hair and his eyes, he can pass as a Gentile. I know a farmer who will give him a job. Joe is already a man in many ways. He should be helping the family. They would put him to work during the summer. They'll pay Joe in food, and that means the family will survive. Would you like that?"

My mother acted as though she had been shot out of her chair.

"Oh, yes, yes, yes, yes, yes, yes," she called out as she jumped up, almost weeping.

I was astonished. I knew if I could pull off this deception, I could help save my family. To save them, I'd kill, I'd do anything. If this plan worked, I wouldn't have to register and the Germans wouldn't know about me. I also knew if the ruse didn't work, then the farmers and I would all be shot immediately.

Money was worthless now. Food was the key to survival, and my passing as a Christian meant my family could survive.

A week later, the farm family's oldest son came to the house. His name was Olszeck Zbanski. He was slender to the point of being skinny, perhaps five feet, nine inches, but with a real intensity in his face.

Our family gathered in the living room.

"We'll take care of Joe, and he will take care of us. We're agronomists, my two brothers and me. The Germans have us hopping from farm to farm figuring out how much crop each farmer should give Germany. We haven't time to do the farm work, and the Germans won't let us. We'd like Joe to come work for us when it gets a little bit warmer," he told my parents.

"And what will Joe do?" my mother asked, sounding a little skeptical. This offer was almost too good to be believed, and she was looking for the catch.

"Joe will do what needs doing: plowing the field, painting the barn, fixing the machinery," he said.

"He's a good boy," my father said, nodding his head. "He'd like to help you out and by him helping you, I'm sure you're going to do something for us with food in the wintertime."

Both my parents held their breath. Food was the key to the deal. "Yes, yes," Olszeck said, nodding his head in unison with my father. "That's exactly what we had in mind."

My father stuck out his hand, and Olszeck grabbed it firmly. The deal had been made.

For now, I still had to work for the Germans. They had my father listed for work at the airport, though I was substituting for him.

I made it through the next two months, and the Zbanskis sent word they wanted me to come in late April. I packed my few belongings, mostly a jacket, a couple of shirts, and a pair of shoes. I could see frown lines deepen in my parents' faces and foreheads. But they and my brothers and sisters also were happy.

"Look, we've known our neighbor for many years, and he says the family we're sending Joseph to are fine people," my father had said the night before.

"I know, I know. And he'll be bringing us food, which we sorely need. Even when you go out to the farmers with what little we have to barter, they don't offer a lot. We have five people here to feed. We need to do it," my mother had said.

That morning my family cried for joy because I was going to bring home food. They kissed me, hugged me. It was almost as though I were going to America. As it turns out, my mother knew the family anyway. She was well known as a trader. When farmers went to the city, they would visit her and she would find some clothing for them, or whatever else she had to trade. A lot of merchants had stashed goods, so Mother also traded with the merchants for their goods and for food she got from the farmers. I could see my family didn't want me to leave home at such a dangerous time, but they had no choice. They hardly knew how they would get our next meal, even with all of mother's trading.

I walked to the marketplace and met Olszeck, who took me out to his farm. When I arrived, I was introduced to the whole Zbanski family. It consisted of three brothers, a sister, mother, and grandmother. The father was dead. As the eldest son had said, he and his brothers couldn't work on the farm. They were all agronomists, too busy deciding how much of their neighbors' food would go to the Germans.

When we reached the farm, I was astonished at how big it was. They had a barn, four stables, a little warehouse, six head of cattle, a dozen pigs, one hundred chickens, turkeys, three horses, and 150 acres. By the standards of that little community, they were rich.

The Zbanski family was actually run by the grandmother, who was seventy-two years old, a quite advanced age for that time and place. She had only a few wrinkles in her face, which was so radiant she looked as though she had scrubbed it only moments before. She was almost austere in the way she carried herself. Her back was always very straight. Her gray hair was pulled back in a tight bun. Her voice was raspy.

Though she looked prim and severe, she soon was almost to adopt me. She would wash my clothes and make sure I had some extra food and also saw to it that I went to sleep on time. It was almost like having a second Jewish mother. She made the sons give me some of their old shoes and she gave me warm, sheepskin-lined jackets to wear. Eventually, she even wanted me to marry one of her granddaughters.

The two daughters-in-law who lived on the farm were both fine-looking ladies, blonde and blue-eyed, very clean. They also treated me kindly. They would give me some lunch when I went out to the pasture. They always asked me with a smile if I was tired.

The grandmother, her daughter, and two daughters-in-law, all did the planting. I arrived there just before planting time, when the snow stops melting and the ground is at its most receptive to new little seeds. Sometimes I would plant seeds; sometimes I would drive the horses. In three days, the planting was done.

The family described me to neighbors as a nephew from Warsaw. This ruse was easy enough to pull off because they had lots of family in Warsaw.

After the planting, my basic job was to take care of the cattle and horses, to keep the stables and barn clean, and to feed the pigs and other animals. However, there was a lot more to be done. The brothers had been away so long there were numerous planks to nail down and cracked windows to fix. The barn and stables were filthy.

When the sons returned, they constantly told me war news. They said some of the Polish army and air force had escaped through Romania, and some of the Polish air force had escaped in their planes to England.

The Zbanski family knew English and they started teaching me, mostly by example. The family talked politics in English and I'd listen. I learned that the British knew what was going on here but nobody wanted to help the Jews.

The days quickly settled into a pattern which was to be my life during the spring, summer, and fall of the next three years, 1940–42. I would work for the farmers from 8:00 A.M. to 3:00 P.M. I plowed their fields. They had many crops: wheat, potatoes, corn, carrots. The farm had three horses, which I rode while they pulled the plow. I also fed, watered, and groomed the horses; in addition I fed the chickens, cows, and pigs.

I had been around only horses before. Other animal smells and noises were new to me. But the cows mooing, pigs oinking, and horses whinnying were such a contrast to the beatings and clubbings and whippings I knew the rest of the year, I thought of the sounds as music, a quiet punctuation to the peaceful countryside silence.

I didn't do all the work. The women milked the cows and made butter and cheese. They also did most of the cooking.

On collection days, when the farmers had to deliver the portion of livestock and harvest the Germans required, I would drive the allotted number of pigs, chickens, or whatever, to the collection point. We delivered the animals live, and the Germans would load them onto trains bound for Germany.

I'd hate to have to clean out those cattle cars after they arrive, I thought. A few years later, I would be cleaning the debris of human cargo out of cattle cars, but I had no way of knowing that then.

The German soldiers milling around the collection point looked at me as though I just blended into the scenery. My blond hair and blue eyes, emblems of the Aryan race, were a perfect disguise.

These were my days from April until late November. Mostly the weather was in the mideighties. Come September, the temperatures dropped to sixty-five or seventy degrees during the day, usually accompanied by drizzles. By the time November rolled around and I would have to return home, the temperatures would have fallen into the midforties.

For now, that time was far away. About a week after I started, my hard work paid off in a lot more food. I was watching the cattle in a pasture which had belonged to the puppet Polish government. Nearby, a half dozen families had their cattle grazing on their individual lands while their sons kept watch.

The boys were restless. They gathered together and started playing soccer instead of minding the herds, which were milling about in little clumps, gently mooing and chewing. As I watched the boys playing, one of them looked up, then came running over with a brown sack in his hand.

"Here, Joe, watch my cattle," he said. "Have my lunch."

I thought of how many of my brothers and sisters could be fed on one of his lunches, fixed from foods that grew in what was essentially his backyard. The food was fresh and ample. I almost cried. I wrapped my hand around the neck of the bag and nodded. The others, struck by the idea, quickly gave me their lunches. Then they ran off to swim in a small nearby lake. I now had a pile of small lunch bags at my feet, and the smells of bread, cheese, and bacon filled my nose.

"I could feed my family for days on what I've got here," I yelled to the indifferent cattle, which were happily chewing grass.

As long as the cows were healthy and produced milk, the families didn't care who was tending them. Eventually the families discovered what I was doing and made it official. I would take the Zbanski cattle past each family's gate, where the sons would be waiting for me. They helped merge the new cattle with the cows I already had. Then I moved on to the next farm on my way to the Polish government pasture.

I would take the cows there twice, first at 3:30 A.M. Then I took them back to their owners at 8:00 A.M. because that's when the flies started getting bad. After I was finished working for the farmers, I took cattle out again at 3:00 P.M. and herded them back at 8:00 P.M.

Only Gentiles were allowed to have cattle. The Jews who had owned them were forbidden to have them, so they'd sold or slaughtered them, then moved to the city.

Ironically, the families had unwittingly entrusted fifteen cows to me, a Jewish city boy who had never dealt with a live cow before. Using the pasture wasn't exactly legal, but that wasn't the point. It worked, and everybody liked the results. The boys told me their parents were ecstatic because the cows were giving double the usual amount of milk.

The Zbanskis were especially pleased because their own cows were also getting fat. To add to their bounty, after I walked the cows back from the second shift, I cleaned the barn and stables, then chopped wood so they would have winter kindling. Meanwhile, I got plenty of food to take home to my family. Every day each family for whom I tended cows gave me a small sack of food as payment, food I kept to feed my parents, brothers, and sisters.

I saved as much food as I could by hiding it under the straw in the barn. At the end of a week or two, I would have little bundles of food with bread, salami, whatever I could preserve.

One nearby family was having a very hard time. Their farmland flooded almost every time it rained. They were a kind of community project, and I would often give them one of my sacks of food. They had three children, and I couldn't stand to see them go hungry.

I felt very lucky. I had work to do, a roof over my head, food to eat, and extra food on top of that. I followed the same routine during the nine months I would spend on the farm. I also learned a lot of skills that would save my life later on.

I always made my family visits on a Sunday. When I was ready to go, I would tell the Zbanskis, and they would fill up a nice sack with whatever food they could spare.

I had a little more food in autumn, enough so sometimes my mother and Hymie would come to the farm to take some food back. They would dress in plain clothing so no German would know they didn't belong there. Every time they came, I could see they'd lost some meat on their bones.

When they did come, I would have perhaps twenty pounds of potatoes, some cabbages, carrots, eggs, and old bread. The Zbanskis baked their own bread. To my family, coming out to the Zbanski farm was like a holiday. They would start out early in the morning and walk three hours through the forest to the farm. They'd stay until about 2:00 P.M. A few times I caught my mother crying because times were so bad. Her husband was supposed to be providing for the family; instead, their fourteen-year-old son was keeping the family alive. She was both proud and ashamed.

When I went to see my family, there was no festivity attached. I would know about two weeks ahead of time when I would go to visit. I would tell the Zbanski sons, who could move around very freely. Then they would go into the city and tell my parents to be ready for my arrival.

Usually I left for home about 1:30 in the morning. By that time the Germans, along with the Jewish and Polish police, would be asleep. I would have a big burlap sack of food around my neck while I walked the six miles to the city through the woods. I stayed fifty feet inside the forest, so the constant patrols of Germans and Polish police wouldn't see me.

When I was about half a mile from the city, I'd step out of the forest and cross the river. If I could find a shallow place, I would wade across. If not, I would wade in even though the water was chest high; if it was even higher, I would swim. I always tied the sack of food around my neck and held it in one hand and my clothing over in the other hand and put both hands over my head so none of it would get wet.

When I arrived, my family would be waiting for me in the kitchen. I was glad to see them, but the sight tore out my heart. Their faces were stamped with the daily agony. I could see lines in their cheeks and forehead. Although I know they didn't want me to see it, my parents had tears in their eyes. I could see that inside they were crying out, "Help us, Joe. Help us." When I put down my sack of food they almost jumped at it, they were so hungry. What I had was enough to give each of them one meal a day, the difference between life and death.

My mother would tell me what was happening to the rest of the family. My father was working on highways, then on rivers, digging the banks wider. The

Germans assumed they would take over the world. Our city was surrounded by rivers, and they wanted to fit the biggest cargo ships possible into the port. Hymie still was taking photographs and painting portraits of the German officers.

I also learned that France had fallen in June. It was now the summer of 1940. When the Germans took over France, they confiscated all the French armor. Because we lived between Berlin and Moscow, when I would go to see Yudel, I also would see thousands of trucks and tanks with French markings lumbering toward the Russian front.

"Joe, the way Hitler is going, Russia's in bad shape. It's surrounded by the Germans. The Nazis got the French already, and England is next. After that the United States is going to be the last big country to fall," Yudel would tell me, his cherubic face sagging. "The way they're going, there's no stopping them."

I could see Jews marching from the train station by the thousands. My parents had told me the Jewish police were always pushing their way through our front door, trying to see whether any more people could be squeezed in.

A few miles from us were the buildings that used to be factories. My parents told me that as the Germans conquered a new territory, they'd send more cattle cars full of Jews to our city.

"Why do they send them here?" my father asked. "We are small. We cannot hold this many, not even close. Why here?"

If we had known the answer to that question, these days would have felt even more hopeless than they already did. All day, every day, my parents could see Jews being marched toward the now-abandoned factories. The Jews would have small, crumpled sacks and tiny, battered suitcases, with knapsacks on their back to carry their small children.

When I came home from the farm one Sunday in late summer, I saw cattle cars full of refugees rolling in repeatedly. Every time I passed the factory section, I would see new faces. People were always coming to our door, wanting to sell some small item, jewelry, anything they had carried with them. Sometimes they just begged for food.

When people are in danger, they need hope they will come out alive. I always had the feeling up until then that the Germans could be beaten. But now, when I saw thousands of captured French vehicles, along with the Germans' own armor, winding like a long splotched caterpillar without end along the highway, and the German planes blackening the sky, I felt drained of hope.

My father was now working on building airports. We had seen the planes. My father told me the Germans were getting ready for a big splash. We were only a little more than thirty-five miles from the Russian border, and the Germans also had our people out in thick numbers fixing highways. Still, most of us had no idea the Germans would try to take Russia. It should have been obvious. France was the major power, in our minds, and if it fell, only Russia would be left to stop the Germans in our part of the world.

I myself was beginning to wonder about Russia. Something very strange was happening near the Zbanski farm, which was near an open field. About November, the Germans strung barbed wire around it. The field was a huge space, half a mile long and half a mile wide. The Germans were pounding poles twelve feet high into the ground, then unwinding huge quantities of concertina wire between them.

This looks like a prisoner-of-war camp, I thought. *There's nobody around here who isn't a prisoner in one way or another. I'll bet they're going after the Russians.*

I kept such musings to myself.

Soon it was time for me to go home. Even though they had nothing for me to do, the Zbanskis offered to let me stay through the winter. They had become fond of me. They were all crying. They loved me. They swore I should marry their daughter. But I had to return to my own family. The Zbanskis gave me a big burlap sack of food, including bread, cheese, and a few pieces of bacon and potatoes.

"I love you all, but I can't stay," I told them. "My family needs me. Especially my father."

The Zbanksis nodded. They understood all too well. They saw my father more often than I did, and they knew far better than I what awaited me on my return.

As I was walking back through the forest, I saw the Germans had started a ghetto, confining Jews to a small corner of the city. Fortunately, our house was inside the boundaries, so we had not been dispossessed.

When I saw my father, he had become even older and more frail. He was in his early forties and he looked eighty. His hair was completely white. He stooped; wrinkles and lines crisscrossed his face. I couldn't sleep that night. The deep lines in my father's face, the white in his hair, sickened me. I tossed and turned. The next day, I called a family meeting.

"I have to take over for you again, father," I told him. "I'm younger. I can take the beatings. And I've been fed pretty well for the last six months."

Even though I had done the same thing the year before, my father was still surprised. His eyes brimmed with tears. He had faith in me, but he also knew how his own health had suffered.

"Stay away from groups," he told me, as though he were passing down a piece of great wisdom from the elders. "When the Germans see people congregating, they think we're planning to attack and they start beating."

"I know, Dad, I know," I replied softly. "I did that last year. I always watched my head. I can outsmart those dumb bastards any day."

Even so, the year before, I had been beaten almost every other day anyway. I never said anything to my parents or showed them my blotchy bruises. It would only have made them feel more helpless.

My father still had a lot of fight left in him, but he had no clothes for the job he was being forced to do. He had to wear summer garments, no matter how cold it was. There was no money to buy winter clothes, and we had traded all of ours for food.

My father had recently been working on the highway, where he had to use hammers and shovels to pound rocks into gravel. He also had to rake gravel and apply blacktop. So did my sisters, part-time. The women worked under an Austrian firm to whom the Germans supplied slave labor. Every city was responsible for working on the highways in its own geographic territory.

Now it was my turn to substitute for my father again. The Nazis never knew who actually worked there and didn't care, as long as they had the designated number of people.

It was night work. Every night, we reported as ordered to the German collection point. They would call out my father's name: "Rosenblum, Samuel," the soldier barked.

"Here," I would say, and the deception was complete for that day. I was never afraid the Germans would find out how my father and I were duping them. Every time the workers met at the collection point, we would be shipped to different places where we worked for Germans who never saw us before and didn't care whether they ever saw us again, so long as we did the work and they could take credit for it.

For food, Mother gave me the usual piece of bread and a small container of water. There was something ironic in my own family's putting me on bread and water, which is usually what jailers give to a prisoner. But they gave it to me with love. It was all they could spare. I understood, even as my stomach rumbled through the night.

The work was hard and ugly. We cleaned out ditches and scraped mud off runways. We worked in the rain and snow and ice. By now I had learned some survival tricks, some of which were made possible by my having lived on the farm. I discovered the Germans had to think you were working even if you weren't, and that meant moving around constantly.

I knew how to do that. On the farm, I was always fixing or digging something, changing toilets, replacing straw in the barn, fixing up the yard, chopping wood for the winter, cleaning horses, plowing fields, or feeding animals. I knew how to look for things to do to keep busy. While working on the airport, I learned to look for similar things to do. There was always work to be done: digging ditches, raking dirt, shoveling snow, covering potholes.

The Germans would position each of us so we were ten to fifteen feet from our fellow workers. I was alone so much of the time on the farm I'd learned to do without workday conversations. That was a good thing, because if the Germans caught us talking, they'd beat us with a piece of wood.

If we then chose to run, we had to scamper like animals. We were always in the middle of ice or rain or both, and we had no shoes or food. We would have to run in a crouch so we wouldn't be beaten over the head, our greatest fear.

We were not human beings to them. We soon learned we had to run just fast enough so they would start chasing somebody else. They were like predators trying to catch an animal: If they couldn't run fast enough to pull down one, they'd go chase another.

Even though I knew enough to stay out of trouble, the Germans still would beat me. The word passed around that we had to protect our head and groin. My height of five feet, five inches, was a big advantage then. The Germans ended up beating the taller guys a lot more. I could bend down and run between the tall ones. I also could duck behind the big guys or under them. They'd get hit, their bodies shielding me from the blows. Sooner or later they got around to all of us, though, including me.

All night long, in weather that felt about twenty degrees below zero, we worked. Germans weren't the only ones beating us. There were Polish Gentiles and even sometimes fellow Jews. Usually it was the rich Jewish kids who beat us as much as the Germans. They wanted to show what a good job they were doing enslaving their own brethren.

Working at night made our situation even worse. It was pitch dark out, and the Germans felt they could get away with whatever they wanted without anybody's seeing them. One particular night, one of the Germans who was walking around with a long stick suddenly attacked me. "Yehuda, you Jew, you pig Jew," he was screaming. All the time he was hitting me. "You have to work, you pig. Work harder, work harder, you scum." I felt my body parts swell.

Two or three times a night, every night, they'd start beating one of us, then they'd move on to someone else. We would run. When they got tired of beating us, we would go back to work. We could run maybe one hundred feet, and that was allowable, as long as we didn't head for the fence. If we tried climbing it, they'd shoot us. A lot of us, too tired to run, were assaulted until we fell over.

The Germans wanted us to work harder so we would finish the work faster, making them look good. They didn't care how hard or often they hit us to do it. If one of us died, there was always somebody else they could force into slave labor to take our place.

After the shift finished, we were all herded into the green military trucks and taken back to the collection point. One night, my mother and father both had awakened, and they saw my bleeding face streaked with clotted blood. They said nothing, but they saw my arms and legs swollen and purple from the beating. My mother cried. After that, she cried almost every time she saw me because I was black and blue almost every night when I came home.

My father was still going out once every two weeks, gun in hand, to barter for food. He didn't try to buy winter clothing, and that was just as well—there wasn't any to be had. Food came before clothing. Food was life. Every time he'd return with only a few pounds of potatoes and vegetables. It hurt my heart.

One night I was home sleeping; that was very unusual for me. I was deep into a heavy sleep, when I heard an odd sound. It sounded familiar, but unfamiliar, too.

"Are the Germans sneaking up on us? Are they trying to kill us in our sleep?" I wondered.

Holding my breath, I listened closely. I heard it again.

"Moooooooooooooooooo."

A cow? In the middle of the night? Walking very gingerly, I sneaked toward my parents' room. I timidly knocked on the door. To disturb my parents in the middle of the night was almost like breaking the German curfew: It was a dangerous proposition, and we would never know how angry they would be. My parents cherished their sleeping time. Still, it had to be done.

"Father? Mother?"

"Yes? Is that you, Joe?" my mother's muffled voice answered through the door.

"Mother, I hear a cow in the back yard. What's happening? Are the Germans after us?"

"It's all right, Joe. Go to sleep. I'll explain it tomorrow."

She did. The man across the street, a Mr. Koch, was a German Gentile who spoke Polish. He was a janitor who used to clean the *yeshivas*, the Jewish religious schools, before the Germans shut them down. A Jewish butcher had moved in up the street after the Germans threw him out of his own city. The butcher paid Koch to go to the surrounding farms once a month to buy a cow. The cow would be slaughtered at night in my mother's warehouse in back of us. It had enough room, and, with the warehouse door shut, no light would leak out to alert the Germans or anyone else that something was happening there.

"It's a good deal for us," my father said. "The butcher gives us the cow's legs, the stomach, all the discards. Of course, if we are discovered, the Germans will kill us all."

Death was always a looming shadow in our lives. At the end of 1940, I saw something which changed me forever. One night I was part of a work crew which was straightening boards to be used for building firing ranges for the Germans. For some reason, or perhaps for no reason, guards started beating one of my crew.

He screamed and screamed, but that was normal for such things. We were always afraid to see what was going on, and we would move as far away from the person being beaten as we could. After finishing one beating, they might gang up on somebody else.

This time was different. I could hear the crunch and crack of bones, the slap of wood on skin. Despite my best instincts, I looked over. I could see blood gushing from his head, streams of blood raining down from his nose.

"They're killing me. They're killing me," he screamed.

The others and I pretended we were working. I kept looking up to see where the Germans were, to make sure they weren't headed toward me. Otherwise I kept bent over with my back turned, looking as though I were working hard.

I glanced back and was shocked at the way the man looked. I could see more and more blood coating his head. His screaming had stopped now, and all I could hear was the thud, thud, thud of the clubs hitting him. I turned my back again, fearful the Germans would aim for me next. We never saw him after that. He couldn't have lived. The Germans probably killed him when we turned our backs.

Every one of us felt riddled with helplessness and guilt. We were afraid we were going to be next, but a human being had been destroyed, and we had done nothing to stop it. I was ashamed, but I knew that to help would have been to die. Not to help was to be ashamed but to live.

Soon after, my father was assigned to loading boxcars again, then quickly was reassigned to a project which looked as if it might be long-term. The Germans were starting to build a train ramp, and my father was assigned to carry cement. I took his place.

The ramp was a foreboding gray color, about seventy boxcars long. Nobody thought to ask what it was for. Because the Germans were so active in their war efforts around our city, we all assumed it had something to do with shipping tanks or guns. We hadn't heard about the crematoriums yet. Later, the sinister reason for this ramp was to become too painfully clear.

We knew the Germans still were dumping thousands of Jews from other parts of Poland and even from Czechoslovakia, Belgium, and France into our abandoned synagogues and factories. All the people the Germans poured into our city were people with kids.

Males between the ages of about fifteen and thirty-five now were shipped off to labor camps. A lot of the teenaged girls escaped because their parents bought them false passports which stated they were Gentiles. The girls then volunteered to go to Germany, where they did factory and farm work. It was better than working on highways in the brutal Polish winter. The boys couldn't get away with it, though, because the Germans would check their penis to see whether they were circumcised.

The flow of uprooted Jews into our city never slowed, and neither did the endless parade of bleak faces at our door. We'd hear an embarrassed knock, and we knew what would follow. When we opened the door, almost always there would be a mother or child.

"Help me. We're hungry. Please help me and my family to live to see another day," they would say, their cheeks quivering as they held back the tears.

Our city was known to be very charitable. Everybody who had survived, including us, would say, "We'll do the best we can. We have very little ourselves."

Nobody went away from our house empty-handed. My father and mother strongly believed in helping other people in trouble, a tradition they learned proudly. They were especially distraught at the idea of a child's going hungry. By this time, the farmers had only potatoes and bread to barter. They were the staples of life.

I envied Lazar, head of the Jewish Council. Because he was such a good traitor for the Germans, he had all the food and luxuries he wanted. He had even disbanded his burglary ring.

Only two people in our family were doing well, both named Hymie. Hymie Kronhartz, the photographer and artist, still had his privileged position as the one who memorialized the Nazis in photographs to send home.

Then there was Hymie Firman, the furrier, who had fled to Russia but had returned and married my sister Fay. Both of them now lived in our family's house. Hymie Firman was a skinny guy, almost six feet tall. Quiet, clean-shaven, he stood very straight and had a round face. He was a snappy dresser, always wearing a jacket, tie, and very expensive shoes. Hymie had lived in a far-away city, but he had relatives a few streets away, and he visited them often. He walked through our street, and that's how he met Fay. As it turned out, our mother and his sister were girlfriends. Fay and Hymie had decided before the war they would marry and finally they did, six months after Sara had married and left for Russia.

Now Hymie Firman and Fay, along with their new baby, would visit farmhouses. He was a terrific furrier. He would kill sheep, then Fay would sew and cut the fleece, turning it into jackets and other clothing. The farmers gave him meat, potatoes, and eggs.

Soon it was time for me to go back to the farm. My father now was being assigned to do small jobs, such as washing streets and repairing potholes. I was sad to leave, but we all knew the family needed the food I would bring. I had to return to the Zbanskis.

Just before I left, the army was about to go through our city, and the Germans wanted the streets in top shape. The Gestapo, Heinrich and Dietrich, were showing up more and more. Most cities didn't have any Gestapo, but we had two. They became an increasingly dark presence.

Like vicious dogs, they were trained to beat, tear apart, even kill people. We called them "The Murderers." When they came to town, everybody would hide in their homes. They were unmistakably Aryan, though hardly impressive to look at. They did have blond hair and blue eyes, but they were a puny five feet, seven inches. They both were slim and wore calf-length leather jackets and snappy-looking hats. A blind man could recognize what they were.

One night, Heinrich came barging through our door, along with a Polish policeman. Sometimes the Gestapo went around with the Polish policemen because they were local and knew their way around the streets. Most times the Gestapo just went with Lazar, who knew everybody and every place.

"Where's that damned Firman?" Heinrich yelled at my mother. Firman was now Fay's last name now that she had married Hymie. I knew why the Germans wanted him. Hymie was a young guy and he belonged to lots of clubs, both athletic and religious. We knew by now the Nazis wanted to get rid of anybody who stood out in some way, who might be a hero or a role model. That included doctors, lawyers, priests, rabbis. But it also included athletes. Hymie played soccer and lifted weights.

My mother instinctively shielded us from Heinrich.

"We don't know where he is," she told him.

Heinrich moved forward to beat us, and Mother blocked his way. She stepped in front of him crying out, "Why my children? Why?"

Heinrich pulled out his whip, which was hanging next to his gun on a black leather belt. He lashed out, smashing the black, checkered whip handle into the bridge of her nose, crushing it. Blood squirted all over her face, and she put up her hands to protect herself.

I could see my father seething, but he didn't dare do anything or he might be killed. Heinrich could shoot us all in seconds, and nobody could stop him. We were all white with fear. My father froze, then ran to help my mother. We cringed in a corner while Heinrich and his policeman looked all around the house, turning over mattresses, tossing cabinets and toys into scattered heaps. They looked for Hymie outside. We could hear them yelling how they would find him and whacking things with the rubber whip handle.

They didn't find anything, so, shouting and cursing, Heinrich and the Polish policeman stomped out of the yard. After they left, we were all crying and upset. I looked at the others and saw they were as white as any snowfall I'd ever seen. They were shaking and shivering; I suddenly was aware I was doing the same.

I wanted to urinate badly, but there were things we had to do. My father ran to the medications and pulled out some bandages and alcohol to clean my mother's face. Gently, hesitatingly, he applied a bandage to her gushing forehead.

"We're in for a real ride with those bastards," my mother muttered, using language I hardly ever heard from her.

She looked at us in pain, but with the clear courage that was one of her hallmarks.

We're more afraid for her than she is, I thought.

The next morning a grave digger was giving his morning report to a group of us, relating whom he had picked up and what had happened to them. We were worried about Hymie, and if anybody would know the worst, it would be the people who dug the graves.

"Yes, they found Hymie working a few blocks from your house," the grave digger said. "They tossed him into the trunk of a car, and he suffocated in a half hour. Apparently he screamed and yelled and tried to force his way out, but he couldn't make it. The Jewish police threw him into a mass grave this morning, along with a lot of other corpses."

When we found out, we all broke down, weeping. My mother cried, my sister Fay cried, my father cried, we all cried.

"We might be next. We can only hope we find a brighter day, a better day," my father wailed.

Personally, I didn't feel we had long to live.

Chapter 4

Revenge Denied

We certainly didn't have long to wait before our lives got worse. From the news we were getting from the newcomers who had been dumped into our city, we knew the war was going badly. The Germans now occupied almost all of Europe except Romania, and they were getting ready to swallow that up as well.

The Germans also were close to invading Russia, and their hostility toward the Russians aggravated our troubles considerably. During the first few months the Germans occupied our town, it was possible to pay someone to take you in a boat across the Bug River, the same one Sara had crossed. That was the only way to escape to Russia, and it was used fairly frequently. It cost the equivalent of fifteen to twenty dollars in German marks or Polish currency.

In July 1940, the Germans and Russians closed their borders. After that, neither country would let people from the other's territory across. In fact, the borders sometimes were thick with guards, making sure neither the other side's soldiers nor even a single refugee would invade. Our last escape route had been slammed shut. We knew there was no place to go, and the whole world seemed unable or unwilling to help us. Years later, I learned that the only place that helped us was the Dominican Republic, which took in perhaps one thousand Jews, including one of Yudel's sons-in-law.

The more the Germans dumped uprooted Jews into our city, the more we learned about the outside from them. During the summer, the Zbanski sons told me news they had gleaned. They said a lot of Polish officers, politicians, and other intelligentsia had fled to Romania, then England. That made me feel good. But when they told me my own little city was clotting with even more dispossessed Jews, I was sickened.

Our little city is like a small tugboat surrounded by warships in the middle of the ocean, I thought, with acid splashing all around the inside of my stomach. *We're going nowhere. We're trapped.*

The only person I knew in my city who still had a job was the father of a girl who was an acquaintance. He was in a factory which made leather for shoe soles and fur linings for winter jackets. Both items were essential to any attack on Russia. Most of the assembly lines in the city had been shut down, except for this factory.

As for me, from January to March that year, 1941, I worked on the train ramp. I had to lay track, install the ties, and pour cement. Sometimes we had to work nights, sometimes days, in twelve-hour shifts. The Germans didn't give us any food, but beatings were always on the menu. Starving us to death while working us as much as possible was what they had in mind. They deprived us of everything a human being needed to survive: food, water, decent shoes.

There were eighty to one hundred boys in my shift. I knew most of them. They were my age or a little older. They were neighbors, schoolmates, people I had known for years. We would all help each other out on the job if we could.

We now were being placed only a few feet away from each other at work, so we'd talk out of the sides of our mouths. A typical conversation would be about how we would finish this job and then they'd let us go out and earn money. Then we could start buying shoes and food again. None of us could have grasped that the Germans had no long-term use for us or the goods our factories produced. So we talked about finding or building a home, about having a better life. All that time the Germans were occasionally marching past us singing, "Today Germany, tomorrow the world." We should have known.

While we were dreaming of a better life that was never to be, we all had to deal with hunger. We each had pathetic little sacks of food for our midshift meal, along with little containers of water. We all had the same problems at home. Our families were starving, we were starving, and we did what we could to survive.

I never asked about other people's situations. They never asked about mine. The unwritten rule was that we didn't want to know if someone we knew was doing worse or better than we were. The knowledge in either case would have been too painful. In fact, my family probably was in better shape than most. My father was still going out at night to trade with the farmers. He had a small bag of gold, which he traded coin by coin.

My parents also had been selling off some of my mother's jewelry, much as it pained them. I never asked where the valuables were or how much was left. Even though I was doing a man's work, I was not entitled to know everything. I certainly never asked. I did know my uncle had a lot of money hidden away, and my mother had some, too.

Though I knew our family had the means to last for some time, if the Germans let us live, I was still feeling depressed. My father aged more every day. My mother somehow stayed beautiful.

She must have some kind of special spirit within her, I thought as I dug more ditches or poured more concrete.

We all figured the Germans were building this train ramp to help win the war by shipping their supplies farther west. By this time, spring of 1940, we all knew they were going to attack Russia. The signs were all around us. The Germans had hundreds of armored carriers loaded with tanks and other armored vehicles. The Germans also had hundreds of planes stashed in various places, ready to ship to the Russian front when it was opened.

As the snows started to turn to slush, and its melting began to form little water trickles all along the sidewalks and streets, it was time for me to return to the farm. The parting in spring 1941 was almost joyous. I felt as though I were a departing hero. Unlike the first time I had gone, the family was all smiles.

"We know you're being treated well, Joe," my mother told me. "We know you are a credit to our family. You are well behaved, you are helpful, and the Zbanskis appreciate those qualities. You also are bringing food into the house, food we need desperately. You're doing a kindness for the Zbanskis, and you're saving our lives. You are doing your duty as a son, and we could not ask more of you or be more proud of you."

My face turned hot. Such praise from my mother was rare, and I knew she meant every word. Her words also meant I didn't have to feel guilty that my father would have to return to the labors that aged him so, where he would be beaten unmercifully. I felt as though a load of rocks had been lifted off my back.

I felt sad at what the Germans would be doing to my father, but at least I also knew my family approved of what I was doing. They all gave me hugs and kisses, and then I set out on my secret walk, wading through the river and walking fifty feet inside the forest along the road, until I got to the Zbankski farm.

They were ecstatic to see me. It was like visiting my second family. The grandmother threw her arms around me and gave me a giant hug which knocked the breath out of me. The brothers all shook my hand and slapped me on the back. It was about lunchtime, and they all waved me toward the table, as though I were their own child or brother.

As I sat down, I felt a giant wave of guilt wash over me. I was about to spend several months being fed well, working with dignity and appreciation and respect.

As I was basking in the love and affection of this family, I couldn't help but feel bad.

My own father is probably being hit with a closet pole and my sisters are out raking gravel on the highway. It's not fair that I should be doing so well and they are suffering such abuse. But that's how it is, I thought, stuffing another roll into my mouth.

After lunch, it was time to survey what needed doing. What I saw didn't surprise me. The stables were littered with horse manure, the barns with cow manure. The horses and cows themselves were dirty, and the family had no wood for the winter. I turned to the oldest brother, Olszeck, who hung his head, looking a little ashamed at the uncleanliness.

"Guess I better get to work," I said, and Olszeck nodded. He and his brothers had to leave for another long trip to do the bidding of the Germans.

A few weeks later, my brother Hymie came to visit. He worked while he was there, of course, and the Zbanskis accepted him as well. After a few weeks he would go back to our family, feeling guilty about his return because he would be another mouth to feed. He at least had the freedom to move around, because he was too young to register.

One night, while I heard Hymie's heavy breathing, a thought struck me: *Maybe I can get Hymie a job like mine. He would be out of the house and he could bring back food to our parents.*

The next day, I approached Olszeck after breakfast. He looked preoccupied, but I needed his full attention.

"Olszeck, can you help me?" I asked, standing in front of him.

He looked at me, and his forehead wrinkled. I did not often ask favors, so he knew it must be important.

"Can you help Hymie? He needs a job, a job like mine. Can you help him?"

Olszeck, a very deliberate man, thought through every decision. I knew he was considering the dangers of being connected with another lie. To lie about me was bad enough. They all would be shot for that if the Germans ever found out, but they could control the situation. They knew where I was at all times and they knew me well enough to trust I wouldn't do something stupid like blurt the truth to one of the other kids. If I had done that, the kid would have told his parents. Then I would be dead, and the Zbanskis would be, too.

Hymie they knew only a little, and he would be completely out of their sight. They'd have to trust his ability to keep quiet even more than mine, because they would have no control over him.

After what seemed like an hour's silence, Olszeck nodded his head. "Let me see what I can do," he said evenly.

He could do quite a bit. The sons had considerable influence because of their godlike authority over food allocation. People wanted to stay on good terms with them.

In a few days, Olszeck came to see me.

"I think we have something for Hymie," he said. "It's only part-time, less than a month's work, but it's something."

I wanted to hug him. Though he was a man who tried to do right, he was not very demonstrative. I just nodded, though we both knew how much this gift meant for Hymie and our family.

Hymie's reaction was sincerely dutiful.

"Finally, Joe, I can take some food back to our family."

June of that year, 1941, was a very big month. I heard the Germans finally had invaded Russia, bringing to fruition all the buildups in our little part of the world.

By now the prisoner-of-war camp near the Zbanski farm was finished. When the Germans finally did attack Russia, we could hear the hollow "thunk" of the bombs. Three days later, thousands of Russians were taken prisoner. One morning I was herding the cattle to pasture and I saw endless prisoner columns being marched to the camp. Some were limping; all were ragged.

In two days the camp was filled. There was nothing there but thick knots of people with no room to lie down, no cooking facilities, and no toilet. I saw some prisoners move their bowels right on the spot. Three or four days later, as I passed the camp with my cows, I saw many prisoners sneaking under the barbed wire, then creeping out of the camp and running away.

Even so, the situation was rapidly getting worse. By the end of June the enclosure was almost choking with prisoners. There must have been fifty thousand Russian soldiers in that open space, forming about ten small camps. The enclosure was situated between the railroad tracks and the woods. By now it was abundantly clear that there were too many prisoners for the Germans to deal with.

There were still no barracks, only the skimpiest of cooking facilities, and only a huge hole in the ground for a latrine. The Germans didn't recognize the Russians as human beings, and so the Russians were being treated the same as Jews.

As 1941's summer moved along, I could see that in the camp space between people gradually grew, and they could move fairly freely. Clearly, there were fewer and fewer people in the camps.

I soon discovered where the prisoners had gone. Every night, when I fed the villagers' cattle, I could smell a certain odor that didn't belong to the cows. I saw figures flitting through the woods, doing a nimble ballet between trees and bushes so they wouldn't be seen. I knew I was looking at people, and they were looking back at me. I didn't know who they were, and this was a neighborhood where everybody knew everybody else. They weren't neighbors, so they had to be strangers.

The only strangers here were the Germans and the Russian prisoners. The Germans weren't exactly shy about making their presence known. They would bluster, bully, beat, and use bullets. It had to be Russians, who had very good reason to be ghostlike.

The first time one of them came to talk to me, he introduced himself as Sasha. He clearly was an intelligent guy and was used to communicating with people. He was about five feet, six inches, with brownish hair and a round face. The three soldiers with him had much leaner faces. He probably got first choice of the food.

They all were fairly small, no more than five feet, eight inches, and scrawny. They dressed oddly, but of necessity. Some wore jacket or pants from their Russian army uniforms. All wore some piece of civilian dress. The odd jumble of shirts, pants, jackets, and shoes made them look like people preparing for a masquerade party. Clearly they had been getting the civilian clothing from the farm families. Whether the clothing was stolen or freely given, I didn't know.

Sasha apparently was respected by his fellow soldiers. When he talked, the others would hang back and let him speak. He started talking to me in Russian, a language whose basics I grasped quickly because certain words in his language are similar to Polish words. Also, my father spoke some Russian, because his commercial travels had taken him into that country.

"No food. Hungry," he said to me.

I've always had a soft spot for people in need. I had shared with people all my life, as had my parents. I could see Sasha and the people with him were trembling slightly. They were more afraid of me than I was of them. They'd never bothered or hurt anybody I knew of. Besides, I knew the Germans were after them, and that fact alone was enough to win me to their cause.

I constantly was in fear that the Germans would catch me, so I slept in the barn in a hard-to-find food storage room. At night, I could hear Russians moving around, very lightly, and sometimes I could hear Germans and their heavy boots. I knew anybody who was against the Germans was somebody I would help.

After thinking for a few moments, I tried to speak his language as best I could.

"I do not know if I will have any food for you. If you want to look, I will leave food I can spare behind the barn at the farm where I work," I said, in very halting Russian.

He kissed me for it. He said in Russian, "Fine man." After that, whatever food I could scrape up, I would leave. After a while, the Russian soldiers would approach me occasionally. They all looked skeletal. They told me in their halting Polish they had largely been eating any scrap they could find. Once again, I felt bad I was eating so well and they looked as deathlike as my friends and neighbors who were doing slave labor for the Germans.

When the other boys would give me their lunches for watching the cows, I would leave some of those lunches behind the barn, plus potatoes, carrots, vegetables, old bread. I knew I was taking some food out of the mouths of my own family, but my father had always taught me to be generous, especially when it came to food. Occasionally the Russians were so moved that when they saw me at night, they would kiss me. I never saw them take the food, but after I left it behind the barn at night, it was always gone the next day.

Sasha was particularly emotional.

"I don't believe in God," he told me. "But God bless you. You're saving our lives."

I didn't think much about it. I had to do it. They were human.

Every day I fed the village cattle in a different part of the Polish government's pasture. Each time, when it was still dark out, one of the Russians, looking ever skinnier, would sneak out of the woods and in their language thank me for the food I had left.

I knew the reason they stayed in the area was that so many villages dotted the landscape. They could dash out of the woods into a farmhouse or yard, grab some food or clothing, then run for the woods again.

I also knew they felt they could safely approach me at night because the nights were almost deep purple, and I was alone. If they could take a risk on talking to anyone, it was a fifteen-year-old tending cows in the middle of a very dark night.

I knew life was dangerous for all of us. Every couple of days, I would see German patrols, with rifles and snarling dogs, roaming through the woods. Their rifles were always cradled in their hands, ready to fire at a moment's notice. They were looking for Russians, and the Nazis would shoot whenever they saw one.

I personally never saw any shootings, but I heard from the Zbanski family about Krullur, a local spy for the Germans.

"That man brags about taking Germans to hiding holes where the Russians are. He showed me where the Nazis shot into those holes while the Russians begged for their lives. He is a despicable man," one of the Zbanski brothers said.

So numerous were escaped Russian prisoners in the miles of forest near the camp that the area became known as "White Russia," though I don't know why. After a while, communication between the Russians and me got easier and easier. The Zbanskis looked the other way as I became more generous with what I left behind the barn. At first it was just potatoes and bread. Then I added cattle food and raisins, whatever I could.

As time went on, the Russians began carrying pistols and old rifles. Every time I saw them, they had more weapons. They stole cattle from the rich farmers and gave them to a poor farmer five or six miles away in exchange for weapons. Many of the farmers knew where the Polish army had stashed their weapons after the surrender so the Germans wouldn't find them. In exchange for a good cow, a farmer was happy to tell the Russians where to find those arms.

Then I made a bold leap. I didn't just leave them food. I myself sometimes found a few Polish army weapons stashed in the woods. I started leaving the

Russians those guns and ammunition. Eventually, I found out the way many of the Russians used to survive. They had dug a tunnel network so they could drop to the forest floor and move without encountering the German patrols.

But I couldn't just stay in farm country. Sometimes I would go back to visit my family. One night I returned home and found two people my father knew. They'd all had the same job, picking up tobacco products from the Polish government warehouses and delivering them to stores. They all had been issued guns.

The two men had just escaped from Treblinka, which at that time was just a penalty prison for Jews and political prisoners.

"We've been there a couple of weeks," the darker of the two said with a scowl. "Damned Germans had us packing clothing taken from the people they're bringing in from Belgium, and even a few from Warsaw. It's going to be a big place. They're clearing hundreds of acres."

My father had helped other Treblinka escapees passing through our city. The ones who came to see us already knew my father would give them refuge. They also sought out my father because they knew he was respected in the community. They had a plan.

"We've got guns. Why don't we organize a partisan group?" the darker one asked.

They wanted to form a militia to harass Polish Germans who were living well in our country under Hitler. We had heard of Jewish partisans. Our area had villages with a large number of German families, where the German men had farms and businesses. The men had volunteered to become SS and Gestapo. The women and children now were running the businesses. They would be easy to harass, and I wanted my revenge.

"Let's get horses and go burn the villages of the German families who are profiting from our misery. Their men are all at the Russian front. What remains are women and children. We're younger and stronger than they are. We can burn their villages and kill their cattle. It's no worse than what they're doing to us."

My father and I were all for it. They wanted my father to call a meeting with twelve more people, people in our community who had been dealers in diamonds, coal, and other such things. My father called a meeting in his house for a couple of days later.

My anger simmered. I knew the German families were profiting because the cities were being emptied of Jews. Before Hitler mobilized them they were snitches, pointing out to the Germans who the Jews were and which were their businesses.

We had seen them several times in our city and overheard them talking about how Hitler had liberated them. They worshiped Hitler. Because they were such zealots and wanted to prove what a terrific job they could do for Der Fuehrer, we were more afraid of them than of the regular Germans.

"Let's do what they did to us. We can burn barns, beat the women, and burn down entire villages. We can ride in with horses, set fire to the villages, then leave. For what they did to us, there's no forgiving," one of the escapees said.

When that plan was proposed at the meeting, my father thundered approval.

"Let's get organized. I'm a military man, and I know how to shoot. Every year the Polish government would call me up to retrain and refresh my skills. Let's put them to good use," he said.

Even though my father and the two Treblinka escapees had been soldiers, the rest of the men were merchants who had sold diamonds, coal, or shirts. They weren't used to hardship or brutality.

"We Jews have never killed. We especially don't kill children," one of them said.

"We've got to kill. They're killing us," I retorted.

The arguments bounced back and forth for hours. Jews love to argue anyway, and when the stakes were this high, the debate was particularly intense. Finally, my father called for a vote. We lost ten to six. I could see my father's shoulders sag. I felt sick inside.

The two Treblinka escapees shook my father's hand.

"We have to go," the darker one said. "Maybe we'll join the Russian partisans. Or maybe the Jewish partisans. We have guns. They'll take us in."

I went back to the farm and started leaving even more food for the Russians because they were the only organized opposition to the Germans. Now they would approach me even during the day and ask for food. I learned more of their language. No matter where I was each day, they would find me.

The Russians particularly feared Krullur. He was short, a little taller than five feet, and skinny. At most he weighed 120 pounds. Krullur, whose nickname was "Kink," was a forester and an informant. He was dangerous because he had grown up in our city and knew many of the people. He also knew the forests because he had been a forester before the war. Now he was the Germans' forester. They gave him a rifle for patrolling and for making sure forests weren't sabotaged.

There were signs plastered all over trees, big buildings, and street corners: "If you see a Jew or a Russian runaway, report it to us and we will give you sugar." Kink must have had lots of sugar.

He knew every corner of the forest and he lived next to it. He had a phone in his house, and he was looking for Russian prisoners of war in particular. There were many thousands of them there, many of whom by now had dug themselves into bunkers in the forest. When Krullur spotted any of them, he called the German garrison, which came running with pistols and rifles ready, along with their leashed dogs, which growled deeply and displayed their fangs.

He didn't bother the farmers because many of them had been in the military, and one of them would gun him down if he were to harass them. He was too cowardly to trouble somebody who could fight back, such as my mother.

Kink knew the whole village, and he zoomed in on any strange faces, wanting to know what they were doing there. Occasionally my mother would come to the farm to pick up food. On one trip, Krullur sneaked up behind her, grabbed her, and tried to haul her away to the police station. She let him have a fist in the face so hard he flew backward. He didn't have his gun with him, so my mother escaped. She ran to the Zbanksi farmhouse. They let her in and hid her in the basement.

"I was lucky, Joe," she told me. "I had some heavy rings on my fingers, and that's what knocked him off his feet. But I'm never coming back here, my son. I can't afford the risk."

Now, when I went back to my family, I could see the city was filled to capacity. Wherever there had been an empty spot, the Germans had shoved more people into it. The number of dead mounted as well. Many days when I was back in my city, I saw the grave diggers. We all knew who they were, but they had a uniform anyway. It was a little round gray hat, with a black band around it. Three or four grave diggers accompanied the corpse wagon every day.

The grave diggers would carry out a corpse by its hands and feet. Nothing could be spared to wrap them, so I saw all too many faces of death. Generally they were children up to age nine or so, and the old. I could tell just by the length of the body whether it was a child. Many died of sickness. They looked skeletal, with ribs almost poking out of the skin. Their teeth stuck out from underneath their shriveled lips, and their eyes were deeply sunken in their head.

We all knew that grave diggers pushed their little cart right to the cemetery. There were no stops where the corpse could be made presentable. No, they were not to have their bodies washed and dressed in nice clothing or their hair combed. The corpse was not intended to be dressed up for family and friends, few of whom were alive anyway. Instead, one end of the cart was put up in the air, and the dead tumbled in a jumble of arms, legs, and grinning heads into mass graves about 125 feet wide and 6 feet deep.

For the living, life only got worse. The beatings, bad enough to begin with, were now administered for all kinds of infractions. If the Jewish police caught us trading among ourselves, trying to stay alive, that was provocation enough for them to crack down on our bodies with whatever they had. Same with the Germans.

The beatings always aimed for the face, usually the ears, nose, or mouth. So we quickly learned to cover those parts of ourselves as well as our groin, at all costs. It was the same on the job. Any excuse the Germans could find to whack us in the face, they took.

"You inferior Jews, you goddamned Semites," the Germans would yell while they beat us. "Your people in England and the United States are supporting the war against us. How dare you, you goddamned Jews."

I and many others would be subjected to this same verbal lashing in many places I was to be during the next several years. The Germans hated the idea that Jews anywhere actually could stand up to them, could actually help the Fatherland's enemies, and they took out their anger on us.

My father was still doing odd jobs for the Germans, cleaning off highways, widening ditches. Sometimes he would come home and describe how the Gestapo would beat him and the three neighbors who were working with him. Usually he didn't have to say anything. The scrapes and blood on his face, the tears in his clothing, the clumps of hair pulled out of his head said it all.

One day, when I was home from the Zbanski farm, I saw something that left me shaken to my core. I heard some noises in the street, and I peeked around the corner. I saw the father of a family I knew well.

This family had been butchers for generations. The Nazis also saw the family and started chasing after them. The father stopped and turned around, and one of the Gestapo raised his pistol and fired from four feet away. The German shot the man in the head, and I could see a pink and red color near his ear. But even though blood was pouring from his ears, he was still breathing. His wife went running to him, and he was still alive. "Please, please, leave him alone," she screamed at the Germans. "He's alive. Let him go. He's done nothing to you."

The Germans shot her and she fell to the ground like a sack of wheat. Then their daughter came, screaming, "Look what the murderers are doing." They shot her, and she fell backward. Then their son, a schoolmate of mine, came running up, screaming and waving his arms. They shot him. He fell in a heap.

I was frightened. For the first time, I could feel deep, cold fear rush through my bones. I realized the Gestapo would return and kill others, including my family. I ran into our house and vomited in the toilet.

My father had seen it all.

"Look what they did. Look what they did," he screamed. "It's the end of the world. It's coming fast, and there's very little we can do about it," he said, his eyes bulging, his face flushed to a bright red. "We have to see what we see, shut up, and hope nothing like that will happen to us."

Then he bowed his head, and his grimy neck showed. "But that's wishful thinking," he said in a small voice. "It will. It will."

I was terrified. We had come to the point where we didn't have any tears. We had no voice to scream. Everybody in the house was numb. We knew that our whole future was gone, that the daily, slow process of liquidation would continue to take everything away from us, our lives, our freedom, our existence. I was numb.

We are harmless fish caught in an ocean of sharks, I thought. *We cannot swim past or around them. If we try, we get eaten. Whatever we do, we're waiting to die.*

Chapter 5

The Noose Tightens

A few months later it was September 1941, almost time for me to go back to my family for the winter. The temperature was dropping to the midforties; frost was coating the stubble in the fields. German soldiers were visiting the farm frequently, taking inventory of all the livestock and food. Their appetite for fresh meat and eggs seemed to have multiplied since the attack on Russia began. We knew the Russian winter was harsh, just as ours was, and the German army's appetite might become even more voracious.

I was still leaving food behind the barn for the Russian partisans. By now they had formed armed bands. I saw them in the forest with old rifles, pistols. One man even had a hand grenade.

One day in October 1941, two German soldiers were doing the usual three-month inventory at the Zbanski farmhouse. They also followed the Zbanski sons around all day. The soldiers had been farmers, so supposedly they knew enough to check on how accurate the Zbanskis' estimates were. The soldiers themselves went by wagon all over the county, independently checking on all the farms.

I was curious about the conversation between the sons and soldiers, so I went into the farmhouse to get a glass of water and some bread. Actually, I was just eavesdropping.

I saw the soldiers sitting at the dining room table with the sons. The Nazis were looking over their list of farmers in the county and of the crops and animals they had to surrender.

"Why is the contribution your farmers make to the Fatherland so small? Are you holding back?" one of the soldiers yelled.

"No," Bernard said. "It's cheap land. It doesn't hold water very well, which you yourselves ought to know. You've been around this area many times. You know what the land is like. It's low, and when the rains come they flood out the wheat and other crops. We can only make so much out of the poor land we have been given."

The Germans didn't say much. But I saw one of them nod his head a little. They did know the land was bad. What they didn't know, as I did, was that the sons were giving the German army the most miserly portion they could get away with.

The sons were well loved in this county. They were covering for everybody, and all the farmers knew it. In other counties, people in their position tried to show the Germans how loyal they were by squeezing their fellow farmers for every last piece of grain. Not the Zbanskis. As a result, the farmers had more food to feed their families and to trade on the black market.

I knew the soldiers from the many other occasions they had visited the farm, but I avoided any kind of relationship with them. They had tried to be friendly, but I knew the snake's bite that lay behind their smiles. I could have talked to them in German, which I knew. But then the Zbanskis would not know what I was saying and might become suspicious. Besides, if the soldiers thought I was on their side, they might want me to spy on the Zbanskis. I couldn't have that. I just pretended to be a Gentile who understood only Polish.

We had a huge lunch before the soldiers left. The table was piled with cheese blintzes, bacon, bread, milk.

This one meal would feed my family for several days. I feel like a criminal, eating so much when they have so little. But I must keep up my strength to do the job, I thought.

After the soldiers finished their work, they came to me as they always did. I was raking out the stables. One of them said in Polish, "Get the wagon and the horses ready."

The Zbanskis had made a seat of straw bales across the back of a wagon and there was also a blanket to shield the soldiers from the forty-degree winter air. I straightened out the bales and smoothed the blanket, and they kept saying, "Good, good," in Polish.

I hitched the gray, well-muscled horses to the wagon. Usually the Zbanskis used the horses for plowing, retrieving wood, or going to church or to my city. The soldiers and I then got into the wagon, and I started driving them to the next county. The soldiers were the standard-issue Aryans: blond hair, blue eyes, stern jaw, white teeth, pink face. Strangely, they looked just like me. But their young faces had worry lines, and the confidence that usually spilled from their eyes seemed to be shot through with streaks of doubt. They were unhappy.

They didn't give me a thought. I also had blond hair and blue eyes, and their Nazi teachings told them I couldn't be anything else but Aryan.

The temperature now was dipping into the thirties, and they were not dressed for that kind of chill. They had only thin coats, thin pants, and a sweater. The cold was biting now, so they appreciated the blanket even more. On the way, they kept talking to me in German.

They kept calling out to me, "It's cold. It's cold. Hurry up, hurry up." They made shoving motions with their hands and kept yelling at me to speed up. I did have the horses gallop a little faster after the soldiers made hand gestures. It wouldn't be good for them to think I understood German, because they wouldn't talk around me. I had come by my German honestly. My father spoke it in order to converse with the German merchants who sold his tobacco. Yiddish also is close to German. Still, the speed wasn't enough for them. So we played what became almost a game.

"Yes, yes, yes," I kept saying in Polish.

"Speed up, speed up, speed up," they kept saying in German.

"What is that? What is that?" I kept asking in Polish. I knew exactly what they meant, of course, but they didn't know that.

One of the soldiers pulled out a wrinkled pack of German cigarettes and offered me one. I smiled politely and shook my head. Then they both lit up. The pungent smell of their harsh tobacco hit my nostrils like a punch in the face, but we were out in the open, so the odor quickly blew away.

"Ja, we'll win the war. We'll beat those fucking Communists, that's for sure," one soldier said with uncertainty in his voice.

"When we do, these ignorant Poles won't know the difference."

At that point, they started talking about how the war was really going—it wasn't going well. Soon, the truth about their war against Russia started to creep into their conversation.

"Damned Communists are holding us up."

"We've been in this whole damned war three years now. The British are starting to bomb our cities. We thought we'd be in Moscow before the cold weather started. We aren't there. It's not happening. Our troops are not moving forward. The Russian winter will kill us. We thought we would live off their horses, pigs, goats, and crops. But the Russians have burned everything they left behind. They've even poisoned the drinking water. There's nothing left for us."

"Whatever will happen, will happen," the other one said. "Right now there's no telling which way this war is going. Our glorious leader, Hitler, wanted a war. He got one."

"We didn't win the First World War. If we lose this one, it will be a lot worse. Now all of them hate us."

"It's worse because now the Russians have partisans all over the place. We're surrounded, and we never know where we are."

I thought about the skinny, almost skeletal men I left food for. These were the fierce warriors these two Germans were so worried about. But it made me feel good to know I was sabotaging the Germans, and to hear that my small contribution was making the Germans afraid to sleep at night.

My stomach burned to call out to my Russian friends, to scream at them to come murder these two pieces of scum. I had to choke back my words. It was the only way to survive.

Then the soldiers' conversation drifted to the liquidations. I understood every word they said, and I wanted to shout at them: "You German sons of bitches, you're killing us. You should be shot yourselves for what you're doing to our people."

I could feel the words leap into my throat. I clamped them there, knowing if I said anything that betrayed my Jewishness I would be killed and the family I was staying with would be murdered as well. The conversation turned to how it would be with the Germans if they lost the war.

"Well, how would it be if we lost to Poland? In the First World War, the people respected us. We didn't kill people. Now we're hurting people, a lot of them. We're hurting Gypsies; we're hurting Russian people. We're surrounded."

"You're right. You're right."

"Three years and we're nowhere. We didn't take England. Russia is far away. The United States may be in the war at some point. Then where will we be? They got Indians, Pakistanis. The English got all the people from North Africa. They're all fighting us."

They talked about how the war in Russia was already beginning to stalemate. That their soldiers didn't have warm clothing because the Fuehrer thought the fighting would be over before the winter set in and the German troops could rape the Russian people and their lands for whatever was needed.

"This war isn't going to turn out the way we thought. We have no choice. We're just soldiers," one of them whined. "We have to fight on. Look what we're doing to the Polish people. We're taking away everything they have. We come here every three months, we strip them naked, and they've got almost nothing left over for themselves or selling to other people to make a living."

Suddenly, I heard them start chattering about how life was in Germany. I kept my eyes ahead, but my ears were tuned in to the conversation. One asked the other, "How's everything at home?"

"Everything is rationed. The military still has food because we take it away from people. Our army is freezing. They're going to go to Stalingrad."

"My wife gave up all my heavy clothes, my jackets, my winter coats, to the army."

"Don't know what my wife did, but she probably did the same."

The conversation went on and on. They were feeling sorry for themselves. My insides were churning. They knew about the death camps. They knew about the concentration camps; they knew Jews, Gypsies, millions of people who weren't Aryan were being liquidated. They knew everything, and they were feeling sorry for *themselves?*

The journey took about ninety minutes. At the end, I dropped them off at a large army barracks, which bristled with guns and jeeps and shiny uniforms.

They waved good-bye. I waved in return, but I wanted to burst into song now that I knew the Germans were hurting—maybe "Havah Nagilah" would have been the right tune. We had to trade away our winter clothes for food. The Germans were losing their winter clothes to keep their shivering army in Russia warm. I slapped the reins on the horses and had them almost galloping home, I was so happy.

I didn't tell the Zbanskis about the conversation. God forbid, maybe they might unintentionally tell the wrong person about it. I knew how to keep secrets, one of the many skills I learned from the partisans. It's not that I thought the Zbanski brothers enjoyed their work. I had heard them talking too many times to believe that. They hated the Germans almost as much as I did.

They obviously were not anti-Semitic. Because I went with them to church most Sundays—I had to keep up the appearance of being Gentile—I could see how religious they were and how much loved in the church.

I loved them for the chance they were giving me to get out of the city and to help feed my family. They liked me because they only had to tell me once what to do, and then I did it, often just as well as they did. I also kept myself clean and washed my own clothes. I didn't expect the grandmother or any of the other women to do that for me. They were always sneaking me little bits of food, worrying that I wasn't getting enough to eat. My own Jewish mother could not have been more attentive to my diet. The daughter, Karza, was particularly attentive.

She was always crying for the suffering of my people. She was the one who made my meal when I was about to plunge into the forest on one of my visits to take food home to my family. One day I was shivering with cold, and she brought out a fleece-lined jacket belonging to one of her brothers and gave it to me.

The warmth that enveloped me was more than just from the fleece. It was a feeling, however fleeting, of being loved, well-fed, and hidden from the Germans. But I knew that was an illusion. Every day I had to be careful of Krullur, who watched the pasture where I grazed cattle. It was illegal to use it, but I got there earlier than he did in the morning and later than he was there at night. My schedule had a comforting pace. I knew I had to be watchful, to make sure Krullur didn't get me. I became confident he wouldn't.

Soon, it was time for me to go back to my family for the winter. All of the Zbanski women gathered around me. They kissed and hugged me, their tears splashing on my shoulder. They knew what would happen to me when I got back home.

We had talked about the beatings, about how my father had traded most of what we had to get food, which was the number one priority, even beyond warm clothing. I could see the pity in their eyes, and I could see they genuinely hurt to hear about what my family had to endure. I also could see their helplessness.

"Good-bye, good-bye," the grandmother mouthed as I started out on my journey through the back route at night. No sense running into the Germans if I didn't need to.

The Zbanskis had given me as much food as I could carry in a burlap sack, but I could carry only so much. I took some potatoes, cabbage, flour, carrots and corn. And I took my usual route fifty feet inside the forest, wading across the river with the sack tied around my neck and my clothes held over my head.

When I sneaked back into town, I noticed there had been many changes. Everything was neglected. Our streets, which had been almost spotless enough to eat off, now had so many garbage piles that the stench reached back into my skull, almost tearing out my sinuses. Between the corpses and the garbage, thick clusters of buzzing flies were accumulating everywhere. Eye sockets were being eaten out, faces devoured, but the dead never stirred.

The streets were empty. Even the Gentiles weren't going out, and they were allowed to move around quite freely.

Later, my father told me the Germans had rounded up one thousand of us who were bristle makers and shipped them to Majdanek, which I later discovered was a death camp. Our townspeople were there as slave labor to make brushes. They were my neighbors, my friends.

Life was disintegrating in our area. There were two reasons my family had any food at all. One was that I was able to provide sacks of food. The other was that Uncle Willy in America had sent us gold pieces and dollars before the war. He would send perhaps fifteen or twenty dollars for our major holidays, Rosh Hashanah and Passover. Now we used those gold pieces to buy food.

My cousin Hymie, the artist, was still doing very well. He occasionally went to Yudel's house, taking some food, and told Yudel what was going on. But even Hymie didn't know much. He lived in the main section of town, but he just closed his windows and tried not to hear or see anything—exactly what the Gentiles did. They didn't want to know what was happening. Hymie, however, had to talk with the all the Germans who came to his studio, so he couldn't help but know some things.

What he heard, and what the Jews in our town knew all too well, was that the Germans were beating us harder, longer, and more often. The Japanese had bombed Pearl Harbor, and America had entered the war—a fact that infuriated the Germans. Now, when the Germans hit us with bone-crunching anger during our forced labor, they would spit out, "You goddamned Jews and the ones in America are dragging out this war, making it worse, to hurt the Reich."

They also had found out the Rothschilds in England had allowed the military to park its armor and planes on their private land. And we heard a lot about that, too, as one German after another assaulted us, on the streets, in our homes, wherever their evil whims dictated.

We were still trying to survive. My father would still put his gun into a summer jacket—we had almost no winter clothes left by now—and walk out into the night with empty sacks. He'd return hours later, usually when most of us were asleep, with potatoes, bread, carrots, chicken, even an occasional piece of beef, a rare prize.

Once every week or two he would say in a quiet and determined voice, "I'm going." We knew that meant he was about to sneak past the Germans and the Polish and Jewish police, and go out for food. I would always offer to go with him, and his response was always the same: "It's a man's job to do it, and it's very dangerous." I thought my substituting for him was doing man's work and quite dangerous, but I was silent. He would have been offended if I had pushed.

I had plenty of work to do. For our family, I would carry water from the wells and wash and dry the dishes and clothes. For the Germans, I was still working on the ramp.

Then the snows started falling, and so did our spirits. The Germans wanted to make a bigger push into Russia. Their war in that country still was not going well.

Our own lives continued to deteriorate. Suddenly the Jewish Council put up signs that all Jews in certain areas had to get out—and they had only a couple of days to do it. We were being squeezed into an even tighter ghetto about two miles long and three miles wide next to the river.

The Germans were taking over the movie theaters, fire departments, a fancy bakery, shops, and bars and allowing Gentiles to open all of them again, replacing the Jewish owners.

Meanwhile, the ghetto the Germans had first created now was slashed by two-thirds. I saw even more strangers walking for fresh air in the twilight hours. I saw the grave diggers carting away more and more corpses on their little wagon.

In a way, our family was lucky. We were in the area where Jews still were allowed to live. The family who had been forced to move in with us were still there, though they kept to themselves. The father continued to work for farmers at night and to get enough food to feed his own family, so we didn't have to worry about them.

For other people, the situation was far worse. The Germans didn't care where people who were living in the now-forbidden zone ended up. That was the Jews' problem, not the Germans'. The Jews could live on the roofs for all the Germans cared. Many people moved in with friends or relatives.

A few people had no friends or family they could turn to, so they had to pay rent. Many of those people had somehow acquired American dollars or English pounds. Polish money was worthless because there was essentially no Polish government. We were not considered human beings, so the Germans didn't trade with us and we never acquired German marks.

Even if people had money to pay rent, finding space was a severe problem because very few people in our city had any space left. The Germans had jammed as many people as they could into our homes, which generally were only between 450 and 550 square feet for a middle-class family.

Yudel had two thousand square feet and lived right across from the Jewish hospital. But the Germans hadn't forced him to take anybody in, and that meant he was paying off someone very important.

The menace was increasing, like a darkening shadow, over our lives. Heinrich and Dietrich, the Gestapo, had been assigned to liquidate us. They roamed the streets all day, with a license to abuse and to kill quite freely. They increasingly whipped people or shot them in the street. With them generally was Lazar, still telling Heinrich and Dietrich who had money, who had worked in the government, who was politically active, who was a professional, or who belonged to the Zionist organizations.

It hardly seemed possible our lives could get worse, but they turned from miserable to desperate. The Germans put up a razorlike barbed wire around the ghetto. My parents and everybody else in our shrunken little area were appalled.

"They're closing in on us. The next time, God knows what they'll do," my father said.

He's right, I thought sadly. *We can't escape death. It's just waiting for us.*

Now the Jewish police patrolled inside the barbed wire at irregular intervals. Outside, the German soldiers patrolled. At any given time, they might be anywhere. When stealing wood at night, I always got through the wire surrounding our ghetto by using a screwdriver and a rag, or gloves, to pull out the bottom strand of wire where it was pinned to the pole.

After I had stolen enough wood, I would put the tip of the strand back, but I would leave it loose so I could pull it out again. I was even less safe while stealing wood than I had been before. Once again, I often heard shots, and the "thunk, thunk" noises near me as the bullets were fired. Whenever that happened, I dropped the wood and escaped through the barbed wire.

I was still working on the train ramp, which turned out to be more than a ramp. It was an entire railroad line, and there were just a few sections left to go. Now, while I took my father's place, he rested during the day, then went out almost every night to trade with the farmers.

A new terror began to besiege us. Every so often, a siren would wail as a few hundred SS men would surround our ghetto, then descend on it. They would go house to house, screaming, "*Raus, Juden; raus, Juden*" (Out, Jews; out, Jews). At first people didn't hide, because they didn't know what was happening.

When the Germans stormed into our homes, they knocked on the walls and floors. They scoured roofs and chimneys. They would take all the people they found in the house, hiding or not, to the train station, then cram them into a train of cattle cars. We didn't know where they went. Many times people knew the raids were coming, though I don't know how. Three times, my family escaped these raids, which happened every several weeks.

Now we weren't safe, even when the Germans weren't raiding us. If they caught people out in the streets with some food, or for any reason whatsoever, the Germans took them to the courtyard of the Tisch house, which had become German headquarters. We knew what happened because the grave diggers would go there daily. My father knew some of the grave diggers, who were eager to share their grisly information. The word spread very fast.

We tried to conceal our existence. We stayed at home until it was almost dark. We put wooden shutters over the windows so people couldn't look in.

We're prisoners in our own homes, with no end to our sentence, I thought. *This has been going on almost three years, and the Germans are still crushing everyone. Right now, they're deep into Russia, and who knows when Russia will fall?*

We—my father, Jacob Wilder, who had married Sara, Yudel's oldest daughter, and I—were taking defensive measures. My father was treating me as an adult.

"We've got to build a bunker," father told me. "We have to hide. We can put a little food and water in there, and, if we have to, we can conceal ourselves from the Germans. At least until spring. Then we can join the Jewish partisans."

I agreed. It was too cold to be in the woods. There was no heat, and we would freeze if we didn't starve first.

Jacob's being in the family was very lucky for us. He was a carpenter, and he started building the bunker underneath the sleeping room in the house. It took a few months. I went out at night and ripped old boards off the factories. Some were to be used to construct a sleeping room eight feet wide and long. It also was about six feet deep, a chilling reminder of many neighbors who now resided in mass graves of a similar depth.

Late at night, I would make several trips through the frigid air to the riverbank, dumping the dirt at the water's edge so the water would wash up on the banks and claim it. I never came near getting caught because I pressed myself close to the buildings. That way, I was always in shadows. We also built a false wall in my father's warehouse. The job took four months, even though we were at it seven nights a week. We finished in April 1942.

Other people were building bunkers, too. A couple of my neighbors told me about theirs, but even if they hadn't, I would have known. When I took my evening runs to dump dirt on the riverbank, the night calm was punctuated with sound of hammerheads banging nails into wood.

In spring 1942, I returned to my farm family. When I arrived, one of the brothers let out a wild whoop, and the women hugged and kissed me.

"Oh, God, we're glad you're alive; we're glad you're alive," the grandmother sobbed. "We'll make up for all that terrible winter you had with kisses and with kindness."

"God, I'm glad to be here," I said, with fat tears of relief streaming down both cheeks. "At least here I can breathe, and not worry about Germans ready to kill me around the next corner."

However, life was becoming a little desperate for many farmers. A lot of husbands were still in German prisons and the women and children needed help with livestock and harvesting. Pretty soon, the families around us started hiring Russian partisans to help. The rail-thin Russians needed the food, desperately. Without the help, most of the livestock would suffer and the crops would wither in the field. If that happened, then the farm families would have proved themselves useless to the German war effort and would have been shot.

But the arrangement was dangerous, just as dangerous as having me work on the Zbanski farm. If the Germans found a Jew or Russian working for a farmer, the Germans would kill everybody, because farmers were supposed to turn in Jews or Russians. Still, the farm families took a practical approach. They needed the work done.

The Zbanskis knew what was going on, but they took a chance and kept me. They were selling pork on the black market and making vodka. They had a distillery in back of the barn where I slept. Occasionally I got tipsy on the vapors, and I would sing songs and stagger. I even sipped some of it here and there, but not much.

The Zbanskis must have had much closer ties to the underground than I suspected. They had made for me a gray and black false passport which said I was an Aryan. It even had the seal of the Third Reich on it. I carried it, but I never got to use it.

Meanwhile, when I went back to visit my family with sacks of food, I discovered Jacob Wilder now was building a false wall in the warehouse attic and a double wall inside our barn, which was about ten feet from our house.

Jacob built a wall three feet from the real wall, so there was space for up to five people to lie down. The door to it was camouflaged. In the house, the bunker was hidden by a toilet which could be swung away from its position, revealing the ladder down to the sleeping room.

The hidden rooms saved my father's life. He told me that one night he was sneaking past the fence to trade with the farmers. A member of the SS caught him and tried to arrest him. Arrest meant certain death. My father found a two-by-four and hit the SS in the head, knocking him out.

When the German came to moments later, he called for reinforcements. The German had a gun, of course, and chased my father into the house. By this time, the bunker under the house and the double walls in the warehouse were completed, along with some false ceilings.

The German and his friends searched the entire block. Everybody was hiding behind bunkers, false ceilings, and double walls. The Germans searched for a couple of hours in pitch darkness, couldn't find my father, and gave up.

From her many contacts, my mother had found out that death camps existed. She had said many times that the farm family I worked for were genuinely good people. At that point, she started giving jewelry, glassware, sheets, pillowcases, and clothing to the Zbanskis when they were in town. She wanted them to store all these things for us.

"I trust them. Who knows if we're going to live through this? I want something there in case one of you survives," she said.

One day, when I returned to my family's house, I walked the streets. They were all paved with cobblestones, but now the cobblestones were littered with corpses and blood. I couldn't tell which people had been shot and which ones had starved to death. I didn't want to know. After a while, all corpses looked the same. They seemed as though the last ounce of life had been wrung out of them until their heart gave out. Their cheeks were sunken, their teeth bared into a hideous grin underneath shriveled lips. Their contorted features displayed the pain they'd been in. Their skin tone was the color of ashes, and they were always, always skinny to the point of resembling shadows.

I'd see one corpse here, a couple there. Usually I ignored the bloated and jaundiced bodies because they had become part of the scenery. I couldn't think about them. The living were my concern. People were starving and sick. We had no food and no medicine. When that happens, your whole body shrinks, including your face, and your eyes bulge out. I saw sticklike arms and legs, children shrivelled to nearly the width of a broomstick with no meat on their bones.

Most of the corpses were naked, because the living had stolen their clothing. As a result, I saw bare women, even though they were dead. It was a sight my parents would have forbidden me under almost any other circumstances. Now I saw them and didn't care, not just because they had died, but also because whatever teenaged sexual interest I might have had was overwhelmed by a tidal wave of hunger and massive indifference to seeing corpses.

71

My feelings were not completely numb. Occasionally, I would imagine for moments how these people died, fighting for their survival, for another week, another day, another hour. But I couldn't let myself dwell on that too long. Every time I did, my head would feel as though it were being split with an ax, and my heart felt as if it were being ripped out of my chest. I couldn't breathe. The only way I could stop the pain was to think about my own family, think about getting food and staying alive. For my own survival, I couldn't afford to dwell on the deaths of complete strangers.

Instead, I would start thinking about myself. My feet were many sizes larger because they were so swollen from starvation, although my hands had shrunk. Even though I had begun to eat well at the Zbanski farm, I had been home all winter. We had many mouths to feed, and very little food to feed them. The bakery still often ran out of bread. My father's trips to the farmers scarcely yielded enough food to help us survive. Even when I was at the Zbanskis', I could look down and count my own ribs.

As I walked home, I could feel my whole body slowing down, like a car running out of gas. I was gasping for breath, feeling the pain of hunger and the headaches and my body hurting all over. I knew I wasn't far from being one of those naked people lying in the street myself.

Chapter 6

Very Bad News

One day in midsummer 1942, I was scrubbing the Zbanski stables when my brother Hymie came running in. I was shocked. Hymie never visited the farm without advance notice. His face was flushed, and was gasping for every breath. His eyes bulged. His face filled with pain. I knew I didn't want to hear what he was going to tell me, but I faced him.

"Our family has been taken to Treblinka. I escaped from the market square where they took everybody. But they took our whole family, Mother, Father, Fay, Rachel, Benny, and our nephew Harry. They pushed them into train cars filled with the smell of chemicals. They were going to push me in, too, but I ran away from the marketplace. Mother yelled, 'Run, Hymie, run. Try to save yourself. This is it. Run to Joe.' They were shooting after me, but I zigzagged and escaped."

We collapsed into each other's arms, then grabbed each other tightly. We were two of the few people left in our family. Suddenly we were orphans. We were clinging to each other so hard that clothing muffled our wails. I could feel Hymie's body jerk and heave while his moaning bombarded my ears. I'm sure he felt the same upheaval, heard the same noises, from me.

The wailing of two terrified boys who suddenly had lost their parents to murderers moved even the normally placid horses, who interrupted their oat chewing to look at us in wonder. I could sense their tossing their heads and snorting. When I looked up, I could see they were watching with mildly curious eyes.

After Hymie and I sobbed and cried for what seemed like hours, we collapsed on the barn floor, emotionally and physically drained. After a stretch of time, I could hear my voice, so choked with emotion and phlegm it resembled the raspy tones of a fifty-year-old, asking Hymie what had happened.

He said the Nazis had pushed and shoved thousands of people into the market square.

"The Germans kicked open the door to our house and started screaming, *'Raus, raus, raus.'* They took everybody. Old, young, sick, healthy, men, women, children. They told us to keep our chands on our heads, and everybody did. There were hundreds of German soldiers there, and they all had rifles. There was nothing to do but obey. We didn't stand a chance," Hymie said, before breaking into long, sharp sobs sounding as though his very soul was being ripped out of his body.

I held him in my arms, feeling his body heave and knowing I had to be strong, because I now was the oldest man in the family. I felt that weight as heavily as I have felt anything in my life.

After Hymie stopped sobbing, he continued his story.

"We couldn't move. It was such a hot day and we were all sweating so much we began to stink. More and more people were shoved into the square, and the moaning and the weeping and the crying and the screaming got louder and louder. Even the children and babies were crying. Everybody knew they would be killed."

"The Nazis were waiting until they had found all the people they could find. Then I ran. Finally, after I knew I was safe, I found a place to look at what was happening. The Germans marched everybody to the station, crammed everybody in cars, then locked the doors. The cars lurched out of the station toward Treblinka."

Hymie and I looked at each other in silence. Almost all of our family was dead, and we could easily be next.

I led Hymie into the Zbanski house. Our faces streaked with tears and rumpled clothing probably spoke volumes. I told the family we had to meet in the living room. Such household gatherings were only for important matters. The brothers, who were there that day, and the grandmother all looked at us. They saw us holding tightly to each other, and their faces turned ashen.

We all adjourned to the living room, where Hymie told his story. I could see their eyes moisten, then tears form. They, too, started sobbing. The family knew my mother and loved her. The brothers knew my father and respected him as a man of honor.

They all cried. The wailing and sobbing must have reached the neighbors. Such noises were not uncommon now, even in this remote part of the land, so nobody paid any attention.

One after another, the family hugged Hymie, then me, then went back to their seats, their faces in their hands, sobbing. Finally, Olszeck spoke. "We are saddened beyond words for your loss," he said somberly. "We knew and loved your parents. Hymie, you must stay here for a time to gather yourself and make your plans."

Hymie and I were relieved to hear that. He really had no place to go but home, and nobody was there.

Hymie was increasingly distressed. He was in pain, and I, even as the eldest male, could not make it go away. A few days after he came, Hymie became restless. He approached me just before I went out to work.

"Joe, I've got to leave," he said, his young face looking very old and very bewildered. "I cannot rest. Maybe a miracle happened; maybe our father survived."

Hymie left in the blackest part of night. Two nights later, he was back, about dinnertime. As dark as the night was, his face was shining right through it. We were all at the table, but I jumped up as soon as I saw him.

"He's alive, Joe. He's alive," he screamed at me, then jumped on me and wrapped his arms and legs around me out of sheer joy. I couldn't believe it. After Hymie and I hugged and squealed, he unwrapped his arms and legs, falling back into a straw chair. He told me our father had escaped, but at high cost.

"The Germans packed people into the cars like a cargo of roasted ducks. People were screaming, yelling, and crying even louder. He said the chemical smells in the cars were so intense, and people were packed in so tightly, that after a few miles, our brother and sisters were barely breathing. Mother was almost dead. Her eyes were closed, her breathing was shallow, and she was coughing and coughing and coughing. He said he could see she would die even before the train arrived at Treblinka. 'I wanted to die, but I knew I couldn't allow myself to do it,' Father told me," Hymie said, his eyes flooding with tears.

We both sobbed and sobbed at the thought of our mother, smart, beautiful, and loving, her life reaching an end like some diseased pig in the midst of human filth, misery, and chemical vapors.

Father told Hymie he hated to leave Mother and the rest of the family, but they were nearly dead anyway. So he broke a small window about five feet from the floor of the cattle car. The window was covered with a thin piece of metal, but no glass. He punched it out with his fist, then somehow wiggled through it while the train was speeding along the tracks. Then he jumped and was safe.

"Father looked at me and said, 'There's a very dark future ahead, Hymie. We can't ignore or get rid of it. We have to live each day and hope we can escape the death chambers so we can live to the next day,' " Hymie sobbed. I could feel his shoulders heaving as I held him.

My end is next, I thought. *Sooner or later they'll catch up with me and I will die in a some twisted pile of people in the gas chambers. God, whatever my death is going to be, please let it be quick.*

I dared not express such thoughts to Hymie. After he and I had stopped crying, Hymie said Father had walked through the forest back to our city so the Germans wouldn't detect him.

When Father had seen Hymie back at the house, they both clutched each other and hugged, crying and laughing at the same time. After Father told Hymie what had happened, he fixed my brother with a look that could have turned most people to stone.

"Go to Joe," Hymie said Father had told him. "Stay on the farm. Stay away from the city. I must stay. Maybe somebody else by a miracle survived, and I must be here for them."

The Zbanskis cried for both of us, and for the relief that knowing our father was alive must have brought.

"Hymie, we'll find you a temporary job," the grandmother said, a hardened look on her face. Hymie did get a job, but only because of the Zbanskis. The sons still determined how much food each farmer gave to the Germans. Nobody wanted to be on their bad side.

Because it was midsummer, much of the work had already been done at most of the farms. Hymie got his job only because the Zbanskis used their influence. In September, after the work on the farm where he was living had finished, Hymie returned to our home to be with Father.

I felt I had to follow.

"I've got to go see him. I've got to know how he is. I'll be back as soon as I can," I told the grandmother.

"You have to do what you have to do. It's your father. We understand," she said, hugging me closely. She packed a sack of bread and cheese for me and my family. I left that night.

I knew getting into the ghetto would be rough. The ghetto was still fenced in, with Jewish police and German soldiers watching over its entire circumference. My usual route inside the forest and through the river let me slip into the house undetected.

When I stepped inside the battered door to our house, Father's back was turned.

"Father?" I whispered. He spun, saw me, and ran to me faster than I had ever seen him move. We hugged. He was crying, and I cried with him, our chests rising and falling almost at the same time, both from relief for having each other and as an expression of profound loss now that Mother and most of the family had died. After we were drained and had no more tears, father said Yudel was now living there.

Someone from the Council had gone to Yudel and told him to leave the house. Yudel didn't take any of his furniture, just whatever was portable. Considering Yudel's wealth, that was a lot. He carried clothing, bolts of cloth, shoes, pillows, blankets.

Yudel was a smart man. He and his family had hidden in the basement of Yudel's bristle warehouse during the German roundups. Yudel also was very rich. Along with all those household goods, he had managed to take a treasure trove of dollars, gold pieces, British pounds, and even several boxes of bristles, which had become quite valuable again.

At night my father, Yudel, and I dug a pit in the back of the house to hide what Yudel saved from his eviction. A few days after Yudel moved in, so did his son Morris, as well as Sara and Rachel, his daughters, along with their two daughters and Jacob Wilder. The Germans had already snatched Yudel's wife and another daughter, Liche.

Shortly after, Yudel saved my life. He may have been fifty years old, but he was built like a barrel. One night I was pulling wooden planks off an old factory one block from our house to use for kindling. Suddenly, in the lemon moonlight, I heard a Jewish policeman yell at me, and I heard his footsteps thudding. I dropped the planks and fled into our house.

The policeman ran after me, eagerness and anger flashing from his eyes. Yudel was standing inside the house, wearing a suit and tie. He was always a sharp dresser. When he had been an important international businessman, he had always worn a suit and tie as a sign of his wealth and prominence. He saw no reason to let the degrading circumstances the Nazis forced upon us dictate what he should wear.

Yudel leaped forward and inserted himself between the policeman and my path. His bulk was puffed up, like a bull's.

"If you touch my nephew, I'll choke you to death and I'll bury you in the stable," he said, his voice hoarse with anger.

The policeman had bounced off Yudel when my uncle got in his way. That bump had told him how big my uncle was and how hard his muscles were. Yudel could kill him as easily as snapping a twig.

The man was also at another disadvantage: Like all Jewish policemen, he carried only a blackjack, which would have been as effective as a flyswatter against Yudel. The policeman backed up, quickly.

"All right, all right, I'll leave him alone," he cried out, then spun on his heels and fled out the door.

Yudel and I looked at each other, tasting this small moment of triumph as though it were the grandest of dinners.

"Thank you, Uncle, for saving my life," I said, as respectfully and as gratefully as I could.

Yudel waved his hand dismissively, as though what he had done was what anybody else would have done in his place.

"You're my nephew," he said, straightening his tie and tucking his loosened shirt back into his pants. "You're my flesh and blood. I don't have many of my people left now."

After my father came home, all of us talked about what to do next. Father was undecided. At first he wanted to melt into the woods and join the Russian partisans. Then, when life was quiet for a few days, and he thought the danger was over for the time being, he decided we should wait until spring before joining the partisans. It was a lot warmer in our house during the winter than it was in the woods.

Jacob Wilder continued working on the bunker under the master bedroom and the false wall in the warehouse attic. I gained a new respect for Jacob. He had been a foreman for Yudel and had run his egg business. Jacob was a good-looking man, almost six feet tall. He knew everything about carpentry and bristle making.

It was late summer 1942. I felt it was my duty to the Zbanskis to return to work to finish out the season, and my father agreed. I had to admit I wasn't just returning out of duty. I knew someday I would be caught. Still, I admired the Russian partisans and felt emotionally attached to them. I even believed I might someday join them. On top of that, the Zbanski family loved me as though I were their real son.

I have so much to go back to in the countryside. If I wait in the ghetto, all I have to look forward to is Treblinka, I thought. I could not dare utter such selfish words to my father or Yudel. They both loved me enough to be thinking the same thing.

When I told my father and Yudel I was leaving, they looked sad, but understanding. They both nodded.

"Do what you must. Save yourself if you can," Father said.

When I got back, I told the Zbanskis what had happened. They said even more of the farmers had hired Russian partisans to do the things I was doing for the Zbanskis.

I was passing as a Gentile, but even so, the menace of discovery was always there. I slept in the hayloft, the stables, behind haystacks. I made a hole in the back fence where Germans couldn't see me if I had to escape. Some days the weather was so dry and warm I would take a blanket into the highest cornfields and sleep there.

There were perhaps eighty farms near the Zbanskis'. The ones using partisans were located along the forest, where the Russians could run if they saw a German patrol. The partisans would work at the farms during the day, then return to camp at night.

Most of the partisans didn't look able to hold up a sack of wheat, let alone bring in crops. Their eyes had sunk into their sockets, and they had stringy arms and legs. But they had a determined look that said they meant business.

So did the Germans. They had made it plain that anybody harboring a Jew or Russian partisan would be shot, but many farmers had no choice. If they couldn't bring in a crop, they'd be ruined financially and the Germans probably would shoot them anyway.

The partisans are just like the Jews, I thought. *If the Germans find us, they'll kill us and the people we're working for, too.*

One afternoon I was bringing the village cattle back from grazing. Suddenly, I heard a crack from the farm next door. The husband was a prisoner in Germany. A mother, her two young children, and a grandmother were living there. They'd recently had a partisan help them with the harvest. Then I heard more sharp cracks.

"Damn. Watch out. Somebody's shooting over there. Watch out. Whatever it is, it won't last long," I told myself.

As I drew closer, I saw a wagon pulling away fast, leaving little puffs of dust clouds. Through the clouds, I saw what looked like multicolored sacks lying in the driveway. When I got closer I saw the whole family: The grandmother and the daughter and the children were lying with their legs and arms flung out.

I saw pink and realized their heads had been blown off with a single shot at close range. The Germans had taken them outside the house and executed them in the driveway. Ironically, the Russian had escaped.

I was in shock. I now fully grasped the danger the Russians and I were in.

"It's just a matter of time. I'll wind up the same way the people next door did. I know there's a God in heaven who's watching over me, but for how long, how long?" I cried out.

Filled with panic, helplessness, and despair, I vomited over and over and over again. I was so afraid I could feel the urge to go in my pants. I held it, but the vomiting didn't stop.

All the time I was throwing up, I kept thinking, *I'm living in fear. I know I'll be killed.*

After the nausea quieted down, I sat by the side of the road near the bodies of my neighbors. A tear worked its way out of the corner of my eye and spilled down my cheek. I knew what I had to do, and it broke my heart to do it.

Chapter 7

Compassion Rewarded

T he first thing I did was shoo the villagers' cattle back to their barns. I had fifteen of them to deal with, so it was a good thing they knew their own way. I had trouble seeing through my tears, and my body was shaking.

I ate breakfast with the family but didn't tell them what had happened. I tried to keep complete control of myself, though it strained every part of me. Right after the meal, I called a meeting of the entire Zbanski family. We met in the living room again.

They all looked astonished. They knew it must be something very important. I couldn't stop crying, and tears simply kept rolling down my cheeks. Anguish and concern for me shone from their eyes. They waited until I stopped crying. Then I stood up. I knew my face was whiter than the fresh milk I saw every morning. I wanted to compose myself, but I knew I would be babbling. Still, I had to speak.

"The family next door has been killed by the Germans for using a Russian to help them. Who knows if the Germans are coming back tomorrow? What if somebody squeals on me? You might be just as dead as the people next door. I love you people very much, and I can't endanger your lives just to save mine,"

I blurted out. Then my eyes sprang more tears, which again rolled down my cheeks in rivers.

I put my hands on my face and felt my shoulders heaving. I knew the grandmother would be heading for me to comfort me, and I held up my hand to stop her. If I felt her warm embrace, if I felt their hugging and kissing, I could never say what I knew I had to. Through my tears, I could see they were all back in their seats again. I felt like a lost little boy, but I knew I had to be a man. I cleared my head, and composed myself.

"My being here endangers all of you," I finally said, in a voice husky from tears and fear. "One soul like me is less than the nine of you. I don't want you to die. Those bastard murderers might get you. I cannot be another day here. I have to go into the forest. Every day I see a lot of Russian partisans in the woods. I don't know whether they will let me join them, or what's going to happen. If I survive, you will be deep in my heart for what you have done for me, my parents, my brothers and sisters," I said.

I could see the worry in their eyes, and I knew I had to complete what I had to say while I still had the will to say it.

"You showed kindness to other human beings who were being destroyed and starved to death. You showed there are still good people left in this world. If I live through this, my feelings for you will never go away. There won't be an hour that passes that, with God's will, I won't be thinking about you."

I stopped. I was emotionally drained. There was a stunned silence. Then they all cried out, "Joe, what's going to happen to you? What's going to happen? You're so young, so nice, so good. We all love you very much."

But as they cried out, I could see not only their love and their pain for me, but also some relief for themselves. They, too, were frightened the Germans might catch up with me and kill them. They had a moral as well as an emotional commitment to me, but they also knew my leaving would put their lives much less at risk.

Then I started crying. I felt bad. I was sixteen years old, and my parents had taught me that men don't cry. But my neighbors had been killed, and much of my family had been liquidated. Now the family who had treated me as another son could be exterminated just because I was living and working on their farm. I was terrified for my own life, but I couldn't carry the shame and guilt if these beautiful people were to die because of me.

A few hours later, I was gone. The grandmother gave me an old jacket and a shirt. She also made a small packet of food, including bread, cheese, and pork. I was never so fastidious a Jew that I didn't eat pork. Right now, I was glad I had some to sustain me.

I plunged into the leafy green silence of the woods. My head swiveled to the left, the right. I stared forward. I didn't dare look back over my shoulder or I would start crying about the security and warmth I had left behind. Still, I knew this choice was the only choice.

I plunged between some thick-trunked trees and started running. I knew my way around the forest after three years of being on the farm and grazing cattle. I ran deeper and deeper into the heart of the forest, past broad trees and bushes, past animals darting away from my path.

I knew if I went to the ghetto, I'd wind up like most of my family. That's what the Germans wanted. One time, when I sneaked into town, I had found Hymie, the artist. He was visiting Yudel. He had told me that my father was in hiding, and that every three or four weeks, the Germans were ransacking homes and pulling people out to be shipped off to Treblinka. "Selections," they called it, as though they were sniffing out spoiled pieces of meat to throw in the garbage.

I knew the only safe place for me was in the forest. I knew from the very first that I had company. I could see black specks on my skin and on the jacket, and I heard mosquitoes buzzing. At first their bites were only annoying as I ran and walked deeper and deeper into what seemed to be the forest's safety.

Finally, that night, drained and exhausted, I went to sleep against a tree, rough bark cradling my ear. When I woke up the next morning, I could feel my whole body itching. I dug my nails in and scratched, hard, causing the bites to bleed. I tried not to scratch. Then I'd dig my dirty nails in and scratch some more.

"I can't survive the rest of the summer like this," I mumbled to myself as I ran into more trees, more bushes. I knew mosquitoes don't like smoke. In our halting conversations, the Russian partisans had told me they used wet wood for campfires so the smoke would keep mosquitoes away.

I had eaten some of my food during the first day, and I had only a few pieces of bread left. My religion taught me suicide was wrong. Now, I had no destiny. I could feel death's shadow on me.

Maybe a miracle will happen, I thought.

By the end of the day, I knew I was in bad trouble. The mosquitoes were attacking in bunches, like German bombers. I had bumps on bumps. I was bleeding and sore from head to toe. It was like being adrift in the ocean. No matter where you are, you're far away from shore and there's nobody there to save you.

"Oh, God, what's going to happen to me?" I called out in the empty forest. There was no answer.

On the morning of the third day, I woke up and my body was almost entirely covered by red and swollen mosquito bites. My whole body hurt, and I felt as though I were covered with boils from my scalp down into my shoes. Finally, I stood by a tree and lifted my swollen eyes toward heaven:

"God, what are you doing? What are you doing? Why us?" I cried out of my cracked and swollen mouth. "Why anybody? I have no way out but to die."

The sun was bright, dappling even the most remote corners of the forest. My spirits, though, fell into the darkest pit of despair. I cried. Every city was being wiped clean of Jews. There was no place for me to go but death.

Then I saw the shadow of a rifle barrel. I looked up and saw three people, each behind a tree. I could see they were wearing parts of Russian uniforms: pants on one, a jacket on another. A third had nothing remaining of his uniform but the once-shiny shoes; the rest was civilian dress. The pieces of uniform had fraying threads and dirty rips. The faces were masked by shadows.

I heard a voice yell, "Who are you? What are you doing here?"

Every hair on my head felt as though it had been electrified.

"I work on the Zbanksi farm," I called out, crying.

One guy behind another tree yelled out, "I know that guy. He gave us food. He hid food for us. If it weren't for him, some of us might have starved. He helped us. Oh my God," he yelled, while slapping his head in disbelief.

Out stepped Sasha, the Russian I had met in the woods many months earlier. He looked me over.

"My God, you look terrible. You're so chewed up the mosquitoes made a lot of meals out of you."

"Can I go with you?" I begged. "If I go to the ghetto, they'll kill me there. If I go on in here, Krullur the murderer will get me. Please, can I go with you?" I realized I was pleading for my life. Just a moment ago my life seemed to be ending. Here, at least, I had a chance. Seeing Sasha was like putting a new soul into my body.

Sasha's round face tightened.

"I can't decide that, my friend. Only captains can make those decisions and I'm merely a lieutenant. I'll go talk to the captain myself. I will tell him exactly what you did for us. We don't really want to take in outsiders. That's our rule. I'll be back in a couple of hours. It's quite a distance, but I'll see what I can do. I'll leave this man to make sure Krullur doesn't harm you."

My strength, my will to live, had been almost drained. I had been hopeless. Sasha represented hope. If they killed me, it was no more than I had been ready to do myself.

I spent the time waiting for Sasha lying on the damp ground, exhausted, almost unconscious, against a tree. My miserable life was ready to drop over the edge of existence, and I didn't care. The soldier stood next to me, his eyes swiveling all around to make sure Krullur wasn't there. He told me in Russian that he couldn't say whether I would be accepted.

"In our company, most of them are soldiers. Sasha knows how to talk to the captain and tell him what you did for his people. Maybe they'll let you live. You deserve it for what you did for us," he said, real sympathy showing in his eyes.

He gave me a small piece of bread. I still had a few crumbs from the Zbanskis in my pocket. I told the guard I appreciated what Sasha and the others were trying to do for me.

"We're in the same situation as you," he replied, wearily. "We're trying to survive. Your problem is you're alone, with no weapon and no food. If we get you into the group, we'll have to train you."

I also knew that I was familiar with the terrain and they weren't. The Russians needed me to show them where to get food, and how to get around German patrols. I had something to offer. I just hoped they recognized it. Then I fell asleep, my head buzzing as though mosquitoes were trapped between my ears and couldn't get out.

Suddenly, I felt a foot nudging my leg. I looked up. It was Sasha. I started to shake. I thought this was the end. I prayed to God to help me.

"You're a lucky little bastard," he said with a big smile. "Come with us."

I walked with them about two hours. My bite-riddled body hurt, but I was still alive. We arrived at guarded camp half a mile in diameter. I was told to surrender my boots. With every square inch of my body coated with pain and itching, I removed them. I had only a thin pair of pants and a worn cotton shirt. I was ashamed to see how bites had made my feet red and bulging. I had always tried to keep myself clean and neat. Now, I hurt and I looked ugly, and I knew it.

They gave me some sturdy used clothing and let me wash in a bucket. They gave me soup and bread on cracked dishes. After I had shoveled the food down my throat, Sasha took me by the hand.

"Now you'll learn how to earn your place here," he said.

I joined a class already in progress. There were thirty-seven people in camp, and, soldiers or not, all of them were training constantly. For the next several hours I learned to shoot a rifle, climb trees, and hide in the forest. I learned how to surprise an enemy by hiding in a tree, jumping down on him, then grabbing his throat and choking him.

We needed to know how to do this because the Germans had better weapons than we did. We couldn't beat them in armed combat, so we had to choke or stab them. We had a crash course in sneaking up on four guards at railroad bridges, then snatching and killing them one by one.

Finally, class was over. I dropped onto the ground next to the fire, grateful to be alive, wondering what my parents would think of their son learning to be a killer, but mostly feeling the limp exhaustion of every part of my body.

Three hours later, the others and I were being shaken awake.

"We have to do this," Sasha whispered to me. "You must learn to operate on only a little sleep in case the Germans find us."

We did a lot of running with packs on our back. We chopped up bushes, then learned to use them as mattresses and to burn them to keep away mosquitoes. Then we learned to dig bunkers and to camouflage them with trees.

Over the succeeding days I learned more about the fine points of running, hiding, and getting around the Germans. I learned that if I were carrying twenty pounds of baggage, ammunition, and guns, how often I got to rest depended on my cover. If I were in the forest, I could use its camouflage to rest more often. If I were in an open space, I had to run fast and frequently. This knowledge was a necessity, because we had to move quickly when the Nazis and Polish police surrounded the forest. We also had long runs to make sure we had the speed and stamina to run far and fast if needed. I was glad I was young.

I particularly enjoyed weapons practice. I learned how to slip a knife between a man's ribs, and how to stab or cut him in the neck. During the exercises, we had to crawl up near the pretend guards, then grab them by the neck and hit them in the head so they would fall unconscious. A few days after I arrived, I was carrying weapons—a knife, a hand grenade, and a submachine gun, all stolen from Polish army caches. That fact alone told me I had their complete trust.

I felt a new power as I learned to fire submachine guns, using trees deep in the woods for firing practice. We were about ten miles inside the forest and had piles and piles of bullets left over from the Polish army, so we were surrounded with miles of trees which muffled our gunfire, preventing it from reaching German ears. And we had enough firepower to give the Nazis problems if they did find us.

The more I practiced using my weapons and fighting skills, the more powerful I felt.

"If there's anything I can do to help destroy the Germans, to help kill Hitler, I'll do it," I told Sasha.

I felt a bond between my fellow soldiers and myself that I had never felt, even in my own family. Every fiber in me felt filled with power. We had weapons and we were fighting together for our survival. If the Germans discovered any of us, we would be killed.

When I was learning how to kill Germans, I lost all track of time, my pain went away, and I felt a surge of hormonal exhilaration I had never felt before. I liked the feeling of learning how to kill Germans. It filled me with hope, with power. My tired muscles felt stronger just thinking about sinking my knife into a German heart.

I wouldn't have killed a chicken before this. Now I'm ready to execute hundreds of Germans. I hope I get a chance to kill the bastards personally, I thought.

If you have revenge in mind, it doesn't matter how you carry it out. I almost embraced my gun and my knife as though they were lovers. They gave me strength. I wasn't afraid to die when I had my weapons with me. The Germans were fighting for power and glory. We were fighting for our homes, our families, our lives. The Russians taught us you have to channel all your agony into fighting the enemy to the death.

All during my training, I could see that Sasha was the man people looked up to. He was like a father. He shared his food; he always told us to be careful to check out a target on a raid, not just run toward it blindly. He was always telling other people about how I had left food and guns for them.

"You didn't have to do it, but you did it," he told me, always nodding approval, a brightness shining in his eyes. "There was always some kind of food at the back of the barn. Nobody came to help us except you. You did your share and more."

One day Sasha walked over to me and said, "Joe, you know the terrain. You know how to read the road signs, how to speak Polish. We need your help. Come with us."

This was my chance to prove my worth. Sasha took seven men as well as me. We would know the purpose of our raid when we got to wherever we were going. Suddenly we found ourselves surrounding a Polish police station. We burst in the door and took the police by surprise. They were cleaning guns, polishing uniforms, checking records, doing everyday tasks. Sasha whispered to me and I yelled out what he told me to say.

"We're only here to take the weapons. Anybody who jumps up will be shot. Let us take the weapons and nobody will be hurt."

The police instantly threw up their hands. "Help yourself," one of them cried, hoarsely. We did.

Several times I led the partisans to Polish police stations. I knew where the stations were, in both the little cities and the countryside villages. The first time I personally kicked in the door of a Polish police station, gun in hand, I expected a blaze of gunfire in return. Instead, the police, as before, politely held up their hands and showed us where the keys to the weapons storage were.

I found out that usually the police put up no resistance, and we didn't shoot anyone. It was an unspoken pact among us all. It resulted in our getting huge batches of rifles, ammunition, handguns, and grenades while shedding not a drop of blood.

The Russians always had plans, mostly on how to get food. A group was always leaving for somewhere to scout the Germans or find something to eat. I was a teenager, but I was going on missions that made me grow up faster. I went with them on raids. I knew where the bridges and railroad stations were, so I led them there. Usually we went through the woods to cloak our movements.

Most of these sneak attacks were the same. Sometimes the Nazis were jittery, and we had to be extra careful that they didn't see us. We were camouflaged with branches and leaves, so we could move closer. We had to choose places close to bridges or shrubs so we could keep ourselves hidden until the last minute. Some nights were freezing, and we had to lie in snow.

The Germans weren't stupid. Lots of times they smelled something and swivelled their heads back and forth like watchful hawks. Sometimes we had to crawl half a night in order to sneak up behind them, or wait for them to march past us.

We had to crawl in pitch-black darkness. We usually would crawl up near a German on two sides. When we got close enough, one of us would leap up, put a hand over the German's mouth, then drag him off the road or bridge. Several of us would surround the flailing form and stab it to death.

The first time I helped murder a German it felt good. I wanted revenge: I wanted to cause them pain and death as they had caused the pain and death to my family, friends, and city. Just before I was going to make my moves, I hesitated. I was still queasy. I'd never done this before, and Sasha had told me the first time is the worst. Sasha whispered to me, "You must do it. It's for our survival. We have to inflict misery on them."

He was right. We approached a small railroad bridge which had only one guard. I sneaked up behind him and jumped him. I grabbed his head and hung on as he tried to throw me off. He was a big man, and I wasn't sure how long I could prevent him from shaking me loose. Some of the Russians started stabbing him, and I could see blood spurt and splash. More burst from somewhere and drenched my shirt.

I could see knife blades rise and fall, and I could feel the man's strength dwindling. He wasn't trying nearly as hard to toss me off, and he wasn't even swinging very hard at the others. Finally, he crumpled, and I landed on top of him.

His eyes rolled back in his head, his wounds bathing his body in blood, and I felt proud. I was taking revenge. I was repaying the Germans for what they were doing to my family and my people.

Sometimes we would shoot a guard. It was a lot easier to kill them with a bullet if we were positioned above them. Aiming while the Germans were above us was not quite so easy.

Sometimes, if we only wounded the German, then the others would hold his squirming body while one of us stuffed rags into his mouth, then taped it shut. Then we'd tie him up and leave him there to freeze to death. The prospect of his slowly dying, lungs filling with ice and body numbing, didn't bother me. It felt good to let them die slowly. Mostly, though, we just killed them outright.

When the snows came in October 1942, we used slightly different tactics. We took white sheets we had stolen from clotheslines and put them over us as we crawled along hills and slopes to get near German guards. Then we would leap on them, clamp one hand over their mouth and throat, then choke them with the other hand. Then one or two others in our group would stab them in the stomach. A few times we let them live, saying to them, "Tell your superiors this is just the beginning of what we'll do to you."

Usually the other partisans would do the killing, because at five feet, five inches, I was light and small. But I killed several Germans myself by choking them from behind.

One time I crawled through some ditches—our favorite way to sneak up on Nazis—and jumped three Germans. I had a gun and killed one with a single shot, then stabbed the others. They shrugged off the wounds I gave them, so others beat them to death. After we killed the guards and dumped their bodies in a ditch, we dynamited whatever they were guarding.

Usually, however, my job was to get food from the big farms. There were about sixty of them in the area. I had lived with the Zbanskis, and the brothers went to all the farms. Because I had listened to the brothers' conversations, I knew where all the farms were, including the big ones.

By local standards, these particular farms were huge. They had perhaps one hundred head of cattle each, a couple of hundred pigs, and thousands of acres. They had Polish people working on them. The Poles who owned the farms had fled, and now Germans already living in Poland had taken them over—as representatives of the Germans.

My Russian friends and I would sneak up on the farm foremen, who were always alone. We'd pick different times, so nobody could figure out exactly when we'd strike. We knew that about 9:00 P.M. the foremen usually checked on the cows, horses, and pigs.

We were pretty fearsome-looking. We carried machine guns and had bandoliers of bullets across our chests, hand grenades on our belts, and sticks of dynamite nearby. We would sneak up on the workers at night and hiss, "We won't hurt you. We just want to know who your foreman is." They would eagerly tell us. Then we'd wait until the foreman showed.

I spoke German, and so did all of the foremen. As spokesman, I would step forward and look directly into the foremen's eyes. Usually they were several inches taller and humiliated to hear threats uttered by someone so short.

"We have come here to steal food from you," I would tell them. "We're not going to kill you," I would say in a very low but firm voice. "We're not here to kill anybody. It's cheaper and easier to give us the food. But if you squeal on us, we'll know you did it. Then we'll come back and slit your throat and disembowel your wife and children. We will need food every time we come. Do you understand me?" I would say in an even tone.

We were not the only partisans they'd encountered. We knew others were in the area. Usually the terrified foreman would just nod his sweating head vigorously. Most of the partisans by then had hand grenades and rifles, so my threats clearly could be backed up. In most cases, the threats worked. As far as we could tell, none of the foremen ever told the Germans what we were doing.

Instead, with the foreman watching mutely, we would take a couple of wagons and some horses and cart off sheep, or pigs, along with about ten loaves of bread and potatoes they had with them to feed their workers. We would tell them where they could pick up the cart and horse after we were through.

We would pick up food at these farms, sometimes in the night, sometimes during the day. Sometimes we took three or four sheep, then led them off at the end of a rope. This was difficult, because most of us were city boys, not shepherds.

We figured out that having the impoverished farmers on our side would be good for them and us. Sometimes when we took a sheep or calf from the rich farms, we would take one of the animals to a poor farmer in another village. Because I was the only one who knew Polish, I would be the one to approach the farmer with a sheep or calf.

"We know you have weapons," I would tell the farmer, who generally was trembling to see all those armed men at his doorstep. "We don't want to take the arms for nothing. We'd rather be on good terms with you. It's dark. Nobody has seen us come here. So, take this gift in exchange for telling us where the weapons are."

Sometimes we'd even give them pigs or a horse, if we thought they knew some especially good locations. One poor farmer was so happy with the pig we gave him, he told us where the other farmers had hidden their arms. He was especially poor. His house had big holes in its roof, and his clothes were ragged. So we gave him and his family food and shoes, for which they hugged us.

The partisans admittedly were using harassment, threats, intimidation, and bribery to get their way. Still, they were nice about it, and they didn't hurt civilians. That seemed fair.

"The Germans were doing a lot worse to people," I told Sasha.

I saw further evidence that war could be conducted on civilized terms. Sometimes we needed horses. If we did, we would take them from a farmer at night but return them by the next morning. I was very good with the horses. One time, the Russians and I were out riding early, when we heard the clatter of some Germans in a wagon drawn by two horses. We pulled our horses behind some trees.

The Germans drove past us, but I saw one of them turn his head, and I noticed we were throwing shadows across the trail. I saw the German driver raise his whip and start flogging the horses. The Germans were scared to death we were going to shoot them. We just laughed the kind of hysterical braying that spoke of the violent emotions we felt underneath.

I did manage to make some friends. A few weeks after I joined the partisans, we ran into a boy who was a little younger than I was. Ragged and half-dead, he saw us and started crying. He was about sixteen years old and was blubbering in Polish. His clothes were torn, and he stammered out that he had been in Warsaw and had leaped from the train taking him and his family to Treblinka.

I talked to Sasha, who said, "We will take him temporarily. We'll get him fed and back in shape. Then we'll try to find a Jewish partisan group for him."

There were plenty around. I knew from people I talked to when I returned to my city that there were a lot of partisans spread out in Poland and Russia.

I was glad the kid was going to be saved. I showed him how to climb trees and crawl on his belly. We didn't take him on raids. After a couple of weeks, I went into town to see my family, and when I returned, he was gone.

About five weeks later, we ran into a guy a few years older than I who had lived near my mother's orchards. He said he had jumped from one of the death trains, had no place to go, and wanted to join the partisans. I talked Sasha into letting him stay for a while. He was there a week, then went to work for a nearby farmer.

Some other people we didn't treat so gently. One time a group of us ambushed an SS man who would ride a bike to see his girlfriend. Her neighbors told us what his schedule was, and we were watching the house. When the time came, we surrounded it. We wanted him to know we were still alive and on the hunt for him and his fellow Germans. We weren't going to kill him. Instead, we wanted him to take back the message that we were going to kill as many of his kind as they had killed of us.

We kicked down the door, and the two of them were in bed. He started to reach for his holstered gun, but I yelled out, "Don't go for your gun or we'll kill you."

He held up his hands, looking comical with the sheet clinging to his body and his girlfriend's, while his naked arms stabbed into the air. She was poor, and he probably gave her packages of food or whatever. A lot of the women sold themselves, but they were only trying to survive, just as we were. We had no quarrel with her, just with him. She ran to the living room.

We shut the door, then grabbed his arms and pulled him out of bed. We just wanted to send a message. So we worked on him for ten minutes, punched him, kicked him in the balls, and heard his strangled screams. Blood was flowing freely out of his eyes and his ears. When we finished, our group commander told him, "Go to your superiors, scum. Tell them this is the beginning of this kind of medicine, and we're going to give it to every one of you."

It was a pleasure to see his blond hair streaked with blood and to see fear in his Aryan-blue eyes. We took away his bike. The SS man crawled, naked and bleeding, out the door. We didn't do a thing to the woman. We were laughing to ourselves for hours about what a pitiful figure he must have been when he finally got to camp.

Shortly after that, I went into town to visit my family. Of course, I told them nothing about what I was doing. My father had been a military man, and he knew what it was to have to kill or beat the enemy. Still, these were my father and my uncle. They knew me as a gentle and polite boy. I was fast becoming a man, understanding and doing things they never would have believed I would be part of. I stayed only a few hours, then returned to camp.

A week later, it was time for my revenge: It was time to call on Krullur. I remembered what he'd done to my mother, how he'd grabbed her and tried to take her to SS headquarters to be killed.

"I want to get that son of a bitch," I told Sasha and my other Russian companions. They, too, particularly wanted Krullur, who was personally responsible for shooting many of their friends in their winter bunkers while they begged for their lives. He had turned in many more of their friends to the Germans. They hated him even more than I hated him. We all wanted to quench our hatred with his blood.

We walked, almost ran, to Krullur's cabin. We didn't say much. We wanted to feel the depths of our bitterness toward him, like filling up a bottle with gasoline before you stuff a fuse into it, light a match, and throw it. Five of us surrounded his house and stood at his windows. I yelled for him to come out.

"No, I won't," he screamed in his high-pitched voice. "My wife is here. Leave us alone."

It was a lie. I knew he was a bachelor. What decent woman would have him?

"Not a chance," one of us yelled, and the soldier at the front door rushed at it, splintering it with a deadly cracking sound.

Krullur must have weighed ninety pounds at most. He was in his underwear and looked small as a mosquito. He had a double-barreled shotgun hanging inside the window. He started to run for it, when I yelled out in Polish, "Don't touch that gun or you're a dead man." He froze, and we descended on him like a pack of wolves tearing at wounded prey. We hit him. Hard. He bounced off the walls, leaving his smeared blood behind.

"This is just a sample," I yelled at him. "If you see one of us in the forest, then I guarantee you're dead. No more punches, no more warnings. You're responsible for killing our friends. Next time, we're going to kill you," I yelled as I punched him in the face, cracking his nose. Blood spurted.

"I didn't do that. I didn't bring the SS and the Gestapo in. I didn't do it," he shrieked, in between punches. As little as he was, he screamed like a pig.

We knew better than to believe his denials. Several of the people in the bunkers whom Krullur had betrayed had lived after they were shot. They had seen his face. The Germans would yank off the bushes covering the bunker, see the Russians, then start shooting. The Russians would glance up and see who it was.

"Our people, the ones you showed to the Germans, they lived, you fucking bastard," Sasha yelled. "They know you did it. They saw you. Shut up, you bastard. This is our revenge, and you deserve it."

After we finished, he looked like a small lump which had been bathed in blood. We looked down at him in contempt. Anger leaped from all of our eyes.

"We'll let you live, you bastard, but not too long. If you bother any of our people ever again, we'll tell everybody. If they don't kill you, we will," Sasha growled at him.

"You're a menace to humanity," I said in Polish. The Russians repeated it in their language. Krullur understood.

I looked at Krullur and wanted to dip my hands into his blood.

I could have survived if it hadn't been for this bastard. I could have stayed with the Zbanskis. The people next door were killed because of him. Krullur is responsible for their deaths. He respected the Zbanskis, but you never can tell when an animal will turn on you. This son of a bitch killed his own people, I thought.

Out loud, I said, "You deserve to die for the deaths of many people. Those people are not the murderers. You are."

He was lying on the floor, crying, bleeding, and screaming. The Russians would have shot or killed him, but they weren't murderers, they were human beings, not like the Nazis. When we left, Krullur was in a bloody heap on the floor.

In early September, I started worrying even more about my father and brother. Hymie was still going back and forth to a farm, doing odd jobs. At some point my Russian partisan bosses had gone into our city and met my father and had taken an interest in my family. I also sometimes went to visit my relatives on weekends, so I knew Hymie was still in the ghetto. I wanted to see him again.

I worried about getting in and out. The ghetto was still fenced by barbed wire, with the Jewish police patrolling the inside and the Germans patrolling the outside. I knew my father, my uncle, and two of his daughters were still there, along with Jacob Wilder. Jacob was still working on the bunkers, constantly improving them, making them more invisible. He made their outer appearance so natural the entrances were impossible to find unless you were right on top of them. I was amazed that he had built the two hideouts we had discussed. In the attic there was a false wall which seamlessly fell into place when it was not pulled back. There was also a sliding wall in the loft.

The partisans had told me my brother Hymie had already returned from the farm to the ghetto. When I entered the house, I saw my father on the couch, and the others a few feet away. They ran to me, and we all hugged, kissed, and cried. Yudel, too, though he was normally not emotional. We gathered in the living room and talked about what to do next. We talked and talked. The topic: how to survive. None of us had an answer.

"Maybe Hymie and I can wait until spring, when it's warmer, then go into the woods. We can try to join the Russian partisans with you," my father said. But the problem, as we all saw, was that Yudel and his daughters could not leave. It was too cold and dangerous for women. Yudel was too old and had to stay with his children and grandchildren. Jacob, who had married Sara, Yudel's oldest daughter, couldn't leave his wife and daughter behind.

A couple of days later, I was chopping wood for the Germans, substituting for my father. The Germans didn't watch us closely. A woman who was passing as Gentile kept sneaking us food. She would whisper to us, "I'm a Jew," then leave a bit of food and rush off. Knowing she was Jewish comforted us. One of our own was looking after our well-being.

Suddenly I heard the air raid siren splitting the air, and everybody around me started running. I saw one thousand people fleeing. The girl who had been bringing us food called out, "You look Jewish; you better run." She told us to head straight for the post office. "A decent man works there. Find the post-master," she yelled.

I didn't want to head for the ghetto. I knew the Germans would pile in there and I'd be caught right away. I ran for the post office, along with fifteen boys and girls my age. We ran in. The postmaster, an old man with a stooped back and wearing a German military uniform, was right inside the front door. As we piled up inside the dark vestibule, we cried out, "Save us, save us, help us, help us."

"Up, up, up," he yelled, motioning to a ladder in the back of the post office. "Climb up the ladder. Get up there. I'll take care of you," he bellowed.

He ran over to the ladder in the vestibule and pointed at it, then said to us, "After you've climbed it, pull up the ladder. This will blow over after a couple of days. I'll try to bring you as much food and water as I can. Let the ladder down when I come. Otherwise, just don't move."

Then he gave one of us a bucket for a toilet. We were terrified, but even more than that, we were astonished a German would help us.

His word was good. Three times a day we heard him hissing at us to let the ladder down, and he would bring up a bucket of food, with potatoes and bread and a little bit of meat.

This is a miracle, I thought. *I've almost been killed again, and a German man has saved me. This is an absolute miracle.*

We all used the toilet bucket. Then at night, when the post office was empty, we would lower the ladder, and Morris, one of Uncle Yudel's sons, would carefully descend, holding tightly to the incredibly smelly bucket. He would dump the contents in the post office's public latrine, then return.

The shooting and the roundups went on for three days. At the end of the third day, the old man hissed at us once again. We lowered the ladder and he climbed up with another bucket full of food.

"Run, my little friends. Run. Hide wherever you can. Please stay alive. Get away from here. This city is a graveyard."

Then he climbed down the ladder and was gone.

When I climbed down from the attic, I went home for only a few days, then headed back to the partisans. Shortly afterward, I heard that the Germans grabbed Morris and nobody had seen him since. A few months later, I returned to see my father for a brief visit. After a couple of days, I decided to go back to the partisans. I took my usual route. Then I walked the back roads until I reached the entrance to the forest where my Russian partisan friends were. Just as I was about to plunge into the leafy protection of the trees, I heard shouts in both German and Polish, telling me to stop.

German soldiers and Polish police had surrounded the woods. I could see rifles and pistols dully bouncing the sun's reflection off their barrels.

A thought quickly shot through my mind: *I can't stop. If I do, they'll arrest me and I'll be killed. I've got to run hard. If I don't, I'm dead. They'll shoot me where I stand.*

I took off like lightning into the woods. They kept on shooting, and I kept on running. But after several minutes, I could feel my legs turning rubbery and the sound of the yelling soldiers growing closer and louder.

Chapter 8

Captured

I heard shouting behind me: "Stop. Stop. Stop," the voices yelled in German and Polish. But I didn't stop, and I could hear the rattle of rifle fire.

Suddenly my left arm felt as though it had been run through with a burning stick. I could feel hot blood streaking down my arm as I kept running. I could hear the pounding of many feet behind me as I dodged through the forest.

I kept zigzagging so they wouldn't get another good shot, but I could feel my legs becoming ever more rubbery. The pain from my arm was consuming, and I could feel the blood now trailing down to my fingertips. Suddenly, although every part of my body was screaming at me to go on, I collapsed, my breath gone and my strength leaking out my bloodied arm.

The Polish police and German soldiers surrounded me, rifles and pistols pointed at my blond head. They could have shot me right there, and I was astonished they didn't. Instead, they searched me, then marched me three miles to an elite German military police station. I held my arm, onto which I had tied a handkerchief, while I was marched directly to the commander.

"We were looking for partisans in the forest. This is what we found, *Herr Kommandant,*" one of the police said. The commandant was about five feet, three inches, with a big nose and black wavy hair. "We thought you might want to question him yourself."

"Come in," said the Commandant, sternly. I quietly shuffled into his office, which consisted of a couple of rooms with deep, dark, finely carved wooden furniture and chairs of thick leather.

I thought the worst: *I'm going to die today. People like me are being taken to the Tisch house at night and being shot to death. Why should I be any different?*

The threat was so real that the Jewish police now threatened us with being dragged off to the Tisch courtyard if we didn't obey their orders. We knew what went on there, through the grave diggers or others. We knew. And we were afraid.

"Who are you and where were you going? And why were you going there?" said the commandant in a rumbling and commanding voice.

"I was just coming back from seeing my brother and father. They're the only ones left in my family," I said.

My lips trembled. I started crying. It wasn't fake. I was frightened. I was surrounded by Polish and German police. I could see in his eyes an emotion I never expected from someone in a German uniform: sympathy, even compassion.

"Where were you going?" he asked.

I knew saying I was with the partisans would get me shot. So I stopped crying, pulled myself together, and told him, "I work for a farmer near the village where I was captured: the Zbanskis." Then I started blubbering, as I wheezed and sputtered: "I lost most of my family. I want to live."

With my blond hair and blue eyes, I obviously looked German. He must have been very confused. He looked me up and down as my body heaved from my crying, which was coming out of the innermost pockets of my soul.

Finally, he went outside his office and called out to one of the police who brought me in: "Did you find anything special on him? Weapons? Anything else?"

"No, we didn't find anything," spoke a voice from someone I couldn't see. "Just a small bread knife and a handkerchief."

He walked back into the office. I could see the sympathy was still in his eyes.

"Magst du leben?" he asked. In German, he was asking me whether I wanted to live.

"Yes, *leben*, live," I said, still blubbering.

He walked over to his office phone and almost snapped the spring on the rotary dial as I heard him whip the dial around and let it go with a brisk whirring sound.

"Hello, my friend. Do you need a young man, strong, hardworking?" he said in German to the person on the other end.

He nodded and hung up the phone. I didn't know the answer just yet, but I did know that every night many people like me were being shot to death in my ghetto, or even outside it.

He pulled open a desk drawer and solemnly handed me back my handkerchief, my little knife, and the few zloty I had with me.

"I will give you a piece of paper so no one will bother you when you go here," the Commandant said. He quickly wrote out something on his German police stationery. "The man I am sending you to runs a distillery which makes vodka, beer, and wine. He says he has work for you. Here are the directions," he said, scribbling on another paper and handing both pieces to me.

I couldn't believe it. I decided not to go to the bathroom before I left. I sorely needed to—my back was aching I had to urinate so badly—but I didn't want to spend any more time than I had to around the Germans. I walked two miles, reading the note. It said, "I'm sending this man to you. Give him work."

I was astonished.

"Either it's plain luck or there's a god in heaven. I think it must be God. I must believe it," I mumbled to myself.

Nobody stopped me, probably because I looked like the rest of the Germans. I looked more Polish or German than they did.

The distillery was located only a few miles from my hometown and my family's house. When I reached the area where the distillery was, I was amazed. There were German soldiers running all over the place. There were stables where rich people had kept their horses, and all kinds of factories were there, too. This was a town doing very well under the Germans. I found out later the previous owner had owned a private plane before the war.

The area was a huge place which had been owned by some of the richest people in Poland. It was about a mile and a half wide and a mile long, surrounded by barbed wire. Inside was a large palace with close to a hundred rooms. No wonder almost an entire German division was housed there. The family who owned it had fled to England. As I looked around, I suddenly realized this was the same place I had groomed horses when the Germans first took over my city.

I opened the door to go ask where I was supposed to work and bumped into a pasty-faced man in his midsixties who was limping and dragging himself around. I knew of the man. His name was Michalek. He'd already gotten a message that I would be coming. I loathed seeing him. He hated Jews and wasn't embarrassed to let anybody know it.

He used to work for a lot of the Jewish people in our city transporting goods from one place to another. The Jews all knew him and knew he was a bigot. They employed him because it was strictly business. They had a lot of wealth and he had nothing. Despite his bigotry, they hired him because he was useful and he didn't beat people.

When Michalek talked to my father, fire almost sprang from his mouth. He would tell my father Jews didn't pay enough; they kept everything for themselves. Michalek said this to lots of people. He was fired a lot of times, too, but people would always take him back. He was so pitiful nobody could take him seriously. Besides, he was old and ragged, and it was impossible to find anybody else willing to groom horses or drive wagons. Everybody else had a trade. When Michalek needed money, he'd apologize. The apology wasn't real, but people felt good that he had to eat his words.

When I first saw him again, I thought, *Out of the boiling water into the fire.*

But when I looked closer, I could see this was a tired, worn-out old man. I had been a child when I last saw him. Now he asked me my name. I debated whether to lie to him. I knew that he knew me. If he recognized me and grasped that I had lied to him, he might have me beaten or killed.

In addition, I had the Commandant's letter. I felt I was under the Commandant's protection, and Michalek wouldn't dare defy him however he felt about me personally. But Michalek hated Jews so much, even the Commandant's letter might not shield me, especially if I lied to Michalek and he later found out.

Whatever is to be later, let it be now, I thought.

I told him my real name. As it turned out, Michalek didn't recognize it, and I did conceal that I knew him. I was only interested in finding out what my job was, then doing it. I found out quickly enough.

"You're going to be working with me," Michalek said in a wheezy, tired voice.

He showed me where to work and what to do. His job was shoveling potatoes into a sluice filled with running water. The water washed the potatoes, which were used to make vodka. The potatoes were carried in from all over by horse-drawn carts and wagons. I took a closer look at him. He could barely stand, let alone work, on his now-spindly legs. Despite his anti-Semitism, I pitied him and offered to do his job as well as my own.

"I'm young. I can work. You sit down and relax and I'll do most of the work for you," I said.

I didn't hold a grudge. They sent me to do a job, and that's what I intended to do. What else could I do? He was too old and sick to do his job. I had little choice. If I weren't nice to him, he might sabotage me and I would be shot for not doing my job. When you're drowning, you catch hold of anything you can. I was nice to him, but he didn't know my motives.

He looked at me strangely, unbelievingly. He looked me up and down suspiciously. Then he said, in a monotone, "Yes. All right. Go ahead and do it."

And I did. Soon I was doing his entire portion of the job as well as my own.

A few days after I arrived, I recognized some villagers who brought potatoes. I thought there might be business to be done.

"What do you need? Maybe I can get it for you," I said.

"We need leather to make shoes," one of them said.

There was one leather factory left, out of nearly a dozen before the war. I had heard about the still-open factory and found out I knew one of the men who still worked there because that man's younger brother used to work for Yudel. One day, I asked Michalek to cover for my absence and I made the short walk into town. I went to the factory worker's house and waited. When he returned, I took him over to a corner.

"Mr. Tama, I've got a proposition for you. I'm going around as a Gentile. I can use leather. If you give me leather, I can bring you butter, cheese, bread, and pork. Can we do business?"

"Sure, I can steal lots of things and we can use the food. What do you need?"

"I need leather for shoes and for soles. How much cheese, bread, butter, or pork do you want for enough leather for a pair of shoes?"

"A pound and a half."

"Done," I said, and we shook hands.

It worked out well for both of us. I got three pounds of food for enough leather for a pair of shoes. I gave half to Mr. Tama. I left some of it with my father and uncle.

I was even getting along better and better with Michalek, who started to like me. He lived nearby. Every day his wife, a small, plain woman, would humbly bring him a loaf of fresh bread and some soup in a little bucket. One day when she arrived, he told her, "Tomorrow, bring some food for this young man. Bring him a shirt. Bring him some soup. He works for me. He keeps me alive," and he almost blushed when he turned around and saw me. He knew I had probably overheard him.

I also figured out how to protect myself at night. I slept in the potato piles inside a large warehouse, where thousands of potatoes were stored. Sometimes I slept on the roof, or in the stable with the horses, or with the cows in the fields. I believed if I moved my sleeping place every night, I would be harder to find and kill.

In the meantime, my brother Hymie had found a job cutting lumber in a lumberyard which was a mile from the distillery. Every day, when the farmers carted in their potatoes, I begged for food.

"Just some bread. My brother and I are hungry," I whispered.

I took whatever they gave me, usually a piece of bread, along with some potatoes I'd stolen. When dark began to fall, I'd cut up potatoes and the pieces of food for which I had traded leather and stuff them into my pants.

Then, when the distillery closed, I'd take my little bundle and crawl through a mile of ditches between the distillery and the lumberyard. If I'd been caught, I would have been shot instantly.

The entire trip to the lumberyard took an hour. I left when it got dark and I always let Hymie know when I would be there. We met in a dark corner of the lumberyard, but we didn't talk much. I just gave him the food, and we would look at each other sadly. We both knew, even while we were sharing these brotherly moments, the Germans were cutting the size of our city's ghetto almost daily.

When I returned to the distillery each time, I'd find a different place to sleep. The nights were freezing, but I had a strong will to live. I also used luck and ingenuity to keep myself warm. I covered myself with straw, rags, potatoes, whatever was close at hand. When I was sleeping on the roof, which was eight feet high, I would lie down next to the chimney, next to the side with no wind. I used straw and rags to cover myself. I'd even hide in the barrel-making factory. Most of the time I didn't manage to sleep, no matter where I lay, because I was too cold.

When the weather got even colder, I usually slept in the potato warehouse. I even buried myself under a layer of potatoes, so the Germans couldn't find me at night and I could try to stay warm. It was just me, the potatoes, and a little straw, trying to stay warm in temperatures that felt like fifty below zero. Fortunately, sleeping inside the potatoes wrapped me in a layer of warmth. Vivid thoughts of my brother passed through my mind before I fell asleep.

On what would be my last run to the lumberyard, I saw floodlights. I ran to the barbed wire surrounding the yard and peered through it. About twenty-five yards away, I saw more than thirty boys lined up, including Hymie.

I saw that their hands were over their heads and tears were streaming down their cheeks. I was behind the Germans, so I could see the boys. I also could see the Germans had machine guns.

Suddenly the loud metallic chattering of machine gun fire burst into the night. I could see some of the boys' faces erupt into blood. In two seconds, all the bodies, including Hymie's, just folded over and fell to the ground.

Now I have nobody but my father who is alive, I thought to myself. I could feel a stabbing pain in my heart, a wound that really never has healed from seeing my Hymie gunned down. *What will I do without Hymie?*

For a few moments my grief so overwhelmed me I felt as though I were drowning. But I had to take care of myself, and I crawled back in the ditches. Along the way I stopped to sob, and I could feel my shoulders heaving as wave after wave of grief washed over me. I knew Hymie wouldn't want me to get shot. I was back at the distillery in an hour.

I knew the grave squad would take the corpses to the cemetery the next day. I went there before work, about five thirty in the morning. Of course, I walked in back of houses and close to the riverbank so I wouldn't be caught and executed. I waited by the cemetery, and the grave diggers brought Hymie and the others about an hour later.

I hid behind a tree near the wagon as the grave diggers shoveled clod after clod of dirt. They saw me, but they were Jews, too. They understood why I was there. I could see in their agonized faces they were sorry for my pain, and my pain was their pain. The bodies had been piled into flat bundles and looked like logs with shoes on. Nobody would have stolen the shoes: they were filled with crusted blood and flies. The shoes also probably had absorbed the stench of death permeating the wagon.

I couldn't see my brother at first. After the metallic sound of shovels hitting dirt stopped, the grave diggers grabbed the hands and feet of individual corpses. On a count of three, they flung outward each limp vessel, its arms and legs floating, into the mass grave, the twisted faces terrible to see.

After the diggers had pulled off a few corpses, I saw Hymie, his face covered in blood, and part of his skull blown away. I cried without shame. Hot tears tumbled down my cheeks and landed on my shoe tops. I felt weak and helpless.

"Oh, God. Oh, God," I moaned, as I stood looking at Hymie's body minutes before it was to be flung into space, only to land in a twisted pile in the ditch. "How could one people be so barbaric to another? Please, God, please let me stay alive long enough to see the Nazis run for their lives."

As I looked up, I saw one body in the pile twitching its leg. A couple of guys were lying on top of him. I heard a muffled voice mumble, "I'm alive. I'm alive." Then both legs moved. Then the other leg and the other arm. Then the body's head began to move.

"Help, help. I'm alive. I'm shot in the arm. Help me get off the wagon," the body yelled. Then, when the grave workers had removed the corpses on top of him, he sat up. I recognized him as Simon Fleishbein, someone from my hometown. I could see blood had clotted around his left shoulder, where he must have been wounded. His clothes were wet from where the corpses had leaked blood onto his arm and the rest of his body. Simon looked like a badly painted carnival doll.

I felt my blood freeze inside me. "I'm alive; I'm alive," he yelled. "I'm trying to get to whatever is left of the ghetto."

The grave workers told him to go in back of the factories where no one would see him, and Simon hobbled off. I went to our house to tell the family of Hymie's death. Father, Yudel, Rachel, Jacob, Sara, even the children, all cried. Loud wails and sobbing filled our little house. Hymie was a good boy, and we would miss him.

The only news they had for me was that no more Jews were being shipped into our city because there was no more room.

When I returned to the distillery, the first thing I did was wave hello to the barrel makers. There were six of them, all Jewish. Three of them were brothers. The Germans left them alone because they knew how to do something the Germans wanted. The six made the casks for the vodka and other spirits made in the distillery.

Some of them were my neighbors in the ghetto, and we had become fairly good friends over the four weeks I had been there. At least this was a little touch of home. They had a little shack where they worked and slept. I used to steal potatoes, then go visit them. They'd cook the potatoes using a little hot plate and share the spoils with me.

One day, about eight in the morning, a Ukrainian who was manager of the whole distillery called the six barrel makers and me. He hated Jews, but that wasn't surprising. Ukrainians are notoriously anti-Semitic, and they loved to beat us. He marched all of us to a warehouse, then motioned us inside, where we saw piles of wheat.

"Put the wheat in those sacks," he said, almost hissing. "And do it right. I'll be back around noon. One o'clock at the latest."

Then he strode outside and closed the warehouse doors. We could hear the "snick" of a metal lock being snapped shut to prevent us from escaping.

We weren't concerned. Locking us in was standard procedure, especially if we were to be left unguarded.

The numerous skylights provided plenty of illumination, and we set to work packing the sixty sacks. One of us had a pocket watch, so we knew we were done about noon. We waited for him to return. Then the time was two o'clock. Then three. We were just waiting, lounging on the wheat sacks.

I could feel my pores begin to gush sweat. I could see the others fidgeting with worry. They were thinking the same thing.

"Guys, I know the Nazis' tricks. This doesn't look good at all," I whispered, suddenly afraid someone might be standing outside. "Let's pile up the sacks to the ceiling. When we reach it, we'll punch through the roof, then run in different directions. If we run in a group, we'll just be a bigger target."

We all started throwing sacks against the wall near the doors. I figured the wall would hold up the sacks while we piled them higher and higher. After an hour, the stack was about twenty inches away from the roof. Three of us were standing on the stacks. I told the other two to start pulling boards out of the roof trusses, and the room was filled with the cracking of breaking boards.

One of us had a penknife; another had some kind of scraping instrument. We sharpened the ends of the boards. Then everyone used the carved points on the end of each board to poke through the ceiling. It worked. We could see dusk through the ragged holes.

We all scrambled up onto the roof.

"Jump down in different directions," I yelled out. We all moved to the roof's low point, then jumped, landing unhurt.

As soon as we landed, though, armed Polish police surrounded us. By the grim looks on their faces, we had no doubt they were taking us to the Tisch courtyard. A cold drizzle was falling. The police said nothing, but motioned for us to put our hands behind our backs. Then they roped our hands and attached us to each other. The police tied us so tightly I could feel my hands go numb.

The Nazis started marching us toward the courtyard, as a little snow began to mix in with the gray rain. I was in the middle of our small group. My hands grew increasingly numb. I could see the hands of the others turning black and blue, and I assumed my hands were becoming the same color. The Polish police were on all sides of us.

We marched for about two miles, and the pain shooting through my hands and arms was so intense I had trouble breathing. We were being marched in the middle of the road, probably as some kind of perverse example to any Jews who might see us. My head hurt. My armpits got squishy.

We entered the city, and we were two blocks from the execution square. We were right near the ghetto gates. As the drizzle and snow turned to a hard rain and slush, I could see a mountain of old clothing, all of which had been stolen from Jews, stacked high right near the gates.

We passed by a small alleyway, and I saw Lazar's broad back. He lived a few houses from us, and he owed my father many favors. Now it was time for Lazar to pay my father back. I yelled out to him so frantically I could hear my voice squeak:

"Lazar, Lazar. They're going to shoot us. In two minutes we will be at the execution square."

Lazar's head swiveled around. He didn't take more than a second to size up the situation. He called out to Heinrich the Gestapo, who coincidentally happened to be passing by.

"Stop, Heinrich, stop," Lazar called.

The Gestapo man was in no mood to listen to anybody, even the head of the ghetto, with whom he was forced to have a working relationship to get the amount of slave labor he needed.

"Go away, Lazar. These boys will be dead in three minutes."

"Oh, Heinrich, what a waste," Lazar said, mustering all his thief's cunning to put on a face which appeared to be consoling Heinrich for some kind of loss. "Think about the piles of rags. They're supposed to be clothing to help Germany. That clothing was probably brought in by the trainload and dumped there. If the clothing stays out in the rain, it'll get wet and rot, and then what good will they be? You've got to get it into the railroad cars and shipped out—fast."

Heinrich's head snapped upward. I could see he was thinking hard. He did not want to account for a loss to the Fatherland.

"You're right. You're right," he said, sounding surprised he hadn't thought of it himself.

He turned to the Polish policemen and started issuing orders:

"Have these Juden bastards start loading these rags so the rain won't ruin them," he shouted.

The Polish police silently marched us to the clothing piles. A few Jews were already working there, but by now darkness had wrapped itself around the city.

"There's not much we can do now," the Jews already there called out. "It's so dark we can't see what we're doing. Come back tomorrow and help us."

Lazar then walked on his way. Amazingly, the Polish police nodded and waved their guns at us to go home, then cut the ropes binding our hands. I was shaking from fear. My hands were black from having been tied together so tightly. I kept trying to use one to rub some circulation into the other, though they both hurt so much I could barely flex my fingers.

When I arrived at our house, I swung open the door, and my father was standing near it. He glanced down at my pitch black hands and instantly sized up most of what had happened.

"Oh, God, Joe, oh, God, I almost lost you too," he cried out, grabbing and pulling me to his breast in the dearest embrace he had ever given me.

I could feel his chest heave and his throat catch as he sobbed like a baby. Yudel was there, too, as were his two daughters and Jacob Wilder. They all formed a circle around me, and, for a very brief moment, I felt like a child shielded from the evils of the world. I knew it couldn't last, but feeling what was left of my family embracing me made me feel better than I had in a long time.

_____ Chapter 9

Fall
of the
Jewish
Police

I had mixed feelings about being rescued by Lazar. He had been our neighbor for many years. However, during that time he often was in jail two or
three times a year for running a burglary ring. Those were the times when
my father would send food over to Lazar's wife and two children.

Several times I had heard Lazar talk about his ring. People would order something they wanted, whether it was a coat or a bristle, and Lazar's guys would
steal it. He never hurt anybody, but he didn't mind running a ring of thieves.

"Your father was good to my family," Lazar had told me once, with his arm
around my shoulder. "Every time I was in prison, he made sure my family, my
precious wife and children, were fed."

It was true. Every Friday my father returned home with a lot of money after
the merchants had paid him for his tobacco. He would walk in the front door,
his pockets bulging with cash, and boom out, "Is anybody hungry?"

What my father wanted to know was whether anybody in the neighborhood
was not getting enough to eat. He was away most of the week, and this question
would be among the first he would ask when he got home. My father was a
generous man. If he had a penny, he would give away the penny.

Often we would tell him Lazar's family was hungry because Lazar was in jail.

My father made sure they and others who were too sick or poor would have food for the weekend. Often, I delivered those bulging food sacks.

There was some advantage to my father's generosity. My father often would carry home a lot of merchandise: pots and pans, soap, candles, along with jelly, plow blades, and tobacco products such as cigarettes and fancy cigars. The manufacturers trusted him to sell their products and send them their price.

Father often would go into Warsaw or the smaller cities to sell what he had. Many days, Mother's small warehouse next to our four-plex was piled to the bursting point with merchandise. But Lazar never let his gang break into our warehouse. It was a point of honor, a way of repaying my father for helping his family.

When Lazar was out of jail, he always carried a gun. Of course people were afraid of him, but he never actually hurt anybody. When he saw any member of our family he always said, "Hello, how are you? Good morning." He was excruciatingly courteous, and meant it sincerely.

However, that courtesy of not robbing us did not extend to the rest of our family. Yudel once told me Lazar's thugs broke into his warehouse and stole three thousand dollars' worth of goods, which Yudel had to buy back through a mediator for eight hundred dollars. I heard many similar stories.

Those same hoodlums, however, had been our city's protectors. Nobody had dared start a pogrom in our city while Lazar was there. Several times he and his men chased whoever was beating a Jew out of town.

"If they think they can beat up one of us, then they think they can beat up three or four of us. We have to stop them before they start thinking they can attack us whenever they want," he had told my father.

However, this was the same man who now occasionally would extort money from people by threatening to have them sent to the camps unless they paid him. It was a funny thing about Lazar. He did both good and bad, and there was no simple way to look at him.

My father couldn't say much about Lazar's saving me from being executed in the Tisch courtyard.

"I don't approve of what Lazar does," my father said. "But he saved your life, he is polite to us, and he protected our warehouse."

My father didn't see Lazar's saving me as repaying his generosity. It was my father's pleasure to assist Lazar's family when they were in need. He ignored the people who said he shouldn't feed Lazar's family.

"Lazar loves his kids and nobody cares about them," my father would say. "It's not the children's fault their father is what he is. Why should they be forced to suffer? They're innocent."

Even if my father couldn't recognize it, I knew Lazar saved me because of my father's kindnesses. Lazar had much greater matters on his mind than my safety. He respected my father, so he respected my father's children.

A few days after he saved me, Lazar and I bumped into each other, and we talked about his rescue.

"You're a lucky guy I was there just at the moment. Your father always made sure my family had food to eat, even when I wasn't there to do it. He is a beautiful man, and I owe him the lives of my children. I am glad to do this for him," he said, both gratitude and contempt edging his voice.

"I really appreciate it, and so do the six guys who were with me," I told him. He just shrugged.

One afternoon a few weeks later, I looked out our window and saw a sight which chilled me down into my bones: Lazar, his hands handcuffed behind his back, surrounded by two Jewish police and the two Gestapo. The Gestapo had their guns drawn.

The Jewish police later told their friends and relatives that Lazar had been captured and taken to the Jewish police station, where he promised to show them where his gold, diamonds, dollars, and pounds were hidden. He was being marched from the police station when I saw him. I heard him saying, "It's somewhere right around here. It's somewhere around here."

While the Jewish police were looking in various houses, Lazar broke into a run right in front of my house. He was a big man, and his long legs pushed him very far, very fast. The Gestapo screamed and yelled at him, but they'd been too astonished to fire until he ducked into a house and ran up a ladder. They couldn't find him.

Frustrated, the Gestapo started firing blindly into windows. Wherever they saw someone, they would fire. People would look out to see what the commotion was, and pieces of their skull would go flying. Other Jews no doubt had ducked into their bunkers, feeling like frightened rats. Heinrich and Dietrich were particularly vicious. They didn't care who or what they shot.

The Gestapo thought people in the neighborhood had helped Lazar to escape and wanted their revenge. To the Gestapo, killing was as casual as lighting a cigarette. Their thinking was that if Lazar escaped, all Jews must be guilty of helping him.

Lazar was on the roof of an abandoned home. We saw him hiding behind some boxes. Finally, the Gestapo spotted him and shot him through the head, then threw his body, still handcuffed, down to the ground. It made a squashing sound.

After that, the police and Gestapo started a shooting rampage. We knew it was going to be a slaughter, so our family ran to our bunker. A half hour later, the shooting stopped. We knew the Germans weren't subtle enough just to stop shooting to deceive us into thinking they weren't there. After hearing the quiet for several minutes, we and the neighbors all sneaked out into the street to see what had happened.

We saw a few bodies, including Lazar's. Then we withdrew back inside our bunkers. It was winter, and we closed up our shutters so the Germans wouldn't see any light. We all dropped off to sleep, exhausted.

When we got up the next morning, our situation was bleaker than ever. Lazar's body was gone, of course. We had no food, no water, and we didn't dare go out on the streets. We had to hide every inch of our existence. The cold was so glacial it made our heads hurt.

We were always on guard. We also had a false wall in our attic, where we could quickly run if a rampage started again. Jacob Wilder and I stood lookout every day. The family had long ago decided that we'd divide up between the attic wall and the bunker. If the Germans found one pocket of us, perhaps the other group would survive.

I thought long and hard about Lazar's death. He had saved my life and the lives of the six barrel makers. He had, as a matter of honor, not stolen even a piece of candy from my father's warehouse. But he was also an evil man.

"He was a thief, a blackmailer, and he cooperated with the Germans," I said to myself. "I also bet Lazar never stole from my father because he thought it was a good way to make sure my father kept on feeding his family."

All in all, Lazar was a man who chose being a thief and blackmailer as a profession. He was good at it, but that didn't mean I should grieve for him now that he was dead. As a fellow Jew and a man who saved my life, he was entitled to some regret for his death, but I also felt better that he wouldn't be squealing on people anymore.

I sensed a twinge inside me, because I felt so little for a man who had saved my life. But there was so much grieving to be done about people I really cared about, there wasn't time for someone who was as bad a man as Lazar.

We were all vulnerable. There were selections every couple of weeks, and we all had to hide. Yet we all needed water. There had been two wells available: the well most of us used had wild dogs and cats running loose near it. The other was across from the former synagogue, now the Jewish police station. People didn't want to use the well near the station because the Jewish police often beat those of us who went there or grabbed them and shipped them off to slave labor. One of my household jobs was to fetch water. I figured that if it came to a choice between the wild dogs and the Jewish police, I could outrun the police.

Now, there wasn't any choice. The Germans had shut down the other well, so we had to use the one near the Jewish police station. I decided to go late in the afternoon. That was closing time for the office, and all the Jewish police had to go there to get their orders for the next day. They would be too busy hurrying to their meeting to bother with me.

I waited until I saw the police running toward the office before I approached the well. Some of the group looked at me curiously.

I scooped up water in each of my two buckets, then walked down the street. The office was on a corner. I walked past it, buckets in hand, then stopped to look in a store window. Out of the corner of my eye, I saw three men in leather coats on the sidewalk directly opposite the police station. They appeared to be lounging, and that was odd. Lingering invited suspicion, and suspicion invited arrest and interrogation. I'd never seen these men. They were strangers in our small city. I was very suspicious.

Just then, the meeting broke up. The police filed out and all turned left. That was unusual. Maybe they were all going to a nearby restaurant. Why they all made that turn, I couldn't say. The strangers, though, were waiting until all the police were walking along the wall of the station, blocking any chance of flight. I stopped to rest for a moment. I was ten feet away from the corner of the building, thirty feet away from the Jewish police office door. That pause may have saved my life.

The strangers flipped open their leather coats with one hand and whipped out submachine guns. They were ugly: black stock, black barrels, black cartridge chambers. Then each man put his other hand underneath his gun and opened fire. They swung their guns back and forth, spraying bullets. The Jewish police were defenseless.

In seconds, the police were all lying on the sidewalk in a river of blood. The three men shoved their guns back under their coats and walked, not ran, away. They probably had a truck nearby.

"I hate killings," I yelled out, as I looked, almost in a stupor, at the more than one hundred bodies in front of me. "I hate blood."

Still, I knew the Jewish police enjoyed their work, and I felt twenty feet tall after seeing our people fight back. I had no use for the traitors who had become police for the Nazis.

Maybe some people will survive because these bastards have been killed. I have no pity for them or their families, I thought.

I knew I was the only witness, but I wasn't gunned down because I was a Jew. I was one of the executioners' people and a youngster, no danger to them. I could have been a tree stump. They made no gesture to me, just walked away. I knew of three hundred people in hiding, three of whom were in the attic of Gestapo headquarters. Because these policemen were executed, all those people might live.

I remembered just a few weeks before the assasinations my cousin Hymie, the artist, had come to visit our house with some food.

"Where are our people?" he asked me, looking sorrowful. "Why doesn't anybody help us? Why don't they do something?"

Now our people had fought back, and my pride tasted sweet.

The silence of the dead screamed in my ears. Then, in a moment, most of the Jews in hiding, including my father and Yudel and the rest of the family, came running to see what the sounds were about. They were all bewildered, though everybody felt the Jews who had betrayed their people deserved to die. I saw many neighbors whose fate I had wondered about. The ghetto had been cut even smaller, and I could only wonder how those who lived outside it would survive. As I mingled with people I hadn't seen in months, I heard the same sense of resignation filling them all.

"The Germans will just do the selections themselves," some of the Jews muttered. "They're already bringing their own guard dogs."

Within ten minutes all of the people had disappeared from the carnage. It was late in the day, and we weren't supposed to be seen in the streets after 5:00 P.M.

Later I found out through Hymie the artist that the Warsaw resistance had been behind the attack. Hymie had predicted that sooner or later, Jews in some place would fight back. Now they had.

Hymie also had Warsaw underground contacts, and that's how he knew who had done the executions. He said the underground wanted to make the Jewish police pay for betraying their people.

Though I hated the Jewish police and considered them traitors, they also had been a valuable source of information. They knew when raids were coming, and they'd warn their friends and relatives. By watching those people, we had a sense of when the next raid was.

Even so, there are very few of us left. There's never any good news, only bad news, and bad news spreads fast, I thought, darkly.

I could hear the Polish police running back and forth outside the ghetto, and I was sure they'd heard all the noise. After all the onlookers slipped back into hiding, I ran the five blocks to my house and slipped inside the bunker with the water buckets. My father, Yudel and his two daughters and their children, plus Jacob Wilder, were all there.

We were all quite depressed in that black pit which was our bunker. We had to prevent any illumination from getting out so the Germans wouldn't find us. So, in the dark, except for one small candle, our voices spoke, seemingly unattached to our bodies.

"At least we've got a bunker. It's saved our lives quite a lot," my father said, trying to be cheerful.

"After four years, I hope this war is over fast. Otherwise our lives will be," said Yudel, who sounded more hopeless than I had ever heard him.

We all started crying. I could hear everyone weeping in the dark, and I could only imagine how contorted with fear and pain their faces must be. "What is there to live for?" I asked myself. The only answer was the sobbing, amplified many times by the closeness of our quarters.

That night, none of us slept. There really wasn't enough room to lie down, just to sit up. The bunker was only eight feet long, six feet wide, and four feet high. With seven people in there, only the children were small enough to stretch out and try to sleep.

Strangely, the executions hadn't changed me very much. We had become numb to killings and shootings. This one had a different flavor, though. These people were traitors; they deserved to die.

The sense of gloom filling the bunker was darker than even the night. I knew we all figured the Gestapo would find our bunker and clean us out. There was no place to run, no place to hide, no way to survive without food or water, no place really to sleep.

"Even rats, cats, and dogs have a better chance to live than we do," I said to no one in particular.

The following morning the grave diggers picked up the bodies of the Jewish police. Their corpses were treated no differently than anyone else's. They were dumped into a mass grave, then dirt was shoveled on top of them.

All this time, my cousin Hymie was doing well. He was in his downtown house on the main street. He now was being transported to various cities so he could photograph German victories, documenting the slaughter of tens of thousands of Jews and others. He was college-educated, successful.

He would show up at our house or Yudel's once every two weeks, and always with sacks of food: bread, butter, cheese, flour. He was willing to share. He, his wife, and their children could get whatever food they wanted, sleep in a comfortable bed, and wear fine clothes. We envied him, but we didn't hate him. He didn't do anything wrong. He was a fine person, and the Germans didn't have anybody else to do this work.

He would also keep us up to date on the war: where the Russians were, what the Germans were doing. He would tell us about Palestinian Jews fighting with the English against the Germans. His food and conversation kept our morale up a little.

"Why doesn't the rest of the world do something? They don't lift a finger to help the Jews," he would say almost every visit.

A few weeks after the slaughter of the Jewish police, the Gestapo went on another rampage. They were rousting people out of their homes and chaining them together for the trip. We could hear the shooting and yelling for blocks. When we heard it moving toward our area, I ran into the leather sole factory attic.

I foolishly went up on the roof and hid behind a chimney to watch the whole thing. I should have been spotted, but I wasn't. I saw and heard the Germans promise to spare the lives of Jews who would tell them where other Jews might be hiding. Some did squeal. I saw more than one hundred men, women, and children taken down from roofs, attics, and other hiding places, then shot right in the streets.

I winced the first few times I saw it. Then I just watched, trying hard to put my emotions somewhere in my mind where I couldn't feel them. I knew my father, Yudel, and Yudel's family had already taken refuge in the bunkers.

"Oh, God, please spare my father and uncle. Please spare Yudel's family, too. God, let my family live, please," I prayed.

Three hours later, the rampage was over. I looked down into the streets from the rooftop and saw the cobblestones littered with corpses slick with blood. I felt a truly unspeakable sadness.

The days were getting worse. I still went out at night to break boards off old factories for firewood; Father would still trade Yudel's gold, diamonds, and currency for enough food to keep seven souls alive. He had some Gentiles who were willing to trade with him once a week, and that's what kept us going. Father would return with a few loaves of bread, a small sack of potatoes, sometimes butter.

When I was home from the distillery, having had Michalek cover for me at work, we all kept looking out the window. Now, every couple of days, Heinrich and Dietrich would come into town, get drunk, then chase down and shoot any Jew on the street.

I despaired: *If life is worth fighting for, then why are we so miserable? We've gone through so many dark, ugly years living like animals. How long can this—and we— continue?* I bitterly thought. I didn't dare say this aloud to my family, who already had plenty of their own gloom to deal with.

I did know we all had seemed to lose the little bit of religious faith we had left. We kept asking ourselves what was going to happen to us. We wanted to survive and tell our children and grandchildren stories of what happened, but we were sure we'd never see that day.

One day, I hit bottom.

Death would be a lot better than going on living like this, I thought. *We pray every day that some of us can live to talk about what happened. But there is no hope, no way out, no hope at all.*

Then I lowered my head and cried.

PART II

SCRAMBLING FOR LIFE IN THE CAMPS

Chapter 10

Snatched
and
Shipped

Even without radios, we knew about the Warsaw Ghetto Uprising in April 1943. The Jews there had launched an armed rebellion against the Germans—a revolt which ultimately would be crushed in three weeks. A few Jews were acting as Gentiles, traveling between our city and wherever they were living now. They spread the news.

We heard about it from the Stein cousins, who had been in school with me. They had a lot of luck going for them: Their family was wealthy and they had blond hair and blue eyes. They were living away from the ghetto. Their parents had probably paid for phony passports as well. When the Germans started taking Jewish kids in 1942, the Steins also knew many Jewish policemen who made sure the cousins were left alone.

They were two of perhaps one hundred people who passed as Gentiles in our city, most of whom were women. I didn't dislike the Steins. They were nice fellows and intelligent. It was no crime to have money. My cousin, Hymie Kronhartz, also heard about Warsaw from his travels documenting the supposed glories of Nazis crushing their opponents.

The Warsaw news made us shiver all the more. We had good reason to be afraid. Soon afterward, in the same month, the Nazis completely enveloped our ghetto with soldiers one night. We had heard this might happen. My family slipped into the bunker beneath the house. All night and all day we heard the Germans knocking on the ceilings, walls, and floors. We heard their sharp raps and pounding.

They didn't care whether they damaged our house or us. We could hear them scraping away at the floor above our heads. When Jacob had built the bunker, he'd intelligently built a false floor underneath the first false floor and put a lot of dirt in between. When the Nazis found the first false floor, then lifted it, all they saw was dirt. We heard them cursing and screaming and yelling in frustration.

Still, we were all frightened to the point of paralysis. My cousins had three little girls, ages two, three, and five. The women put their hands over each child's mouth. The children were frightened, and their contorted faces showed they were ready to cry. If they had, we would have been discovered instantly.

Every one of us was still. Even our breathing almost stopped. All we heard was the splitting, cracking, and chopping of boards above our heads. We knew what would happen if they found us.

But we had a little food to share: a few loaves of bread and two buckets of water. We didn't need much to eat or drink because we were so still. The Nazis stopped looking for us when darkness fell, so we would use our toilet at night when they weren't around. We knew they would be back when the edge of daylight appeared.

Inside the bunker, after the Germans had left, my father and I had another long talk. We decided we couldn't flee because Yudel was too old, and his daughters and their three young children didn't have the stamina.

"Maybe a miracle will happen," I said, in a low voice.

"Maybe it will, God willing," my father said hollowly.

About 5:00 A.M. the next day, May 1, 1943, we heard a noise. We could tell it was the Germans, and they were cursing and screaming again. This time they didn't bother digging. They called for us to come out. When we didn't, they started firing into the house.

We could feel the sound of each bullet's firing magnified many times in our little space. It hurt my ears to the point of bursting. After several shots, Yudel was hit badly in his right arm. We heard him cry out. We could see the blood gushing.

"If you don't come out, we're going to throw a hand grenade into your bunker and burn your house to the ground," the Nazis yelled in German. *"Raus, raus, raus, Juden,"* they screamed.

We could tell they knew we were there. We all looked at each other in despair. I said what we all were thinking: "We have no way out. If we don't leave the bunker, they'll kill us with fire or hand grenades. They'll kill us here or they'll kill us in Treblinka. This is the end of it."

We saw that Yudel's face was becoming more and more white. We took out handkerchiefs and wrapped them around his wounded arm. He was badly in need of medical attention. Yudel kept waving to us not to surrender, but we felt we had no choice.

"Kids," Yudel groaned to all of us. "This is the end of that."

We popped up the ceiling of our bunker, and the Germans reached in and grabbed us any way they could. They pulled us all up into what had been my parents' bedroom. As we were being pulled out of our hiding place, we could see Nachem, one of our neighbors, standing nearby, shaking, surrounded by Germans, with his head hanging in shame.

He didn't really belong there. Nachem had lived outside the ghetto, but when his aunt and uncle were taken to Treblinka, he moved in. He was a Jew, but he did small favors for the Germans in exchange for an extra loaf of bread or sack of sugar. He knew about our hiding place because he and his girlfriend had moved into our four-plex. They had heard us shoveling and seen us carrying dirt, so they knew we had a bunker.

I heard the Nazis talking to him in German, and they were saying they might let him live if he found some more bunkers. He told the Germans he would show them where quite a few bunkers were.

Meanwhile we were marched down to the marketplace. There were already about seven hundred people just sitting there on the ground. Shortly after we got there, they forced us to lie on our bellies and put our hands on top of our heads. German guards were pointing rifles and pistols at all of us. We were almost the last people to arrive. During the next hour and a half, the Germans collected another ten to fifteen of us. The latecomers whispered to our family that the Germans had killed Nachem anyway, despite all his betrayals.

Then the Germans started marching us toward the train ramp my family and hundreds of others were forced to build. It was a little less than three miles away, but some of us never got that far.

About eight of the traditional Orthodox Jews, all wearing black *yarmulkes* on their heads, refused to march and stepped out of line. They knew they were going to die, and they wanted to lie with their own kind in the family graveyard. I had no idea who they thought would give them a proper burial, but the Germans obliged. All eight were shot and left on the road. The rest of us were forced to march.

During that time, the forty-five to fifty guards, many of them teenagers, were visibly nervous. Their trigger fingers twitched and they kept shouting orders in high-pitched, harsh voices. The Warsaw Uprising was still going on, and many Germans had been killed there. These Germans were in charge of liquidating ghettos, and they had been in Warsaw days before. They were afraid we were going to jump them. Their eyes never stopped moving. They had a row of guards on each side of us.

It's not as though we needed a lot of guarding. We were mostly women, children, and old men. The young men of working age had already been taken. We were just remnants. After about an hour, we reached the train station. The soldiers leaped up on the ramp and threw open the doors to grimy cattle cars. We climbed in, slowly, but they kept pushing and packing us: the young, the old, the sick, the healthy—it didn't matter. Inside, there was not a piece of food, not a toilet.

The cars were filled with dust stirred up by so many bodies. There was a rank smell composed of cow dung and urination, sweat, dirt, and straw. We were not very different from the cows. We sat down like animals, and we were sixty-five people packed in so closely there was no place to lie down. People were crying, "Help us. Who's going to help us? Where is God?"

He's on vacation, I thought, shocked at my own blasphemy. There was no water, and the hot summer air plus the smell of fear made the stink in our car even more sour. We waited to die.

We could hear soldiers climbing up on the roof, and the clicking of safety catches on their submachine guns. My armpits started to gush. When the train started up, the guards started firing into the cattle cars, and we all tried to hide behind each other. Two people near me were killed. I cringed, along with the rest of my family, and wondered whether I would live to see out the day.

After a while, the firing stopped. By now it was nighttime. My father kicked out a metal window, as he had done before, the noises hidden by the clackety-clack of the train.

I heard him whisper to me, "Joe, you'll follow me and we'll meet in front of the village."

Then he flung himself off the moving train. A lot of people had been jumping off the cars and the guards kept firing. Just as I edged my way to the window and was getting ready to jump, I could hear the train's brakes squealing. The Germans were stopping the train and shooting. There was no way for me to jump off. My father had departed when the guards had still been unprepared. Now they'd recovered. The shooting stopped, and the train lurched ahead.

Then I could hear the popping of gunfire as the guards on the roof—Germans, Ukrainians, and Lithuanians—again started firing mercilessly into the cars. Two of my neighbors were wounded. The screaming and shrieking filled my ears. People huddled up against each other as protection, crouching as low as they could. Still, the blood welling up around my feet felt as though it were going to wash over my shoes.

The smell of people dying and letting go of their bladders and bowels, the sound of screaming and wailing, were almost like being in hell itself. Six or seven of us were killed, and twice that many were wounded. I felt numb, but I was never touched. I crouched down, lying between the dead and wounded, waiting for the Germans to shoot again.

They did, and the screaming and the flowing blood went on. I was lying on the floor by this time, and there were people on top of other people. The man lying on my legs screamed, then slumped, dead. The guy lying on my shoulder was shot, too.

This is the end, I thought.

Then the shooting stopped, and the train lunged on into the darkness until daylight. We all had thought we were being taken to Treblinka. The train paused in the middle of our trip, stopping ten minutes for no apparent reason. Later, I learned the Nazis were killing so many people in Treblinka the trains were backed up for miles. We had been diverted to Majdanek.

That was another piece of luck. Had we been sent to Treblinka, I would have been executed before the day was out. Instead, at Majdanek, I had a chance to live. When the train stopped there, those of us who were still alive and weren't injured were ordered to carry out the dead and the wounded.

The injured and even some of those who were still intact were yelling at the Germans, "Bandits, gangsters, murderers." It didn't matter whether they were silent or not. The Germans were going to kill us just the same. A couple of people who had been shot in the leg pleaded with us to shoot them. Instead, they were loaded on a wagon and taken to a crematorium.

The Germans marched those of us who could still walk a couple of miles to the camp. We had never heard of Majdanek. We never knew it existed. Learning this bit of knowledge was going to cost many of us our lives.

We were all lined up in rows, five abreast. Our family was all in one line. I spotted someone I knew from my city. I was astonished. He had disappeared three years earlier, and we all thought he was dead. I tried to speak to him out of the corner of my mouth. He did the same.

"What goes on here?" I asked.

"They're gassing people every day, bringing in people from all over. If you go right, you live. If you go left, you die. But even if you live, you may not survive. I came here with fifty of my _landsmen_. Now I'm the only one left."

I saw several wagons with wounded people outside the gas chamber. We had heard about gas chambers from Treblinka escapees. I knew what was happening to them. The wounded were crying, screaming, pleading to be shot. The crematorium chimney shot flames, like hell's fire, and its smoke smelled like frying bacon—but I knew it was human flesh.

Yudel said, "This is the end." He was almost speechless. We were all trembling in fear.

The SS man at the head of the line motioned for Jacob Wilder and me to go to the right. I knew what that meant. I could see the women, the children, and the old and sick were being sent to the left. They were headed toward the crematoriums.

121

Sara's and Rachel's children were crying. As young as they were, they could see what was coming. They could see the ashen looks on their mothers' faces, and they were afraid.

I looked at Jacob and said, soulfully, "We have to stay together. Now it's just you and me."

"Absolutely."

The gas chamber and the crematorium were in the middle of the camp. There were two lines. One led straight to the gas chamber. I saw my uncle and his family start to shuffle into it.

"Uncle, I don't know what to say and what will be for all of us. This is the end of the road," I yelled.

Yudel was speechless, the women were speechless, the cousins knew this was it. Yudel, Rachel, Sara, all were walking with their heads down. They knew. Then they entered the building.

I was taken to a delousing station, which also was in the middle of the camp. They gave us a little bit of water in dirty buckets to drink. All the people here were men and boys from fourteen or fifteen up to about forty-five. The guards told us to take off all our clothes except our shoes.

Then we went into the building and our hair was cut off with hand clippers. We saw a lot of lumber lying around. The old-timers said it was from Jewish single-family homes.

"They chased out the Jews, and now they're tearing down the houses to build barracks. Hitler is getting ready to put a lot of people here," one of them said. "Every once in a while, you'll find some Jewish books in there."

But we had yet to receive any order. We were waiting there so long in the heat I was ready to pass out. An hour after I saw Yudel and his family enter the other building, the crematorium spewed black smoke. I knew where my family had gone, and I felt sickened.

"Almost the last of my relatives are disappearing. There's very few of us left—I don't even know whether my father is alive or not. My brothers are dead. Now, I may be the last male, the last in line," I told Jacob.

They gave us striped shirts with crosses on the back, which made us an easier target if we ran. Our pants had a big red stripe up the side, making us visible if we fled. They gave each of us a patch with a number on it to sew on, and some needles and thread.

Each patch had a symbol in the middle and a number to the right of it. A triangle pointing downward was the basic symbol. A red triangle meant a prisoner was there for his politics, such as being a Communist or Socialist. Jews had a six-pointed star, representing the Jewish Star of David. Those labeled who were antisocial had a black triangle. Some Gentile murderers had a green triangle. I very shortly would find out more about murderers.

122

When darkness came, we were marched into the olive green barracks. We had to grab whatever bunk we could.

At 4:00 A.M. we had to get up. The guards turned on the light, then yelled, "Up, up, up." We were herded quickly to the toilets and showers and back. Breakfast was a small amount of gray material in a bowl and imitation coffee, which was mostly water. The coffee was in a big barrel. A few prisoners dunked cups into the coffee, then handed the liquid to us. We had to eat on the run.

Lunch actually wasn't bad. It generally was a fairly thick green soup made from a grass or plant and served in a small bowl. It was somewhat filling.

Dinner was perhaps a third of a piece of bread, sometimes with a small piece of salami on top. Each time, the people serving us never spoke a word. We had to grab our food and eat it, fast. For camp food, the meals were pretty good.

During that first breakfast, though, I found out some of the prisoners were not like the rest of us. They were murderers. They taunted the Jews. They yelled, "Jews, now you're going to die," and they pointed and laughed at us.

There were hundreds of them there, maybe thousands. They had raped, stolen, even murdered, and had been put in prison for it. A background that would have labeled people as gangsters and trash almost anywhere else was a first-class pedigree to the Nazis. The murderers considered us material to be killed, not human beings. In a sense, we had already been dehumanized. They addressed us only by our numbers, and we used the German designated numbers to address any prisoner we didn't know by name—a system I was to find in all of the camps where I lived.

The murderers were different from us. I could tell they were mostly Ukrainians, but there were Germans and Poles, too. Often, they were either foremen or *Kapos*. A *Kapo* was in charge of a work group of 50 to 150 prisoners. Several foremen under a *Kapo* watched to make sure the men were working and hoped for opportunities to beat them. Murderers were both *Kapos* and foremen.

The *Kapos* and foremen slept in front of the barracks entrance. Their privileges included getting enough food, getting better clothing, and not being beaten. There were twenty-five to thirty people packing, sorting, and disinfecting clothing in the camp. The *Kapos* and foremen also got their pick of clothing from that packing station. In theory, the rest was shipped to Germany.

Although *Kapos* and foremen had only those four privileges guaranteed, those privileges were the ones that counted, the ones that let people stay alive.

Kapos got prisoners to work, took orders regarding who was to be selected, submitted their reports to the SS on who died and who committed suicide. They were also in charge of making sure prisoners marched past the guardhouse gate in the morning.

The foreman was the *Kapo*'s second in command. *Kapos* in charge of fewer than one hundred men had only one foreman; those in charge of more than one hundred had two.

Strangely, perhaps 10 percent of the *Kapos*, foremen, and others in charge of prisoners were Jews. Half of those were real bastards and were even more cruel than the Germans, just to prove how loyal they were to the Nazis. Those Jews would hit us with a stake or a whip harder and more frequently than the Gentiles.

A person who was in charge of other prisoners usually was someone who had worked his way up through murder, beatings, and sadism. *Kapos* and foremen had the same job: to drive Jews into the ground and kill them.

After breakfast, some of us were sent to work. They were lucky. The rest of us were taken to a no-man's-land between two barbed wire fences. The strip was about a mile long and seven feet wide, with an electrified barbed wire fence around it. Then the murderers, of whom there were about thirty, formed a gauntlet more than a half a mile long. Each person in the gauntlet was about one hundred feet from the next one, and each one had a closet pole with nails sticking out of it or a two-by-four.

We were grouped in bunches of twenty to fifty people, between the two rows of the gauntlet. The murderers started cursing us, yelling, "You fucking Jews, you goddamned Hebrews, we'll kill you," and other such things. Then, they shouted, "Run." We had to speed through the gauntlet. Sometimes we fell over one another or got our feet tangled with somebody else's and fell down.

Whoever was on top got beaten very badly. We each had to untangle ourselves, then keep running. A lot of us just passed out. When, exhausted, we reached the end of the gauntlet the first time, we had a surprise. "Run back, you fucking Jews," we were told. And we did. Running the gauntlet took about twenty-five minutes, if we survived.

The big guys got it worse than the short guys. I was so short I could hide behind most of the other people most of the time and not get hit. But even I got whacked. I could feel the biting hurt of a nail piercing my skin. There was a kind of hot buzzing, like fire touching my body, when the nail first impaled itself in my flesh. Then the buzzing started again when the nail was pulled out. Blood was pouring from all of us, especially the tall guys, leaving the grass in the gauntlet looking like a splotchy red carpet.

Three hours passed. Most of the guys fainted, and they were tough. Some were Warsaw Uprising veterans. Blood was gushing from their eyes, their mouths. The bastards kept aiming for our heads. This went on almost every day, several hours a day, for two weeks.

My God, how long do we have to suffer like this? How long do we have to run the gauntlet, zigzagging back and forth, being beaten to death? I see blood gushing from their mouth, their eyes, their ears, their arms and legs. God, how can you do this? I screamed inside my head.

There was no answer to my beseechings.

Occasionally, however, some of us got a break. Every day a few us were shepherded off to build barracks for the army. There were some Jewish buildings there, single- and double-family homes—some only two or three years old—which Jews had owned until quite recently. There were groups of thirty-five to forty-five prisoners ripping apart the Jewish buildings to use the lumber for barracks. We would either straighten the lumber into piles or move it. There was no particular way to know whom the Germans would pick for this job. They would just choose twenty-five or thirty of us, then march us to the work site.

It wasn't much of a break from the gauntlet. The murderers and the guards usually beat us ferociously while we worked, and we would return with bloody noses, chopped-up ears, bruises and gashes in the head.

One day they were beating us, but not severely. Then three SS and some murderers decided to try a different game. A group of twenty of us were called to a part of the camp where barracks were to be built. One of the murderers had a steel plumbing pipe, about four inches in diameter and fourteen feet long. They told everybody to straighten some lumber piles, and I could tell something was going to happen. We were spread out among fifty piles, one prisoner to a pile.

A few SS were there, too. Suddenly, one of the murderers leaped for a prisoner and threw him to the ground. Then he and another murderer took the piece of pipe and forced it under the screaming prisoner's chin and onto his throat. Then the murderers stood on each side of the pipe, rocking it back and forth while pressing it down harder and harder.

The boy screamed and yelled, but that sound turned into gurgling as the pipe slowly crushed his windpipe. The screaming deafened me. Then they grabbed the prisoner in front of the next pile and did the same thing. The SS sometimes would take a turn at standing on the pipe. If they weren't participating, they were applauding, laughing, and having a good time. They acted as though this was a carnival game.

When I saw what was happening, I kept moving farther and farther away. I had been standing in front of the fourth pile, but when they started murdering people, I was always one or two piles away. Every time they grabbed one prisoner I would duck around the back of the piles and move three or four piles away from them.

They kept coming toward me, but always there were other prisoners and lumber piles between us. Suddenly I looked up and saw there were only three other prisoners left besides me.

Just as I heard their voices heading toward me, the shriek of the lunch siren sounded. I was amazed. The murderers and SS simply stopped what they were doing, dropped the pipe, and walked together in clusters toward the mess hall. They didn't say a thing. All I heard was delighted laughter at their morning's entertainment.

When I was sure they had all walked away, I dropped to my knees and prayed. "God, God, God, please don't let them come back. Please don't let them find me."

My prayers were answered. They didn't return. I and the other prisoners who survived all found each other in a matter of minutes. We didn't say anything. We just looked at each other and knew this was not the end of our misery. We surveyed the field in front of us, the broken bodies, black faces, tongues sticking out, bulging eyes, bruised and broken arms and legs. We knew nobody would get out alive.

We didn't huddle around each other or talk. We were in shock from seeing people murdered so brutally. We waited, all in a little group but each one sitting apart from the others, until the 4:00 P.M. quitting siren blew.

While I was waiting, I looked over at a fenced-in area and saw what seemed to be familiar figures moving around. I squinted: They were bristle makers from my city. They were friends and neighbors.

I was astonished. Later, after dinner, I went to get water in a latrine and bumped into Morris, Yudel's son. I had thought he was dead. I told him what had happened to Yudel and the rest of the family, and he told me that he and the others had been there since the Germans had snatched him from our home town. He and our former neighbors had been making bristles for German brushes, combs, and other uses. Later, I found a shortcut to their area.

When I finally got there, everything was in disarray. The gate to the camp was open with no guards, so I could run into there and hide for a few hours during the day. The Germans had taken in so many people they had trouble keeping track of them all. So much for German efficiency.

A few nights later, guards told us some of us would be transported elsewhere for a special job.

"All Jews, report to the infirmary tomorrow morning," one guard said, with a sneer.

I wanted to get out of there fast, and I was willing to do almost anything. The camp was near a highway. Several times I tried to edge close enough to it to run. However, the camp was ringed with German shepherds that the Nazis purposely underfed. Those dogs followed me when I started to get too close to the camp's borders. If I'd tried to escape, they would have ripped me apart.

The next day, there was a marked change in the camp. That day and the following few days people were being poured in from Warsaw and all over Poland and elsewhere. The camp had held perhaps 20,000 when I got there. Now it held about 100,000 people. We were told all these people were here because Treblinka was overloaded.

I wasn't so sure. Still, the changes were amazing. Now, if we didn't have a job, we still had to run the gauntlet, but only two to three hours a day. If we had a job, they would still beat us, though not nearly so often.

The guards and murderers had lightened their abuse for a couple of reasons. First, the camp's population had expanded so the guards and the murderers were no longer plentiful enough to torture us personally.

Second, we were undergoing physical examinations. We were told to form lines. Then doctors in white coats, with stethoscopes hanging around their necks, checked us. We were naked, except for our shoes. The doctors felt our muscles, then examined our skin to make sure it was clear. They also put a finger up our rectum, then looked in our mouth and eyes with a flashlight.

The doctors inspected us every couple of days, showing each time about the same interest as if they were inspecting cattle, sheep, or pigs. But the decisions on who was still in the running to go on the special assignment were up to the SS and Gestapo. We knew that because those who were still prospects were gathered in a group by the SS and told to come back the next day. The SS told each reject individually, "You don't have to come back."

The group to be examined for a special assignment was pared down to 50,000. Then 40,000. Then down to 25,000. Then 10,000. Then 5,000. Then 1,000. As the group grew smaller, the physical examinations grew more thorough. The doctors looked over our legs, ears, fingertips.

After each round of examinations, the rejected prisoners disappeared, probably shipped to different camps. We never saw them again. Those of us who still might be chosen were treated to another round of running the gauntlet for two to three hours.

"Thank God, thank God," I said to myself, every time I knew I was still in the group they were considering. We talked among ourselves, and we figured they might send us to fight in Stalingrad. Or perhaps to a supersecret weapons factory.

"It could be the moon where they want to send us. I don't give a damn," I told one of my fellow sufferers during our endless speculation over where and what the assignment might be. We figured whatever it was, it couldn't possibly be worse than where we were. That small ember of hope by itself helped those of us who remained to look forward to going wherever our destination was.

Jacob and I were still together. We talked about getting out of there and other fantasies. Meanwhile, I found out my father was dead. One day, the niece of my sister Fay's husband walked up to me. She was toiling in the Majdanek vegetable gardens. Sometimes men were taken through that area. When I was walking past, she recognized me. Watching out for the guards, she whispered:

"Joe, Joe, I have some terrible news for you. Your father is dead," she said, weeping.

My heart ached, my head hurt, I felt dizzy. I always felt I could rely on my father, that having him as the head of the family was comforting. I had felt the weight of being the oldest male once, and a miracle had taken that weight off my back. Now, I could feel it again.

She talked to me quickly.

"I saw your father limping back to your house after all of you were captured. He said he'd jumped off that train and the Germans captured him a second time. Then he jumped off the train again. Then they caught him a third time. When he jumped off the last time, the Germans shot him in the leg. When the Germans came on another raid a few days later, the one where they got me, your father was so badly wounded, he couldn't escape them and their dogs. He obviously couldn't work, so they probably shot him, Joe, they probably shot him," she uttered, crying.

My head started pounding. I could feel my whole body throb. My shoulders felt as though they had a ton of rocks on them. My eyes started to mist.

"I'm the only one left in this world. I'm the last man of the family. Thank God Sara has escaped to Russia, but I don't know whether she's alive or dead," I told the girl.

She nodded, then quickly ducked back to her work.

When I went to bed, I could feel my tears flowing down my cheeks and across my nose. My thin blanket bobbed up and down as I sobbed, wailing inside at the loss of my family, the loss of my innocence, and the likely loss of my own life. Nobody comforted me. Although those of us in our barracks were theoretically living together, in fact, each of us was quite alone. Every day was a rainy day in our lives. We each had to live that day by ourselves.

Finally, at the end of June 1943, the doctors made the final inspection. The examination was not really as thorough as many we had endured already. They checked our hands, pinched our muscles, shone flashlights in our ears and eyes, and that was it.

After so many examinations, I could tell the Germans were looking for young men in top physical condition. The people in the group now numbered 465: I counted them. I have always been a curious person, and there wasn't much in the way of mental exercise to pass the time. We were mostly men and about twenty women in our late teens or early twenties. Most had been fighters in the Warsaw ghetto.

We're going to be special, really special. I wonder what they're going to do with us, I mused.

After the final inspection, nobody was cut from the group. I guessed the Germans didn't want to admit they might have been mistaken. They gave us the most superficial inspection, just to confirm they were right in choosing us. They wrote our names and numbers down on a clipboard. A doctor called us together and said, "You'll have to wait another day to find out what's next."

We looked at each other in wonder. We couldn't imagine what would happen. A day later, one prisoner in each barracks called out the names of people assigned to the elite group. A couple of hundred were chosen from my barracks. Then

128

members from the other parts of camp were marched over to my barracks, because we had so many prisoners in that group.

"You will be marched out of here tomorrow afternoon," we were told. "Be ready."

I wryly wondered whether he was worried that we might take too much luggage with us. After all, none of us had anything more than the clothes on his back, a fact I joked about with Jacob Wilder. I went to sleep with a smile on my face.

Late the next day, we were marched into a shower, and we were allowed to soap up and wash ourselves for a full ten minutes, about three times as long as usual.

While we were lathering up, we asked the guards where we were going. "We don't know," they replied. "We only know you're going on the train."

However, we naturally had no towels, so we had to put on our clothes while we were still wet and soapy. Then we were forced to lie in our barracks in our wet clothing.

The following day at 1:00 A.M., the guards lined us up. Ten guards were waiting for us. One of the guards started to chat with me and the guy next to me.

"Where are we going?" I asked, out of the side of my mouth.

"This is supposed to be a secret," he said, his voice dropping to a whisper, a crooked smile playing across his face. "You're going to Auschwitz."

I could feel my blood freeze. We had heard about Auschwitz. The Germans— or, rather, their slave labor—had already built part of Birkenau, the death camp there. I knew Birkenau was where they sent the intelligentsia, doctors, lawyers, politicians.

This time they took away our shoes. To replace them, they gave us wooden clogs, the kind the Dutch wear. We put them on, but they were tight and heavy. Then we had to run more than ten miles to reach the train station.

The Germans rode bicycles and were carrying submachine guns, which they used to club us if we didn't run faster than the bikes. Some of the Germans were drunk. Their bicycles were spaced every fifty feet or so, making it completely impossible to escape a beating.

They ran us out of the camp and right through the local city, Lublin, to the train station. People looked out from the windows in their apartments and their houses to see what was going on. It was dark, but I could see illumination in some of the houses. The wooden shoes clomping on the highway had awakened the residents.

They didn't know who we were, nor did they seem to care. They just gawked at the spectacle of us running in Dutch shoes from Germans on bicycles armed with submachine guns. There were lots of camps in the area, so they probably had seen such sights before.

The shoes pinched our feet so much, and the insides were so rough that the blood in our feet started flowing like water. We ran ten miles, awkwardly lurching forward and from side to side as we tried to stay upright. Every so often one of us would stumble and fall, and the others would pick him up by the elbows while still in motion. I helped three or four people this way. We tried to help each other as much as we could. Fortunately, I never fell.

By the time we got there, our shoes were filled with blood. I looked down and saw my own shoes streaked with dirt and small clots sticking to my shoes and toes. Now that I had stopped, I could feel the streams of blood in my shoes, and I could see some of it flowing out the sides.

I looked around to see what was happening to the others. By the pain on their faces, and the puddled crimson around their shoes, I could see they were experiencing the same thing.

The funny thing was that the Germans, so proud of how they made things work, apparently couldn't make the trains run on time. We still had to wait five hours.

The train, consisting of about fifteen grimy cars, finally approached the station. It arrived slowly, so slowly it almost glided into the station. Then it stopped. The engine wheezed and shot out black smoke. It was the standard cattle car parade.

Then the guards opened up the car doors.

"*Raus, raus, raus,*" the guards yelled, beating us with whips.

The cars again had carried coal before they got to us. Three inches of coal dust sat on the floors, but we were so exhausted we flopped down into it anyway. The weight of our bodies threw the dust into the air, almost choking us. I was next to Jacob, and that was a comfort. A little daylight crept in about an hour later.

There was no toilet. We didn't have much to drink or eat. It was summer, and our bloody feet and our sweaty bodies made living inside that cattle car very unpleasant. The only agreeable part was the almost soothing clickety-clack of the wheels on the tracks.

We could see in the developing gray light that we were so coated with coal powder, only our teeth were white. I had hoped being part of this elite group would improve my life.

"From the looks of this train, and the fact we're almost suffocating, it looks as if our lives are getting worse, not better," I told Jacob Wilder.

Still, nobody tried to escape. Even though guards were standing on the roof, I talked to Jacob about fleeing.

"Let's break out of the window and jump," I whispered to him.

"You can hear them on the roof. You don't know how to jump. Even if you make it off the train, you don't know the terrain well enough to dodge them. They have Nazis all over. You'll be shot."

I was feeling giddy and stupid from fear and fatigue. Summoning my courage, I said, "I'll steal a horse from a farmer."

Jacob laughed a small laugh. "By the time you get to a farmer, you'll be dead."

I shrugged. He was one of the most levelheaded people I knew. I was so dazed I couldn't think clearly. I knew Jacob was right.

After about eighteen hours, we got to where we were going. Even though it was still dark, we could see even more clearly that each of us was colored pitch black, except for our teeth. We'd had no food, no water, and we looked like grim shadows. Soon the car doors were flung open, and we could see the people on the other side were wearing prisoner uniforms, too. We started chattering Yiddish to each other.

"Where are you from?" They asked us.

"We're from Majdanek," I said. "Where are we?"

"You're in Auschwitz-Birkenau now," they said grimly.

It was July 1943. I turned to Jacob and the others. "Damn. For once, the Germans told the truth. We are in Auschwitz."

Most of the other people in the car swooned. There was mumbling, even crying, over what we knew would be our fate.

We were taken to a bathhouse to wash. It was a huge building, eight feet tall and made of brick. We were handed bars of hard soap which smelled like oil and felt like lime. We scrubbed and scrubbed. We were astonished that we were given so long to wash, perhaps ten minutes, and the soap actually removed the coal dust.

After rinsing off and getting dressed, we lined up outside a barracks, then were let inside a few at a time. Workers asked us what our occupation was. I took a guess at what they might want and I claimed to be a mechanic. Jacob said he was a bristle maker. Apparently they would occasionally call people to go to Auschwitz Number One, which was a work camp.

Inside, three French Jews were tattooing numbers into everyone's forearm. One started talking with me in Yiddish.

"Where are you from?" he asked, in a voice that said he wasn't all that interested.

I told him I was from Poland.

His eyes widened.

"What city?"

"Miedzyrzec."

"My parents were from that city," he said, excitedly.

Then he sneaked me a piece of bread under his tattooing table.

"Come over and see me," he whispered. "You're going to be in a quarantined barracks and that's very tough. I'll give you a few more pieces of bread. You've been through Majdanek, so you're already toughened."

After we had all been tattooed, they gave us each a half-cup of soup. We met the barracks leader, a French-educated man who had been born in Poland and was the son of an important rabbi. His name was Greenberg. He was strikingly handsome. He also was the Senior Block Inmate, the barracks boss. The Germans had taken him from France to Auschwitz. He assembled us together, five abreast in our barracks.

"Don't even raise your filthy heads, you goddamned Juden," he screamed at us. Then, with our heads properly bowed, he told us how to live at Birkenau:

"You have to do whatever you're told. If you don't, you'll be whipped. This is not a sanitorium and this is not a hospital. This is a concentration camp, and you're here to die," he screamed.

Then he introduced us to his *Stubendienst*, who was in charge of daily barracks life, and told us what the other rules were: "When the time comes to go to sleep, after you hear two whistles, you'd better be in bed. And no going to the bathroom during the night."

His *Stubendienst* held up a cane, then slashed it down across the face of one of the men in the first line.

"Stay in formation, Juden; stay in formation," the *Stubendienst* yelled as he used the cane to slash and bruise prisoner after prisoner.

Our sleeping quarters were three-tiered bunk beds with no blankets. The bunks were three inches thick, the width of a brick, which is what they were made of, and perhaps eighteen inches high. We could squeeze into our beds by positioning ourselves on the edge and pulling ourselves backward. Once we were in, we were in. There was no turning over.

We learned that our situation was typical, that inside the barracks there were two kinds of officials who oversaw the prisoners: Senior Block Inmates and *Stubendiensts*. The Senior Block Inmate was the top dog. There was only one of these per barracks, and he was in charge of making sure everything in the barracks was neat and orderly, the way the Germans liked it. The Senior Block Inmate made sure the rubbish was cleaned up and the food delivered on time. They sometimes had a mattress made out of wood chips, the height of comfort by death camp standards.

Under the Senior Block Inmate were the *Stubendiensts*. There were generally five or six of them, some of whom, I later learned, also were Jews. The *Stubendiensts* controlled the barracks and gave out food. If a prisoner had a question, these were the people to ask.

Stubendiensts also called out the numbers of the people who had been chosen to die. They got their jobs the same way the Senior Block Inmate got his: being thrown in the camp early, then being crafty and lucky enough to stay alive long enough to get promoted. They had the same privileges as the Senior Block Inmates. Both slept in the same section as the *Kapos* and the foremen and had the same privileges.

During the four weeks we were quarantined, the Germans took us out to do a lot of jobs. Sometimes we would pull leaves from trees for cooking. Sometimes we'd sweep the road or pick up garbage, all in the rain and cold, and all while we were being beaten.

Each barracks had a barber, and ours was a short Polish Gentile who hated Jews. He would spit on us, hit us with a stick, whatever he felt like. All we could do was duck and cringe.

"No matter where we are, even in the barber's chair, we're always the punching bag," I told Jacob, who just nodded, quietly.

We had been given old shoes, but that wasn't much help. We soon discovered the ground was laced with lime, which seeped into our leaky shoes. I could feel the lime's sting on my naked, bleeding feet. The trouble was, once you put your shoe in the lime, the wet ground had such suction, pulling the shoe out was difficult.

Meanwhile, many of us lost our shoes in the lime and became barefoot. The weather was cold and rainy, and the combination of wet and lime made the clinging soil burn on naked flesh. One time I lost my shoe, and I still had to run. If we didn't run at the Senior Block Inmate's command, we would be beaten, shoes or no shoes. Our clothes also took a beating. They were constantly soaked and often fell apart like paper, rotted by the lime and rain.

The only advantage to the lethal weather was that we were forced to work only a few hours a day. Even so, the phlegm-filled hacking and wheezing in the barracks were testament to the pneumonia we all were getting from the cold and wet climate.

One of the few consolations I had in quarantine was the tattoo artist. He was a specialty worker, so he got more food than most of us. He also had free time, and during those occasions, he would always manage to find and give me some food, whether it was a piece of bread or some salami.

Few others were so fortunate, and many of us died. Although that was sad for the deceased, it was useful for the living. When we discovered that one of us had expired, we would strip the body of its clothing and shoes.

I felt disgusted pillaging the dead at first, but my feelings soon numbed as I felt more and more desperate, recognizing that survival meant doing things I wouldn't do under any other circumstances.

One time I took one shoe apiece off two corpses, because each one had only one shoe left. The shoes were different sizes and neither one of them fit right, but having them was better than having one shoe or, worse, no shoes at all. I followed the basic law of survival: Whoever found the corpse got the clothing. I, like everyone else, wanted to stay alive for another day.

"I'm doing no harm," I would tell myself. "They're dead."

So corpse-robbing was how I improved my wardrobe. After my successful shoe theft, I vowed I'd try for jacket or pants next. Even if they were wet, I could dry the clothing in the sun. I never talked about this feature of camp life with my fellow inmates. We all had the same attitude: the dead didn't need the clothing and the living did. There was nothing to discuss.

Meanwhile, our food situation continued at subsistence level. We learned to find worms in the soil, or swat mosquitoes, then toss them into our mouths. We'd pick up roots and leaves to fill our stomachs. I learned to peel the bark off trees while I was still moving. Personally, I liked worms and roots best. They seemed to be the most nutritious.

Even so, we were always hungry. Back at the camp, we could at least get water out of rainwater barrels. Solid food, however, was hard to come by. Fortunately, nature had provided an answer, though not an easy one. The thousands of acres we worked consisted of mostly grass, and the sounds of frogs croaking after a spring or summer rain were never far from our consciousness. Of course, they disappeared in winter.

I quickly learned the French Jews considered frog legs a delicacy. I saw one of them popping a live frog into his mouth and I almost vomited—until my rumbling stomach told me any food would do. The French Jew showed me how to peel off the skin, even while the frog was still alive. After I learned, it took only seconds to skin an entire frog.

I could only catch the smaller ones because I was younger and had small hands. The Germans, French, and Dutch were generally bigger and older. They caught the big frogs.

I also quickly learned there was no time to peel off the skin. You had to pop the frog into your mouth fast, or another prisoner would grab it from you and eat it. That happened often because many prisoners didn't have the strength to chase the creatures. These prisoners were just waiting to grab frogs somebody else had caught.

I sometimes felt almost that weak. We were getting even fewer calories a day now, and sometimes we felt too feeble even to crawl out of bed. My heart was often beating so hard it was like a carburetor sucking for gas. I would just pop the live frog into my mouth, chew it, and swallow. The taste was quite bitter. I thought a lot more about the taste than about the frogs, which I assumed were asphyxiated before they hit my stomach.

Our diet was helped a little more by eating grass. We also dug up tree roots and peeled bark off trees. The roots were bitter, and the bark tasted like wood, almost sticking in our throats. We tried to find smaller trees because the bark was softer and we could chew it. We also would break it into small pieces to go down our gullets more easily. Because of the constant rain, the ground was almost alive with worms as long as five inches. These we would grab and swallow, with no chewing. We desperately ate anything we could get our hands on.

The beatings were constant. The Senior Block Inmate's assistant lashed out with a cane at his whim. I myself was beaten many times.

I did find someone I never expected to see: Morris Tisch, son of the Tisch family, whose house was being used as German headquarters in my town and whose courtyard was the scene of so many executions. I met him one Sunday as we were both washing in the latrine. We were astonished to see each other.

Finally, after four weeks of quarantine, about four hundred of our group were still alive. When our four-week isolation expired, we were moved to a barracks we ourselves had built. We had constructed barracks without benefit of roads; the floors were packed dirt. When it rained, the floor was soaked. The only good aspect was that there was only six to eight feet of space between bunks. That meant many people stood often on whatever floor space was there. That compacted the earth, making it less sloppy after the rains.

After being moved to the new barracks, we were herded into a large field of perhaps five thousand acres. For miles, we could see only grass and trees, all green and wet. The foremen and guards were standing in formation. One of them stepped out and pointed to the large empty space in front of us and smirked.

"Here is where you will work. And here you will die. Don't expect to live through this. You won't. We have brought you here to be worked to death. None of you will survive."

Our stunned silence was punctuated only by the never-ending croaking of frogs throughout this lush land on which most of us were to shed our blood and lose our lives.

Chapter 11

Construction
for
Destruction

After our mocking introduction to the site where they would force us to work ourselves to death, the guards marched us three miles to the train station. We saw some men were already there unloading pre-fabricated walls. After seeing a number of walls being placed against each other, we figured it out.

My God, we're going to build more barracks, a lot more. We're going to build a whole goddamned camp, I thought.

I heard other prisoners murmuring. They'd had the same realization. We could see the work was going to be massive. Each wooden wall was about twelve feet high, four inches thick, and as much as two hundred feet long. Each wall weighed more than two tons and required fifty to sixty of us to carry it. We were told we had to carry each wall three miles to an area about a mile from the construction site.

The walls were killers—literally. Every time we carried one, we lost some of the boys. We carried the walls on our shoulders, but some people just slipped or were so exhausted they fell and were crushed. Almost every time we carried one, we dropped it at least once, pinning or crushing some of us underneath. I also figured out early that when the wall fell, most frequently it would be the people at the front who had lost their grip. If I was in the back, I had a lot more time to decide which way to jump than the people holding the wall in the front. If I took a position in either of the back corners, I could backpedal or run to either side because I wasn't hemmed in by people.

A group of about forty of us from my home city, including Jacob Wilder, banded together. There also were Hymie and Nuftul. I hadn't known them very well when we were all living in the same city. Now we were all in Birkenau together, and we depended on each other for our lives. I had seen them in Majdanek, but we hadn't been able to talk to each other much.

Hymie and Nuftul had handsome faces. Nuftul had been a demolitions expert in the Polish army. His parents had been fish peddlers. Nuftul would come home every year on leave in his Polish soldier's uniform and help his parents sell fish very close to our home. Nuftul was about twenty-two, four years older than I. Hymie's father had worked in a movie house, where Hymie, who was about seven years older than I was, had learned to be an electrician. I had often gone to the movie house where Hymie worked.

We instinctively knew that, in a concentration camp, we all needed to be as close as possible. The only people you could really trust in a place like this were those people you knew from your own city, plus your relatives. Hymie, Nuftul, Jacob, and I all found food for each other occasionally, and each also tried to watch the others' backs. If one of us would get assigned to a good job, he'd try to get the others in there, too.

After work, we'd all meet for a while to talk and figure out how to last one more day. I was always the optimist, constantly saying to them, "Guys, give it all you have. We can do it." I believed we could, and my optimism seemed to cheer them up daily.

I worked the day shift, starting at 5:30 A.M., no matter what the season. We had no heat, and in the winter, nights seemed as though they could get as cold as twenty below. When we arose in our barracks, which held almost a thousand men, the chill inside would force us to move fast.

All of us were wobbly from hunger. However, the guards started cutting a bigger portion for themselves, so we actually were getting even less than our allotted portions.

We learned very quickly what the pecking order was. Once again, the Germans addressed us by our numbers, and we addressed our fellow prisoners the same way, unless we knew them well. Of course I called Jacob Wilder by his name, but most people were numbers to me and everybody else as well.

The *Stubendienst* would wake us up by turning on the light. We didn't have to go far for our clothing: We wore it to bed, both to get some warmth and to prevent it from being stolen. When we arose, we would line up in formation, then march to the bathrooms.

If we had to go to the bathroom during the night, there were some barrels about five feet high and three feet in diameter for us to use. There was a wooden bench next to the barrel. If we had to urinate, we would stand on the bench and leak into the barrel. If we had to move our bowels, we would stand on the bench, turn our backs, drop our pants and hang over the barrel. Amazingly, the barrel wasn't very smelly—probably because of the bitter cold—and nobody ever fell in that I knew about. We used anything we could find to wipe ourselves, paper, rags, whatever. A *Stubendienst* emptied the barrel every morning.

The regular bathroom facilities for the whole camp were in the middle of the grounds. The bathroom was about two hundred feet long by sixty feet wide, with around 150 toilets in two separate rows. The toilets were long pine boards with holes in them. We had three minutes to do our business. There were prisoners watching us whose job was to make sure the latrines were clean and that we didn't linger too long. We knew we had to finish quickly.

The bathroom itself had a trench underneath, with water running constantly through it. Right across from the toilets in the same building was a wall on each side. In a line across each wall, there was a metal sink every two to three feet. We had two minutes to wash. If we didn't do it quickly, the latrine workers would beat us. I saw someone beaten bloody for taking too long on the toilet. I got the message, and other prisoners learned just as fast. At the sink, we would take off our shirt, then wash ourselves anywhere we could, as long as we could do it quickly. Some of us had little pieces of soap, about the size of a fourth of a candy bar.

Then we had to march double-time back to the barracks, usually in five minutes or less. We slept on a board with a blanket over it, but no mattress, no pillow. The bed had to be made up precisely: straight and with hospital corners, no uneven edges. Then German soldiers would go through and give the *Stubendienst* a warning if any of the beds weren't done right. That meant the *Stubendienst* immediately would beat up the unfortunate Jew who had failed to make his bed correctly.

After inspection finished, some prisoners carried in a barrel of coffee-colored water. Three guys ladled it out, about three-fourths of a cup per person. Then we'd be gathered into formation to march double-time in groups through the camp's gate.

The Germans wanted military precision in almost everything. They had captured a Jewish band from Paris, complete with instruments. The band played German marching songs at a brisk pace. To their tune, each working group had to goose step past the guardhouse as *Kapos* called their own name and the number of prisoners with them. Work groups could number from ten to two hundred people, depending on the job. It took less than an hour for twenty-thousand people to march through the gate. If we didn't march fast or correctly, we would be beaten. Out of sheer terror, we learned to march better than the SS.

The Germans were thrilled they had a military band to keep time for the work groups going and coming. We could hear the band and its brass tones, the drums, and the tuba's "ooompah," sounding a "zum, zum, zum," all the way to our work site—and again when we returned.

They've got a hell of a great job, I often thought. *They play once in the morning, once in the evening, and they've got nothing to do for the rest of the day. I wish I played the tuba.*

I have no doubt I was only one of tens of thousands of prisoners who thought the same thing as we marched to our job, a trip taking an hour or more. Even many miles outside the gate, we could still hear the band's "Zum, zum, zum."

Most of us wore clothing ill-suited to the frigid conditions. We usually had light summer shoes which leaked whenever we stepped into the weekly rain puddles. To prevent our shoes from leaking, we lined them with empty cement bags.

Usually we had a thin shirt, thin pants, and a summer jacket. If our clothing wasn't wet from the rain, it was wet from the snow, which fell on us almost every day. We also wore the cement bags by making holes for the head and arms in them. Even so, many of us had frostbite from the glacial chill, which could reach biting subzero temperatures. We had no gloves, so we just kept rubbing our hands for warmth.

Food was always on our minds. In the middle of the shift, two guys would show up carrying vats with big metal handles. Sometimes they arrived in a horse-drawn wagon if we were far from camp. We all had metal plates hanging from our belts. We'd use the cup to pour the soup onto a metal plate. *Kapos* and foremen got all they wanted, of course. Sometimes, the supply ran short, and then the people at the end of the line got nothing. The soup was sometimes warm, sometimes cold. It was 98 percent water, with a few sprinkles of potato or barley. After we ate the soup, we were all still hungry.

Sometimes the bigger guys would try to muscle the smaller prisoners out of line. The Russians, who generally were bigger than most of the rest of us, were particularly belligerent, and I had to stand up to them several times so smaller friends of mine could get their rightful share.

The work itself was building roads, laying railroad track and ties, erecting electrified fences, building barracks, and also digging graves and sewers. Other prisoners packed clothes stripped from corpses.

When our work lagged, we were beaten. The *Kapos* and others used a cane or rubber whips. They would raise their arms as high as they could, then bring them down fast and hard, slashing at us with the whips. The more they beat us, the more they were rewarded with better jobs and food. Foremen were particularly vicious because they were so eager to be promoted to *Kapo*.

Finally, when our shift was over, we were marched double-time back to the barracks. We marched past a table holding some food. We'd grab our share, then move on. There was no time for chatting or asking anyone for a second helping. We also got a slice of bread made from a half-sawdust, half-flour compound. The bread was originally an eight- by six-inch piece, but then that piece was cut into four slices. However, the _Kapos_ cut a slice out of the middle for themselves. On the bread was a lump of coal-based margarine. Sometimes we got a tiny piece of horsemeat salami.

We did have some chances to sneak extra nourishment. Near the end of 1943, I was called to the kitchen with a few other guys to peel potatoes. I knew what to do. I leaned hard on the metal peeler, to make sure there would be lots of potato in each peeling, which I would throw into my mouth. I whispered to the others to try it; they did. The peelings didn't taste good, but they were food.

We were prepared next time. We tied our pants cuffs closed. As soon as we arrived at the kitchen and started to work, we opened our flies and, making sure nobody saw us, started tossing in the peelings, so they would go down our pants legs. The cooks and their helpers were there, but they were too busy eating to watch us.

The guards didn't pay us much attention, either. They had plenty of food, they were constantly coming and going, and it was night. I learned to eat bites of raw potato and showed others how to do it. We got a little cocky about getting away with almost anything in that kitchen if we were careful. One night, we had a surprise. The SS was waiting for us by the kitchen doors.

"Stop, you Jewish pigs," one of them yelled as we were walking out of the kitchen. Then, one by one, they pulled the strings on our pants legs and all the potatoes and peelings dropped out.

"Pigs. Greedy Jewish bastards," they yelled, then used sticks and canes to drive us behind a barracks. Then they smashed our heads and our bodies using their sticks and the whips with wires in them hard enough to peel our skin off in ragged chunks. This beating went on for an hour, and I almost passed out from the pain.

The Germans weren't the only ones to attack me for my potato thieving. One night I returned to the barracks and two Russian prisoners jumped me and tried to take away all of the peelings I had. Both started screaming at me, though not very loudly because they didn't want to attract the Senior Block Inmate's attention. I kicked one guy in the balls, paralyzing him. Then I pushed him over. The other one I held by his windpipe until he pleaded with me to stop.

After the fight was over, I untied my pants legs and let all the peelings spill out. "Come and get it," I whispered to the several people in the barracks who were waiting for me. They knew I'd share with them. In fact, I had already eaten several raw potatoes in the kitchen. I was full, and my stomach was having a hard time digesting what I'd eaten. I even let the two Russians have some food.

Why not? I can't eat any more food, and I can't carry it around with me. They're trying not to starve, just like the rest of us, I thought.

Neither the Russians nor their friends ever bothered me again. They were typical bullies. Once they learned you would fight back, they would leave you alone.

After dinner, we were allowed to go to the latrine and wash up sometime before 9:00 P.M. We had to shave. The Germans insisted their prisoners be clean-shaven. Some of my Gentile countrymen were getting razor blades from home, and when they had almost used them up, I begged for them. I was young and had a soft beard, so I didn't need as sharp a razor as the older men. I'd also find razors lying around the bathrooms, then use tiny pieces of soap I would find there for lather.

The Germans didn't worry about whether we might commit suicide with our razors. In fact, they probably would have welcomed it. Strangely, nobody ever did use a razor to kill himself. At least, nobody I knew about.

Most prisoners didn't wash after dinner. They were too tired or too sick, or they were giving up on life. As for me, I went there every night. I'd take off my shirt, then wash as long and as much of me as I could. Then I dried myself off with my shirt. After that, I'd take off my pants—of course I had no underwear. I would wash myself there, then dry off, using my pants. By the time I was finished I was half-dry. My body heat dried out the rest by morning.

Staying clean was important. The Germans liked cleanliness, and it was good for my morale and for conversation. I met quite a few people at night who were cleaning themselves. We'd talk about everything, especially food. Dying seldom came up, because we all knew this was a death camp. Food was a way to live another day, to cheat death, maybe even live long enough to be liberated.

I had been having dreams recently, dreams I would be somebody. I would have a wife and children and would have a business with lots of people working for me. I believed that I would get out of this camp and have a future I could be proud of, and I believed that some of my friends could make it too.

That's why I kept urging them to try to make it through another hour, another day. Nobody in his right mind would think that any of us was going to get out of this alive, but I did. I didn't tell any of the other guys then. I knew they'd think I had gone crazy.

Between 8:30 and 9:00, we'd have to go to our bunks and sleep. Nobody had any trouble dropping off to dreamland. We were exhausted from the day, and we only got to sleep for five hours.

That time was one of the few when the Germans left us alone. Beatings throughout the day and night were common. The *Kapos* would beat every one of us at least once a week. The *Stubendiensts* also would beat us, and the SS would attack us, too.

Even our fellow prisoners joined in. This was a place where the strong clawed the weak to death, and that went for the prisoners as well. I was less than five feet, five inches, tall. Tall and well-muscled Gentile prisoners from Russia, the Ukraine, and other places would beat me two or three times a week. The worst were the Ukrainians and the Polish people who lived close to the German border and were largely loyal to Hitler.

I wasn't the worst-off prisoner. I had some respect. Prisoners, Jew and non-Jew, often came to me for advice. They all admired me.

"You're so tough. How did you make it?" Hymie once asked me.

"We had to in the ghettos. They did every monstrous thing to us they could think of. There are a lot of decent, God-fearing people here, too. Maybe He will take care of it," I told them. I left out the parts about the partisans and passing as a Gentile. That was the real reason I was tough, but telling anybody anything was dangerous.

We also thought about other things, such as women. Thinking was as far as it went. Some of the men worked with women packing up old shoes and clothing. Sometimes we saw women and got to talk to them briefly. But you couldn't associate with them, let alone have sex. It was forbidden.

Sometimes, when we went out on jobs, I saw a woman whose father had worked in Yudel's factory. We were being moved in different directions, so we would exchange just a couple of words.

A friend of mine there had a girlfriend from my home city. He was a Polish Jewish prisoner who had been dumped into my city along with lots of other people. He had been an officer in the Polish army. One day he confided in me.

"I'm dying to see my girlfriend. What can I do, Joe?" he asked, out of the corner of his mouth.

"I know the foreman of the *Leichenkommandos*. I'll ask him whether he's going over to the women's camp to pick up the dead."

I approached the foreman and asked him about going over to the women's camp.

"Do you want to go, Joe?"

"No, a friend of mine does. Can you do me a favor? He has a girlfriend over there. He's eager to see her. He's going to die, and so is she. Can you arrange for them to see each other?"

"Sure, Joe. Anything for you."

When I told my friend he almost jumped out of his skin. A few hours later, he was helping the *Leichenkommandos*, whose job it was to pick up work camp corpses, pull their cart over to the women's camp.

He returned several hours later.

"Thanks, Joe, you saved my life," he smiled, giving me a huge hug. He told me they'd hugged, kissed, cried together, and, no doubt, had sex.

"A couple of the girls stood watch outside her barracks to make sure the SS bitch with the whip didn't come around," he said.

143

Still, the business of Birkenau went on as usual. We got very little food, very little water, and we were being beaten every day. People also were dying daily by the hundreds and coming in by the thousands. Birkenau was a distribution point for manpower. When people were transported in, one-third were allowed to live to be sent to work camps. The other two-thirds were gassed, then burned.

Even so, the number of people there permanently was expanding. The Germans had us building more barracks, more camps, more roads. There were more *Kapos* and *Stubendiensts*. The number of electrified fences multiplied, just as our misery did.

Some people couldn't wait for the Germans to kill them. One morning I was lying on my bunk, feeling both legs pounding with pain because they were swollen a fourth larger than normal. I turned around to talk with some of my friends about it. I looked up and down the rows of beds, and I saw a number of my friends were missing. Inside myself, I felt more despair than I had ever felt before. I knew what had happened, even before I saw their bodies dangling on the electrified fences right outside the barracks door.

"They couldn't go any further. This was the fastest way to get it over with instead of being gassed. But they were my friends, and I hurt because they're not here," I told Hymie and Nuftul. They nodded. Eventually about 10 percent of us took this way out.

People started talking more openly about committing suicide.

"What's the sense of living? I hurt, my whole body hurts, and there is no other way out," they would say.

As the days went on, I would see two, five, ten, sometimes twenty bodies of my friends slumped over the fence in the morning.

"Don't do this," I pleaded with them when they started talking about suicide. "This is murder. Our religion says so. To kill yourself is to assassinate a piece of God, because He created you. Besides, God can make a miracle happen. We just have to hang on until it does. Don't kill yourself. Just get through tomorrow. Just get through the day."

Most of them, even Morris Tisch, Hymie, and Nuftul, would just shake their heads.

"You're a sweet guy, Joe. You're the best. But you're naive. You're crazy. A miracle? The only miracle is we've lived this long. This is a death camp, son. Sooner or later, we all die here."

I kept trying to convince them to fight. I told them I knew they were fed up, hungry, and desperate and probably would die. But I kept urging them to try one more day; maybe it all would change.

However, my own situation was deteriorating rapidly. My legs were swelling to twice their normal size, and I was very worried. I knew that people who couldn't work were gassed immediately.

Our conditions grew still worse. We were getting less bread at night as the

Senior Block Inmates and *Stubendiensts* started cutting even bigger pieces for themselves. I awakened every morning to find more bunks empty, the bodies hanging on the electrified fence.

We did catch one break. About thirty of us were digging a ditch. The temperatures generally were around zero. The ground was hard, the work was tough, and, as usual, we were getting little or no food. About 150 yards away from us were guards' barracks. The cooking smelled rich, like my grandmother's. They had so much food they put barrels of it uneaten outside to be lapped up by the dogs or taken away as garbage. I analyzed the situation. I noticed that after the afternoon meals were delivered and the guards ate, it got quiet and the guards took a nap—after leaving out whatever food remained for the dogs and pigs.

I calculated that they ate a half-hour after the food was delivered, then got an hour for rest. There were bushes near the guards' barracks, and I kept going in there quietly. I knew the guards were resting.

One afternoon, after the meal had been delivered, I sneaked close to the barrels of uneaten food. I said a prayer. Because everybody was so hungry, only God could help us. I took out the bowl from my belt and scooped up real soup and beans, with potatoes and meat in it. I sneaked back to where the other prisoners were, and they all helped me eat what was in my dish.

"Go one by one," I told them after we had all finished my plateful. "They're sleeping in the barracks."

We crawled there one at a time while the guards were still sleeping. Each guy in turn filled up his plate. It was like a new soul in our body, to have meat and potatoes, to have the same food as the murderers had. I could see the difference in every one of us. Our color was a little more pink and our eyes lost some of their dull glazing. Just that one big plate of food made us come alive.

But the triumph was only a temporary victory. Generally, all of us were starving to death. I started dreaming my dream again: that when the war was over, I would have a wife, children, and my own business. Every night I kept on dreaming the dream. And during the day I would visualize these hopes over and over again. It was my nature to think this way. It was my nature to think that my life would go beyond the electrified wires and the smokestacks belching flames fueled by corpses. It was a hope I clung to no matter what happened, and I believed it. I believe in miracles.

It had been three weeks since we began carrying the walls, and both Jacob Wilder and I were suffering. So was a man named Frank. I liked Frank, who was near my age.

"We can't go on like this," I told both of them. "I don't know what to do. If we don't get a job where we won't be beaten, we'll wind up in the crematorium."

Jacob's leg was swollen even larger than mine. That night, a miracle happened, at least for Jacob. The *Stubendienst* called his number. Jacob went to see him and came back smiling.

"Joe, I might have a job in Auschwitz Number One. He asked me whether I am a bristle maker. When I said yes, he said I'd be taken over there tomorrow morning," he crowed, trying hard not to look happy. Frank and I were still in bad shape. We could be killed any day.

The next day, Jacob was called out again by the *Stubendienst*. We hugged, then he left. I later heard he indeed did have a bristle maker's job.

In the meantime, Frank and I got weaker and weaker. My leg started swelling even larger and became spongy. Frank's legs, too.

The days were too hard for us to endure. My leg was so swollen I could hardly move. One night we looked at each other's pitifully thin bodies and enormous legs and we were scared.

"Joe," Frank said, "if we don't do something soon, the Germans will gas us."

Chapter 12

Hoodwinking
the
Death
Merchants

We were desperate. Every morning after the work crews had gone past the guardhouse and out to work for the day, about fifty *Kapos* and SS men formed a line standing shoulder to shoulder to go from the back side of the camp up to the guardhouse. Whomever they found, they sent to the crematorium.

The sweeps generally caught twenty or thirty people daily, though as the war went on and conditions grew worse, they caught more. Later, I would see the sweeps at work. The SS, *Kapos*, and Gestapo would cover the entire width of the camp, with their hands held out to their sides, almost touching fingertips.

Whoever they caught had to walk, limp, or crawl in front of them, like sheep being herded to slaughter. Most of them couldn't walk. At best, they were limping, but crawling was something they refused to do unless their bodies were too drained of energy to do otherwise. Instead, holding their arms around each other for support, the doomed men wobbled upright on spindly legs, using their last ounce of strength to lose their lives with dignity. They were pushed out the gate and to the hospital, which was about a quarter of a mile away. There, the prisoners were picked up by trucks and taken to be gassed.

One exception to the death sweep was the night shift people, who worked in an area called Canada. They gathered food and baggage and helped to unload boxcars when the death trains rolled in. They slept in a special area in one of the barracks, and none of the SS or Gestapo dared to disturb them. The *Stubendiensts* controlled who got in and out of that section, so the guards had no reason to go there.

I knew about Canada, and I knew that nobody could get a job in there because it was filled with people who had been there much longer than I. Largely the people who were there seemed to be tradesmen, including bricklayers, plumbers, and electricians. They knew what kind of haven Canada was because they had helped build it, so they quickly got themselves assigned there. I also discovered the hospital had the best jobs in the camp.

Then we got lucky. We spotted Hans Eistenstein. Hans was a golden angel, a Jewish *Kapo*. He had a reputation: If you couldn't find a job, see him. He would take care of you. He had lots of connections, and he looked German. He must have had women all over him before he ended up in the camp. He knew a lot of people in Birkenau and had compassion for young guys like me. He was fifteen years older than I was, a big man with a big heart. Later, he would be demoted to picking up rubbish, probably for being too soft.

He had been here a year before I arrived and had been made a temporary *Kapo* to move stones on the road near the hospital. Frank and I were desperate to find a new job. That day we were wandering near the hospital, along with several other people who looked as thin and full of pain as we were. Somehow they also had avoided the morning death sweep. Hans raised his arm and motioned for us to come over.

"I need some extra people to help clean up in the hospital and the barracks. It's only for a couple of days. You guys interested?" he asked with a smile containing the brightest teeth I'd ever seen and a look that radiated compassion. He knew we'd be gassed if we didn't find a safe job very fast.

I learned during my work under Hans that there was a sudden flurry of activity. A lot of barracks had been built quickly near the hospital, and I had helped build them. About half of them had thirty to forty triple-decker bunk beds. The others held seven hundred to eight hundred people. The big ones were for the dying. The smaller ones were for those who had a chance to live. They had all been built in about eight weeks.

Now, everybody knew the hospital was being opened and that Josef Mengele was moving to our camp. I had heard many things about Mengele from some of the *Kapos*, who knew him from Auschwitz Number One. They knew what kind of monster Mengele was.

I heard that Mengele was the reason new offices and a laboratory had been built in Birkenau. I also heard a lot about the rest of the camp. I could see that droves of new construction crews were being brought in after my group arrived.

What I saw during my few days working near the hospital startled me. I had been around dead people a lot by now, but this was a new experience. I knew only Gentiles were there, never Jews. Jews and Gypsies didn't get sent to the hospital. Germans wouldn't waste valuable bed space or medicine on them.

When the murderers weren't looking, we used to run into the hospital to urinate, and we would look around like animals sniffing for food. I saw teachers, lawyers, white-collar workers, all European nationalities. These people, mostly middle-aged, weren't used to this kind of life. Before I returned to use the toilet again, many of them were dead.

I also saw that they got food packages, and these were thrown out. The Jews had no family left, and nobody knew where they were, so, even if they had been in the hospital, they never would have received food packages. What a discovery! I tried sneaking food out of those packages, but the Germans were watching too closely. At least I knew the packages were there.

While I was working near the hospital, I kept looking for a steady job. I knew this job was temporary. While I was cleaning the hospital, I saw a detail working on the hospital roads.

I asked the guys which barracks they were in and who their *Kapo* was. They were in Barracks 8 and their *Kapo* was an old Czech guy. I saw him once wobbling by on a cane. I didn't approach or say anything to him. He would have killed me if I'd tried. Still, I figured out I wanted to be in that old Czech's squad.

After several days, Hans told Frank, me, and several others he had bad news.

"I hate to tell you this, all of you, but the temporary job is over. I've got to hire people I already know for my permanent work crew. I feel bad about this, I really do. But you know how it is in here. First you have to save the people you know."

We all nodded, with our eyes down. This could mean going back out in the winds, the snow, the rain. It could mean our death.

I've got to find something for Frank and me. We've got to stay alive, I thought.

We had to scavenge for jobs; we had to find a way to work that wouldn't expose us to the cold, the starvation, and the beatings. I knew that a few prisoners actually worked in each barracks every day, cleaning up and carrying in soup pots.

That's what we can use. An indoor job. No rain, no snow, no beatings, and maybe we can sneak a little food on the side, I mused to myself.

Then I was struck with an inspiration. I knew there were some prisoners who worked inside the camp cleaning up the roads, garbage, papers, and clothing that littered the grounds every day. They went to work after the death sweep. People who had jobs were in the buildings or in their barracks, so they were unharmed.

I had spotted a wheelbarrow, two shovels, and a broom, which were lying in back of the guardhouse every day. The guys who used them were supposed to clean up after the line went through. They usually left their equipment in that spot.

I created a plan. The next day, Frank and I reached the guardhouse before the line did and picked up the wheelbarrow and shovels.

"We've got to do this if we're going to last for another day. No questions asked, we have to do it," I told Frank. I could feel my heart thumping so hard I thought it would burst out of my chest. God forbid anybody should figure out Frank and I didn't really have a job. Every day I prayed, "God help us. Look out for us. This is our last chance. If we get caught, we are minutes away from death. God, please answer my prayers."

When the SS, Gestapo, and *Kapos* saw us, they dropped their arms, creating a space between some of them, so we could get through. As we did, they just waved and said, "Hello," figuring we belonged on the job. Then they walked around us.

As soon as we passed the line, we walked as rapidly as we could, without drawing attention, over to an alley, then headed up toward the guardhouse. By that time, the line had disbanded. There was no window in the back of the guardhouse for anybody to see us, so we put the wheelbarrow, shovels, and broom back where they belonged in exactly the positions we'd found them. Shortly afterward, the prisoners who were actually supposed to use them showed up.

There was a drawback. Out on the jobs, the Germans brought us some lunch, little as it was. Here, we had no food, so we had to go find it. But by now I knew about the food packages at the hospital.

Now that our wheelbarrow and push broom trick had worked this first day, Frank and I were free to do what we needed to do: look for food.

"Let's go to the garbage bin," I told Frank. "Who knows? Maybe we'll have an international banquet."

There was only one garbage bin, about six feet high, fifty feet long, and twelve feet wide. Frank and I picked up garbage and litter around the grounds, slowly edging toward the bin. Several Germans passed by without saying a thing. When they saw us working, they figured we were on an assigned job. We picked up garbage for about a half hour. We knew the garbage was thrown out first thing in the morning, and we wanted to get to the top layer while it was still fresh and we would be the first ones to plunder it.

After looking around to make sure nobody was looking, we climbed in. The smell hit us right in the face. It made us gag so much, we had to cover our nose and mouth.

Most of the food was coated with bright green mold. When we opened up the bread, sometimes there were a few bites that hadn't turned green. The odor nearly burned my eyes out, but I couldn't afford to let that stop me. I knotted a handkerchief over my mouth to keep from gagging and then went on digging through the debris.

The food usually was wrapped in brown and stained paper. Sometimes it was just lying there. We ate every unmoldy crumb we could find: bread, potato peelings, meat left over from the guards' table. We would shove the small crumbs into our mouth while we looked for more. I drooled and coughed and licked my fingers.

I knew I couldn't eat the mold itself. It tasted like poison and burned my mouth. I did, however, eat most things. I tried a piece of bread with salami. It had been there so long it had worms on it, gluing the pieces together. We ate whatever we could, even the food that was congealed and gummy. Much of it had maggots on it. We brushed off the maggots and ate.

I thought of my mother and how much she once would have disapproved of my table manners. I knew she'd understand now. I also knew I'd sunk about as low as I could sink in order to survive.

"If I've become only a little better than an animal, is it even worth saving my life?" I confided to Frank. "What have I become? How much longer can I survive this way? Somebody's going to catch on to our wheelbarrow trick or figure out that if we're in the garbage bins we don't really belong in camp, that we should be out on work details. How much longer can I survive this way without being gassed?"

While we were gagging and rooting around in the garbage bins, I knew we had to find a permanent daytime job. To have no work was to invite suspicion and death.

Another inspiration struck me. All of the dishes in that camp were washed every day, but there was a constant shortage of clean dishes—or dishes of any kind—even so. In my barracks, I found a *Stubendienst* in charge of getting our quarters cleaned up and getting food. I asked whether he had any dishes to wash. I'd also noticed my barracks was short of dishes.

"Do you need any help or do you need more metal dishes? Do you want us to wash the dishes?" Frank and I asked him.

"Ja, ja, we need dishes. They're dirty, they've all piled up, and even when we have them all clean we don't have enough," he said. "The bastards never give us enough. If you can get dishes, I'll give you some soup and a little bread."

I started washing the dishes, feeling my hands and arms luxuriate in the cold water, which my body heat turned warm. Meanwhile, Frank went to the next barracks and, when nobody was looking, stole about twenty-five clean metal dishes and brought them to our barracks. When the *Stubendienst* saw all the old dishes were clean and there were new ones, he was thrilled.

"Take some soup for yourselves. You've done us a big favor," he said, waving his hand magnanimously at the soup kettles.

The next day we made the same offer to another barracks. Then Frank stole the twenty-five dishes he'd taken the day before from our barracks. The barracks were perhaps twenty feet away from each other. While I was washing dishes, I also watched to make sure the *Stubendienst* in the barracks where Frank was stealing the dishes didn't come into view.

This routine went on for six or eight days. We always got the same response. The *Stubendienst* was so grateful for having all the dishes cleaned and acquiring a lot of extra ones that he let us take some soup and a little bread. One time when I talked to a *Stubendienst*, I got a big bonus. I asked him whether he needed some dishes, and whether he could help me.

"Where are you from?" he asked, his eyes narrowing just a little. In this camp, you learned not to let your emotions show in any way, shape, or form.

"Poland."

"Where in Poland?"

"You wouldn't know it."

"East Poland?"

"Yes."

He started trembling.

"My parents were taken to eastern Poland to a small city near Treblinka. Name me some names."

I rattled off several, then said, "Miedzyrzec. My city."

"Oh my God, you're from that city?" he said. I could see his eyes widen, and his hair almost stood up. His eyes moistened.

"Yes. I was born there. Why would I lie to you?"

His hard face softened at the edges, and his voice began to crack. "My whole family wound up in that city. They put my family in the synagogues, they put them in the factories, they brought in Jewish people from all over. What went on there?" he said in a wounded voice. "I've never seen them since. What can you tell me?"

So I told him the story of my city, how the Germans had occupied it, how the ghetto had been shrunk and shrunk and shrunk, and how the Jews who had no place to live had been crammed into synagogues, factories, warehouses, as though they were pieces of meat or piles of clothing. How the Jews who had been uprooted would go from door to door, begging just a crumb from the Jews who had homes there.

I told him how we would give them whatever we could, although we knew it wasn't enough and that more people just like them would come knocking on the door that same day. And how, even though we were all in desperate circumstances we all treated each other with dignity through our pain. And how most of us eventually were hunted out and shipped off to Treblinka or Majdanek, then gassed within an hour. I told him everything.

"Now I know what happened to them," he said, softly, little bits of moisture rimming his eyes, his shoulders sagging. Then he pulled a ragged piece of bread from his pocket. He could do nothing more for me, though. I had nothing to trade. If you didn't have something to trade, few people would lift a finger for you.

Several days after I created my wheelbarrow trick, I saw two of my friends get caught up in the sweeps. Samuel and Benjamin, both nearly my age, had come through Majdanek with me. They had been in my construction crew. They had carried the walls with me. When I had still been able to march out to work, Samuel would say, "Joe, you look good."

It hurt to hear that. I knew they looked ten times worse. They were ragged and dirty skeletons. That day, both of them were so sick, so tired of trying to survive for another couple of days, they could do nothing but prop each other up. I watched as the sweep line forced them nearer and nearer to the hospital and the death trucks. As they rounded a corner, I could see them holding onto each other, limping, crying, but determined not to crawl or beg. They were treated as animals, but they, like many others, chose to die as men.

I prayed, "God, let me live just a few more days. Maybe a miracle will happen."

Then, as the fires of the crematoriums shot upward, like hell's fire, I thought about Samuel and Benjamin again. I felt deep and bitter despair, and I cried out, quietly.

"Maybe Samuel and Benjamin are better off. Me, I keep going. Someday the Germans will catch me, and then I will join Samuel and Benjamin. Why do you let these things happen, God? Why? Why? Why?"

I watched the fires stabbing higher and higher into the sky, as though they could almost scorch God Himself. Then, I turned away.

Chapter 13

The
Fifty-Dollar
Break

Two weeks after I had started picking through the garbage, I spotted a dull green which was not mildew. It looked familiar. I had an uncle in Detroit who used to send us money during the Depression, so I had seen American money.

This small bit of green looked very much like that. I crawled over rotting apples, bread, and potatoes. With the stink rising into my brain, I clawed at the pile where this hint of green was almost winking at me. I picked it up. It was an American fifty-dollar bill.

I almost wept, though I knew I could not betray such emotion, even around Frank. This money would be stolen if anybody knew about it. I went into Barracks 8, where all the good jobs were. I talked to the guys in charge. One guy was from Slovakia. He was a *Stubendienst* in my barracks, but he lived in Number 8. He was the one whose parents wound up in my city. I knew he knew most of the Senior Block Inmates, and if anybody could help me, he could. I pulled him aside, and he looked at me suspiciously

"And what can I do for you?" he asked, knowing with the sense of someone winning the game of survival in Birkenau that this conversation had not happened accidentally.

"Can I trust you?" I asked.

"Of course," he said, giving me a small smile. "You gave me peace with my parents. Now I know what happened to them." Tears dribbled down one of his cheeks. He had been deeply touched.

It was my turn to cry. I was shocked to feel my chest heaving, my eyes dripping, and my voice so filled with sobs. "Can you help me, please? I want to get a good job. I want to be in the hospital group. Do you know the Czech?"

"Morris the Hasid knows him quite well, Morris is the Senior Block Inmate. He talks with the Czech every day. The *Kapo* is a murderer. He's been here for years, not just in Birkenau but in several other prisons. They brought him in to beat and kill us. I'll talk to Morris and see what I can do. What do you have to trade?"

"Can I trust Morris? I have fifty dollars in American money. I want a half loaf of bread, a stick of margarine, a whole salami, a job in the hospital, and fifteen dollars change. Do you know Morris well?"

I knew if I asked for a lot, I wouldn't get it because there wasn't a lot of bread or salami to steal. They had enough for themselves but not enough to be extravagant. If I asked for more than they could deliver, there would be no deal and they'd just beat me up and steal the money. Still, I'd heard good things about Morris.

He nodded, his eyes widening with new respect.

"I'll talk to Morris tonight."

That night, exhausted as I was, I could barely sleep. I kept the bill in the lining of my pants. I knew this piece of paper, manufactured thousands of miles away, was my passport to staying alive. If I lost it, I would be lost. I also had confidence.

I've got a good way with people. I work when they want me to work. I never stop. I keep myself clean. And this guy needs good workers so he can look good and save his job. I can do his work and outsmart him, too. I have faith, God willing, that this will happen, I thought, hoping I wasn't overconfident. Being too confident in a death camp could be a way of hallucinating away reality. If anyone else found out about my fifty dollars, I would be dead.

The next day I met the *Stubendienst* after work. He introduced me to Morris, the Hasid. Morris had been a thief in Lodz but was a well-respected Senior Block Inmate in Birkenau. I could feel my spine tingling, my bladder pulsating, and my sweat gushing. If this didn't work, I knew my life expectancy was short. And what was to prevent them from just stealing the money?

"Maybe you can help me," I told Morris in a voice almost husky from fear. "Here's the situation: I've got fifty dollars American money. I would like to get a good job with the Czech, a loaf of bread, some margarine, a salami, and fifteen dollars in change."

Morris nodded his head. "OK, come in tomorrow. I'll talk to the Czech tonight."

I went to bed again with great hope. But in here, anything could go wrong.

I went to see Morris the next day. My wheelbarrow-and-broom trick had worked again, and I'd spent more hours in the garbage bin. Morris knew none of that. He looked at me thoughtfully.

"I talked to the Czech," Morris said, his voice emotionless. "All he said was, 'We'll see.' Come see me tomorrow night."

I left Morris and felt my heart soar. If only my trick would work for one more day, I thought this deal might happen. I knew the Czech couldn't fight Morris. Morris controlled the food, and that meant all the extra salami, bread, anything extra the Czech wanted to eat, Morris could give him—or not. Morris had a reputation for doing well by people who did well by him.

In the morning, Frank and I waved at the SS and Gestapo as usual. We almost ran back to the spot where we dropped off the equipment, then went diving into the garbage bins, wiping maggots off food and looking for something not coated with mold. I hadn't told Frank about my fifty-dollar bill.

That night, my body felt as though it were liquid. I tried all day not to think about Morris. I couldn't afford the luxury of hope, but I did offer up several prayers. When I finally went to see Morris, his slender face broke into a big-toothed grin. "You've got yourself a deal," he said. "Give me the fifty dollars."

I reached into my pants lining for the bill, which I had wrapped into a ball no bigger than a pill. I gave Morris the money. He motioned me over to a small sack in the barracks corner. In it were a loaf of bread, a stick of margarine, and a bulbous salami. He also gave me forty reichsmarks change. I looked at the coin. Anything German was considered worthless, because it often had been devalued.

"I can't use the German marks. They're good for nothing. I need dollars," I said, looking him in the eye. I was feeling frantic. I could see him sense my hostility and helplessness.

He looked darkly at me and said with some impatience in his voice, "Look. I just gave you food and a good job. You'll eat, you won't have to go outside the camp, and you won't be beaten as much. There's nothing more important in here. Nothing."

He was right. There was nothing I could do anyway. I just shrugged and put the reichsmarks into my pocket. I hid and took a few bites out of the margarine, salami, and bread. I had to get rid of the food because anybody who smelled it would steal it. I gave the rest of my food to Frank and Noah—who was always asking me for advice—along with Morris, who was the guy who had a girlfriend, and another five or six people.

"Boys, come on. I have something," I told them.

I had already sliced it so I could hide it. I pulled the salami and margarine out of my pants and shirt.

One of them asked, "Where did you get it?"

"Don't ask questions," I replied, an impatient edge in my voice. "I'm going to work inside the camp."

"What about us?"

"You'll be there soon."

"What happened?"

"An uncle from America sent something. Now go eat somewhere. If anybody catches you, he'll steal it," I whispered.

They hid behind corners and bunks, and in five minutes, everything was gone. I had kept two slices for myself.

The next day, I moved into Barracks 8. There wasn't much to move, just me and my empty pockets. I said good-bye to Frank. I couldn't tell him how this change of luck had come about. I felt as though he might do something stupid, and if somebody found out, I might suffer. In there, people turned into animals.

I had to abandon him for the time being. I now had a steady job and he would have to figure out how to survive by himself. I could see he was glad for me, but frightened for himself.

It was now late 1943. I approached my new work feeling I had liberated myself and life would be a lot easier. I was put to work using a sledgehammer to break rocks as big as barrels. The rock pieces were then fitted together to build roads to the hospital.

At least I'm escaping the sweeps. If I had to keep using my wheelbarrow trick, eventually they'd find out and I'd end up in the crematorium. At least I'm safe for the moment, I thought, but I couldn't help but worry about Frank.

I found out fast that our *Kapo*, the Czech murderer, walked with a cane because he had a double hernia. Even though he was lame, his cane was lethal. He would sit in a little trailer with a cooking plate and a heater. He also had a window which looked out on us. Always, some of us were too exhausted to work. Guys would just lie down, their arms and legs sprawled like rubber.

When the Czech saw that, he would hobble and hop out of his shack, then quickly move toward the offender. He would raise his cane and strike, using the thick, round brass knob on the end to crack guys on the head. The cane made a whooshing sound every time he would strike. Sometimes we could hear a dull thud as the cane struck a man's head, maybe even his nose or eyes—again and again and again. We could see blood flowing from the victim's head, often trailing off in snakelike streaks. Sometimes the beaten man would die with a caved-in skull, his eyes bulging out so much the whites looked like golf balls.

Every day three or four guys were hit and blood would flow as the Czech raised his cane and whipped it downward with an anger I wouldn't have expected from someone who looked so old. Though he was in his midforties, in some ways the Czech looked like somebody's grandfather. He was about my size, maybe five foot six, very skinny, and a face so white it looked drained of blood.

He looked as if he were going to a funeral: he always wore a heavy knit cap over dark black hair and black clothes, and he stood very straight, though his hernia made him take gingerly steps. The story was that when the Germans overran Czechoslovakia, they found him in a prison. Like many others, he had a ticket out: beating and murdering Jews. As long as he did his job, the Germans were happy and he ate and slept well.

Fortunately, I wasn't beaten at all. First, I figured out that if I were one hundred yards on the other side of the work site with 120 people in the squad between him and me, the Czech couldn't see me very well. The site was about half a mile square, with several streets in it. When he wobbled out of his little trailer, I tried to keep even more people between him and me.

The second reason I wasn't beaten was that I quickly figured out how to break rocks. On the farm, I had learned how to calculate the fastest way to get a job done. Now, I quickly spotted out that every rock has a vein which, if hit, makes the rock explode. I could do it better than anyone else. Most of the others were swinging their hammers and getting only small chips, while my rocks turned into pieces and pebbles with one blow.

Lots of guys noticed, and I gladly showed them the trick. I felt sorry for them. I showed the people working near me how to grip the hammer for maximum force and how to find the vein. Then those people showed other people. Pretty soon, everybody in our work group knew how to break rocks. I found out the Czech knew I was responsible for this productivity burst and was pleased.

From my time in Majdanek and on other work squads I knew how to stay in motion so I didn't look tired or sick. "Keep moving, do a little something, just look like you're on the job so he won't hit you," I said again and again.

But we were all tired, if not exhausted. Sometimes one of the guys was just too drained to move, unfazed by the possibility that the Czech might beat him to death. I noticed that a man named Josef paid attention to me, followed my ideas, and started asking me for lots of advice. Josef was a Polish Gentile. He was quiet and well behaved, and I didn't think he was an anti-Semite. He had become a kind of casual acquaintance. He would get a little bit of food from home, even though his parents were quite poor. He willingly shared his food with me, no matter how little. The food generally had been dried out to prevent mildew and was hard to chew. Still, it was food. I was learning to trust him. Later, he was to help me execute a bold scheme.

During this time, I came to notice Max Stein, the Czech's secretary. His job was to make sure the work squad of 120 was fully staffed. If people were lost to selections or got sick and were carted off to the gas chambers, he had to find replacements. I noticed that Max, like me, tried not to be around the murderer very much.

Guys were always going to Max for advice. He was a good-looking man, a big personality. He was a convert. His parents had become Catholic, and he didn't know much about Judaism. Still, the fact that he had been born Jewish was enough for the Nazis to throw him into Birkenau. He never beat or cursed anybody, just tried to keep track of manpower. I wondered whether becoming his friend would help me.

Max had already noticed me. Once, when I had to be near the murderer, I overheard Max saying, "This guy Joe is the best. He shows people how to work, he's always clean and neat, he always does his work."

I was ecstatic. I had a feeling there was something special about Max. I was glad he liked the way I kept up morale and productivity. Two days later, Max purposefully walked all the way across the work site to talk to me.

"Where are you from, Joe?"

"Poland," I said, using the terse response all prisoners learned to use. Saying more than absolutely necessary to someone in charge could mean betraying secrets you didn't mean to betray.

"I'm from Poland. Lived in Krakow."

He asked me a few more questions, such as how I was doing and when had I come here. Then he left.

A few days later he was back. "I want to ask you how you came to be here," he said, his eyes betraying nothing but mild curiosity. I couldn't imagine why he was so interested.

I told him about working on a farm, being captured, working in the distillery, then being caught up in a massive selection. I didn't tell him about being with the partisans. That was a dangerous secret even here.

Max wasn't satisfied with just a small answer. He kept asking, "And then what? And then what?"

After several minutes he left me, but I knew with instincts honed by surviving in Birkenau that Max was up to something, though I couldn't imagine what.

After that, Max passed by me frequently during work. He didn't say much, just nodded to me. Then one day, Max pulled me aside. He wanted to know more about where I had been working in the camp. Where were you? Working in the hospital? In the barracks? He had a kind of mocking, yet serious look in his eyes.

"I want to talk to you about how you have managed to make it through all of this so far," he said.

I told Max again about working on the farm, and how I had substituted for my father in winter because I loved him. I told him about the day the farm family next door was killed. I still didn't tell him about the partisans. I just told him I'd run into the woods.

160

"You mean you didn't join the Jewish or Polish partisans?" Max asked, looking very stern.

I really didn't want to answer, but I couldn't see many ways around it. "Not exactly," I said.

"Any other partisans?"

I took a deep breath. "Well, there were Russians in the woods. I gave them food when I was on the farm. When I was in the woods, they helped me." I didn't tell him the Russians were partisans.

Over a period of about two weeks, Max had several more conversations with me pressing for more and more detail. Finally he stopped asking and started bringing an occasional piece of bread.

Why is this man so curious about me? Something's going on, but I'll be damned if I can figure out what, I mused.

In the meantime, I finally had a chance to help some friends. The Czech was pushing hard to get the roads done. One day Max came over and asked, "Do you know anybody? People who will work as hard as you?"

"I know several. They're working in bad jobs, very bad jobs." I picked Frank, Noah, Hymie, and Nuftul. A few days later, I got Morris Tisch and two other men transferred to our group.

Later Samuel, who had noticed Max was talking to me a lot, asked me what was going on. I told him truthfully, I didn't know. Samuel and his son had been in the Czech's squad long before I was. He was a tall man with a lean and friendly face, and his son resembled him. They were just nice people. I asked Samuel and his son what they thought was going on, but they had no idea either.

About a week later, Max was complaining to me about the murderer. "I can't do much with him, Joe. He's got a vicious temper, and he hates the world because of his injuries. I just try to stay as far away from him as I can."

A plan started forming. It was daring, and I would need some very good help. Samuel and his son were the perfect helpers, but I wasn't sure they'd go along. Several days later, Samuel approached me.

"Joe, you're an expert on keeping people out of trouble. That bastard murderer is going to kill us all. Any ideas on how to get closer to him so we can avoid getting beaten to death?"

This was my time. I already had the plan, and now Samuel wanted to hear it.

"I have an idea," I said. "I don't know whether it will work, but let's give it a try. We can't be any worse off."

"What have you got in mind, Joe?"

The plan was simple: drench him in kindness. He was a bitter, sour person. I figured he wouldn't know what to do if people he had abused treated him well in return. I thought back to Michalek, the anti-Semite in the brewery. I saw from that experience that if I treated people nicely, they would treat me nicely. The murderer was tougher than Michalek, but it was worth a try.

I knew the rest of the group wasn't going to think I was turning against them by kissing up to the Czech. I was friendly to everybody, and people liked and respected me. I felt that even though times were bad, I still had to keep some humanity.

"He's handicapped," I whispered in Samuel's ear. "He can't pick up wood when it's cold, so we'll get him wood. We'll give him fresh water. A man that age, sick with a double hernia, needs help. He can't do much for himself. Besides, he wants to keep this group together so he can stay a *Kapo*."

Samuel nodded.

We executed the plan in stages. First, I carried the Czech water in a little bucket. Then I found some potatoes from the kitchen through a friend of Samuel's. When I gave the water to the Czech, his eyes grew very large. He didn't know what we were up to. He nodded at us, then grunted. I offered to get him wood for his little wood stove. He looked surprised, but pleased. He nodded his assent.

A week later, I asked the murderer whether he'd like a haircut. I had a pair of scissors I used to cut people's hair. Then they'd use the scissors to do mine. He nodded his head. It would cost him too much to thank me. He nodded in a way that said, "That's nice." I started giving him haircuts. By now he wasn't suspicious of me.

As I snipped his hair, I saw it was clean and shiny. I wanted to plunge my scissors into his throat, but I resisted. I kept thinking of Michalek, and I just kept snipping and combing.

Two weeks later, Samuel and I asked the murderer whether we could get him some soup. Our job description had been broadened. By this time, part of my job, in addition to breaking rocks, was to take food from the main camp's kitchen in stainless steel kettles to the hospital patients.

On this occasion, while we were there, Samuel and I loaded up our pockets with potatoes, then took back enough to give a couple to the murderer and several to our friends in the group.

"Let's put the potatoes behind the corpse pile," I told Samuel. "Nobody will find them there."

The corpse pile was where the bodies of men who died on work sites away from Birkenau, including the coal mines, were dumped. The bodies piled up until trucks hauled the corpses away. It wasn't a place where anyone volunteered to go, and that's why hiding food there made so much sense. We wrapped the potatoes in newspaper, then stuffed them behind a corpse which had a particularly hideous grin.

The pile was a fenced-in mountain of bodies about 7 feet high, perhaps 250 feet long, and 100 feet wide. The corpses were all squashed together like herring, and buzzing flies gathered in black, glistening clumps all over the pile. The smell, especially in summer, was rank, requiring a handkerchief or rag over your nose to prevent vomiting. Sometimes you threw up anyway. The corpses didn't mind, though. They never complained.

The next day we retrieved some potatoes and took them to the murderer's shack. On his hot plate, I made him potato soup, which became his favorite. The murderer smiled at me a little, the corners of his mouth barely crinkling.

The Czech language was close enough to Polish that we could talk a little. "Thank you, thank you, thank you," he said as I stayed in his shack for a half-hour, making soup and cleaning up. As I left, I made some hot water so he could wash up later. Then we started making him tea and stealing him more kitchen food.

A few weeks later, Samuel, his son, and I started polishing the Czech's shoes and shining the little shower he had in his shack. About a month later, we worked on his clothing. The Czech used to wash his clothing so he always had a spare pair of pants, shirt, and underwear. Now, one of the three of us would wash the spare clothing, then hang it from a rope over the hot plate to dry off.

Every necessity we could think of, we provided to him. I thought if he had so many comforts in his shack he wouldn't want to leave it, so he wouldn't go around and beat people to death.

After several weeks, I noticed the campaign was working: People were sprawled out on the job, not doing work. Everybody knew the Czech would beat anybody not working, but now nothing happened. I'd told the others about our campaign, and they could see it was working, too.

However, we were running out of road work. If there wasn't any more labor for us, then our work squad would be disbanded, most of us would be gassed, and the Czech wouldn't even be a *Kapo*. Alarmed, I took Max aside.

"Max, we've got a problem. There's not enough work. If we don't have work, you know what's going to happen. What do we do?"

Max stroked his face for a few moments. I had believed he was a smart man. He now confirmed my suspicions.

"I've been giving that some thought myself. But let me first talk to the Czech."

The next day, the Czech took me aside.

"You and the other guys try to find some work in the hospital," he whispered. "Stretch out your work on the roads as much as you can. Keep moving and don't look as if you're not doing anything or you'll get beaten. In the meantime, clean up the barracks, work in the hospital, any way you can find to keep yourself busy."

I now could see there was another reason the Czech wasn't beating us nearly as often or as hard, though I'm convinced he had a sincere change of heart. He had been beating us to make the work go faster. Now he wanted to drag it out. I quickly spread the word to everyone else: the Czech would let us do virtually any work, as long as we were busy, because then he still was a *Kapo*.

Several days later, another opportunity materialized to reduce my beatings. I had been looking at the number on my shirt, and the Jewish star on it always made me a marked man. I knew every guard, every *Kapo*, everybody who considered himself above me, thought I was a target for every insult passing through his mind.

Even with the Czech's anger now tamed, I still was being beaten fairly regularly. If I could just alter my identity slightly, that would help. I had blue eyes and blond hair. I was well behaved and didn't shout or curse. I thought people would assume I was a Gentile if I didn't have a Jewish star showing.

One night I looked at my prisoner's shirt. I resewed my prison number above the left shirt pocket, but very far away from the buttons, toward my armpit. If I could find some clothing with wide lapels, they would almost cover the number.

Fortunately, there were lots of wide lapels available. The engineers, lawyers, doctors, all wore wide lapels, because that was the fashion at the time. These people had a lot of education, but they hadn't worked on farms or fought with the partisans. They hadn't learned the art of living through another day.

Consequently, I saw these people dying all around me in the barracks. I saw their insignia was covered, but their number wasn't. The next day, by the barracks door, I saw corpses of people who had died during the night. We had to find work, so we carried the corpses to the corpse pile. One corpse I was carrying had a crinkled yellow face and no teeth, but it was wearing a wide-lapelled jacket a lot warmer than mine.

I didn't even have to prevent myself from gagging. I stripped that jacket with one hand. After I started wearing wide lapels, I was only beaten half as often. The Germans still beat me, though. They knew who I was.

I didn't let the beatings prevent me from looking for other work, as the Czech had told us to. I knew the hospital had the best jobs, so I started helping to take kettles of soup there. The *Stubendienst* would ladle out the soup. Then, when we carried the pot back to the kitchen, I'd bend down and scoop the pot's inside with my fingers. My posture wasn't elegant, but I got soup.

More food came my way when we cleaned up the belongings of the dead there. They always left behind food packages containing rye bread, which was hard but quite edible. When I got a piece of bread or potato or whatever scraps I could find, I sneaked out of the hospital, wrapped the food in newspaper, and put the scraps behind the pile of corpses. The dead eyes and empty grins on faces yellow from disease, or black and blue from beatings, or both, never bothered me.

Nobody ever found my food there. I would put it between corpses, then tumble another corpse over it. I knew exactly where the food was, but it was impossible for anyone else to tell. If I didn't hide it, people would steal it, so I figured the dead were doing me a service.

I'd retrieve my food about 4:30 in the afternoon. Samuel and I would eat, along with other friends. I always gave away much of my food. I liked kitchen work. It was clean, I didn't get beaten, and I could steal some soup from the kettles. I also started carrying corpses from trucks to the corpse pile.

In addition, I helped with the mine workers. Every couple of days, the Germans took used-up men from the coal mines and dropped them off at the far end of the camp, near the corpse pile. Appropriately, the pile was at a dead end, surrounded by wooden boards. Some of the miners we helped down, others fell down, and some jumped down. There was always one truckload from each mine. The Germans waited until late in the day, then I and others, including Frank, would help them onto the trucks to be gassed.

About a quarter of the time I would work on roads, and maybe 15 percent helping with the miners. Mostly I worked around the hospital, which really was a collection of buildings resembling a small village. Mengele had his office near the hospital wards.

One particularly depressing hospital task was _Schrott_ duty. _Schrott_ means junk-yard scrap. I and others had to move the sick whom the nurses and doctors decided were terminal over to the barracks for the dying, which we knew as the _Schrott_. Many times the patients died before we could move them, so we took them directly to the corpse pile.

No matter how disgusting our duties, we still had to eat. We scavenged in the hospital for the dirty potato peelings. There wasn't any water available, so the potatoes were unwashed, with dirt clinging to them when they were thrown out. I still was going through the garbage bins, along with Frank, Hymie, and Nuftul. We discovered we could eat soft bones from chickens or pigs. The sick patients ate the meat, then the bones were discarded into the garbage bins. We also enjoyed apple peelings and an occasional fish head.

Sometimes we would get food even before it was eaten. When we went into the hospital, the intelligentsia were often the patients: priests, doctors, lawyers, engineers, and such. We could spot the priests. We talked to them, gave them water and a few crumbs, then they'd start talking about God.

No matter what part of the intelligentsia these people were from, they had lived delicate lives and couldn't stand up to the hardships of a death camp. But they did have food packages, so we would tell them we'd get them water, but they had to trade for it.

Water came from rain barrels sitting next to the outside wall of the hospital. Actually, they were for the sick to urinate into, but they were too bedridden with typhus, pneumonia, and other diseases to go, so they urinated in their beds.

When we offered water, the patients by then didn't have much to trade. They usually had only a piece of bread, perhaps a little soup. Some offered a cigarette.

The hospital barracks was as big as a regular barracks but with far fewer people. Hospital patients were too weak to climb up bunk beds, so there was only one bunk per floor space. The wards themselves were eerie, shrouded in an almost deathlike quiet. Patients were so sick they had no strength to moan or cry. They were sprawled out on the bed, waiting to die.

During the summer, the three doctors Mengele was training would dissect Gentile corpses—they wouldn't consider touching Jews or Gypsies—for one to two hours every day, to learn about anatomy. The autopsy tables were outdoors, just outside Mengele's office. I knew the Czech was nervous because our work was running out. I also saw the autopsy tables were far away from the Czech's shack.

Germans hate sloppiness and messes. Autopsies are messy and they have a stink that fills the air and doesn't go away. They'd love to have that mess taken care of, I thought.

It indeed was a mess. All the corpses had been cut into bloody pieces. There were piles of body parts on the wooden tables, which were about twelve feet long and four feet wide, peppered with numerous bloodstained nicks. I thought I'd use a stiff brush to scrub the blood off.

I told my plan to Josef, the Polish Gentile. He had continued to share his food and I thought I could trust him with my plan. Besides, I needed another guy to handle the corpses. I had worked with him on the roads, and he was a good worker. After I talked to Josef, we immediately started cleaning the autopsy tables, which were about three feet from Mengele's office window. I knew nobody was going to object.

It was a tough job. The stink of decaying human arms, legs, livers, and heads of what, days before, had been assembled as human beings, made me gag repeatedly. But I couldn't risk the Germans' thinking I couldn't do a job. I would put the body parts into waterproof paper bags, then put the bags on the corpse pile. I excelled at this kind of work. I'm a perfectionist. When I take on a cleaning task, whatever I set out to clean comes out sparkling. It's always perfect.

A couple of days after Josef and I started to scrub the autopsy tables, the young doctors complimented us in German. Then I heard them talking to Mengele about how fabulous we were.

A few days passed. A thin German in a particularly shiny uniform walked over to us while we were scrubbing. He had been looking through his office window, overlooking the autopsy area.

I knew it was Mengele. Through Max Stein, I had come to learn a lot about him. One of Max's friends was Mengele's secretary. One day, Max had pointed out the "Angel of Death." "Watch out for your life around that man," Max had said. "He'd as soon shoot you as breathe." Now the monster himself was standing almost in my face.

"Clean the windows, straighten the office, wash the floors, polish my boots and those of my three doctors. Empty the wastebaskets," he said to me in German.

I understood him, but I didn't want him to know I knew his language. I played dumb and answered him in Polish. He ended up pantomiming what he wanted me to do. Basically I made Mengele act like a stilted puppet trying to show me what he wanted done. I loved the feeling of making him look stupid, but I knew I shouldn't press my luck. I pretended his pantomiming had worked.

"_Jawohl, jawohl_," I told him. Everybody in the camp knew _jawohl_ meant "yes" in German, so I wasn't betraying my deeper knowledge of the language by saying it.

I knew I was playing a very dangerous game. I wanted to keep busy, and I wanted to stay in the hospital, so I could pick up crumbs of food. This was a steady job, at least. In a way, I had deliberately picked Mengele to work for. I had a certain charm, and so did my friend, Josef. I was always good at guessing what was in a person's mind and what he would do next.

"I'm not afraid of Mengele," I heard myself saying to nobody in particular. "Mengele is here to kill us all. I'm going to die anyway. Once I've accepted that, what can he do to me?"

It was October 1943. Only four months after I had been taken to Auschwitz-Birkenau to build the death camp, I now worked for Josef Mengele himself. For the next eighteen months during 1943 and 1944, I worked for him. For several months, I had the same basic duties I'd had on the day he motioned to me and Josef into his office. I cleaned the windows inside and out, dusted, washed the floors, then polished his boots so they gleamed. I also washed down the roof and the walls inside and outside his office. Autopsies were finished by 2:00 P.M. Then I'd do my duties there, plus cleaning barracks and carrying the dead to the corpse pile.

Mengele always talked at a very slow and deliberate pace. Even so, whenever he or his doctors or any of the Germans addressed me in their native language, I just continued to act puzzled. They all spoke to me in pidgin Polish when they wanted to tell me something. Otherwise, they lapsed into German, talking as though I were nothing at all.

I grew to like the three doctors Mengele was training. They were young and very naive. They didn't beat or curse us. Every morning we came in they said, "Good morning." The three young doctors all wore German military uniforms. Mengele and the doctors always were very cordial. Mengele would just point to the table or to the office windows or whatever else he wanted cleaned and we did what he wanted. When we were done, he would say, _Danke schön_.

Usually, though, Mengele's three assistants didn't speak much to me or anybody else. A Jew had about the same value to them as a rat. In fact, a rat had a better chance to survive because he could hide.

Josef and I also started taking on hospital duties. The Czech, intensely wanting to remain a *Kapo*, let us be assigned to the hospital. The good part was that all the doctors and interns liked us. We were clean, we shaved, we didn't smell. We were thankful and cordial, and we both looked Aryan. We did our jobs with no commotion. They kept thanking us, though they never gave us food.

We still were taking soup or water to the sick. We also continued carrying out the dead from the hospital and elsewhere. Other corpses were straight from Mengele's autopsy tables. These corpses were in various pieces plus intestines which had been piled up outside the bodies. We had to put the dismembered corpses in separate bags for legs, lungs, livers, and stomachs. These bodies were so light they weren't much trouble to move.

We knew exactly when it was time to clean the tables. We would pass by the doctors several times during the afternoon, keeping a close watch to determine when they finished. We had to act quickly, because flies would cluster around the bodies almost immediately.

No matter where the corpses were from, we had to carry them to the corpse pile. Once a week a truck would come. Then we'd dump the corpses, whole or in body bags, into the back.

This is a good job, I thought. *I get a piece of bread and hide it under dead people. Nobody beats me, and the doctors, including Mengele, are nice to me.*

However, Father and his good graces were the most valuable commodity of all. All of us who worked in and around the hospital had reason to be thankful for Father. He was built like a stubby barrel, about five feet tall and 250 pounds, with more jowls than a bulldog. He was only forty-five years old and one of the sweetest people imaginable. His pudgy arms were always wrapped around somebody, so kind was he. He wandered the camp all day, looking out for people.

"Stay away from the wires," he'd tell us. Or, "I know you're hungry but you'll get beaten. Watch yourself," he would say.

Father was a Socialist and didn't believe in dictatorships, Nazi or otherwise. For that heresy the Germans had thrown him into prison. He wore the red badge of a political prisoner. He also was German and a doctor. In fact, he and Mengele had been in medical school together.

Father ran the hospital for Mengele, who was always talking to him. When they conversed, Mengele would nod his head emphatically, occasionally even gently touching Father. It was clear Mengele had considerable respect and affection for him.

Father lived a good life there. He had his own room and, as his ample weight displayed, plenty of food. He was basically in charge of making sure the hospital was running right.

He had every reason not to jeopardize his situation, but he did. He was a lovely man who always watched over those of us who worked in the hospital to make sure we weren't beaten up.

After a while, I noticed that Father, Mengele's secretary, and Max were meeting briefly a couple of times a week. The first time I noticed, the meeting lasted about two minutes.

God, what could this be? Something is going on, and it's clearly meant to be a secret, I thought.

Then it struck me.

My God. Maybe they're with the underground.

Joe in Birkenau. Joe estimates it was taken some time in October 1944. He found it accidentally in a book on the Holocaust.

Joe in his cap, circa October 1945, Munich. Joe would get together regularly with Abie and Max (not the Czech's secretary, but a man who also had worked on the ramp). This photo was taken on one of those occasions. Abie took the photo.

Joe and Elke in November 1946. They were visiting Elke's sister, who was living in a Holocaust survivor's camp. The camp was about 40 miles north of Munich. The name, as Joe remembers it, was Feloafink.

Abie and Joe, taken also in November 1946 in Munich. This was another occasion when Joe got together with Abie and Max. Max took the photo. Joe lost track of Max several months later and has no idea what happened to him.

Joe and his American family in Los Angeles, 1990. From left to right: Back row—son-in-law Steven Kort, Joe, daughter Marla, son Sid, and wife Ellen. Front row—granddaughter Molly and grandson Aaron.

Joe's Polish family. From left to right: Back row—Joe, Faye, and Rachel. Front row—Hymie, mother Mendl, Benny, and father Samuel. Missing—sister Sara. The photo was taken, not surprisingly, by Hymie Kronhartz, Joe's cousin and one Jew in his hometown who had special privileges after the Germans moved in. Photo taken in Joe's hometown in the summer of either 1933 or 1934.

The Zbanski farm.

Photo of the barn and forest in the background where Joe hid from the Germans. A Catholic family who lived at this farm, the Zbanskis, helped Joe to survive by providing food.

Joe and Marian, son of one of the Zbanski children who helped Joe to hide from the Germans.

The local post office where a German military officer allowed Joe and some friends to hide in the attic.

Joe standing in front of a barracks at Majdanek Death Camp. Joe was severely and cruelly beaten every day by the German "bastards." He barely survived the many beatings.

Joe standing on the "ramp" at Birkenau where he worked along side Dr. Josef Mengele as the Jews were disembarking from the trains and sent to their deaths. Many times, Joe risked his own life by saving children while working on the "ramp." Joe remembers Mengele assigning him to clean the notorious doctor's office and work areas. The assignment lasted 14 months.

Joe pauses in his cleanup work near the ramp while people from the death trains are lined up to be sent to the crematoriums or work camps.

The "Gates to Hell" at the Birkenau Death Camp where Joe spent three winters. Upon his arrival, Joe was told that he will "work here" and "die here" and that there was no way to escape.

The actual barrack No. 8 where Joe spent three winters while incarcerated at Birkenau. The flames shot up through the chimneys of the crematorium 24 hours a day. The sky was dark from smoke and the air always smelled of burning flesh.

Joe standing next to his actual bunk in barrack No. 8 where he slept without a blanket or pillow. The barrack contained a brick chimney which was never used.

PART III

TIPTOEING ON A RAZOR BLADE: THE UNDERGROUND AND MENGELE

Chapter 14

Healing
by
Butter
Knife

Sunday was usually a day off, so people could visit or talk. But one Sunday the *Stubendiensts* and the Senior Block Inmate showed up and said, "Don't go anywhere today. You've got to stay right here."

We all looked at each other, fearfully. Now the Germans were cutting into our one day of rest, and we were sure it wasn't so they could hand us sugar candies. About eleven o'clock in the morning, the *Stubendiensts* and Senior Block Inmate returned. This time they told us to take off our clothes and stand in rows of five.

"Those of you who are selected will be gassed tonight," the Senior Block Inmate told us.

I could feel my knees shake, though I tried not to let any emotion creep out into my face.

The first time was very much like all the times to follow. The selection ran for three hours. The Jews—non-Jews didn't have to endure selections—had to line up outside five abreast. Usually six hundred to seven hundred of the thousand men in a barracks were Jews. We had to strip naked, leaving our clothing on the ground. Even in the wintertime we had to stand for an hour in deep subzero weather. In a gesture of what Mengele considered compassion, he sometimes allowed us to keep our shoes on.

This time, as occurred most often, each row of five had to step forward to a space three feet away from him, forearms held out to show our tattooed numbers. Mengele would jab his finger at those he selected. His secretary, standing next to him with pen and clipboard, quickly jotted down the numbers. They went through our barracks in ten minutes.

After he went through, we all slumped. Mengele had gone so fast we weren't sure who had been picked to die, but we were prepared. After all, it wasn't as though someone had cancer or heart trouble and was hiding the problem. We had been sent to Birkenau to be killed.

"All the hunger and beatings, and now we've got this to deal with," Nuftul moaned to me.

I knew; we all knew: Every one of us was going to die. What was frightening was that we never knew when or how. That suspense added to our agony. The answer that evening came when we heard the grinding of truck gears outside, and the *Stubendienst* called out, "These numbers come forward and line up."

He called out the numbers. We started shaking hands and hugging those about to be gassed. They had to move fast, and so hugging our friends and our companions had to be very brief. It was that brevity that hurt so much. So quick, and then they were gone.

We all looked at each other with hollow and hopeless eyes.

"God forbid, the same thing might happen to us the next time. Or the next. We never know when, but it's coming," I said.

"Maybe it's better for them," somebody replied, a wheezing, sputtering sound coming from his throat. "At least their beatings and starvation are finished."

After several minutes of murmuring to each other, we went to sleep, all of us sunk deeply into the blackest pit of depression.

As time rolled along, those of us who survived selections got to know how they worked. They were conducted every two to three weeks. Sometimes Mengele would simply walk down the lines of prisoners, or have each line move back, instead of having them move forward. Always, though, he was dressed as though attending a formal state reception. His boots were polished, and his cap visor and holster were shined. I knew just how well they glistened because I had shined them. He always shaved for the occasion, and he smelled of the perfumed soap the German officers used.

My feelings were always the same: "Who knows whether I'm going to come out of this? Who knows whether I will be alive tomorrow? My family is almost completely gone, and I may become ashes, too."

Still, we didn't shake or tremble, though all of us were afraid. We held ourselves ramrod straight, no matter how sick we were, and hoped for the best while Mengele looked us over.

The first time we lost perhaps 350 or 400. The postselection routine was usually the same as the first time. After Mengele was finished, the secretary gave the numbers to the *Stubendienst*. When it got dark, the *Stubendienst* called out the numbers, his voice as emotionless as if he were reading from a telephone directory. One of the privileges of being *Stubendienst* was not having to endure selections, even if you were Jewish.

"Let's see number 50. Let's see 80," they would call.

The men who had been selected lined up single file. They didn't cry. We didn't have any tears left. There was no such thing as people saying, "I don't want to go." In a second the guards would have broken their bones, then thrown them into the trucks.

From inside, we would hear the squealing of truck brakes. As the men marched out, we heard their dull footsteps on the truck floors. Then we heard the whine of one truck pulling away, while another pulled up to take on its own doomed cargo.

Sometimes, because the gas chambers were very close, the selected prisoners had to walk. No matter how they left, about two hours after the men had glumly marched out the door, we would smell the stink of burning flesh.

Selections were worse than being beaten to death or getting a bullet in your head. You never knew who was going to go. The biggest torture was standing and waiting to see who was going to die. At least those of us who were beaten to death had little warning and it was generally over in minutes. In selections, those of us who were spared felt terrible for us and for them. Morale was almost at zero.

Just after selections started, I had a chance to get out of Birkenau. A *Stubendienst* announced in our barracks that we could go to the coal mines instead of staying there. Morris came to me.

"Joe, we've got to get out of here. Here, it's a matter of time and we're gone. I'm taking that ticket out," Morris said. "I'll die in here. It can't be worse, and maybe I can escape," Morris told me, his eyes flashing hope.

I had seen his spirits sagging. His privileged background worked against surviving this life. I, too, wanted out of Birkenau. Parts of my body hurt almost every day from beating, hunger, and work. I stood in line to sign up for the mines. Still, I had a bad feeling. I had seen the shriveled remains of dead miners, and I had helped the living onto crematorium-bound trucks.

I also remembered when I first worked for the Germans grooming horses. I had to feed the furnace with coal, and I saw how dirty it was. I remembered how black all of us who had come from Majdanek looked after so many hours in a car filled with coal dust. I had seen dying miners. I didn't want to die in the cold and darkness.

To work in the dark, with so much dust flying around, I won't be able to breathe. I'll die in the same way those pathetic wrecks from the mine I keep helping off the trucks have died, I thought.

I stepped out of line. Morris, who was standing behind me, was shocked. I simply told him, "I don't like to work in the dark." I didn't think I needed to give him any further explanation.

Morris still tried to talk me out of staying.

"Let's get out of here. This is hell. It's unbearable here," he said, pleading.

"But we don't know what's there. It cannot be better. With the Germans, it always gets worse," I told him, my eyes hurting at the feeling of abandonment stamped on his face.

That same day, Morris left for the mines. I worried about both of us. I wondered whether we'd ever see each other again, and what kind of condition we would be in if that ever happened. By this time, just living another day was all the hope I could muster.

Suddenly, my dream came to me again, and it nourished my hopes. By now the other prisoners were so discouraged I started telling them about my dream. Of course, they said I was crazy—they said it jokingly, they said it lovingly, but they said it—and I think some of them half-believed it. Sometimes, I wondered a little myself.

I also was learning a few more rules of survival. One was that nobody talked to Mr. Mengele. Well, almost nobody. Father, Mengele's three assistant doctors, and his secretary would converse with him. Otherwise, Mengele went about his grim tasks in a businesslike way. Throughout the day, I would see him spending time in his office. If he wasn't there, he was on the ramp, deciding who lived and died.

Personally, I was afraid to talk to Mengele for a most unusual reason: I didn't want any German words to slip out. If they did, he'd know I'd been eavesdropping while he discussed anatomy or politics with his assistant doctors.

I did start talking with Mengele's secretary, a tall, good-looking man who had been a diplomat in the Polish government. He kept the running totals of the number of people dying and their nationalities. He walked the camp freely during selections. He warmed up to me and told me something about himself. He had graduated from the university in Krakow with Max Stein. He said they had gone to the university together and were close.

Strangely, Father now was taking a more personal interest in me. He would stop and ask, "How does it go?" or "How are you doing?" Of course, he used to see me constantly with Max, and I used to see Max and Mengele's secretary briefly meeting with Father. I wondered what the three of them had planned for me.

I took a lesson from the way the Germans referred to the Muslims, or *Muselmänner*, as they were referred to, in Birkenau. They called them "thin, dark, dirty, and unshaven," and most of them were selected for gassing almost immediately. I figured out that not resembling what Germans thought Muslims looked like gave me a better chance.

Being thin was a particular sign of trouble. It meant you might be too weak to work. If you had some meat on your bones, if you had a sparkle in your eye, you were a lot more likely to live another week.

The aches and pangs from hunger always crowed our thoughts. My stomach often felt as if somebody had wrapped his hands around my gut and squeezed very tightly. Some of us were so hungry we couldn't walk because our legs were so swollen. We were living on the equivalent of two and a half slices of bread a day. The bread was not real bread. It made of powdered wood mixed with flour. Even so, I would share what I had with my friends.

Despite these circumstances, I learned one thing that a lot of people didn't: you couldn't give up hope. If you did, you felt doomed, and soon, doomed you were. If you cleaned yourself, you looked better. If you had a good job, then you wouldn't be beaten as much and you ate better. That helped, too. But having hope meant they hadn't crushed your spirit, and that fact alone made you look more alive and vital when time for selections came.

I had taken care of myself for a long time. My mother had gone into business when I was fairly young, and we children had to be disciplined and well behaved because, our parents told us, we were helping to give the family a better way of life. I had an active imagination, and even then I could visualize just how our way of life would be better: better furniture, more clothing, lots of food. Now my imagination fed itself on other dreams.

Someday I will be somebody, I told myself. *Someday I'll have people working for me. I will have a factory, a home, a wife and children, and a truck.* As before, it was a dream that still fed my soul, no matter how much it defied all the grim reality surrounding me.

My daily routine consisted of cleaning Mengele's offices and shining his personal items for the first couple of hours. I also knew the Czech took a nap after lunch. That meant I had to fill in a few hours before the autopsy tables needed cleaning, so I wandered around the camp looking for work. I needed to look purposeful, or the Germans would think I had no job. So, I'd go to the hospital and give patients a little water or a cigarette.

Working in the hospital opened up another avenue to me. The hospital was right next to the Gypsy camp, so I started trading with the Gypsies. They were imprisoned with their families in their own compound, and every morning there was a pile of dead right outside their fence. At this point I had the run of the camp, so I could go pretty much where I wanted.

The Gypsies would go to the fence surrounding their camp and offer in German to sell us cigarettes. Many of us now had German marks, brought in by the civil engineers, who were Polish Gentiles. They usually had suitcases with them because they had to be out for weeks, surveying the land for more camps. In the suitcase generally were clothing, whiskey, and pieces of salami.

The Germans didn't bother the engineers, whom the guards respected. If any of the guards did ask to see what was in their suitcases, the engineers knew enough to say it was their whiskey and they planned to drink it.

The first time I wandered near the Gypsy camp fences, I heard "Pssssssst. Pssssssssssst."

A Gypsy was motioning me to him. The camp was surrounded by electrified barbed wire, but the electricity was turned on only at night. I was about fifteen feet from the wire. I looked all around to make sure nobody was watching, then walked over to him.

"We have cigarettes if you have marks," he said softly.

I still had the change Morris the Hasid had given me for my fifty-dollar bill. It turned out that the German money had value after all. I paid the equivalent of two dollars for a package of perhaps a dozen German cigarettes with an eagle symbol and a swastika on the front. The Germans gave the Gypsies wine and cigarettes, though I never figured out why.

I myself didn't smoke at all. When I got back to the barracks, I told my friends what I had. Hymie and Nuftul were smokers, as were others, who would give away their soul for a cigarette. Hymie and Nuftul and the others hugged me, happy to have smokes.

Once a week after that first time, I'd buy a package of cigarettes and a bottle of wine for my friends, though the wine tasted nearly like water. We would pass the bottle around after the lights were out. I drank a little to be sociable but mostly kept passing it. My friends got used to my having cigarettes with me.

"Joe, I'm dying for a smoke. I've got to have a smoke," Hymie and Nuftul would tell me. Others would echo, "I'm dying for a smoke. Help me, please," they would beg. I obliged them.

I also used the cigarettes to buy bread. Depending on the size of the loaf, bread cost twenty cigarettes or ten marks. Often I would use my cigarettes to buy a loaf, which I would share with my friends.

I didn't forget to do good things for myself. If you had the money or cigarettes, the people who were packing clothing would sell you garments. I bought a long-sleeved shirt a few times, and one time a jacket.

It wasn't always a fair exchange. One day we were digging a sewer with a German woman who was also a prisoner. She said she had bread which she'd trade for cigarettes. We struck a deal.

Sometimes the guards let us have a few minutes to go to the bathroom. She left the bread on her way there, and I left the cigarettes in rags on a nearby rock pile while I walked to the bathroom. On the way back, we each picked up what we'd traded for.

I could feel my stomach growl and my mouth water. Ordinarily we were a lot better off not thinking about food, and we didn't dare dwell on it for very long. I threw back one rag, waiting to pounce on a big, fluffy loaf. I saw a brick.

I could feel the hunger pangs go shooting through my stomach. There it was: one brick. She had cheated us. We all held our stomachs and our heads. Our stomachs were aching from the lack of food, and there was a banging inside our heads for the same reason.

"Nothing is happening the way it should," I told Nuftul. "People are becoming like animals. Everybody is grabbing whatever he can, and there's no justice. If you have a piece of salami or a cigarette, somebody will grab it. I'm not surprised. We're all being starved like animals. It's not a surprise that many of us act like animals."

Shortly after we were cheated out of our cigarettes, I started to feel sick. The September chill was settling into the air, and I was having trouble swallowing. My throat hurt so much I had trouble with even the tiniest portion of water.

This went on week after week. The cold gripped us tighter and tighter. It was ironic that I was working in the hospital but I couldn't get medical treatment. Finally, my throat had ballooned so much I thought I was going to choke. I couldn't swallow water and I had to fight for every bit of air.

I had to see the doctor. There actually was a medical facility for us. The camp even had an ambulance, though it was mostly for show in case the Red Cross inspected us. Occasionally the Germans used the ambulance to carry prisoners to a makeshift emergency room at the end of a row of barracks, where the healthiest of the sick prisoners were taken. That room was about six by seven feet. Inside were a small table five feet long and four feet wide and two chairs. There was one small bulb for illumination. Prisoners had to go here during the day, because it was shuttered at night.

When I went into the dimly lit room, a man stood up. Next to him, in a drawer, I could see small knives, a little gauze, and cotton. The doctor, who also was a prisoner, spoke Hungarian, of which I knew only a little. But he knew a little German, which I understood. I showed him my tonsils.

"My God, my God," I heard him say in German. "It's closed up your entire throat. If I don't cut this out right now, your tonsils will explode like a bomb and kill you."

He reached toward the open drawer and pulled out a badly battered butter knife. Then the guy made noises, the meaning of which escaped me. Then he made pantomined gestures which I meant he wanted a match. I had a few. We prisoners were expert scavengers, and I always had a match or two to light cigarettes for my friends who smoked. I handed him a match.

He scraped it across the table until it sprang into flame. He held the fire for about a minute on the butter knife, sterilizing it. Then he made other gestures, pointing to the only table in the room, then grabbing it in a death grip. I knew he was telling me I had to hold this table hard, really hard. Then he showed on himself how I would have to open my mouth wide, then he'd insert the knife and cut out my tonsils. By the grimace on his face, I knew this operation was going to hurt like hell, but I knew he didn't have any anesthesia or scalpel. I didn't give a damn what he didn't have. What he did have was a more or less sterile knife and, I prayed, a very steady hand.

"Go ahead. Take them out. I won't survive another two days like this. Do it, dammit. Do it," I rasped.

So I put both hands on the table, opened my mouth wide, leaned forward, and closed my eyes. Then I pictured myself standing in a factory, my factory, showing my wife and children what I had achieved.

"God, God, please let me live." I mentally beseeched Him.

I could smell the stink of my own burning flesh rushing up through my nostrils. I could feel the knife cut deeply into my throat. I couldn't breathe because his hand was blocking off the air, and I was in such a bad position I could scarcely draw breath through my nose. I wanted to scream but couldn't.

All I could hear come out of me were little squeaks, and I could feel the blood gushing into my mouth as he frequently dabbed with cotton and gauze to soak it up. Finally he huskily told me, "It's done, my friend. It is done."

I fainted.

I woke up a few minutes later, and the doctor gave me more gauze and cotton to take with me. I knew from other prisoners that recovery would take a day or two. Then I returned to Barracks 8.

Too bad there's not a taxi service available, I thought, with my usual humor. *I'd probably give the driver a nice tip.*

A few weeks later I got sick again. The hole in my right bicep where I'd been shot trying to escape from the Polish police into the forest had become infected. I'd only had a handkerchief to put around it. Eventually it got red and pus-filled. It was throbbing so hard I felt I had a drum beating inside my arm. Once more, I returned to the emergency room, wearing a jacket.

This time there was a Polish guy inside. He was young, perhaps in his mid-thirties. He said he was a doctor or intern; I don't remember which. He examined my arm for about ten minutes.

"This arm is filled with pus," he told me. "If I don't cut it out now, it's going to spread to your whole body and kill you."

My sense of humor somehow kicked into gear.

Same tune as the guy who took out my tonsils, I thought. *I almost wish he would tell me something new. Life in a concentration camp is monotonous as it is. At least I'd like to get a little variety in my medical problems.*

Out loud, I told the guy to cut out the infection, then took off my jacket.

The guy pointed to the same badly scarred table. *Don't tell me. Let me guess.*

He's going to tell me to grab that table and hang on tight, I thought, smiling a little to myself.

"Grab that table and hang on tight," the guy said. "This is going to hurt like hell, but I don't have any anesthesia."

Can't they think of something original to say? I mused, just as the guy put a match to a short, but very sharp knife.

"I wish I had some anesthesia to give you, but you see what I have to work with—nothing. Just a little knife and some cotton. You're young. If they let you live, you may survive this."

Once again I smelled the stink of my flesh burning as pain pounded through my head and flashed up and down my arm and plunged into the rest of my body. This time I could hear myself screaming. I jumped around while holding the table.

As much as my entire body felt as if it were being ravaged by hot iron spikes, I dared not yell too loudly. Had the Germans discovered I was not well, they might have gassed me.

"There, it's done," he said.

Again, I fainted.

This time I was awakened with a chill. The guy had a basin of water and was splashing it on my face. I looked at my arm, and it had a clean rag wrapped around it. Nothing fancy, and blood was certainly staining it. My arm throbbed so hard I could feel the pounding through my entire body. At least the operation was done.

I walked back wearing my jacket so the guards wouldn't notice the bandages. You couldn't tell anybody anything in there, for fear the Germans would find out, so I didn't shower for three or four days until the pain subsided. Then, for several days, I washed myself, skipping the arm. I noticed I was down to maybe 115 pounds.

Several weeks later, the Czech beckoned Samuel, his son, and me into his shack. He had a serious but almost angelic look on his face. He didn't seem to be the same man.

"From now on, I'm not going to hurt you or anyone else in the squad anymore," he said, pausing to take a deep breath and stifle what could have been a sob. "I became a murderer. I was the outcast of my family, and I killed people before the war. In Czechoslovakia, they gave me life in prison for my crimes."

He paused again, the lines in his face wobbling as the struggle inside him turned his face an alternating gray and pink. He composed himself, then went on.

"Then Hitler came in and took me out of jail and to the army. When I was injured, they brought me here. And I still killed people. But no more, no more," he cried out. Then his composure started to crumble, and he waved us out the door. When we closed it, we could hear his crying.

One day later, Max pulled me into a corner. "Joe, I see you're getting along pretty well here. You finally tamed the murderer, though how you thought of flooding him with kindness is beyond me. It was a brilliant idea, and it's made my life easier. Yours, too, and all the other men's. We think you're a smart guy who can think on his feet. From what we can see, you can do a lot of things."

He paused for a moment, looked around to make sure nobody was listening, then locked his eyes with mine. He had glasses. I hadn't noticed before, but his eyes had a purple cast to them.

"Can you work with us? You've got to be able to think fast and know how to handle dangerous situations," he said. His voice was quiet, but tinged with menace. We both knew the consequences if either one of us were found out.

I took a very deep breath. Becoming part of the underground could save my life—or get me killed a lot sooner. There was no choice. My people were being killed for the crime of being born Jewish. I was angry with a world, Jews and non-Jews alike, which ignored what was happening to us.

I wanted the world to know what was happening here, no matter how small my contribution. Max was a dedicated and sweet human being. He also didn't like the killing he saw.

It was September 1943. My tonsils and arm had almost healed, and we both could see our breath in the air as we spoke. It was a good thing those little puffs of vapor didn't form words for people to read, or we both would have been dead.

"What do you want me to do?" I asked, surprised at the eagerness in my voice.

"As you know, every day we send out the *Leichenkommandos*, the death squads, to pick up the corpses of men who have died from beating or starvation or whatever, out on the job."

I nodded. I had seen the death details go out daily with a farm wagon, about twelve feet long. Seven or eight guys pulled the wagon. The Germans couldn't be bothered to provide horses. When the prisoners returned, the wagon was a heap of arms, legs, and heads. Nobody paid any attention to it. The industry here was death, and everybody knew it.

"Once or more every week, we're going to send you on the corpse patrol. We'll tell the commander you're going to be there to help them out."

I nodded again. So far this made sense. It was almost an adventure. I was going to go on a work detail outside the camp, but I wouldn't be in any danger of being shot or beaten to death. It was almost thrilling to have that kind of freedom.

"Before you go, we're going to give you a little letter inside a condom. Put that condom up your behind. We will tell you the spot to leave your letter. At that same spot, there will be another letter. Put that letter in the condom and bring it back."

"Sounds easy enough. Besides, I could use a little exercise and fresh air, as long as the corpses don't mind not my not attending to them for a little while." I chuckled a little at my gallows humor.

"One more thing, Joe," Max said, laughing a little. "If you get caught, you don't know us, and we don't know you. You're on your own, my friend. We will not be able to help you."

I could feel my bowels and bladder quiver. This was the tough part. My protection, even as an underground member, would only go so far. Once the Germans detected me, I would be dead within minutes—after they tortured me first to find out who my confederates were.

Still, there was no choice. To keep my life as it was, to wait for the Germans to decide when and how to kill me, was unacceptable. If I joined the underground, at least my life—and my likely death—would have a purpose. The faces of my dead parents, my sisters, my brothers, my uncle and nephews and nieces, all swam through my mind. Something my father told me popped into my head.

"This is going to be a tough war against Hitler," he had said. "I went through a war before, but this one is worse. Whatever happens, do what you've got to do."

I went out on my first trip the following week.

Max called me over. "You'll find a message at the second work project, three feet away from the south side. You'll see a rock and a little dirt. The rock will be next to two stones and a tree with branches around the bottom. Look underneath the fifth branch, and you'll find some wood with rubbish on it. The message is in the rubbish," he whispered. "I love you. God willing, we might be liberated in January or February. But who knows what they're going to do with us in the meantime?"

He handed me a condom.

When I showed up for the trip at 7:00 A.M., my fellow *Leichenkommandos* greeted me heartily. "We need you. Glad to see you. Strap yourself in and let's go. There's plenty of business for everybody," the leader called out, more cheerily than I expected.

I quickly understood why. The prisoners were the horses, and we were the ones strapped into the harnesses. I took my place, strapped myself in, and we started to walk, with me taking his place. Now the leader didn't have to act as a horse, so he walked alongside me.

"How did you get to help out? Who do you know?"

"I worked in the hospital. I just do what I'm told," I replied. I wasn't about to tell him anything, especially because I was the only person assigned to this detail part-time.

We arrived at our first stop, a sewer construction site. Several corpses with their heads bashed were laid in a pile. One of us would grab the head, while the other would pick up the feet. Then we would swing the form toward the back of the wagon, saying, "One, two, three." On the count of three, we let the body fly forward and its momentum landed it in the wagon in a disfigured heap.

Getting used to this work wasn't hard. The death camps were factories for killing people, so death was easy to accept. We ate and slept with it. We'd take in as many as twenty-five corpses a day.

We walked through project after project, following a map. We always found one or two corpses beaten to death by the *Kapos*. Heads were caved in, with blood usually dribbling out of eyes or nose or mouth. Often legs or arms were bent at an awkward angle from being broken. We made up to seven stops a day, depending on how many loads we had and how far we had to walk. I discovered that the actual camp went on for miles. No matter how far we walked to retrieve corpses, we never left the boundaries of the camp.

At every stop we took a fifteen-minute break to relieve ourselves. At the second project, we took a break and I discovered the small rubbish pile under an outstretched tree branch. I reached into the pile and there it was, a packet about three-fourths of an inch square wrapped in waterproof paper.

I pulled my pants down and defecated. Out came the condom. Before I put the message into it and inserted it back into my rectum, I read it. The writing, tiny and precise, was on two sides.

It said, "From now on you will find a message here or some other designated place. We're going to give you all the information we have on how the war is going. In exchange, we want to know from you how many people are killed each day. How many children, old people, and women. We also want to know how many people are sent off to work camps. Send it to us as often as you can."

I was so happy I could almost shout. We were going to know what was going on in the war.

The people who die here will be known. Maybe not by name, but at least their deaths will be counted. Maybe, maybe, they even will be avenged, I thought, with flashes of my mother, father, and all my brothers and sisters hurtling through my mind.

I knew I couldn't keep the condom or the Germans would find it. They were always searching prisoners, looking for weapons, gold, dollars, and other valuables.

Two days later, I went out with a condom-wrapped message in my rectum and orders to leave this message at one place and pick up a message two stops later. The outgoing message said, "You'll get the news constantly. We want to know what's going on. Even God doesn't seem to know, and she seems to be asleep."

Whoever wrote it had a droll sense of humor. After that, in very tiny precise handwriting, there was a list of how many people had been killed, barracks by barracks. Also included was a list of how many people had been transported to work camps, a laundry list of death, dying, and slavery.

The return message thrilled me. It said the Russians were close to Lublin and were marching toward Warsaw. It listed how many tanks, trucks, and planes the Russians, Poles, and Czechs had.

My God, my God, the Allies are pushing back the goddamned Germans. They're beating the bastards. We might be winning, I gloated inside my mind. Of course, I could never tell anybody what I knew. The Germans had spies everywhere. *It feels good to think I'm hurting those bastard Germans. It doesn't nearly pay back what they've done to me and my family, but it's something.*

After I picked up my first message, I knew the Allies were liberating my Poland. I talked to Hymie, to Nuftul, to whoever would listen. I knew telling them how I knew was too dangerous, but I tried to be a cheerleader.

"Have faith. Have faith. We have a chance. Take care of yourself. Do what you have to do. Fight. Survive," I would tell them, though many already were so discouraged they were talking about suicide.

I soon figured out the messages were left by the engineers, of whom there were about thirty. They hated the Germans. However, the Germans never ran out of surveying to be done because Auschwitz eventually was supposed to house one million prisoners after the Germans won the war.

The hiding place for messages almost always was behind a tree or bush which had been marked with an axe cut. Max would tell me where to find it. While the *Leichenkommandos* took their break, I would say, "I have to pee" or "I have to go to the toilet." Nobody asked questions.

I'd go to the spot Max had designated. Depending on the day, I would leave a message, get one, or do both. The paper that was used was waterproof, so I didn't have to leave it in any container. I just had to fold it up into a very tiny square.

Despite my involvement with the underground, my life in many respects stayed the same. Hunger always clawed at my insides. We now received only a quarter pound of bread per person at night. We customarily kept that bread overnight, so we would have some fuel to start the morning. We kept it in a cotton prison cap which we put over our heads while we slept. The cap kept us warm, and the bread we placed next to our head so we could feel movement if someone tried to steal it.

One night I woke up to find my piece of bread gone. I could see some guy I didn't know standing near me, eating it. I couldn't help myself. I started crying.

"My bread has been stolen; my bread has been stolen," I wailed. I was surprised to hear such pain come out of my mouth. I was acting like a little child, but I couldn't help myself. That piece of bread was my lifeline.

The man who stole my bread whispered, "Don't cry. Don't cry. I will fix this." Then he disappeared in the barracks' eerie half-light, while the German guards stood watch outside. There were one thousand people there in an almost deathlike sleep from exhaustion. When he returned, I could see he had a piece of bread in his hand.

"Here's a portion of bread. Eat it up," he said.

To keep that piece of bread would have been to betray a fellow prisoner. Someone else would be deprived of his nutrition because this prisoner had stolen it for me. There was enough light in the barracks for me to see his eyes. I looked at them hard. "This isn't right," I told him. "Show me where you got this bread."

I could see his eyes widen in disbelief. We both crawled to where a boy of twelve was lying. I shook him until he woke up.

"See whether you have your portion of bread," I whispered.

He felt for it and found nothing but empty space. He started to scream. I held one hand over his mouth and returned his bread with the other. I could feel his tears splashing over my face.

"It is nothing," I told the young one. "I would die of shame if I ate another man's bread."

I felt a little virtuous for what I'd done. The same could not be said for a friend of mine. One day a prisoner was brought back from the coal mines. His hair was stringy, his face streaked with coal dust. His eyes were hollowed out, his teeth broken. I saw him sprawled across one of the hospital beds.

"Morris?" I asked, my voice catching in my throat.

He looked up at me with eyes almost vacant of hope.

"Joe, I know you," he whispered. "You make the impossible become possible. You know I come from a rich family. Can you help?"

"Morris, all of us are going to die here. I don't know whether they're going to take you and cure you," I said.

I knew he'd be gassed. I just didn't have the heart to tell him. I could barely recognize him, and I certainly couldn't help. Once the Germans decided they were going to gas you, nothing could stop them. As guards carried him off, I wept.

Chapter 15

A
Happy
Delivery
Man

After three months of working for the underground, I saw a startling change in the way Mengele conducted the selections. The change was in relation to me personally. The first time I saw it, I had to tighten my bladder and anal muscles to contain myself. As Mengele passed by me, he gave me a half-smile. Then his secretary quickly winked as he also passed by me.

Are they kidding me? I thought.

I could feel my toes go cold. Mengele and his secretary probably thought they were being reassuring, but this routine was strictly business to Mengele; it was life and death for me.

I couldn't talk to my friends about it. How could I explain it without telling them I was in the underground? I had to keep it to myself, and wonder why this bizarre turn of events had taken place. I understood why the secretary was trying to reassure me. After all, he was in the underground, too. But Mengele? I could only wonder.

My underground connections came in handy in other ways. I was still buying cigarettes from the Gypsies, but I, like everyone else, knew that if the SS or Gestapo saw us, they would beat us. Occasionally, Father would see me and walk over.

"Be careful. Be careful or they'll beat you to death," he would say in a voice so low only I could hear him. I knew I wasn't the only prisoner Father tried to help. He was well known and loved by all the prisoners as somebody who would slip us a small word of encouragement here, a tip on how to stay away from beatings there. He just tried to make sure people wouldn't get hurt.

Of course, Father couldn't save us from selections. They had become a monotonous, if terrifying, routine. Every two or three weeks we would be called out to stand naked, with our clothing in a neat pile next to us, while Mengele looked us up and down. Wintertime was especially bad. Sometimes there would be as much as twelve inches of snow between the barracks, where we had to stand.

No matter what the weather, Mengele did the job himself. Apparently he enjoyed playing God far too much to delegate. Whenever he came near me, he gave me that crooked half-smile and passed me by.

After I've worked for him for so long, the least he could do is give me a full smile, I jokingly thought. *It probably costs him too much to make the effort.*

I also suspected that even if Mengele selected me, his secretary wouldn't write down my number. Still, I felt no comfort or certainty. I remembered what happened to Lazar, and the wet sound his body made when it landed on the street after the Germans threw it off the roof. I didn't trust anybody. When selections went on, I was just as terrified as anybody else.

Of course, in order to give myself the best chance of surviving selections, I had to make sure Mengele knew and liked me. When he came through his offices, no matter how quickly or slowly, no matter how little or much I was doing, I smiled a big smile, as though he were the most benevolent employer I had ever worked for.

Of course he saw me taking care of the inside of the offices, because he and the three young doctors practically lived there. They met there, they talked there, they ate there. Because they were using the office area so much, I constantly straightened the tables and chairs, wiped the windows, and mopped the wooden floors until they sparkled and gleamed. He would leave his boots to be polished, with the tops and toes practically lined up like soldiers at attention. The boots had to be mirror-perfect.

I knew I had to do my work both fast and well. My reward was that he said nothing to me. If he had spoken to me about my work, I knew it would be a complaint, and a complaint from Josef Mengele could be fatal. He would smile, but only a small upward slanting of one side of his mouth. Then he'd nod his head up and down and purse his lips in approval.

The three young doctors would exclaim German words meaning "Clean. It's very clean." Mengele never said a word. Just his look of satisfaction was all I wanted. The reward I got was his quirky little smile during selections—and being allowed to live.

Others were not so fortunate. With so little else to do and our lives resting on each selection, those of us who had endured several of them had figured out that 20 to 25 percent of us were chosen to be gassed each time. We calculated that our chances of making it through the entire war were not very bright.

"Sooner or later it will catch up with us," Hymie might say, his head hanging low so the Senior Block Inmate and *Stubendienst* couldn't see him talking.

"For some of us, it's all over. For the rest of us who are still here, it's just a matter of time," Nuftul would respond, the thickness of his voice betraying his sadness, though he tried not to show it.

"Nobody can avoid it," I would say. "This is a death camp. Anybody who is sick or skinny gets shipped here. We don't get a lot to eat; the people in the working camp get a lot more. They're valuable, and we're not needed. Still, a miracle might happen. We might get through this. Just keep fighting, just keep fighting."

They'd all look at me with wide eyes, then grin and shake their heads. They thought I was the eternal optimist. I was. Still, we lived with constant torture. Inside myself, I thought that if we didn't get picked for this selection, we'd get nailed in the next one or die on the job.

Every three to four months, there was a mass selection in which about 150 Jews would be picked as *Sonderkommandos*. At first, that job seemed to be a real plum because it meant you could pick the pockets of the dead for food or belongings. After a while, we discovered that being a *Sonderkommando* meant you yourself would die in a few months.

They had good food because they got whatever people threw away or what they could find on the corpses. Even better, they could keep—if nobody caught them—whatever treasure they plundered from the corpses' pockets, underwear, or anywhere else somebody had tucked a jewel, money, or bread, as long as a guard didn't take the loot for himself. As life in a death camp goes, this was pretty soft living. All they had to do was extract corpses from the gas chambers.

As I remember, before Mengele came, prisoners fought to be *Sonderkommandos* because the life was so good. Eventually, though, people figured out that the crew was gassed every few months, even though the Germans staggered the intervals so the *Sonderkommandos* couldn't predict when their time was up.

The Germans never let people know that was where they were going. Whenever they needed a new *Sonderkommando* shift, the Senior Block Inmate would assemble everybody from the barracks and call out, "Attention. The following numbers will stand on the right-hand side in the morning. You will be moving to another job." Nobody knew exactly which job it was until it was too late.

The *Sonderkommandos* had a grisly task: they removed the corpses from the gas chambers and took them to the ovens. Each of the four gas chambers was about ten feet from its own crematorium, like a pair of evil twins. Each pair was connected by several boards slanted downward from the gas chambers so bodies could be transferred easily to the ovens.

When the gas chambers were being heavily stoked with bodies, the *Sonderkommandos* would roll the corpses down the planks into the mouth of the ovens. When there was more time, they'd carry the corpses by the head and feet down the planks, dropping them like garbage sacks into the vast crematoriums.

One time in October 1943, some of my *landsmen*, my compatriots from my city, were picked. I saw them in the *Sonderkommando* barracks the next day. I talked to them occasionally near the barbed wire, when nobody was looking, and that's how I found out what being a *Sonderkommando* was all about.

One of the worst parts, they told me, was that people in the gas chambers would climb on top of each other clawing toward what they hoped was untainted air. The result was a pyramid effect: a mass of people on the bottom and an increasingly small cluster of corpses rising toward the top.

Naturally, people in the throes of terror and death lose control of their bodily functions. However, I was told, a chemical washed the smell from the released bowels and urine and sweat out of the air.

The *Sonderkommando* compound was isolated from the rest of the camp. It consisted of two barracks, one for sleeping, the other for necessities such as washing. It was almost encased in barbed wire, and soldiers tightly guarded every square inch of the perimeter, so supposedly word of what happened there wouldn't leak out. It was futile. We all knew what was happening. When people live so closely together, keeping such secrets is almost impossible.

Still, the Nazis tried. In October 1943, four *Leichenkommandos* escaped. They were from that part of the country and thought they could get away. Germans hated prisoners who escaped for several reasons. First, escapees could spread word of what was actually happening at the camps. Personally, I think a lot of people knew anyway, but the Germans thought anything they wanted to keep secret would stay secret. They certainly had succeeded in keeping the Red Cross from knowing what was happening.

Second, people who escaped obviously had outsmarted the Nazis, a fact incompatible with their being a master race. Third, escapes reflected badly on everyone, from the commander down to the guards, making them look incompetent and stupid at the hands of lowly Jews. Fourth, if some prisoners escaped, then other prisoners might get the same idea. A constant stream of breakouts would disrupt the tidy order the Germans had imposed upon Birkenau.

The four were captured in a few days, brought back to the guardhouse front gate, then put up on a small wooden platform. The German soldiers put ropes around the prisoners' necks, then pulled them up in the air. I watched as the prisoners' heads dropped over to the side after their necks broke. Their faces turned black, their legs kicked at the air, their eyes bulged, and their tongues protruded like long, pink snakes from their mouths.

Finally, they were still. They'd been executed before the day shift returned, so their bodies were left suspended until after thousands of workers had passed by the limp forms. Eventually, the bodies were cut down and tossed into a crematorium.

"I want to escape every day, but seeing what happened to these guys rips the guts out of me," I whispered to Nuftul, my voice filled with sadness. "These people knew the territory. They knew where to run and the Germans still brought them in. We're so tightly patrolled, even a mouse couldn't escape."

Still, two overheard conversations filled me with happiness. The first occurred when Mengele was in his office discussing politics with his three doctors. He had such discussions with them almost every morning. They all had access to daily newspapers, which they read religiously.

The suite was four approximately twelve-by-twelve-foot rooms, each with a handmade rectangular table, some wooden chairs, and a few books. Mengele would sit on one side of the table in his office, and the three young doctors would sit on the other side, sipping coffee from metal cups. The young ones leaned forward, listening intently. Mengele acted as though he were having a casual conversation among friends, discussing politics, the daily routine, whatever.

Almost every day the young ones would ask Mengele what was going on in the Fatherland. They were reading in their papers about staggering German military losses, and they were worried.

Mengele was soothing, telling them that Hitler had special plans, that he was letting the Russians think they were winning the war by letting them capture a lot of little countries, but scientists were working on new, awful weapons which would miraculously change the war's entire complexion.

They listened respectfully but were skeptical. They asked, "How come the Canadians, French, and English all are attacking us? How come we can't protect our own people?"

"We let them do a little bit of damage to us. At the end, they'll be finished. They'll never bombard the Homeland," he said smugly. I knew from the underground messages that Britain had already bombed Germany a couple of times.

I was often around during these discussions, because Mengele still didn't think I understood German. One morning, I went in to clean Mengele's offices. The doctors and Mengele were having their usual cups of coffee and asking Mengele why the Gypsies, Masons, Slavic races, and Jews were being eliminated. One of the doctors earnestly asked Mengele, "Why are we killing Jews? They never did anything to us. They have the best engineers, artists, scientists, doctors, musicians. Germany was built with streets named after Jews."

Mengele looked over his shoulder to make sure nobody was watching or listening. Then he leaned forward in his chair and looked at the doctor who asked the question. He would address them all as *Meine lieben Kinder*" (My dear children). The doctors loved that. Every time Mengele called them that name, they acted almost like dogs rolling over on their back so their stomach could be scratched.

He treated them with such fatherly affection that he often didn't even let them go along when he did selections. Instead they did research, from what I could gather in the snatches of conversations I overheard. What kind of research, I never did find out. I'd heard about Mengele's experiments, but I never saw any. I heard Mengele had stopped them after he moved over to Birkenau. In any case, all I saw were autopsied corpses.

"*Meine lieben Kinder*," Mengele said to the three doctors. "The Jewish people, no matter where they are, they become the best in the world. Yes, you're right. They have all kinds of medicine, music, and scientific discoveries." Then he described how rich some of them were, including the Rothschilds, and how the French borrowed from the Jews so the country could fight a war. "There can't be two smart peoples in the world. We're going to win the war, so only the Aryan race will stand."

One doctor asked a question, to which Mengele replied: "My father fought in the German-Austrian war with the tsar. That was in 1914, when they started fighting, and we kept winning the war. Then the United States came in, and we started to lose the war. Now, the whole world is involved against us and we're only 90 million people."

Still, Mengele said, the Germans had some of the French and Italians on their side. "We didn't realize the Jewish people were going to fight," Mengele said, slowly, deliberately, without any passion.

"Where are they fighting?" one of the young doctors asked.

"Right here, next to the camp, there are all kinds of chemical factories. Take a look. They work right next to us in those camps, those Jewish pilots. A lot of them were shot down. Take a look. All kinds of nationalities are fighting, the English, the Indians, the Pakistanis. There are even some Jewish brigades fighting us."

A lot of what he said just then was correct. Many times when I went out with the death wagon to pick up corpses, we would see and talk to English pilots, American pilots. We even ran into a number of Jewish pilots. Under the Germans they were being forced to build factories. They lived in the work camps surrounding Auschwitz.

Listening hard, I continued to clean the windows, wash the floors and tables, and shine boots.

"Look," Mengele said. "Even the Russians are fighting us. They've brought in Jewish pilots, nurses, and doctors. Everybody's ganging up on us. We didn't think it would happen this way."

"What will happen in this war?" one of the doctors asked Mengele.

"*Meine lieben Kinder*, what can I tell you? You know what the situation is now. Everything is in the open. There's nothing to hide."

Then Mengele stood up and said something that made me want to grab his neck and crush his throat, to kick his balls until they were jelly, then stomp on his face.

"Actually, we never had anything against the Jewish people. But they're smarter than we are. Hitler wanted to be smarter than the rest of the world, so we had to eliminate the Jews. In reality, they never did anything to us. They didn't even have a country of their own to fight against us. We have to eliminate them. There can only be one smart people and it's us. We're winning the war. Our Fuehrer knows what he's doing."

One of the doctors just shook his head, and Mengele proclaimed again that the Fatherland was working on the world's most destructive weapon, which would change everything overnight. The young ones just looked at him pityingly. They knew it was a lost cause. Then the talk ended. It was time for Mengele and his doctors to make their rounds, to see how quickly and efficiently Jews were being killed.

That crazy bastard, that bastard, I thought to myself. It was the beginning of 1944; I knew the end of the war was a long way off. Of course, not a syllable of any of these thoughts escaped my mouth. He would have had me gassed without hesitation.

After the conversation was over, my friend Josef asked me what had been said. But I played dumb with him, too. We went on to clean something else.

In the second conversation that thrilled me, I happened to be cleaning in Mengele's office while the three doctors were there alone. They were discussing how the war was going, and it was going badly.

"We didn't expect the *Juden* all over the world to bring educated people into this fight. Pilots, boat captains, officers: all of them are fighting us," one doctor said.

"What do you expect? People have to fight for their lives. You can see how many prisoners we took in, educated people. Now they're destroying our cities and killing our people."

Another one said: "We didn't realize they had so many Jewish people in England. They're bombing and destroying our cities."

One of them looked very somber. "Well, we're getting paid back for what we did up to now. Why should they lie down and die? Look at what we're doing to the *Juden*."

Another one leaned forward in his chair, forehead furrowed.

"Why are we killing the Jews? What did they do to us?" he asked. "They're the smartest people in the world, and they're the richest people in the world, too. They have banks. Look at what they're doing in England. Rothschild gave them all that land to open up new air force bases. He gave up all that land to fight us. The Jew bastard wouldn't give up that land before."

I could tell what they meant. It was the same old Nazi propaganda. They were saying that the Jews control everything and are greedy, rich, and selfish, so they're getting what they deserve. But I was excited to hear how badly the Germans were losing.

Just because the Germans were in deep trouble militarily didn't mean that the way they treated us had softened. Germany was being blanketed by bombs without pause or mercy. The Nazi mythology said the master race was invincible and Germany would never be bombed. Yet the mothers, wives, girlfriends, sons, and daughters of these soldiers and doctors were being killed, maimed, driven into starvation and homelessness by repeated attacks.

The Germans had trouble grasping the problem. It was beyond anything they had been led to believe. Their world was being exploded, one bomb at a time.

A little later, some of the most pitiful prisoners I had seen in all my time there began arriving. The Greeks had been conquered, and a number of Jews from there were being sent to Auschwitz. They spoke Hebrew. Most were small and skinny, with no meat on their bones to insulate them from the marrow-freezing Polish winter. Being thin and accustomed to a warm climate, they had a life expectancy, even by prison standards, that was particularly short.

Even if they didn't freeze, they were likely to starve. Their small size put them at a big disadvantage against the taller, stronger, and more belligerent prisoners. I saw many of the Greeks walking around with bread and a piece of salami they'd been given. The Russian prisoners, among the biggest in the camp, would punch the Greeks in the face and force them to hand over the food. Whenever this happened, tears would swarm into the eyes of the Greeks as they were lying on the ground, their eyes and nose bleeding and swelling from the beatings.

They looked so frail, so helpless, I had to do something. Being in a death camp meant being next to people from lots of different countries speaking numerous languages. Survival depended at least in part on communicating with fellow prisoners. I had picked up enough Greek to talk to one of them. I knew in particular the Greek word for "eat." Whenever I saw a Greek guy walking around with food in his hand, I would rush over to him.

"Don't keep food. Eat it or somebody will steal it from you," I said in my fractured version of their language. It was enough to get the point across. The Greeks would look around at the numerous Russians and other larger prisoners. They instantly would shove the food into their mouth. With their cheeks puffed out and their saliva showing, they'd try to smile their gratitude.

"It's nothing," I'd say. "We all must help each other."

They would look at me strangely. Because their size seemed to invite people to slap them around, they weren't used to anybody's helping them. But I was as short as many of them, though not nearly as thin. That made me seem like more of an ally. I would just nod my head in acknowledgment, then walk on. I didn't need a lot of thanks.

However, I did desperately want to escape, and it looked as though a gate might be opening. Months after the Warsaw Uprising, rumors started circulating that the Germans wanted volunteers to clean up Warsaw's wreckage.

I can get to Warsaw and run away as soon as I get there, I thought. *I know the terrain, and maybe I'll be able to travel the 125 miles to reach the Russian partisans. I can do it. I can do it. I can get out of here.*

The rumors were true. I volunteered. Usually the German guards handpicked people, but this time anybody who wanted to go could do it just by standing in line. We were told to go clean up, but I didn't want to lose my place. Then one of the Germans looked at me.

"You're a Polish Jew. You filthy Jew. You thought we wouldn't find out you were from Poland? Stupid pig. Get back to your barracks."

I never did discover how they found out, but I felt about as low as I'd ever felt. *This place is going to be my graveyard. I had a way out, and it was stolen from me*, I thought, despairing. My heart sank to my shoes as I heard the Warsaw-bound group march off.

One day, while the winter's ice clamped itself onto trees and bricks and made the snow slippery, I returned from work and noticed a huge gray vat the size of a large swimming pool. It contained chemicals so raw the smell almost ripped out my sinuses, which had been leaking for days. I knew I was getting a very bad cold.

Is this how we end? In a tub of chemicals that will send us screaming and shrieking in pain before we die? I wondered.

I walked inside our barracks. Before we had a chance to eat or do anything, the *Stubendienst* yelled out:

"Today we're going to be disinfecting. Just the Jews."

At that point it didn't matter much. The Gentiles largely had died; most remaining prisoners were Jews. We had to march out of the barracks and line up a half-mile away.

"Take off your clothes. Now. Everything except your shoes."

We did. The wind was gently kicking up puffs of snow and made the ever-present ice seem to darken.

"Now, tie your shoelaces around the clothing so you can find them later. Now throw your clothing into the vat."

The Germans were always frightened of disease, so they constantly stayed three to five feet away from us. The chemicals were so strong they'd kill the worst germs even the Germans could imagine.

We were forced to stand there in our laceless shoes for an hour and a half, while the wind and cold made our flesh swell up into large goose bumps. Many of us started to sneeze and cough. After a while, I heard the rasping sound of people spitting up huge wads of phlegm, but we had to stay in formation at attention.

When the Germans finally let us retrieve our clothing, the pants and shirts and underwear were all stuck together. There wasn't time for each guy to find his own clothing, so each of us had to grab the first bundle we could find and put it on fast. Of course, the clothing was saturated with chemicals. By the time we got back to the barracks, the uniforms had frozen on our bodies.

Naturally there was no heat in the barracks. In temperatures that seemed to be plummeting down way below zero, we all ran around looking for someone wearing clothing with our prisoner number on it. At the same time, the owner of the clothing we each were wearing was looking for his own uniform. It took several hours for everybody to get his own uniform back.

Over the next few days, sneezing and deep bronchial hacking became a kind of ragged melody which played all day and night. Many of us would die of pneumonia during the next few weeks.

I was affected, too. Two days after the vat, my head was starting to feel as though it would burst apart like a ripe melon. It throbbed. My whole body became so feverishly hot I climbed onto the barracks roof at night so I could keep my body cool while I slept. To protect myself from the wind and cold, I wore a summer jacket; I stuffed cement bags all around me and into my shoes.

It wasn't working. I could barely pull myself off the roof in the morning, even though I'd slept next to the warm chimney. I knew I had to keep doing my job, but I tried to beg off carrying messages to the outside. I could scarcely do my hospital work. I saw skeletal prisoners moaning and bleeding in bed, and I almost envied them. At least their suffering was about to end.

The pain intensified, and my strength was draining fast. My head felt as though explosions were going off almost every minute. Then another small explosion went off in my head; it wasn't pain. It was a thought as clear as the forbidding ice that coated the camp.

"I'm going to die. If this hammering in my head doesn't stop, I'm going to die."

Chapter 16

Mengele
Saves
a Life

The pounding in my head made my whole body feel that it might split open and that my pulse was throbbing all the way down to my toes. My body was so hot I was still climbing onto the barracks roof at night. My legs were too weak to work, and my hand felt blistered when I checked my forehead for my temperature.

Next to the hospital was a shed which housed the hot water pumps which warmed the whole building. I climbed up onto the rooftop during the day, hiding behind a chimney which itself had been heated by the pumps. The chimney blocked the view of the guards sweeping the camp every morning, and the side of the chimney where I hid was next to a fence, so nobody could see me.

Still, I couldn't work, and I had no place to go. My head was pounding so hard it felt ready to fall off. I hadn't much time.

I went to see Max Stein.

"Max, I can't go out on my assignment. I think I'm going to die. My head is thundering and I'm burning up. I've been sleeping on a roof during the day. I'm so hot, I can't work. I'll be dead in a few days."

If anything ever disturbed or distressed Max, he never let it show. This time, his eyes almost bulged out. He could see my eyes were closed nearly to slits. He put a hand on my forehead and immediately pulled back. He knew this was serious.

"I've been watching you, Joe. I know where you've been hiding, but I didn't know it was this bad. Let me go talk to Father," he said, worry clouding his eyes.

Later that day, Father came waddling over to me, his pudgy body almost hopping. When I saw him, I started crying. He examined my head and my eyes. Then worry furrowed his face.

"Take it easy. Take it easy. Let me see what I can do for you, Joe. I might be back later today. Tomorrow at the latest," he told me, his voice low and soothing.

I wasn't sure I would make it through the day. I just hid next to the chimney, hoping no guard would spot that I was sick. Later that same day, Father found me just as I was leaving my warm perch.

"You're going into the hospital. Report there at 7:30 in the morning," he said, his eyes sparkling.

I was astonished. I just stood there with my mouth hanging open. Everybody knew Jews were never treated in the hospital.

"Just be there on time," Father said, then waddled away.

That night, a lot of thoughts went spinning through my head. Father must have talked to Mengele. Nobody but Mengele could have given permission for me to be treated. Mengele knew and liked how clean and neat I was and how well I did all his cleaning and polished his boots to almost a mirrorlike shine. But to be treated in the hospital? This was far more than I could ever have expected.

I know what happened, I thought. *Father went to Mengele, and he didn't say I am a Jew, and he didn't say I am not a Jew.*

Later, Father said he'd told Mengele that I was a guy Mengele knows, the guy who does the cleaning.

When I reported to the particular hospital barracks Father had directed me to, I could smell an antiseptic. Then an orderly took me to a bed.

What's going to happen? Are the bastards going to beat me? Force me to watch while they torture one of us? I feverishly wondered.

My fear only increased when the orderly returned and walked toward me with a razor in his hand. Would he slit my throat? Cut out my eye? What was he going to do? What he did was to shave my head completely bald, my blond hair falling like pieces of gold.

Soon I was wheeled into an operating room. I looked up, and my eyes almost fell out of my head. Underneath surgical masks were the faces of Josef Mengele and his three assistants. I could feel fear rise in my throat. I'd heard about Mengele's experiments.

"How could Father betray me like this?" I cried to myself.

Then a mask was put over my face and the sweet-smelling anesthetic was administered. I just didn't care anymore. I was in such pain the faces of my parents, my brothers, my sisters, all bobbed in front of my eyes and I just didn't care whether I died. From seemingly far away, I heard the pounding of a hammer, the scraping of a chisel, and the cracking of a bone. Then I blacked out.

When I woke up five hours later, my head was wrapped in white cloth. I could see out of one eye, but the other one was covered with some kind of bandage which went all the way around my head.

"What happened? Where am I?" I cried out.

As the anesthesia fumes wore off, I realized I was in a hospital bed. All I knew was that Josef Mengele had operated on me, and I was still alive. I still had pain in my head, but it wasn't the kind of feverish pounding I'd had before. It somehow was cleaner, brighter, more hopeful, though my head still felt as though somebody were banging the clapper on a large bell.

"What happened? What happened? No Jew I know has ever been put in here," I said to myself.

Then I remembered that Mengele and his doctors had operated on me. I could feel a chill of fear run the length of my body. I knew Mengele's reputation, so I ran my hands over my body to make sure I still had all my parts. I even grabbed my penis and my scrotum. I touched them all over. I wiggled them. They were all there. All in one piece. I was astonished.

It was Mengele doing the operation. I know it was. He never does anything for Jews, and surely he can see my circumcised penis. It must have been Father. Nobody else could arrange this, I thought in the blackness.

A few hours later, the guards brought in a prisoner and placed him in bed next to me. The rest of the ward's fifteen beds were filled, and some even had two people in them. It was my turn to have a bunkmate.

The man groaned.

"Who are you?" I asked in German.

"I'm a German Jew," he replied thickly, in German.

"Jew? How? There's no such thing as Jews in this hospital."

"I was hiding in Berlin. I was born there and I have friends. They were hiding me and I had to go out to see a friend of mine who also was in hiding. They caught me on the street. Somebody squealed, I guess, and I had an attack."

He groaned again. I didn't know whether his attack was stomach, gallbladder, or what. He went on to say that when they captured him they took him to Birkenau. They had told him they didn't know whether he was Jew or Aryan, and they had to check him out. In the meantime, they had put him next to me.

He looked at me with troubled eyes and trembling cheeks.

"What goes on here?"

"Me and you are not going to be here tonight," I told him. "You're in Birkenau, and here they gas five thousand to ten thousand people a day. Jews, Gypsies, Masons. Everybody."

"You're crazy," he said, hissing. "My people, the German people, would never do that."

"We'll see. Tonight me and you are going to be leaving here," I said in a nasty tone I later regretted. I knew what would happen to him; he didn't. Maybe his last hours should have been spent in comforting ignorance. Still, his protecting the Germans grated on me, so I stuck in my final dagger.

"You won't be coming back," I said.

About midnight, they came for him. But amazingly, not for me.

"Where am I going?" he demanded of the guards, shouting.

Instead, I answered him: "You're going to die, as I'm going to die," I said, this time with real compassion. I could see by his wide eyes and flaring nostrils he now fully understood the truth of what I said. I never saw him again.

The next day Mengele and his three doctors visited me. I figured this was my time to die. Whatever they wanted to do to me, they would do. They saw my eyes were open very wide, and they all walked over, including Mengele. I badly wanted to urinate.

The three young doctors were cordial.

"Hello, how are you?" they said with big smiles. Doing surgery on a live body was a thrilling change of pace for them. Usually they only got to slice up corpses.

Mengele looked hard at the medical chart, then up at me. He talked to me in German, even though he thought I didn't understand. He was trying to demonstrate a warm bedside manner to the young doctors. "You've had a mastoid operation," he told me. I had no idea what that was. I just knew I had a yard of bandages wrapped around my head.

Then the three doctors unwrapped the bandages, which had globs of gray and yellow pus clinging to them. That pus was pouring out of my wounds like water from a leaking faucet.

"Ja, ja. Yes, it's good. It's good. Very good. Very good," Mengele said, looking at the results of his own surgery and nodding approvingly.

Then he called over a male orderly, someone I had seen on the job but had never talked to very much. He knew me because I moved around a lot. Mengele looked sharply at the orderly and said sternly, "Give him farina with milk. Give him margarine and white bread."

I'd not even seen, let alone eaten, such food since the war started. I would have had to bribe or kill somebody to get any of it. Now Josef Mengele himself was ordering me to be fed this delicious, life-giving nourishment. It was too ridiculous.

Either he thinks I'm a child or he's going to adopt me, I giggled inside my mind, half-giddy with fear and the realization that I might live.

I quickly pulled myself together. I understood Father was able to save me because Mengele knew me and I was as familiar a part of his routine as brushing his teeth. Mengele adored sticking to routines, not changing the way he walked, ate, or anything else. I had in an odd way become a part of him. Because I was an underground member, Father had been willing to save me.

I was still astonished that my life had been spared. I thought, *I guess it's not what you know, it's who is looking out for you. I know Max, Max knows Father, Father knows Mengele, Mengele knows me. Simple as that.*

I fell back asleep, but the orderly shook me awake. I opened my eyes in wonder. I saw a bowl of farina swimming in milk, white bread, real margarine. I almost threw the food down my throat.

A little while later, the orderly brought me white bread and hunks of cheese for lunch. I know my eyes were almost bulging out of their sockets. In four years of war, I had never had such a warm place to sleep or such nourishing food. Dinner that night was a thick vegetable soup.

I'm used to scraping the bottoms of garbage bins for food, and now look what's being brought to me in real dishes, I thought. I was overwhelmed. The food wasn't hard to digest, so even my shriveled stomach could handle it.

Most days, I was fighting to stay alive. Now, I could feel my body being flooded with vitamins and warmth and sleep, and I could feel myself tense up—I knew enough to mistrust good things that happened to me in a death camp. But nobody bothered me, I slept well, and I had good food. I was even given water in a small pan and a towel to wash myself.

There must be a God in heaven, I thought. *A few days ago I was ready to die. Now the Germans are treating me as a human being and the underground protects me. There must be a God in heaven.*

Still, I was not treated the same as the Gentiles. I was put off in a corner, fifty feet away from everybody else. I was almost the only patient on my side. I figured Mengele knew I was Jewish but was doing a big favor for Father. He also was letting his young doctors do surgery on a live body. I think that was his idea of a good deed.

All around me were death and sickness. All day and night, when I wasn't sleeping, I heard the phlegmy hacking of people with infections deep in their lungs, groaning and even yelling from pain. Even though this was a ward for the healthiest of the sick people, a few died, and I saw them being carried out.

As for me, I had fine care. Nobody else in the barracks had a sheet or a pillow, and I had both. An orderly walked up to me and silently displayed his forearm: its blue tattooing contained the same series of numbers as mine.

"We have been through Majdanek together," he whispered. "I'm from Warsaw."

For several days after that he brought me a cup of water occasionally, asking, "How are you sleeping? How are you feeling?"

He knew that I was a celebrity of some kind, that there must be something special about this short little Jew.

"Thank God, thank God," was all I could say.

Max visited me a few times. He joked, "What are you doing here, Joe? I need you back there." Then he'd joke about my being placed so far away from every other patient. I'd smile, he'd smile, and we'd make small talk. We'd never talk about the underground.

About five days into my stay, Mengele and his entourage came again. One of the orderlies unwrapped the bandages to show off the surgery results. Mengele peered at the wound and said, softly, "Nice, nice, nice." Then he ordered my bandages changed and the four doctors went on their way.

I was in the hospital for nine days, gorging myself on farina, almost drowning in milk, white bread, and margarine. Every day I was drenched with sweat, afraid being sick meant somebody was going to cart me off to be gassed at any moment.

I said to myself, "This has got to be a fantasy. This has got to be a dream," but I would always feel the lump behind my right ear and I would know the truth.

One day the orderly who had been through Majdanek approached me, looking a little sad.

"You're going to be discharged, Joe. You already have your clothing, but if you want a new set I'll get you some. And you get your old job back. Somebody's looking out after your rear end, and I'm glad," he said.

The next day I woke up, stretched, and looked over to the row of sick prisoners in beds along the opposite wall. I waited until breakfast was served. I slowly lapped up the milk and farina, letting every swallow take the longest time possible to dribble down my throat.

The sweet taste would have to stay with me for what I hoped would be a long, long time. So would the taste of white bread and margarine. I buttered the bread, then tore it into small pieces. I ate each little piece, chewing slowly and letting the rich taste wander down my gullet, savoring every last second of it.

The orderly took off my remaining bandages and put a little bandage over my scar. Then he gave me my clothing. I put it on, then left. I didn't have to check out; I didn't have a bill to pay. I waved good-bye to the orderly who had helped me.

The patients on the other side of the ward just looked at me with curiosity. They had no idea what strange disease I had that kept me isolated. I didn't bother explaining that it was just Jewishness, and that it wasn't contagious.

It's good to have friends, I thought, realizing that without the underground I would be dead by now. I also realized I was the link between the Birkenau underground and the outside world. I was the one who delivered the messages from each side. If not for me, nobody in the outside would know the horrors that were happening here. In my rectum, I carried hope for the underground inside the camp. I was the one who carried the news of how far the Allies had advanced, and how far the Germans were beaten back.

I'm a valuable instrument to them, I thought. _They need me, and I'm thrilled to be needed._

The first day out, I was assigned to a Jewish foreman, a miserable man. He had been a foreman for the Czech for several months. As time went on, he was beating more and more people to death, until the Czech had renounced beatings. Then the foreman had to be careful.

Without a word, he walked over to me and started beating me. He especially enjoyed hitting me in the head. My hair had not grown back yet, and my surgical scars stood out like blood on a bandage. The partisans had trained me how to defend myself. I knew what to do, but my body was too weak to do it.

After he beat and kicked me for a while, he picked me up and threw me into the mud, which was partially icy because winter still gripped the camp. I saw male orderlies who had originally come with me to Auschwitz looking out the hospital window. I could see them frowning in anger as I picked myself out of the soggy mud.

I got my revenge. A couple of months later, when I was even more secure about how the underground could protect me, I walked over to the foreman. He was several inches taller than I, but I leaned up into his ear and hissed, "If you mess with me again, I'll cut your hands off and nobody will do a damned thing to me. And you know what the Germans will do to you if your arms are stumps and you can't even work."

The look he gave me, melding surprise and fear, made me feel almost as good as that first mouthful of farina in the hospital. It was nourishment for the soul.

I had taken heart. Every week I went out with the _Leichenkommandos_, and every week Max gave me the message and the condom. We always had very short conversations, as though we were total strangers. Generally we would meet in the hospital or between one barrack and another. Sometimes we would meet in the latrine after work, and he would just shake my hand, and say, "Hello, how are you?" Then I'd feel the neatly folded oily paper in my palm.

Nobody would bother Max wherever he went. He was a secretary, so he didn't work. He dressed fairly well and had such winter items as boots and jackets, all with no holes. He no doubt got enough to eat because his face still was plump.

When Max and I saw each other after a few days, we would go through the ritual used with all of the people we knew. We'd shake hands and say, "Thank God you're still alive."

That was how we behaved in Birkenau. Forming friendships was difficult, because we knew any of us could be caught up in the Nazi net at any time. But we couldn't survive without the sustenance of human companionship, no matter how temporary. Friendship in here meant almost as much as food. In a way, it was food for the spirit. Often, friendship was all that prevented us from going crazy or throwing ourselves onto the wires.

However, Max and I had something special. When Max and I saw each other and shook hands, either he was passing a note to me or I one to him. Our exuberance at seeing each other was not remarkable here, where just seeing someone you knew after a few days was a small miracle, a blessing, a light in an otherwise dark and menacing existence.

_____

Chapter 17

Death and a Job Switch

The messages between the underground and the outside were a bright beam of light in my life. I always read them before I put them into the condom, then into my rectum. I wanted to know what was happening in the camp. The news was always depressing, but it always made me feel good that the deaths of these people—many of them my people—would be noted by the world, no matter how slightly, through the numbers on this small slip of paper.

What really gave me heart were the messages I picked up detailing the battering the Germans were taking. One day I was face-to-face with proof that the war was souring for the Germans. I was passing by a work camp near Birkenau during my corpse-fetching duties. I had been there so long nobody bothered me much. Some of the work camps had been turned into prisoner-of-war facilities, and I wandered near the fence and asked the POWs where they were from. It was amazing: they were Jewish pilots from all over the United States and England. Some spoke Yiddish. One said he was from New York. Earlier in the war they might have been beaten to death. Now, the Germans left them in peace because the Swedish Red Cross was watching very closely.

"Damned Krauts are running for their lives now," said the guy from New York in a nasal twang. "We're bombing hell out of them."

He assured me that if we could just hang on, we'd be free.

Just then the *Leichenkommando* leader called out and I had to go back to my duties, but the news thrilled me.

By this time, in the winter of early 1944, I knew the Soviets were pushing the Germans across the Polish border. I also knew the Allies were winning important battles. I dreamed my Poland would one day soon be free of these vermin. My personal dream continued, too.

"One day, I will be free. I will have a wife and children, and I will have my own business. I can do this. Miracles do happen. And they are happening," I would almost chant to myself.

I was a mass of conflicted feelings. Often I would picture my dream in my mind, usually when I was cold, wet, and hungry and it was raining or snowing. Then I would grasp reality. I would lie quietly and press my flesh between my thumb and forefinger realizing I had so little meat that my skin felt like a piece of paper lying on top of my bones. I would despair, then think over the messages about the war I had read and dare to think the war might be over sometime soon, and that I would survive.

I will get an education. I'm just as good as the Germans, and even a lot better. There's plenty of land to buy yet. I will build. I will create factories, homes, I thought.

Sometimes I would let my fantasy become even richer. I would see myself with two or three of my friends, maybe Hymie, Nuftul, and Frank, and we had all formed a company and were living nicely, with nice houses, wives, children, and cars. I pictured my house as palacelike, shrubs and flowers blooming in a profusion of colors.

While my soul was being filled with hope, the spirits of many of my *landsmen* were being drained. Day after day I would wake up to find someone's bed was empty. Maybe two or three beds.

I knew right away who was missing just by looking up and down the seemingly endless rows. Also, I'd go near the barracks back door, where the barrel was. That door was always open a little, looking out on the electrified fences, which sat like silent snakes in the dawn.

From that vantage point, I could see limp bodies, the head hanging down on one side, the toes of the shoes touching the ground, draped over the wires. Generally there were one to four corpses. Many of us regularly went to the barrel in the morning to see who had committed suicide the night before. Over the next several months, I would see the corpses of perhaps three hundred men from my barracks alone swaying lightly on the wires. So thin had they become that their corpses bent the wires only a little.

After work, when we were wet, tired, hungry, and had endured countless beatings during a twelve-hour shift, the men often would talk about killing themselves. They'd had only the most meager food and their ragged clothing was scant protection against the freezing nights. They'd look at me and say, "Joe, life is intolerable here. Why wait? Why be tortured? Nobody can withstand such misery, such agony. We'll all be dead very shortly anyway. What is the point?"

Of course, all the people who talked that way were Jews. The barracks had some Gentiles, but they didn't endure selections. They got packages of clothes and food. I despaired. The Allies may have been winning battles, but the world had forgotten about us.

We are Jews. We have no home, no food, no friends, no relatives, nothing to help us. People gave up on us. Some were too busy making millions and some don't care. President Roosevelt doesn't seem to care much, I would often think to myself. _If he cared, a lot of things could have been done to stop the atrocities. I hope and pray the world will have peace, and all I see around me are atrocities. Where are our fellow Jews? Where are the Americans?_

Sometimes I'd say this to my close friends. Mostly I tried to keep up people's spirits for another day. I wanted what I knew to leap out of my mouth, to soothe the hurts, the pain, the agony, the despair, of those I saw around me. But it would mean my death.

All I could do was talk to them. In my seven years in the _yeshiva_, I learned that in both the Jewish and Christian religions, people who commit suicide are murdering themselves. If you kill yourself, you will lie next to the wall of the cemetery, not with your family.

"You have no right to destroy the life God gave to you. I know we all could face the gas chamber," I would tell the prisoners, pleadingly. "In a short while, all of us could be gone. There's always a chance a miracle can happen again. Stay alive another hour. We can live to see these bastards buried in their own blood."

"You're crazy, Joe," they would say to me. "You're a sweet man. Nobody ever tried harder to make things good for us. But this is a death camp. What people do here is die. It's only a question of whether it's going to be sooner or later."

I was nearly dead myself. I was almost a skeleton. I weighed maybe 80 pounds, down from 150.

Will I survive this war? Will I make it? I keep dreaming I will be somebody. But maybe instead of being somebody important, I'll just be somebody who is dead, I thought to myself. Then I shivered.

In the spring of 1944, our food situation began to improve a little. The Nazis had occupied Hungary to prevent the Hungarian government from making peace with the Allies. A few months later, the government there started deporting Jews to Birkenau. The Germans had told the Jews they were being sent to Auschwitz to work, so the Hungarian Jewish committees sent along huge piles of sacked peas and beans to feed their people.

Although many of the Hungarians were not kept at Birkenau, the Germans in some small measure had told the truth. At that point, they were allowing healthy men up to age forty and women up to age thirty or thirty-five to be sent to Germany or to work camps.

However, the peas and beans that the Hungarians had with them stayed in Birkenau, so we ate slightly better for a little while. Then international pressure from the Red Cross, the Vatican, and the Allies made the Hungarian government stop the deportations only weeks after they began. I knew what had happened, of course, because I was reading the underground's messages.

In the spring of 1944, a Jewish boy from Hungary arrived in Birkenau. He was in good shape. Somehow the Hungarian government had allowed him to be fed decently. He was medium-sized, seventeen years old, with auburn hair and some meat on his bones. He came over to me, because he'd figured out I could help him.

"Joe, the Hungarians lost the war on our front and the Germans started deporting us right away. Jews were being taken to the front, but I'm too young. What goes on here?"

Because he had given me some news, I gave him some news and told him what happened there. He hung on to me, but he was smart enough to land a job on the ramp without my help. I had helped several people to get jobs: Frank, Noah—the prisoner who always was asking my advice—and two other guys.

Ultimately, I had more than a dozen men transferred to my area. There were some people I could not help, but who could take very good care of themselves. In the middle of 1944, a transport of Jews was shipped in from northern Italy, where the Germans still held on against the Allies. Among them was Checo, a champion boxer. Checo could speak only Italian. I didn't know that language very well, but he had a friend with him who also spoke Serbo-Croatian. I knew enough of that language to get by, and the boxer and I communicated through his friend.

Already there was a gang of seven Ukrainians in the camp. They were anti-Semites. They also had an amateur boxer in their midst. They told Checo's interpreter that if Checo didn't fight, they'd kill him. Checo refused, but after several death threats from the Ukrainians, he gave in. Though I never could catch him at it, I suspected the *Stubendienst* kept urging on the Ukrainians.

About three weeks after Checo arrived, the two boxers fought. The fight was held on a Sunday between Barracks 8 and 9. There was almost a carnival atmosphere. There must have been twelve hundred people, packed in very tightly. Everybody was craning his neck or pushing toward the front row.

It was a pitiful festivity. The smell of unwashed bodies clogged the air and ragged clothes hung in strips on most of us. Many of us had lost our teeth, and most were covered with scars and caked blood. Finally, a space about eighty by one hundred feet was cleared in the middle of this pathetic and ragged group. The two boxers, stripped to the waist, stepped forward. A *Stubendienst* with a whistle and watch was referee.

"We're going to have a fight," he announced in German. "We don't know who's going to win, but it's all for free. There will be ten rounds, and each round will be five minutes," he bellowed.

The crowd, already in a circle around the men, was probably the most religion- and nationality-diverse group I had ever seen at the camp. It was first come, first served, so Jews and Gentiles were randomly mixed together.

The whistle blew for the first round, and Checo came bobbing and bouncing out of his corner. He was squat, with rippling muscles and a ballet dancer's ability to move on his feet. He was about five feet, seven inches, and weighed perhaps 190. The Ukrainian was about an inch taller but skinnier by 25 pounds.

From the beginning, the Ukrainian clearly was overmatched. Checo bounced, bobbed, and weaved around him, while the Ukrainian just stood there and moved a little. He had no footwork. Checo would jab and run, and the sound of Checo's fist smacking the Ukrainian's face popped into the air several times a minute. The Ukrainian's face kept getting lumpier and lumpier. By the end of the second round there was no doubt how this fight would turn out.

The Ukrainian was tired, his movements more leaden. By this time, Checo was pumping his fist into the Ukrainian's face harder and harder, smothering him with flurries while the Ukrainian kept covering his face and stomach. After smashing the Ukrainian five or six times, Checo would dance away from the man's lunges, which became increasingly awkward and ungainly as fatigue and the pounding of Checo's punches sapped his strength.

The Ukrainian kept shaking his head to clear his mind. After each flurry, he shook his head harder and harder. Occasionally, he would land a solid blow to Checo's head or stomach. We could hear the flesh smack, but Checo didn't budge. By the third round, the Ukrainian was being hit more, getting weaker, and shaking his head harder after each attack. Checo was almost dancing in and out at will, smacking the Ukrainian around, then dancing away from his opponent's flailing.

Checo was obviously toying with his opponent. In the middle of the fourth round, Checo stopped his mosquitolike tactics and started banging away hard at the Ukrainian. Checo's fists were hitting their mark almost unopposed. The Ukrainian's knees started to crumple, his body became wobbly, his eyes started to glaze over, and he seemed to become disoriented, moving disjointedly in several different directions. The yelling and screaming from the Ukrainians grew louder as they shrieked in disbelief that a Jew could beat one of them.

Finally, Checo decided to end it. He slammed the Ukrainian with a rain of blows to his head, breaking the nose so hard blood started spurting. We saw plenty of blood in this place, but this was the first time we had seen it when rules actually applied. With one deep uppercut, Checo nailed the Ukrainian, who flew upward, then landed spread-eagled on the ground. Two glum Ukrainians carried the unconscious boxer away.

The Jews applauded the outcome, but not aggressively. We had to play down our true feelings. If we had screamed and yelled and slapped each other on the back, we would have instigated a riot. There were lots of *Kapos* there. There was an abundance of murderers there, too, and they had knives and brass knuckles. If we'd been too exuberant, we would have suffered mightily.

The Ukrainian boys were clearly angry about the outcome. They'd point at the Italian boxer and make muttering noises, their eyes flashing a bigot's anger. One day, all seven of them sneaked up behind Checo and dragged him outside. Even such a splendid physical specimen as Checo couldn't fight back while being assaulted by several two-by-fours and brass knuckles.

We heard the crunch and slap of the weapons hitting their target, and the Ukrainians screaming, "We're going to kill you, Jew. We're going to fucking kill you."

Checo didn't understand a word they were saying, but he was screaming out, "Help, help, they're murdering me," in Italian, punctuated by loud shrieks and wailing. The only reason I knew what he was saying was that his interpreter was standing near me.

We couldn't help him. No matter what we did, we'd be losing. If we helped him, then our lives would be in jeopardy from the murderers. If we laid a finger on a Gentile, that would be the end of us. We felt terrible that we couldn't help.

The assault lasted about ten minutes. When Checo staggered back in, we couldn't recognize him. His face was swollen. Blood was gushing out of his eyes and through his mouth, which spilled red spittle. There was hardly an inch of his face undamaged in some way. His eyes could barely see out of their sockets they were so bloody and his face was so swollen.

The Jews were upset and angry with the Ukrainians, but we felt we couldn't do anything in revenge. Many of the Ukrainians were murderers and *Kapos*. They could get their own kind of revenge on us, and we couldn't stand up to them nearly as well as Checo could.

I went over to his bunk and put a hand on his shoulder. "God, Checo, we all feel bad about what they did to you. But if we do something to them, they'll kill us," I said, with real sadness.

"Don't worry, Joe," he said through broken teeth and swollen lips through his interpreter. I could hear his breath rasping because something inside his nose had been broken. "I'll take care of this myself. I'm not done with them. I'm going to die, but they're going to be dead before I get through with them."

About three weeks later, Checo caught four of the Ukrainians outside the barracks. Two Jewish doctors who worked in the ambulance later said two Ukrainians died, and the others were half-dead.

I asked Checo why he did it.

"I'm going to die anyway. Now I feel good about it. The whole thing is this: They messed up my face, but I broke their arms and legs and I let them know they can't get away with this. They're going to survive because they're Gentile. I'm Jewish. I'm dead. But until they go to their graves, they will know a Jew was a better man than they were."

A few days later, I saw Checo's interpreter. I hadn't seen Checo in at least thirty-six hours.

"Where's Checo?" I asked, trying to mask my fears.

"I don't know where he went. I haven't seen him. I think they took him to the crematorium because he looked so pitiful," the interpreter said, looking sad.

Brutality here still was everyday fare. On rare occasions, however, it even had a humorous side. Once my friends and I were working all night unloading at the ramp. I and 120 other guys were marching back into camp. We were the cream, the elite, of the prisoners. Many of us had survived in Birkenau for four years, whereas most people didn't last more than four hours. We marched as well as any of the Germans, and we were proud.

That night an SS man was stinking drunk. And he had a whip, one of those with metal wires inside. We were returning a little early, and I guess he thought we were slacking off.

He was staggering, and his legs were buckling. He couldn't hit all of us, but he came after us with a shovel. He staggered around. We were right by the gate on an empty lot, running for our lives.

We couldn't run very far or we would be shot. We had to stay there. He probably didn't know what he was doing. He made us run in a circle. The gate was locked and the guards wouldn't let us in, and we would have been shot for going back to the ramp. So we had to stay there, running around in a circle.

He was howling, "You bastards, you dumb motherfuckers." He was loaded, but he wasn't too drunk to beat us. His lash swung out time and time again in the night.

"Jews. Filthy fucking Jew bastards," he yelled. "Crawl, you slime, crawl on your hands and knees!"

For two hours, the blood ran. The snap of his whip and the yells and groans of pain were almost more frightening than the gas chambers. At least there your death was certain. His whip would lash out, then he would flick it so it ripped off a piece of a man's ear, or pulled out an eye.

Being a small man was a real advantage at a time like this. We were all on our hands and knees, but my size let me hide behind the bigger men. The tongue of his whip barely licked my back once or twice. Mostly I was next to the people who got hit, and I heard their cries.

Suddenly I heard the Nazi shriek, and I looked up. There was a huge welt across both eyes, his left cheek, and his forehead. He was so drunk he had hit himself in the face with his own whip. His eyes had swollen shut, and the rest of his face was starting to puff up.

"I'll get you, you bastards. Think you can fight back? Think you can strike one of the Fuehrer's men? Think you can beat an Aryan, you fucking Jew bastards?" he roared. The pain he was feeling and the revenge he was bent on taking made me sweat and shudder, and I hid closely behind a big man in front of me.

The Nazi snapped his whip again and again, but now he was both drunk and blind. We easily dodged his lash. Every time he lashed out, the whip would snap back and he would hit himself. He would roar in pain and anger, then draw his whip back and lash out again, hitting himself with a snap, followed by a shriek.

By now we all had stood up and were standing in a ragged semicircle in front of him. We were watching a glorious show, and we only longed to have our hand on the whip instead of his. But watching an SS man whip himself while his face turned bloody and the foam poured out of his mouth was a treat we'd never had.

Finally, the SS reared back and let loose with a muscular force that would have felled any man in our group, then whipped his arm back to strike again. The whip curled under itself, hitting him in the head. He fell into a bloody heap in his uniform, now drenched with his own blood and coated with dust. He was a disgusting parody of the military might and racial superiority Hitler claimed for himself and his Germans.

"God paid this man back," I said to Hymie, as we walked away.

Not long after this incident, I got up in the morning and started walking toward the hospital. I passed by the Gypsy camp. The quiet was suddenly shroud-like. There were no children running near the fences, and nobody was trying to sell me cigarettes. I could smell charred flesh.

Something's wrong, very, very wrong, I thought, troubled.

I spent most of the day trying to imagine what the Germans might have done. I was working in the hospital, and we all kept asking each other what had happened to the Gypsies. Back in my barracks, a guy I was sure had *Sonderkommando* connections walked up.

"Guys, guess what? No more Gypsies. They gassed them all last night," he said.

The Allies were rolling closer. Every time I picked up the underground's notes now, I could feel the earth shake from bombing which was no more than forty or fifty miles away. I knew the Allies were gaining ground.

I figured the Germans were getting panicky about the possibility they might lose the war, so they were exterminating as many undesirable people as they possibly could. This was May 1944, and about fifteen Gestapo started taking over some of the selections. The Allies had overrun Majdanek and Treblinka by then. Mengele still did most of the selections. He especially liked the night shift. He seemed to soak up the darkness.

"We're next," I told Frank. "We are having our finger put in the lion's mouth, and we have to wait to see when the lion is going to bite it off."

212

Frank just nodded sadly. We were all depressed. So many people were being transported in and gassed.

A day after the Gypsies were executed, I met with Max to pick up my next message. By that time, we could see the number of trains was increasing, and the Germans were grabbing everybody they wanted from wherever they could. The healthy prisoners were shipped to Germany as slave labor. The rest went up the Birkenau chimney.

"What's going to happen to us, Max? The Gypsies have been liquidated."

"They're shipping people out of here to Germany like crazy," Max said out of the side of his mouth. "They'll either kill us here or send us to Germany, where they will kill us or starve us to death. Getting out alive is not a choice."

"What about the hospital?"

"They'll probably shut down everything. If they're shipping people to Germany by the trainload, they won't have time to give anybody medical attention. If people can't work, they're dead. Things are so bad even the Gentile patients may be in the ovens."

Soon after, one of Mengele's young doctors pulled me aside while Mengele and the others weren't looking.

"Listen, Joe, you're in danger. With the Gypsy camp closed, the hospital probably is next. They'll evacuate every able person to Germany," he whispered, then nodded at me and left the room.

In the next few days, I could see more and more hospital beds yawning empty as the patients died even faster than usual—probably for lack of medicine—and no more patients were being sent in.

The hospital workers, about 120 of us, were panicking. We all tried to find something to do, some way to justify our continuing to be kept there. At night, we could hear bombs exploding.

I knew the Russians had taken Warsaw. They had stopped for a while to regroup, and now they were on the move again.

"What are they going to do with us in Germany?" I asked Hymie and Nuftul. "They're going to kill us one by one by working us to death while we starve. We know the end of the war is coming fast, but it's still too damned slow."

The next night after dinner the *Stubendienst* shouted, "Listen, I have an announcement to make." He called out a lot of numbers, including Hymie and Nuftul's.

"These numbers are to gather in front of the barracks tomorrow and march to the *Sonderkommando* barracks."

They weren't even trying to hide where they were sending us. Then he called out my number, Frank's, and a few others. "Tomorrow, you report to Canada," he said.

Everybody's face went ashen. Hymie and Nuftul looked at me.

"How come we end up in hell and you get Canada?" Hymie asked.

I knew the answer, but even God I couldn't tell.

"I don't know," I said, shaking my head. "They just called out my number and here I am."

Inside, my mind was thinking faster than I could run. I knew nobody had been sent from Canada to the ovens, so I was safe for the time being. I also knew Hymie and Nuftul soon would be in the crematoriums.

The next morning, as soon as the numbers were called out, the *Sonderkommandos* had to go. Hymie and Nuftul's heads bowed. They knew they had about twelve weeks. The pace of the executions had stepped up dramatically, as had the pace of *Sonderkommando* executions. I guessed that the Germans, knowing that the war was lost, wanted to kill as many Jews and other people they considered undesirable as possible.

It was a sure bet that all my friends would die very shortly. I hugged them, then kissed them on the cheek. We were all crying. Then they had to walk twenty-five yards across the street to be swallowed up by the barbed wire fence. The six-foot wooden door of the *Sonderkommando* barrack swung open and they walked in. The gate slammed behind them.

Later, I found out that this same night all the patients were cleared out of the hospital. Most were gassed.

The hospital workers now were in a bind. They'd had the best jobs, but now they had nothing to do. The Jews were sent to the *Sonderkommando* squads; the Gentiles were sent to work on construction. Even in the face of imminent defeat, the Germans just couldn't stop building.

"What's going to happen to me? What's going to happen to the rest of us?" I asked Frank. "I'm scared."

I even thought of killing myself. Fear was the constant undercurrent, and I knew my religion required me to battle it.

"No, I won't give in," I told myself. "I'm going to fight the bastards to the end. It's been almost six years now. I know the end is coming. Maybe I'll be here for it."

Chapter 18

On
the
Ramp

I had slipped away from death once again. I was assigned to clean up at the ramp, and that was one of the best jobs around, especially since the hospital closed. But being on the ramp also forced me to witness more death, desperation, and fear than any human being should have to see. What I saw there made me sick in my soul.

I worked the night shift, from 6:00 P.M. to 6:00 A.M. There were about 140 of us on each shift. The Nazi cause looked worse than ever. Rommel had been defeated in North Africa, and the Germans were determined to exterminate as many Jews as possible.

The sounds, sights, and smells at the ramp were so grotesque the Germans had four six-hour shifts working there. They were not concerned about us, so prisoners had only two twelve-hour shifts.

My new job required me to wear a special uniform of dark green pants, shirt, jacket, and a small round cap, all with white stripes. We wore this outfit so guards would know we were prisoners who were not supposed to be sent to gas chambers or work camps.

Before we went to the ramp for our shift, each of us had to shave and wash. The Germans worshiped cleanliness, especially in this despicable situation. They wanted us to be presentable and neat, as if we were preparing for a day at the office.

The Germans also wanted us to be both fast and efficient. We had to work quickly, because there was almost always another train waiting with its own load of human cargo. Behind that train was another, and then another, in an endless parade of death. The prisoners were almost always Jewish, packed into each car like herrings.

A few minutes after each empty train left, a full one arrived. The whole process, from emptying the train and dispatching the prisoners to their fate, to unloading corpses and baggage, took thirty minutes. Of course there were other matters such as one train's leaving, another's arriving, as well as testing car couplings, all of which expanded the cycle for each train's stay to an hour or more.

Almost every train stretched for half a mile. On our shift, we would go through as many as ten trains a night. That meant Mengele disposed of perhaps ten thousand to fifteen thousand men, women, and children in a single shift, nearly the equivalent of the entire population of my hometown.

The more night's darkness cloaked the ramp, the more frightening the place became. When each train rolled in billowing black smoke and squealing brakes, my job was to jump forward and slide back the cattle car doors. When pulled together, those doors formed a single hinge along their common seam. The hinge had a pin in it. I pulled the pin, which was attached to one of the doors by a small metal chain, out of the hinge, then flung the doors open and jumped back.

We were forbidden to talk to or touch anyone. The Germans didn't want us panicking the people on the train by telling them where they were and what was going to happen. They might revolt, and then the guards would have to massacre them with gunfire. That method, although emotionally satisfying for them, wouldn't be nearly as neat and orderly as herding them off to the gas chambers. Order is what mattered most to the Germans.

The prisoners were processed so quickly they weren't given much time to panic and create a mass uprising against eighty guards. Even with the German-made rifles the guards held and the Lugers the Gestapo and Mengele carried in holsters, the Germans were badly outnumbered.

Still, it wouldn't have mattered. It was like flies on an elephant: the Germans would have gunned down everybody in a second. That's why I never saw anyone try to escape. There would have been no point. The prisoners were always surrounded by electric wires, armed guards, and dogs.

Guards constantly watched me and the other ramp workers from a distance of about ten feet to make sure we didn't talk to anyone. Even so, when the guards turned their backs to patrol another cattle car, the people would always ask me, pleadingly, in Yiddish, "Where are we?" I had learned to talk out of the side of my mouth so the guards couldn't see. With my lips barely moving, I would whisper, "Auschwitz."

Their next reaction was as predictable as it was painful to watch. Their faces would turn gray and bulbous tears would begin to well up. They'd put their hands to their heads and start shrieking and sobbing—especially the old women and men. They knew what a short road lay before them. The word was quickly passed along to everyone else.

Despite such terror, fear made the whole process astonishingly quiet. Fear has many stings. People were afraid of dying, afraid of being beaten before they died, and afraid that if they cried, something even worse than death would happen to them.

The SS all had large wooden poles. If somebody asked them a question, they would hit the person who asked it. If people made noise or started shrieking, the guards would scream and hit them in the head, beating people until they crumpled onto the ground.

Also, the guards always had ten to fifteen leashed and snarling German shepherds. Oddly, I never saw the dogs attack a single person. Their real function was to sniff out anyone who was hiding under the train cars after the selections had been finished.

Just the dogs' snapping and snarling probably would have deterred people from making noise. However, the guards' constant beatings also were sufficient. It only took a few assaults before everyone on the ramp grasped that silence was required.

The result was a strange and passive quiet, punctuated by shrieks and wails which were quickly muffled. There was a constant undertone of people sobbing into handkerchiefs. They would cry whenever they could. Almost all of them cried when they saw the crematoriums spouting flames, but they were too terrified to be very noisy about their emotions.

They had other reactions which could not be suppressed, however. Many times, when people discovered where they were, they would start vomiting or lose control over their bowels and bladder. The results stained the ramp with various-colored messy piles. The smell they imparted mingled with the smell of sweat and fear to create a stench that was as disgusting as it was frightening.

The children reacted both to that smell and to the fear they sensed from the adults. However, the guards with their sticks and dogs so frightened the children that even they were subdued. The kids still knew what was coming and they did cry, though much more quietly than anybody would expect. Young and old knew they were excess baggage to the Third Reich.

As for the baggage and other belongings they had, that's why my crew and I were there. The people almost always were carrying small, battered suitcases or food in wrinkled bags. Large suitcases and trunks weren't allowed. The Germans had told these people they were being relocated. They also told the Jews that they should leave large valises behind, that they would be delivered. Indeed they would be, but not where the people expected.

When the people from the trains heard they were in Auschwitz, they immediately dropped or threw away their scraped and battered belongings and their food bags. Sometimes they would drop them in the railroad cars, sometimes on the ramp, sometimes elsewhere. Dealing with those sacks and suitcases was part of my job. After the people left the train, I and the ramp workers were assigned to run into the cars to clean out debris, whether it be sacks of food or corpses. I was amazed when I entered my first railroad car and saw graffiti penciled on the walls.

Those writings in the smoky and dingy cattle cars were proof that even though the Germans had said the Jews were being relocated, a lot of them didn't believe it. The people would scrawl on the walls who they were and where they were going. They tried to leave some mark, some way for people who cared about them to know what had happened to them. They were making a feeble attempt to find some way to exist beyond their final stop.

People had heard about three death camps. They knew Treblinka and Majdanek were to the east and Auschwitz-Birkenau was to the northwest. So they would write *Treblinka, Majdanek,* or *Auschwitz-Birkenau* on the walls of the cattle car, depending on where they thought they were heading.

They sometimes would write out their names and addresses and their occupation. The handwriting generally was shaky, as though it had been scrawled quickly or by a sickly hand. A typical message would say, "This train delivered people to Treblinka. This is the end of the road. Help yourself in any way you can."

Some people heeded the warning. Often, the train car's windows were broken. Most of the cars held a small pane of glass perhaps three feet high and two and a half feet wide. The occupants would knock out the glass. Whoever was skinny had the best chance of snaking out the window and jumping to the ground when the train slowed down.

The railroad car messages touched me at first, but I quickly coated my feelings over with indifference. There were so many notes, and I saw so many atrocities every night, I became hardened.

It was pure self-defense. I became resigned to my being in a death camp and to the fact that I would die. I knew there was no way out, though my occasional fantasies about having a family and a business sometimes ballooned large enough to blot out my darkest thoughts.

Often, those of us who worked on the ramp would talk to each other about our desperate situation. I myself participated in many such conversations.

"We're going to die," someone would say, bitterly.

"What can you do about it? We can't fight seventy or eighty SS with guns," I'd reply.

"There are electric wires all around us. There's not one chance in 20 million we can escape."

"Why was I born Jewish? We would be better off to be born rats. Any animal has a better chance than we do."

"And we're supposed to be the Chosen People."

I would say these things almost every day. I always hoped to see the Germans run for their lives. In reality, I was just waiting for my own death to arrive.

Even people on the trains who hadn't known their final destination was a death camp realized the facts soon after they got there. Flames from the four chimneys were stabbing for the sky in the night, like giant candles burning brighter and uglier than the flames of hell. The crematorium fires gave off considerable, though wavering, orange and yellow light. The illumination wrapped the whole ramp in a radiance which flickered and danced across the terrified faces in the night. The ramp also was lit feebly by naked bulbs strung up on poles, adding a cool and eerie feeling to the hot, dancing chimney fires.

The smoke was so thick it made everyone's eyes feel they were burning into their skull; sometimes it made the light from the flames shimmer. In addition, the stench of burning flesh and bones was so nauseating that those of us who worked on the ramp had to wrap towels around our faces in order to breathe. We just left the towel loose, leaving our eyes exposed. The fastidious Germans clamped white handkerchiefs over their faces.

Occasionally, when the fire diminished a little and the smoke started to rise, ashes would fall upon us. These were soft, black, wavy flakes of what had been breathing, living human beings only minutes before. Such sights and sounds, happening as they did while the camp was wrapped in the black shroud of night, terrified everyone there to their marrow.

In the beginning of my time on the ramp I often said to myself, "This is the end of the world. It's tearing me apart. I can't stand another minute of it. But if I don't, I'll die, too."

No matter when each new train arrived, Mengele was always there, his boots no longer polished to a high shine by my hands. Even that bow to Mengele's personal fastidiousness had stopped after the hospital had closed. Even so, Mengele still arrived dressed in full uniform, his jacket buttoned to the neck. His three doctors were behind him and several SS captains with chests full of medals stood nearby. All in all, his entourage numbered about a dozen.

He was a very moody man, but when he was at the ramp he was all business. There, he hardly ever gave me his half-smile, though the three young doctors often acknowledged me. Sometimes I would even have small conversations with them.

Before a train arrived, Mengele stood lost in thought, with his arms crossed, watching the train and its cattle cars pull into the station. Once a train stopped, he snapped to attention. After the train had halted completely, the people inside the cars were forced to carry the dead and dying and put them in a pile. If there were too many dead, our group helped. By that time, the guards had taken their place by every cattle car door.

Mengele would stand ready at his usual spot, twenty feet from the train. Whatever he did, he did slowly, methodically, and in small steps. After the trains had been emptied, the people were lined up and marched toward him. He never said anything. He just pointed his finger at the person at the head of the line, then pointed again, designating in which line that person should go. The guards would push and shove, or sometimes carry, that person to the designated line. Then the next person would be presented for judgment.

Prisoners from the trains were assigned to one of three rows: one for able-bodied men, usually between the ages of sixteen and forty-five; another for able-bodied women about the same age but without children. Prisoners in these lines were forced to change into prison uniforms and were shipped out that night, or the next morning, to slave labor camps or factories in Germany or Poland. Germany needed the extra hands. The Allies already had taken back a lot of Poland, Estonia, Czechoslovakia, and Russia, cutting off large pools of slave labor.

The third column was for those who could not work: the old, the sick, the women with children, and the children themselves. People in that line were sent to the gas chambers.

I despised being on the ramp, but I still thanked God I was protected by the underground. They were watching out for me, even though I could no longer deliver secret reports to the outside.

It could have been worse. I could have been a *Sonderkommando*.

Though the underground had made sure I didn't become one, I kept in close touch with the *Sonderkommando* group. On the ramp, my thoughts often would drift off to them, because many of them were my *landsmen*. I slowly had gotten several of them jobs at the hospital after I paid for my own position. It hurt to think about the way they would end, especially Hymie and Nuftul.

Thoughts of my friends often were interrupted by reality. After Mengele had dispatched each trainload, we would continue cleaning up. After we had picked up the belongings, we had to wrap them into bundles to be sent back to Germany. We would put caps in one pile, blankets in another, pants in yet another. Then we'd tie the piles and hoist them onto trucks to be taken away.

I hated the lifting. It was tough work, and I was getting very little to eat. One big benefit of working on the ramp was that we could keep any food we found. The guards were constantly searching us, but if we found something to eat, that was fine with them. Much of the time we ate it right there. They enjoyed seeing us behave like animals, grabbing food from the mud and stuffing it into our faces.

Even with the extra fruits and bread I was finding, I wasn't eating much more than a subsistence diet. I didn't have any calories to spare. I knew that if I continued to do the heavy lifting the ramp work required, I would weaken and might even be injured, making me a candidate for gassing.

I also hated the smell of the people. When the trains carried them in, many prisoners had been in transport for weeks. The stink was terrible. The worst smell I encountered was at almost the beginning of my time on the ramp. A long train arrived from Tunisia and Morocco. We knew which countries Hitler had conquered by the nationalities of the people on the trains. This particular transport had been rolling for more than five weeks, and the people had been given no water, no food, nothing.

When we opened up the cars, almost everybody had died. In fact, some of the corpses had started to decay. Many were filled with maggots and other creatures we could see crawling inside the remains. Some of the corpses had decomposed so much the bodies were no longer whole, and we carried out individual arms and legs. The stench made us gag and vomit repeatedly, so we had to wrap our rags and towels around our faces very tightly.

Then some trucks rumbled over to the ramp and we picked up the intact corpses—men, women, children—by the legs and shoulders and lifted them, while trying to keep a grip on their decaying flesh. We tossed them into the trucks, which then drove to the crematorium.

Even the stink of the live people, who had been on trains for days, and the sweaty smell of fear, were making me feel sad and disgusted. The children's muffled sobbing, though, really stabbed at my heart and made my head feel it was exploding.

"These children are a half-hour away from being killed," I'd say to myself, trying to hold back my own weeping.

To save my strength and my sanity, I created my own job once more. I had cleaned up after Mengele before, and I decided to do it a second time. After my earlier experience creating my own job, I kept a shovel and a broom hidden in some bushes. It was time to get them out again. I knew the German love of cleanliness and order, and the ramp was generally messy. In addition, when the people on the trains saw what was about to happen to them, they would throw away lots of food, including packages of tomatoes, pears, and plums.

The guards and captives moved around a lot, squashing a lot of the fruits and vegetables under tattered shoes, dirty feet, and jackboots, turning the ramp and the area nearby bright with the colors of smeared fruits and vegetables. Germans hate such a mess.

The mess they hated worse was the result of prisoners' losing control of their bowels or vomiting. The small mounds on the ramp would pile up and begin to stink. I decided to take advantage of the German revulsion.

One night, I retrieved my shovel and broom from their hiding place. For about fifteen minutes, I carted corpses out of the cattle cars and loaded suit-cases onto trucks. Then I started sweeping, and all those messy splotches on the ramp and on the grounds began to disappear. Mengele and his people loved it.

I used the routine I established the first night I tried this trick: spend ten to fifteen minutes unloading the train, then get my broom and shovel. Lots of times Mengele, the three doctors and the SS men would be standing near some of these piles. Mengele and his people would back away from the debris so I could clean up.

They look relieved I was doing it. They didn't want to step into any of those clumps. I was keeping all that stuff away from them, they thought, so they wouldn't mess up their boots. My cleaning up appealed to the German sense of order. That was why they thought my doing it had to be their idea.

Each evening, I continued to clean up the ramp; then I would move to the area next to it, and, finally, to the parking lot, where the gas chamber trucks stood. As more and more people finally realized what was happening, they, too, threw away their possessions and food. Even more of them lost control of their bodily functions. At that point, amid the trucks, smells, smoke, and chimneys belching fire, these people didn't have much doubt about their fate.

I had my priorities clearly in mind. I tried in every way to look out for my own good. I first combed the ramp for food among the dead's possessions. Then I looked for things I could barter for food. If I found anything, I always shared it with my friends. That's the way I've been all my life. This is my nature.

Children were my next priority. The best part of this job was that there were messes in many places throughout the camp, so I was allowed to go anywhere I wanted to go, a freedom nobody else had. I turned that fact toward saving the lives of many children.

After the first two months I was on the ramp, the policy on children changed. The Germans needed more and more workers in factories and camps, because they were losing manpower and the war. Mengele now was sending women accompanied by children to work camps instead of gas chambers. However, he still executed the children.

When that new policy began, the children routinely were taken off the ramp and put into a line on the other side of the train. They weren't allowed to return to their mothers, who were being shipped off to detention camps that night. When the Germans had enough old and sick people to be gassed, the children were mixed in with that group and taken off to their death.

The children's ages ranged from infant to middle teenager. Most of them sensed something was wrong. After they'd been separated from their mothers, I heard them crying and yelling, or just making animal-like sounds. From the other side of the train, I could hear the wails of the mothers whose children had been taken from them. Hearing these people cry out made my heart and head hurt. Many nights, even now, I can hear their terrified screams and their hopeless cries.

I decided to do something. One night, I took my broom and shovel over to the side where children were lined up. When I arrived on their side, about fifty children were mixed in with the old and the sick. The old people were wailing, "This is the end of us," and holding their heads and each other.

I saw the children's twisted faces, their tear-filled eyes, and my skin started itching. The kids could sense where they were going. Many were crying, "I want to see Mommy. I want Mommy."

"Come on," I whispered. "I will take you to see Mommy."

I grabbed three of them, all between the ages of five and seven. I put my hand over my mouth to show them they had to be quiet. Then I motioned them to follow me. Like little ducklings waddling after a mother duck, they followed me as I crawled under a railway car. We emerged on the other side, where the women were standing.

It was just the right time. The SS had left. Their main purpose was to be there when a train came in so they could force prisoners to go where the Germans wanted. After a train was gone, there was nothing for the SS to do. By that time, the women would be taken off to work camps very shortly.

Each of the children found his or her mother. Most of the people from the same street in a town would be bunched together. When the children spotted someone they knew, they also knew their mother was nearby. I didn't stay around for gratitude. I had to get back to my broom and shovel so the Germans wouldn't suspect me.

Every night for three months, I repeated the same routine. I only did it once a night. If the SS had spotted me, they would have shot me. I took so many chances doing other things, I couldn't afford this risk more than once a shift.

I deliberately picked children ages five to seven. They were old enough to be mobile and to follow directions. When I told them to be quiet, they listened. They also were small enough that the mothers could hide them on trains until they reached work camps.

There, at least, the children would have a fighting chance. Prisoners were beaten and starved in those camps, but they weren't systematically executed. This was late in the war. I'd heard from Max Stein that Hitler set up Theresienstadt, a model combination work camp and city in Germany, to show off to the Red Cross.

The Nazis wanted a few kids in these camps. If the children were sent along with their mothers, at least they would be left alone. I heard the same thing from prisoners being transferred from one work camp to another.

The risk was worth taking. If the children had stayed in the gassing line, they would have had no chance. I heard later some children I helped did survive, though I have no way of knowing.

I did it for another reason as well. Every night I thought to myself, *These kids could be my own brothers and sisters.* This was just something I had to do. I couldn't save them all. I feel bad I could save only a few.

Aside from food and a chance to save some children, there were other rewards for working on the ramp. I found valuables. One time I found a bag of onion rolls. I started eating, when my teeth hit metal. It was a gold coin. So I bit into another onion roll, then another. There were fifteen onion rolls; each had a gold coin inside.

What could I do? The guards were searching us every second day, so I had to put the coins somewhere. By this time, the Germans were losing the war badly, and the Swedish Red Cross was visiting occasionally.

The Germans now felt obliged to put on a good show. We had never had mattresses before. Now, the Germans had issued sacks of wood chips to sleep on. I wrapped my gold coins in toilet paper and stashed them in my mattress. The next day, they were gone. Some people working in the barracks were probably looking. They always seemed to know. I wasn't upset. It wasn't as though money was being stolen from my parents' house. Here, we all knew we would die soon.

Somehow, my continuing fantasy of having a family and a business still sustained me. But every waking moment, I also faced reality. I continued having these complicated feelings for the rest of my time as a prisoner.

Another time I was cleaning up and spotted a diamond ring. Unfortunately an SS captain, a cripple on a cane, saw me grab it. He stepped right on my hand, and I had to let go.

"Give it to me," he growled. I had no choice. This wasn't the last time he would make me suffer.

Aside from Mengele, the biggest threat to my personal safety was Hans, the *Kapo*, a German Jew. Hans was in charge of the 140 ramp workers on the night shift. He was about five feet, six inches. Pockmarks pitted his face. He liked beating us with the standard-issue cane, about an inch in diameter and three feet long. Hans enjoyed making people suffer and wanted to prove his loyalty to the Third Reich. By this time, Germany was so obviously losing the war most other *Kapos* had stopped beating us. Not Hans. Sometimes, when we would return from work, Hans would make us run double-time. Usually we could keep ahead of him, because we had eaten some food we had found near the ramp and had extra energy. But if Hans caught anybody, he would pound him repeatedly with his cane. He didn't need any excuses to beat us. He also ran through groups, assaulting whoever was in his way.

What Hans and many of the other *Kapos* did to us was beneath human behavior, especially what they did to their own people. The Polish *Kapos* treated the Poles badly; the Czech *Kapos* treated the Czechs badly. They treated us all as if we were animals, they tried to turn us into animals, and they acted as if they were animals themselves.

Once we got inside the barracks, though, we were fairly safe. I had an after-work routine which, I am convinced, helped save my life. By 7:00 A.M., we had to go to our bunks. Nobody dared disobey, but we didn't have to be in the barracks all day. So, after I slept for a few hours, I walked to the latrine, about a quarter of a mile from our barracks. I searched for discarded razor blades and soap chips, and I'd always find some of each.

I'd use the soap to lather my face, then squeeze at least one last shave from an old razor. I'd also wash my clothes and my body and hair. It may have been cold water, but it was water. I'd rinse off my shoes and comb my hair. That way, I felt fresh and clean. Sometimes, I even had a friend cut my hair.

Many of the guys didn't bother to shave or shower or do much of anything for themselves. They were disgusted with their lives, and they looked and smelled dirty. Keeping myself clean is, I am convinced, one of the reasons I survived. The Germans didn't like a man who smelled.

I felt that as long as I kept myself clean and did my work I was reasonably safe—as long as nobody knew that I was a member of the underground or that my sweeping job was nobody's idea but my own. My broom and shovel now let me wander around the camp almost at will.

We still had Sundays off—unless there were selections—and all of us could move around wherever we wanted. It always seemed ironic to me that the Nazis rested on what many people consider to be a day for religious worship.

I could even talk relatively freely with the *Sonderkommandos* then, though such contact was technically forbidden at any time. I knew what went on in their part of the camp. They would take whatever valuables they could from the corpses, then use these valuables to bribe the guards to smuggle them liquor, food, that kind of thing. They also would pay the Germans to let them talk to other prisoners through the barbed wire surrounding their camp.

Because I knew most of this group, I talked to them frequently and lifted their spirits by telling them how badly the war was going for the Germans. The camp atmosphere had changed. By now, the German war effort was in such shambles that the guards were openly muttering about it among themselves, and of course we overheard them. The engineers, still surveying fields for the master race's expansion of Auschwitz, openly talked about it when they were in the camp. And prisoners from countries such as Holland, now arriving daily at the camp in transit for work camps, openly talked about how the Allies were winning. The crumbling of the once-mighty German war machine was an open secret.

The *Sonderkommandos*, sealed off as they were from most of humanity, were unaware. Even though I couldn't deliver and retrieve messages anymore for the underground, what I did know about the war's progress was more than enough. One time Nuftul again asked me, "Joe, how come you got sent to the ramp and we ended up being sent to work in the crematoriums?"

"Just my luck," I replied, with a straight face. Letting even him know my secret was too dangerous. I wouldn't even have told my own brother.

One day I got word that Hymie and Nuftul would meet me at the *Sonderkommando* fence in back of their camp at six o'clock in the morning. When I showed up, one of them embraced me and said, "Joe, come with us."

"Are you crazy? The guards won't let me into your barracks."

"Don't worry."

I never found out how much it cost them to get me past their guards or to bribe the ones in my barracks to ignore my absence. Once inside, we sat down between two bunks in the back of the barracks. My two friends started swigging vodka out of a bottle, then passed it to me. I took a long, long, swallow. There also were pieces of bacon, bread, and salami on small pieces of paper, a feast that could have fed all of Barracks 8.

Hymie looked at me, sadly, bitterly, with a face pinched by fear and the witnessing of too many deaths. Slowly, reluctantly, he said, "This time is the last time you will see us. In a week, two weeks, maybe three weeks, we will be dead. They will gas us."

I looked at them in shock. "What do you mean? You know damned well *Sonderkommandos* are allowed to live longer than that. What the hell are you talking about?"

They both looked at me with sorrow.

"It's the last time, Joe, because we're going to blow up a crematorium," they both said at once. Then they started a frenzied binge of laughing, crying, eating, and drinking. I was stunned. After what seemed like several minutes of silence, I asked, in a squeaky voice, "When?"

I was frantic. These two were my last close friends in this world. The thought of their being gone seared my stomach and head more than I can describe.

"Two weeks. We need your help. We have the dynamite and detonator. Can you get us wires for the detonator?"

"Definitely," I said. "But why? Why are you doing this?"

"We want the world to know what is happening here. And even if the world never knows, we want to slow up the killing. Our deaths have to mean something. There will be one less crematorium," Hymie said in a voice hissing like a snake ready to strike.

Then we drank and ate. We talked about people we knew from our hometown. We talked about the guards, about women. We talked about everything except the awful fate that awaited them, no matter how their daring plan turned out. We spent most of the day talking, drinking, crying, hugging, and kissing each other on the cheek. This, we knew, would be the way our lives would come to an end.

I'm next, I thought, feeling very lonely.

When the party was over many hours later, my legs were too wobbly to stand up. I wasn't used to eating food, let alone absorbing huge quantities of vodka. Hymie and Nuftul carried me over to an ambulance.

They called one of the SS to help. The three of them carried me inside the ambulance and swung me onto the table. Then all the vodka was pumped out of my stomach. When I became conscious, I saw the SS man leaning over me.

"Whew, that guy is really loaded," he laughed.

The SS and Gestapo had become a lot friendlier. The Germans knew the war's end loomed, and they didn't want anybody remembering their brutality—as though any of us could forget.

That night I went to work. The trains carried in people from all over the world, and sometimes their possessions were bound together by electrical wire. After the load of prisoners had been dispatched and the crew was bundling the belongings left behind, I'd find any electrical wire available, then untie and hide it. When nobody was looking, I pulled up my shirt and wrapped the wire around my belly.

I'd arranged with Hymie and Nuftul that whenever I had some wire to deliver, I would go to the back of their barracks, walk casually, then, at a spot we'd agreed on, quickly scoop up some dirt, drop the bundled wire from my palm, replace the dirt, and walk on. The movements required only seconds. After about six deliveries, Hymie sent word they had enough wire.

As the seemingly never-ending parade of black locomotives chugged to the ramp, I was surprised to see how many people from ghettos or even concentration camps the Germans were piling in. This change raised opportunities for revenge, a chance to pay back the Jews and others who had turned against their own kind to gain an extra slice of bread or a more comfortable bed. The most blatant example I saw occurred in September 1944 when the Jewish policemen from the Polish city of Lodz were brought in. Among them was Chaim Rumkowski, president of the whole ghetto, as Lazar had been in our town. Rumkowski was getting the same reward as Lazar: death.

The Lodz Jewish Council, through the Jewish police there, had turned in about fifty Jews who had been underworld members in 1940. These guys had been thugs, thieves, and con men. Like Lazar, they'd have people steal for them, then ransom back the goods. The men had committed all kinds of crimes, except murder. Strangely, in Birkenau they were a closely knit lot, but kindly. A few had become powerful Senior Block Inmates, including Morris the Hasid, to whom I had paid the fifty dollars to get my job with the Czech.

There was also Blackie, who got his name because he was so dark-skinned. He had been a thief and a con man in Lodz, but here he was a man whose word was good and who took care of his people. It was Blackie I went to when I wanted a job for someone. I did it so often he once looked at me and asked, "Who else are you going to bring in here? Your uncle? Your cousin? Your nephew? No babies, Joe. I draw the line there. They're too young," he said, his dark skin framing a smile bright enough to light up the sky.

Even though they usually were good people, Morris, Blackie, and the others had vowed revenge on the Jewish policemen who had captured them. One night, the former thieves had their chance. They spotted the Jewish police contingent from Lodz emptying out of one of the cattle cars.

"We're going to have our revenge," Blackie whispered to me. "We're going to get them gassed."

The policemen didn't know which line was which. Mengele had put them into the group that was going to live and be shipped off to labor camps. Then a couple of the Lodz underground group, including Blackie, walked over to the Jewish police, looked them in the eye, then pointed over to the death line. The policemen, not knowing the difference, meekly obeyed and were marched to their death.

They joined Rumkowski, who was old and lame, and was being carried to the crematorium on a litter.

"Take a look," Blackie whispered to me. "Now he's in a litter. He sent a lot of us to the camps. Lots of us were gassed. It's his turn."

Rumkowski didn't know what was happening. He turned to me, of all people, and asked, "What goes on here?"

"Can't you smell? Can't you see the fire?" I replied, anger and revenge in my voice for what he had done to my friends.

"Where am I?"

"Auschwitz."

"Oh, my God," he said, smacking his forehead with his palm. Then he started reciting a Jewish prayer as two guards picked up his litter to carry him away.

There he was, a man who had been rich and powerful, in charge of a city out of which had poured the products of enormous factories. He thought he would save himself by doing the Germans' bidding. As they had for Lazar, the Nazis ultimately had more use for him dead than alive. I felt no sympathy, no pain. Rumkowski was a traitor and deserved a traitor's death.

Later, I talked to Blackie about what they had done to the Lodz Jewish police.

"You did what you did. I guess you had to do it," I told him.

"We were pushed out of the ghetto because we were in the underworld. I didn't know any better. I considered it my job, which I went to while people were sleeping in their beds. But we had a heart, and this guy didn't," Blackie said, looking grim.

In the late afternoon on a day in October 1944, about two weeks after I made my last drop, the entire camp shook and trembled. We saw a large smoke cloud hanging over the crematoriums. Then the Germans were everywhere, whistles and sirens blowing, machine gun clips clicking into place.

The Germans were in various states of dress, even in their underwear. Even so, they ran to the crematorium. I could see the guards and the SS surrounding the *Sonderkommando* barracks. Then I heard machine gun fire ripping through the afternoon. If anyone escaped, I never saw it. I am sure Hymie and Nuftul, my brave and beautiful friends, along with many others, were executed immediately, then taken to the ovens. A big puff of smoke and fire erupted from one of the crematoriums, even though no train had been there for an hour. The other ovens, though, seemed untouched.

Good-bye, Hymie. Good-bye, Nuftul, I grieved inside myself. *At least you're fighting back. At least you made your death count for something. Thank God people are starting to do something about this mess, even if they are going to die. Let the Germans feel how close the end of the war is coming. That will be our victory, because by the time the war will be over, we will be dead,* I thought.

I was always angry that the United States, England, and France had never launched an attack to destroy the crematoriums. They had the power to do it. At least Hymie and Nuftul died heroes.

Soon after the *Sonderkommando* uprising, I thought my own life was in deep jeopardy. The German war effort had been deteriorating for some time, and the Red Cross from Sweden and Switzerland was inspecting our camp periodically. The Germans apparently felt pressured to show Red Cross workers something which could be passed off as benign, even though it actually was part of their evil plan.

So, the Nazis used some slave labor to build a new gas chamber near existing ones in the rear of the camp. After the new structure was finished, one thousand of us were forced to line up outside it.

"We're going to give you a shower," said one of the guards, sounding almost gleeful.

We knew what that meant. We knew about the other gas chambers, and we knew the showerheads were dummies. We also had watched the building being built. We knew where the gas outlets were, and we knew where and how the gassing would be done. It was very similar to the others. The way they were going, if Hitler had more time, they would use this one, too. All of the others were being used at full capacity.

Then one of the soldiers ordered all of us to march through the doors of the structure. It looked like any other gas chamber. It was built of brick. It was one big room, about 150 feet wide, 200 feet deep, and 14 feet high. The floors were gray cement. The walls were whitewashed plaster, with eighty or more shower-heads each. The lighting heightened our sense of danger. The building had only a dozen low-wattage bulbs whose weak illumination encased the room in a dim, dingy, and menacing aura.

No use wasting a lot of light on people who haven't much time to live, I thought.

We knew what they were going to do to us. Most of us had survived many months, if not years, in this place, and we were under no illusions.

"Go into the extra room, take off your clothes, and leave them there," one of the guards barked.

We shuffled into the room and left our clothing, then went back out. We lined up underneath the showerheads.

We were sure our time had come. Most of us had been together for years. We knew this time would be the last we'd see each other. We started shaking hands and crying.

"This is it," I told people. "Like all the rest of us, we're going to die. Cry all you want, but it won't change anything."

People who shouldn't have had any tears left started sobbing. We heard some prolonged hissing. Then the pipes in the building started to rumble and shake. We knew our time was at an end.

PART IV

DARING AND DEATH

Chapter 19

Hangman

With the pipes in full rumble and a thousand of us ready to die, a miraculous thing happened. Water started dribbling out of the steel showerheads. Just a few drops at first, then a trickle, then a small, clear, steady stream. After about a minute, the water gushed out.

We all looked at each other in shock and amazement. My eyes widened to nearly double their usual size. I sniffed the air. I looked up at the air vents. Not a hint of the lethal cloud this place was designed for. I felt the frigid water hitting my skin. It was almost painful, because we'd not had a real shower in five years. Now, in the middle of this death chamber, the parts of myself I never really got to clean were being touched by water.

Everyone had waited with his eyes closed, in shock, waiting in a tomblike silence which almost echoed itself. When we heard the water dribbling, we opened our eyes and looked at each other, astonished. We'd been prepared to die, and instead our bodies were going to be cleansed. I watched caked black patches on my body and everybody else's turn to beige, then to streaks, then disappear altogether.

There was no soap in the gas chamber. In a death camp, whatever people owned they carried with them. When we saw what was happening, some of us ran for our clothing and pulled little pieces of soap out of the lining. I broke mine into smaller pieces, sharing them. Others did, too. The fact that the water was cold didn't matter. What mattered was that we were alive and rubbing little chips of soap all over our bodies. Feeling soap lather and so many layers of dirt peeling off was almost like being at a party.

Some of us started laughing, the hysterical laugh of the damned given an unexpected reprieve. Some prisoners laughed so hard they pounded the walls and floors and held their sides. The shrieks and roars of desperate laughter burst out of gaunt faces, revealing yellow and gray teeth and blackened gumlines. The sounds we made bounced off the walls, sounding like the braying of a thousand donkeys.

"Those crazy Germans. They were going to gas us. And instead they gave us a shower," one man guffawed, and many of us joined in. For people who had expected to be dead, this was a truly hilarious twist.

The shower lasted three or four minutes. Then we heard an order barked on the other side of the gas chamber door: "Get your clothes on. Get dressed."

As we filed out to the room where our clothing was, some of us whispered to each other, trying to figure out why the Germans had done something so nice. Most of us were silent and bewildered. We had no towels, of course, so we dried ourselves off with our pants and jackets, which immediately became soggy. While I felt my body heat trying to dry the shower water out of my uniform, the Germans' reasoning finally hit me.

"They wanted to test the shower in case the Swedish Red Cross wants to see it," I whispered to Frank. Frank nodded, then out of the side of his mouth, said, "I've never had such a good time being a guinea pig."

We walked outside in twos and threes, then lined up in military formation. There were a couple of guards, a *Stubendienst*, and a *Kapo*. The *Kapo*, an Austrian Jew and a decent man, just shook his head.

"Somebody's crazy here," he said.

Then we marched back to the camps, but most of us were still laughing out of hysterical relief.

Despite their underlying motive—testing out their new shower system—I was surprised the Nazis let us spend so long in there to lather up and actually cleanse our bodies. For them that was benevolent behavior, especially considering how badly the war was going for them. I knew from the underground's notes I carried back to camp that by this time the Allied forces had landed boats in France and Soviet forces were sweeping into Romania and Poland.

As the German war machine deteriorated, it was a time of extremes in Birkenau. Some things got a lot better. Some things got a lot worse. It was hard to absorb all the changes. Before, at least our lives, however short they might be, had some predictability from day to day. Now, it was hard to foresee what was going to happen.

I could see that German morale was shot. I started noticing dirt on the soldiers' necks. Their shoes no longer were shined; some were even scuffed. The guards used to wear the shirts buttoned up to their neck. Now their clothes hung ragged and neglected. Obviously they were sleeping outdoors and running from the Russians and the other Allies. Now, most of the guards had been relocated from lands the Germans once occupied: Poland, Russia, the Ukraine, and Romania.

Feeling the hot breath of defeat, the Germans lashed out in the one matter over which they had complete control: our lives. That was one of the things that got worse—a lot worse. They had stepped up their executions. They also accelerated their appropriation of slave labor to work in German bomb factories and to build bomb shelters for their own people.

The Germans had even found another use for what had been the Gypsy camp. About a week after the Gypsy liquidations, the Germans built a scaffolding about four feet deep and fifteen feet long near the camp entrance. On the platform were two poles standing vertically, supporting a single eight-foot horizontal wooden pole from which four nooses were suspended. Several stepladders waited on the ground nearby. The area was visible throughout the camp, because they wanted the hangings to be an object lesson.

A few weeks after the scaffolding was built, we saw some men forced up on the stepladders, which then were yanked away. The men fell like sacks of wheat, breaking their necks with their own weight. The hangings were done on a regular schedule, so we knew exactly when they would be. One thing about the Germans: they were very punctual. Some people wanted to watch. Not me. Almost always, the soon-to-be dead were people I knew. Almost always, the reason they were hanged was that they had escaped.

A sign of just how extreme was the German desperation, and how deep was their hatred of us, was the number of trains chugging into the camp, wheezing black smoke as they squealed to a stop beside the ramp. The procession never seemed to stop. I could see the prisoners were being crammed into the cars like cows off to the slaughterhouse. Now we were starting to see prisoners from other camps.

One sign of their discouragement was that the Germans weren't watching us closely anymore, so the prisoners would tell each other where they had come from. Some were from Russia, others from all over Poland. What hadn't changed was the Germans' rough rule of thumb: if they were old, young, or sick, they went to the crematoriums. If they were of working age and healthy, they were put in the former Gypsy camp, which now was being used as a kind of holding pen, except for the hanging area.

The need for slave labor helped make our lives a little more tolerable. Prisoners accumulated in holding pens there for a week or two, then were shipped off to

Germany or Austria as slave labor. The *Stubendiensts* and *Kapos* now had to behave somewhat reasonably. As much as they enjoyed whipping and beating us, as much as they enjoyed seeing us run, cringe, and bleed, we prisoners suddenly had become valuable commodities. They needed us to shore up their collapsing war effort, so we had to be in good enough shape to work. Beating a prisoner to death meant losing a valuable worker, a loss the Germans now could ill afford. We were still beaten, but a lot less often and not with bone-crushing, lethal force.

While that much of life was getting better for us, there was some irony for others. In this new situation, prisoners were being hauled in from other camps at an ever-increasing rate. When *Kapos* or *Stubendiensts* from other camps were shipped in as prisoners, they got no special privileges. I was better treated than some of them; I was allowed to live. For them, the same rules applied that they'd applied to others. If they could work, they were slave labor. If they were too ill, they would be gassed. Many of them had committed atrocities against the very prisoners with whom they were sharing space in cattle cars, but the prisoners were too afraid to kill them. It was ironic that the Germans often did the job instead.

In one way, the gassings produced a huge, if grim, bounty. When I was with the *Leichenkommandos*, picking up the dead, I saw enormous warehouses with workers sorting out piles of clothing as fast as they could. Most of the workers were women, some of whom were from my city. I couldn't ignore them. So on my *Leichenkommando* trips, I would slip them pieces of bread. They had soft jobs, but they had to produce work quickly if they wanted to keep their positions. Losing a job meant death.

As the pace of executions accelerated, the clothing warehouses became even more crammed. There were warehouses for men's jackets, for dresses. The Germans had separate warehouses for each kind of shoe: a warehouse for men's, another for women's. Both contained piles ranging from the scruffiest footwear to high-fashion leather. Every pair of shoes had a story and a dead person behind it. I didn't want to know the stories. I didn't have room in my soul for more pain.

However, the Germans also had a warehouse for children's shoes. That place broke my heart every time I saw it. Some of those shoes were so tiny, their dead owners couldn't have been more than a few months old.

So innocent, so clean. They did nothing to deserve this. Nothing. But they gas the children because the children can't work, I thought, mournfully. At such low points I screamed inside my mind, *Why doesn't the world come to save us? They know what's happening here. I carried the letters inside my rectum to the outside. I know they know. Where are they? Where are they?*

My own life had become a little more grim. Because I was on the ramp, I couldn't deliver messages anymore, and even the *Leichenkommandos* had stopped going out. The bright side, however, was that I still would see Max every once in a while. He often brought me good news, even occasional words of praise.

"You're still looking clean and neat, Joe. They like that. And I hear you're still trying to make sure people don't get beaten. You're keeping up the morale there, Joe," he would whisper warmly. "Do you know that?"

"Yeah, Max, I'm just trying hard to stay alive. Maybe a miracle will happen. Maybe a miracle will happen." I hadn't told Max about my dream. I knew he'd just laugh.

"Are you a saint, Joe? Can you predict the future?"

"No, I just try to keep hoping, Max. I just try to keep hoping."

"Things are changing, Joe," he whispered to me. "We can do a lot of things we couldn't do before. We're looking out for our people."

Then he would leave, and I would feel sad. Max was one of the few prisoners who kept up my morale. I had a world of respect for him. He was a fine human being. Not many of those people survived here.

Still, I tried my best to save a few people myself. Abe Blady was one of them. He had been shipped in from Russia. He looked a lot like my brother Hymie, who had been shot in the lumberyard. One night, Abe walked over to me while I was surrounded by other prisoners, most of whom were asking my advice or talking to me about various matters. Abe had a pleading look in his eye that I'd seen all too often in Birkenau.

"Help me, help me, please. I'm hungry, and I just came in. I don't have a job, and if I don't find one today, I'll end up in the crematorium," he said. Then he fell into my arms and started sobbing.

I was touched. I went to Blackie. "I've got a boy who needs a job. I want you to give him one."

"Is he your brother, your cousin?" Blackie said, with just a trace of exasperation.

"No, but the war's coming to an end. He's going to die."

"You already brought in Frank, Noah, and others."

"One more isn't going to hurt."

I looked at Blackie. He stared back.

He asked me, "When are you going to stop?"

"When the war is over. Then I'll stop."

Another man I saved was Hana. He had come from Lodz and followed me around a lot, always asking my advice. He worked in the hospital until it was shut down. He was about six feet, one inch, tall and was considered well educated because he'd finished high school. He liked my preaching about how miracles can happen. He was very religious, and he enjoyed my style. When the hospital was shut down and I was put on the ramp, he wanted to follow me. I had the connections, so I went to Blackie.

"If this guy doesn't have a job, he'll be dead by tomorrow. Give him a job," I demanded.

Blackie looked at me hard, then started laughing.

"Joe, if I don't keep an eye on you, you're going to bring all your relatives in here," he said, then walked away chuckling at his own joke. I knew he'd find a job for my newest friend. I glowed.

Even at triumphant moments like this, I could not help but be overwhelmed by the enormity of Auschwitz-Birkenau. It seemed big enough to me to be a small city. Camps upon camps upon camps. So many rows of barracks packed so closely together that, from an airplane, they probably looked like tiny little beads on a string.

This place is so big, how could the world not know about it? I screamed to myself. *Not a damned person lifts a finger to help us.*

Still, the arrogance of the Third Reich was visibly giving way to caution, even fear. The Germans were running very scared. I heard that Americans had crossed into German territory for the first time, near a place called Eupen.

Shortly after that, almost miraculously, the beatings seemed to stop completely. One of the extremes in this new situation would have been unthinkable even a month before: I knew that the underground now had connections with the SS and the guards. I could see it. Before, if somebody had marched even a hair out of step, the SS would have cracked that man with a cane. Now, if somebody missed a step, the SS ignored it.

During one of my meetings with Max, he asked me, "How are the beatings where you are? Have they quieted down?"

"Hardly anybody gets beaten now."

"That's what I thought," Max said, allowing himself a small smile.

About that same time, a train came in loaded with workers from my city, producing one of my best chances to help save a fair-sized group of people but also producing one of the worst beatings I'd had since I had been in the camp. The workers had been taken to factories outside our town to build German planes. Now the plane factory had been taken over by the Russians. These men were skilled workers—bricklayers, mechanics, tradespeople—and the Germans were going to send them to Germany to help the Nazi war effort.

First they chase us out of Germany. Now they're forcing us to go back into Germany. The Nazis must be getting very desperate, I thought.

Sam, one of my sister Fay's in-laws, was among them. I knew him because he'd been an inspector in one of Yudel's factories. My *landsmen* were put in the Gypsy camp, which was near my Barracks 8. I saw the poor guys standing by the barbed wire, hollow-eyed hunger on their faces, looking for someone they knew to get them food.

"Joe, Joe," Sam called out.

I waved at him, but I didn't dare approach. It was daylight, and I would have been gassed for doing that. I didn't know the rest of the people with him, but I could see they all were hungry.

One day I passed by them on my way somewhere else.

"I'll be here Saturday night, and I will throw things over the wires at this spot," I whispered out of the side of my mouth.

When Saturday night came, I had rolled-up shirts, food, and tobacco tucked away from my time at the ramp. I packed them all into bundles and crawled up to the fence, then threw the bundles over the now-electrified barbed wire. Then I started to crawl away.

"Stop," someone bellowed. I could feel sweat ooze out of my skin. "I saw you throw something over the fence. What did you throw them?"

"Nothing but bread I picked up on the ramp."

"Why?"

"They're hungry."

"So what?" he growled.

I turned around from my face-down position and looked. It was the same crippled bastard who had stepped on my hand and forced me to give up the diamond. He marched me to a barracks where there was a long oven. Almost all of the barracks had these ovens, which were only for show purposes if the Red Cross arrived. By this time, most barracks were empty, as this one was. He swung the oven door open on its side hinges and bellowed, "Put your head in, you fucking Jew bastard."

I did.

The oven had a musty smell from lack of use. I could feel my armpits gush. I knew the guy was just as likely to slam the door on my neck and break it. Instead, he closed the oven door, pinning my head inside the oven. Then he beat my back and rear end about twenty-five times with his cane. I counted the blows as they fell on me. The first few caused such a sharp pain I felt as though he'd cut off a finger. After about a dozen, my body stopped jumping around. I couldn't feel anything anymore.

God, God, is he going to break my spine? I worried, the thought dancing through the cloud of pain in my head.

When he stopped, he yelled at me, "Run, run, you Yiddish bastard. Run on your hands and knees."

As I dragged myself across the camp, I kept thinking about my *landsmen*. I kept thinking about their pain and their hunger and their lack of clothing. It helped my state of mind to focus on other people's pain as a distraction from my own. It also helped to blot out the pain.

"I'm not letting this swine tell me whether I can help my *landsmen*," I said to myself.

Later that night, some of the guys in my barracks surveyed my naked back and buttocks, which they said were black from the blood which had leaked out of my veins and into the surface of my skin. But I still wasn't about to be prevented from helping my people. In here, you gave loyalty to the people you knew. I knew one of the people in that group, and the others also were from my city. I had to help.

The next night, I went again at about 10:00 P.M. so I'd miss the guard, who probably checked at the same time every night. I'd stolen more food and clothing from the ramp. Pain was shooting through my back and legs, but I just kept crawling until I got near the wire at a place different from the night before. I threw rocks through the open barracks window until somebody looked out.

"I want to talk to Sam," I whispered.

Sam came out, and I started throwing things over the fence: shirts, bread, that kind of thing. I did this run about every three nights until they were sent to Germany, two or three weeks later.

One astonishing day, the Germans acted as if they were throwing a party. The *Stubendiensts* ordered each of us to walk toward the front of the barracks and pick up a small cardboard box on a table. Some of the packets contained a liquid which tasted like sweet milk. Other packets had cookies in them. Still a third packet had some sugar.

Each of us wolfed down whatever didn't appear to be too dangerous to our health. Even though the small individual boxes had Red Cross markings, we were always suspicious of generous gestures from the Germans. We couldn't drink the milk because our stomach couldn't take such rich food. We would throw up right away. The cookies were nice, but what we really wanted was bread. Still, we decided to eat what we could get. We all gobbled up our cookies and our sugar packets. It helped for a little while, and it fed us a little hope along with a little nourishment.

About a week later, in another combination of extremes, something happened which gave us a real reason for hope, only to have it crushed. The guards suddenly entered the barracks with some scarred wooden tables and set out a meal of bread and soup. The bread was freshly made, and the soup had been brought to a boil. The smells of both rose into our nostrils, and I almost cried. I hadn't smelled or seen food like this in more than two years, not even during my short stay in the hospital.

My stomach gurgled and growled, as did everybody else's. The gaseous noises almost sounded like a chorus of frogs. We were starving men, and a feast lay so near to us we almost could reach out and grab it.

"You are chosen people," the *Stubendeinst* told us, obviously not understanding the biblical irony. This time, we'd been chosen to get haircuts and a shave. I would give a haircut and shave to one guy, then he'd return the favor.

In addition, all of us also washed our clothes and scrubbed the barracks, made our bunks, and tidied up the floor. We couldn't say anything, and we certainly weren't allowed to eat the food which was within an arm's length. We felt good, though.

"At least we're seeing a little action," I told Frank.

The *Kapo* kept yelling at us to behave and be clean. Because we were two miles from the crematoriums, the bacon-like odor of charred flesh didn't hang over our barracks.

We suspected why the Germans suddenly were making our lives so tidy. The Red Cross had started to make appearances more frequently, and the Germans felt they had at least to pretend they were treating us humanely. On this occasion, which was about the middle of 1944, the Red Cross inspector finally arrived. There was no doubting he was someone from the outside. He wore tan civilian clothing and carried a briefcase. He wore a hat, like a salesman's, and arrived driving a car with the Red Cross insignia painted on the side. The inspector looked us over but didn't talk to us.

God, let them see what's really happening here. Let them know that this is a death camp. Every day thousands of souls are lost here, burning in hellfire flames that rise to the heavens, I bitterly thought. I was only one of thousands of people offering this prayer that day.

It was never answered. The inspector first went to the gas chamber which we'd recently completed. To the untrained eye, it looked like a large shower room. Then he came to our barracks. He walked in, and we were standing at attention, the piles of fresh food still within reach. "*Jawohl, jawohl, jawohl,*" he said, then walked out.

I have no doubt the inspector saw the other gas chambers and the crematoriums, but he didn't know what he was looking at. The Germans showed the Red Cross what they wanted them to see. To the untrained eye, a gas chamber just looked like a room for mass showers, and the inspectors never got to see the crematoriums.

About a minute after the inspector left, the SS just stood there and laughed at our wretched state.

"You want good clothes and food? Too damned bad," they yelled at us. "You think the Fatherland should give you good things? You, who will soon be dead? You soon will be food for the flies, nothing more."

Then they struck us with whips, kicked us with their hard boots, and beat us with their fists. We all scattered and ran out the door. They carted away the food table and chairs. Then the guards came back after us, beating us for several hours with canes, poles, their bare hands, whatever they wanted.

The air filled with the cries of the crushed and wounded. The prisoners yelled and screamed as they were hit, or fingers were crushed, or ears ripped off. I wasn't hurt badly. As always, I put my small size to good use by using some bigger men as shields.

Some things didn't change. The pace of the camp's executions still was at its highest pitch. Trains kept arriving at a rapid clip, largely from other German camps. It was the same every time. If the prisoners were physically fit, they were shipped to Germany as slave labor. If they weren't, they were gassed. The standards for who lived and who died hadn't altered much, even though the Germans needed slave labor worse than ever.

Fortunately, Mengele still acted the same—at least toward me. When he conducted selections, he still gave me that twisted half-smile. He was still trim, and I made sure his uniform was cleaned and pressed.

Despite Mengele's freshly scrubbed appearance, I could see how the war was crumbling even further for the Germans. There were many signs. For one, even the elite SS troops were standing guard. Before, they were considered too important. Now, the guards generally were more ragged. Their hair was growing shaggy, and stubble covered their faces. Most of them had a gaunt look, their boots were dirty, and their uniforms were even stained. I found out they were from the front, and Birkenau had become a kind of rest stop where they could get some food and sleep in a bed for a while.

Then, unbelievably, the pace of the executions got even more frantic. More and more death trains were piling up at the ramp. The people were packed in even tighter. Time was closing in. Other camps were being consolidated into ours even faster. Over a period of a couple of days, prisoners who had been in quarantine were stuffed into our barracks and into what had been the hospital barracks. Increasing the body count to as high as their ingenuity could muster seemed to be the Germans' top priority. The smell of roasted death hung heavier and thicker over the camp than it ever had before.

One morning, in December 1944, everything changed.

"*Raus, raus*, you pigs. *Raus*. Get dressed. Line up," a guard yelled.

We didn't even get the usual meager breakfast. We found ourselves outside, lined up with tens of thousands of other prisoners, all standing at attention. I wondered whether the Germans were going to execute us all in one last orgy of death. Instead, they started shipping us out. Each of us had to line up next to our respective barracks. There were still four or five barracks being occupied, with about one thousand prisoners in each. "Don't move around or we'll beat you," the guards growled.

Otherwise they didn't say much. We thought they'd march us into the woods, then mow us down with rifle fire. About midday, the guards called out, "March, you pitiful bastards, march."

I could feel my body get sweaty with fear again.

Now they're going to kill us. It's now, I thought.

We could feel the shock waves from Allied bombs. We knew Birkenau's end was coming. We were all equally sure our end was coming, too. In another fit of extremes, I was thrilled at the same time I was in the deepest despair.

The miracle I've been praying for has happened, I thought. *The Russians are coming, and soon there will be no more Birkenau. But will the rest of my miracle happen? Will I be a husband and father and have a lot of people working for me and own my own business? I don't think so. The Germans will want to destroy the Jews they have, even if they can't grab any more of us. I'm a dead man.*

Then it was the turn of Barracks 8. We lined up the usual five abreast to march out. Out of the corner of my eye I saw a man walk past me, briefly.

"Go into the sewer next to the pump house. Drop down into the sewer," he whispered in my ear. I didn't even know who he was, but I knew he must be from the underground. I didn't ask questions. The Germans were clearly intending to gas, hang, or shoot us.

I was standing next to Abe. We started marching, then I dropped out of line. Nobody saw me because everybody was absorbed with themselves. I ducked away from the group and flattened myself next to the pump house wall nearest to the sewer opening. A skinny cement square lay over it. I pushed it away and dropped down onto a metal ladder. Then I reached up, pulled the cover back to its original place, and climbed down the ladder.

Once I was inside, I noticed another man in the dim light, a man I had worked with at the hospital. I looked hard at him.

"What are you doing here?" I demanded in a startled voice.

"What are you doing here?" he replied, his own voice hoarse with fear.

We stared at each other for a few seconds, then nodded. We figured out that we both worked for the underground and had been told to jump into the sewer.

It wasn't a glorious way to hide. The stink and gas down there were so penetrating our eyes started stinging, and we had to put a handkerchief over our noses to breathe. I wondered what we were supposed to do when the danger passed and we got out of the sewer. Unfortunately, the guards were constantly counting us, and within thirty minutes they knew we were gone.

"What's going on? Two guys are missing," we could hear them yell in angry guttural tones. A piercing siren shrieked. Suddenly it was quiet. I thought everyone had marched out of camp, mercifully leaving us behind. I relaxed.

About a half-hour later, we could hear a kind of low growling, which got louder and meaner. It was the barking and snapping of a hundred German shepherds the Nazis had used to find us. The growling noise bounced off the cement walls and penetrated my head so much I had to cover my ears. After what seemed like seconds, they found us. The sound of the dogs' high-pitched whining and yipping and full-throated, menacing growls, was right over the sewer entrance.

Suddenly a loud voice yelled in Polish, "Open up, you Jewish pigs. Open up before we throw in hand grenades."

There wasn't much choice. We climbed out. There were perhaps forty guards, surrounded by yapping German shepherds, their gums flashing, their teeth bared and dripping. We put up our hands. Once we'd been found, most of the guards left, taking the dogs with them.

"Jewish pigs. You're less than rats," the remaining half-dozen guards yelled at us, shoving and kicking us toward the hanging area. Suddenly we found ourselves on top of some wooden scaffolding. Surrounded as we were, we couldn't see what was happening. Suddenly a thick and hairy noose dropped over my head and around my neck. The same happened to the other man. They put us each up on a stool, then adjusted the noose.

It's ironic that I, who have spent so much time outsmarting the Germans to keep myself and others alive, should be one of the last men to die in Birkenau. There is no justice after all, I thought to myself, my mind riddled with despair.

The SS guards surrounded us in a small circle, hatred leaping from their eyes. I knew they were already imagining us dead, our faces black, bodies swinging back and forth, pants stained from the loss of control of our bowels and bladder. They tested the stools, making sure they'd support us until a heavy boot kicked them away.

Though I didn't know my compatriot very well, he was the only friend I had in the world at that moment. I wanted my death to be noticed, to mean something to somebody, if only for a second.

"This is it," I told him in a sorrowful voice.

"It was good while it lasted. We lived long enough to see Hitler going under fast," he said, choking back a sob.

Chapter 20

Trapped
in
Concrete

J ust then, I heard shouting. I looked up and saw two figures running toward us, one of them clad in an SS uniform, the other a civilian. They were shouting and gesturing frantically. The SS soldier was screaming, "Stop. Stop. Don't do it."

The SS behind me said to the man to my right, "Let's wait. They must want something."

As the pair ran closer, both yelled out, "Stop it. Stop it."

I couldn't believe it. A blond-haired, blue-eyed man sporting the insignia of an SS captain shouting at the SS men surrounding me to stop my execution. I know my eyes must have been bulging out of my head. I didn't recognize either the civilian or the captain, but I knew what the word *stop* meant.

The two men reached the scaffolding and leaped up onto it.

"Don't. Nix. Don't hang them," the SS captain barked.

All of a sudden, the scratchy circle of hemp around my neck was jerked up over and off my head, temporarily flattening my nose.

"You're damned lucky, Jew. Goddamned lucky. I don't know who you know, but your ass just got saved from a hanging," one of the SS whispered in my ear.

I knew the underground had saved me, though how they found out where I was I couldn't begin to guess.

"This isn't real. This is a miracle," I said to myself.

I'd heard rumors from Max and Father that even the SS could see which way the war was going, and some of them might be captured and shot. I figured they wanted to have some friends on their side after the war, so they were playing both sides, Hitler's and the underground's. Still, this was a miracle, no matter how it had happened. I sent up a silent prayer.

The SS men shoved both me and the other prisoner off the scaffolding. We fell to our knees, and that must have appealed to the SS. The civilian and SS captain disappeared. Then I stood up and walked back to the camp with the man who was almost hanged with me. We introduced ourselves.

"My name is John," he said, offering a shaky hand. I clasped it. "Mine is Joe," I replied.

Our legs were rubbery with fear and relief. I looked out from the Gypsy camp, and I could see the Birkenau camp was largely empty. Just a few skeleton crews were waiting for the next train to move in some prisoners. The grim and forbidding walls somehow seemed smaller, less lethal. They had seen the most terrible sights humanity had ever inflicted on itself, but these walls now were a gesture whose meaning had vanished.

I was almost alone. The echoes of my steps in a barracks built for a thousand men sounded so empty, so pathetic, so small, so inconsequential. Just my tiny steps. Not much else except the man who'd been almost hanged with me and the mice for company.

I put my hands over my eyes and collapsed into tears, sobbing for the relief of having been spared, sobbing for the people I would never see again, sobbing for all the torture I was sure would come, sobbing for the fact I was still alive and so many bright lights had been extinguished. At that moment, I came as near as I ever did to letting the Germans crush my spirit.

John and I stayed there two more weeks. There were plenty of guards left. They had their own camp close to Birkenau. The guards told us the Germans wanted to have enough people gathered to fill a train before sending us somewhere else. But I heard rumors that a famous Russian brigade was heading toward Birkenau. If its soldiers found a German, they killed him. Still, I could see by their confident strutting that the Germans guarding us were certain nothing would happen, and they would still win the war.

We were there for two weeks in December while our barracks and the camp filled up again. It was only a few weeks until the end of 1944. It looked as though I might live to see the end of the year, anyway, and I began to feel a little hopeful.

At half its capacity, Birkenau had enough people for the Germans to transport an entire trainload of human cargo. All during that time, I could hear the muffled sounds of Allied bombs exploding throughout the night and the loud roar and whine of aircraft. No bombs or other explosives were tossed at us.

One day, with no warning, we were marched to the train station three miles away. This was the same station where my fellow prisoners and I had first picked up the walls of Birkenau and carried them to the construction site. They were the same walls that imprisoned me, my fellow Jews, and all the other persons the Nazis had caught. Now we were being marched to this same station to be forced into Germany, where they had tried so hard to eradicate us. The black locomotive, dappled with grime and soot, was puffing huge black clouds. Behind it stood the usual parade of cattle cars, stretching back endlessly. We were ordered into the cars. I stepped in, along with about seventy others. Then the door was shut, and we were bathed in a dusklike darkness. The usual small, dusty pane in each car let a little sunlight through.

The smell was almost overwhelming, a mixture of human and cattle excrement, along with coal dust. Coal powder lay like an inch-thick blanket on the floor of each car. When we entered, the dust would fly up in small clouds. Every time we moved, there would be more clouds. Within hours, we were coated with black.

We didn't know where we were going, but it took us almost four days to get there. Every couple of miles, the locomotive would stop with a hiss and a roar. The train would stand, like an impatient but helpless beast, as the Germans repaired the bombed track. Then we lurched forward again, only to stop a few miles farther and repeat the process.

There was no toilet, and even when we stopped, we weren't allowed to get out and relieve ourselves. Most of us had a bladder filled to bursting and some of us relieved ourselves in our pants. Our temporary home began to take on some indescribable smells.

Finally, the train stopped and we were let out. We looked almost comical, with our bodies covered head to toe with black dust. We were near a site where bombs were falling and it was too dangerous to keep moving. The Germans didn't care about our lives, but they feared they might be killed. The bombing was a strangely fascinating and beautiful sight, with its tangle of exploding lights and multicolored streaks and smoke trails.

The Germans kept us outside until morning. Suddenly, the air seemed vacant. The train cars rested snugly on the tracks and the skies no longer were filled with flash and smoke. The bombing had stopped.

That was excuse enough for the Germans, who pushed and shoved us back into the cars. We didn't start moving again until late that night. The train stopped three to four days later, and we were force-marched to one city. After a seven- or eight-hour march, we arrived at the factory where we were supposed to work. I guessed they didn't know what else to do with us.

From the outside, the factory was just a large concrete hulk amid expansive green woods coated by the whitest snow I've ever seen. By contrast, the factory was an ugly splotch on the land. We could see the percussive effects of the bombing had blown large chunks off the factory's exterior and out of the windows, leaving the remaining glass looking like broken teeth.

The wind was whipping the snow into powdery showers and clamping chill into our bones. The Germans had us march into the factory, which looked like a workplace begging for workers. We saw both order and disorder, a kind of symbol of German neatness and the chaos the Allies were visiting upon it. There were no planes. Some of the tools were hanging in tidy rows on pegs, and most workbenches had a thin layer of dust. In counterpoint, some tools, desks, workbenches, and tables were randomly scattered around the floor.

"My God," I said to myself. "It's empty. The Germans have abandoned it, and they're going to abandon us. They have no jobs for us, and no jobs means death."

I was wrong. The Germans marched us into the factory. Older soldiers were in charge of guarding us. We heard the cavernous factory doors slam shut, leaving us in near-darkness. The dampness and musty odors all rose into my nostrils. We didn't know how long we'd be there. There was no place to run, and I didn't think they were about to give us any food. Again, I was wrong. Once in a while the Germans brought in a few loaves of bread or a tiny kettle of soup. Then they stood back and laughed as we scrambled for the pitiful amount of nutrition.

We acted like animals. There was enough food for only a few people, and there were 350 of us. People would elbow each other out of the way, then push away still others from the steaming food. Whoever was near it had only a few seconds to grab a handful of bread or soup. To hold the food, we used whatever we could scrounge—a broken plate, an old can, anything—before a crowd of grasping hands pushed away the person nearest the food and other bodies surged forward.

As for me, I found a little shard of a broken plate and I tilted the kettle to pour soup into it. I did manage to grab a few slivers of bread.

At night, when I lay down to sleep, my heart pounded sluggishly, like a car engine working on its last drop of gas. My stomach and muscles were knotted and cramped. We all felt so weak that we were sure we'd die of starvation.

We soon learned why the Germans were no longer making planes there. The Allies were bombing the hell out of it. When the bombs would start to fall, the guards would let us stream out of the building to hide in the woods.

We should have been hiding behind trees, but we all took the opportunity to forage tree roots, as well as capture and swallow frogs, and eat red nuts so bitter they made our eyes water. We'd eat anything that would feed our bodies and keep us alive.

The orange, yellow, and black explosions were so near we could see every detail, while we ourselves were hopping around the woods trying to catch frogs. With two or three bombing runs a night, we had a couple of chances to feed ourselves in the darkness.

We were there for two weeks. Then once again I heard, *"Raus, Juden, raus,"* and we complied. Several hundred of us were force-marched once again, this time to another city. It took us four days with no food or water. We waited until the guards' backs were turned, then ate whatever we could pluck from the land: roots, grass, worms, and, of course, birds' eggs.

We stayed in the camp for two days. On my first day, I heard someone cry out, "Joe. Joe Rosenblum from Miedzyrzec."

I looked up and saw a Gentile I had known faintly in my hometown. In these places, the most casual acquaintances became treasured friends.

"I'm hungry. I haven't eaten much in days, weeks," I told him. I hadn't. The bombing runs in the last several nights had been so severe there was no chance to strip bark or hunt birds' eggs. Huddling next to a tree and hoping it would protect me from shrapnel had been all I could manage.

My new friend nodded and said, "Wait here. I'll get you food."

In about an hour, my friend returned and slipped me a few pieces of old bread. I ate two, then shared the rest.

At the end of two days, we marched off again. Every couple of hours, the Germans would stop the march and let us grab snow or slurp rainwater from puddles. The water they carried they reserved for themselves.

Some of us never made it. All along this march people would lie down by the side of the streets, dying, exhausted from the years of torture, beatings, and starvation. The rain came down in endless sheets. We were all drenched, and the weather was about forty degrees above zero.

It was a strange march. We knew we were in Germany. When we passed through the towns, we saw that some buildings had been hit. Their windows were standing vacant, with small shards of glass still in them, like the broken mouth of Checo the boxer after the Ukrainians beat him. Even so, many stores were still open.

The German townspeople, dressed in pressed pants, shirts, and dresses, hurried in and out of the shops. When they emerged, they carried small bundles. Nobody was rich enough to buy large amounts of food. The towns seemed almost normal. I could see youngsters throwing snowballs at each other, dogsleds ready for traveling. Despite all the bombing, the townspeople tried to act as though their lives were simply going to play out, unchanged.

"I'm so damned hungry, so hungry. Please throw us a little bit of food, a piece of bread, a piece of meat, something," I mentally begged the Germans.

Nothing. They looked at us casually and disdainfully, as though we were cockroaches scurrying away from the light.

Then we were again funneled into a long, winding ribbon of grimy cattle cars. The guards gave us each a slice of bread and a small tin cup of water. We had no sense of where we were going. We spent a couple of days in the darkened cars, lit only by the sun's erratically streaking through the usual single grimy windowpane. Quite a few people, drained of all that could sustain them, passed out, never to awaken again.

Often we would hear air raid sirens wailing, and the train would lurch to a stop. The guards slid back the doors and let us out of the cars, only to force us back moments later as the sirens sounded the all-clear. We didn't have a chance to go to the toilet.

Finally, late one evening, we arrived in a railroad station. I looked out the small window of our car and saw a sign saying, *Berlin*. Then, with great hissing and squealing, the train pulled off to a side track and parked. Someone bellowed over the loudspeaker, "Prisoners. The Swedish Red Cross has food for you."

The railroad car doors slid open, and there were barrels and barrels of steaming food, along with people in civilian clothing and metal ladles in their hands. My stomach felt as though someone were trying to rip it apart. I wanted to lunge for the food, but I knew the guards would crack me with a stick.

The civilians were supposed to ladle soup onto plates and pass them to us. As we all filed out of the car toward the waiting nourishment, air raid sirens started wailing louder and louder. The smell of the food was filling my nostrils, and I was standing in line, only seven feet away from the soup, when those earsplitting sirens sounded.

Then I saw Germans run out of a little office, screaming, with smiles on their face. "Take it away. Take it away," they screamed at the Red Cross workers. They reluctantly picked up their food barrels and looked at us soulfully. The workers genuinely wanted to give us food, but they couldn't. So close, so close to the food, but it was not to be. We were rushed back into the railroad cars, and the doors slammed behind us. My stomach, which had been on full alert ever since I saw the vegetables and meat peeking out over the tops of the barrels, began to ache so badly I doubled over with pain.

The Germans drove the train about a mile and a half from the station and brought it to a stop.

"*Raus, raus,*" they yelled as they slid the doors open. We had to walk out the doors. We wanted to run, but if we did, the guards would shoot us down. We took cover as best we could, huddling in bushes next to each other. At least we could use each other's body heat for warmth.

Soon the British bombers came, and we felt the ground shake and tremble with every detonation. It went on all night. I didn't get a shred of sleep. I just lay there with my eyes open, wondering when our liberators were going to do what our German captors had been unable to: end our lives.

The bombing's shock waves made the train cars jump up and down, as though each one had hiccups. None of us was going anywhere near the cars for fear they were too fat a target.

In the morning, when the bombing stopped, our train rolled on. Of course, we were given no food or water. We spent another several days in the train, stopping often for the bomb-ravaged tracks to be mended. We finally reached our new home, Kaufering, near Munich.

We all disembarked, black with coal dust grime. Then we had to march five miles to our new home. Remarkably, nobody died. We were eager to be some-place: we had been bounced around like battered balls, and we felt horribly dislocated.

We were heading for a satellite camp of Dachau. I knew where we were because guards had told us where we were going and said that several thousand prisoners were in each camp. When we arrived there in the late afternoon, we passed the kitchen. We could see big, shiny pots and could smell soup bubbling. It smelled as though it had meat in it.

"God, maybe we will eat decently," I prayed.

The camp consisted of about ten buildings, approximately two hundred feet long and fifteen feet wide. The guards pushed us along to our barracks as if we were animals, yelling the familiar "*Raus, raus, raus.*"

Inside, the buildings were nothing more than trenches in the ground and a roof of straw on top. The inside was built so low that it was only an inch or so taller than I was. The barracks really was nothing more than a series of long planks running the entire two hundred-foot length. The planks, which were about three feet above a dirt floor, were where prisoners slept at night. In the front were a couple of windows providing pale illumination.

I rested, while some of the men went to pick up the soup. We had about four hundred people in the barracks. When the men with the soup returned with a shiny pot, they had plastic cups. We formed a line, and we each got a cup, which was about a pint. After the starvation we had been through, even this pitifully small amount seemed like an ocean.

On top of that, the soup had a quarter of a potato and a few unidentifiable vegetables swimming in it. This dinner seemed like so much bounty, I was almost ready to wash my face in it. About 9:00 P.M., the guards came through bellowing at us to turn out the lights. There weren't many to turn off. There were a few small ones, maybe forty watts, in each corner. Of course there were no blankets, but we had a small stove the size of a bucket in the middle of the room. We looked for little things to keep us warm. The best way, it turned out, was to rip pieces off the wood planks to throw into the stove. We all sagged into a deep sleep.

A little after midnight, the dim bulbs flashed on, air raid sirens sounded, and the guards ran screaming through the barracks, "*Raus, raus.* We're going to the train station. *Raus.*"

In what was to become a nightly routine, we were loaded onto a train with only three boxcars. Loading took only a few minutes. Then the train's brakes squealed, the engine hissed, and the cars lurched forward. We were half-dead from carrying cement, so we just dropped off to sleep right there in the cattle car.

About an hour later, the train began to decelerate. I thought this was some kind of emergency. Many minutes later, the brakes squealed, the motion stopped, and I could see a sign which said we were at the Munich station.

I smelled smoke, and the air raid sirens were blaring. Something was wrong. A small part of the Munich train station was on fire. The Germans were running in all directions. The Allies had been dropping bombs there for half an hour. German commuters were scheduled to go to work around 5:30 in the morning, so our job was to get the train station cleaned up and ready for them.

This first night, fire trucks were squirting small streams of water onto the fire inside the station, which was about a half-mile long and wide. Dozens of railroad lines snaked around the center of the first floor.

"We're all alive," I told one of my companions. "No matter how bad this has been, we're all alive to see this happen. The best gift they could give us is to see the Munich station burning."

He nodded.

Meanwhile, there were huge piles of trash to clean up: bricks, cement, and wood, all the material shaken loose by the bombardment an hour before. The Germans certainly were clean and neat. There were no old sandwiches, peanut wrappers, or any other kind of human debris around, just the assorted chunks of the railroad station which had been ripped loose by the bombing. There were only a half dozen soldiers guarding 250 people, which meant our barracks alone had been forced into this work.

"No talking, prisoners. Just clean up this mess," one of the guards shouted. So we shoveled the debris into wheelbarrows, which we then rolled onto ramps and up into trucks waiting outside. During the five months we did this, we sometimes would end up staying later, even after 5:00 A.M., when the first commuters arrived.

"Please, just a small piece of bread from your lunch. We are so hungry. We haven't eaten in days," I would tell the passersby. Most just wrinkled their noses and ignored us, treating us as a little lower than vermin. Also, the guards were watching.

Only one time did anybody respond. He slowed down in the middle of his rapid walk, then dropped something dark out of his pocket. He dropped it where the guards couldn't see. I waited until the guards turned the other way, then casually walked over to it. It was a piece of dark bread, which I put into my pocket.

A few hours after we returned from our first night at the Munich station , the Germans made us walk more than two miles to go to our daytime job. We saw nothing but fields and huge underground bunkers, along with a train carrying cement. The tracks stopped right at the entrance to a building.

I also saw a huge gray concrete building, maybe two-thirds finished. The building was supposed to be a munitions factory. The Germans still thought they were going to win the war. There were thousands of guys there from all the camps. The train consisted of a half-mile of cattle cars filled with heavy cement sacks. It takes a good man to carry one. We had to pick up the cement sacks, hoist them, then march up a steep hill about fifty feet to the job site.

For weeks they gave us about the same amount of food as in Birkenau, which is to say, not much. The winter winds were blowing, the snow was piling up, and the Germans issued each of us a worn, paper-thin jacket. It was slender protection against the frigid weather and the marrow-penetrating winds.

We had to work with an army of Germans in green uniforms we called Todts, short for members of Organisation Todt. They were engineers, designing and constructing roads and highways for the German government. About fifty of them were there, and they were selfish and sadistic people. They wouldn't give us a piece of bread, or a shirt, or anything. They were part of the killing machine. They didn't lift a finger to help us, even though nobody would have beaten them for doing it.

One of them particularly enjoyed beating us with a pole so we'd keep unloading the trains full of cement. As soon as one train left, another took its place. However, he made it a point not to beat us so much we couldn't carry the bags. We now got a little more food, but hardly enough to keep a man going.

"What a difference," I told Frank. "In Birkenau they didn't care whether they clubbed us to death. In fact, they enjoyed it. They figured there was always somebody to replace us. Now we're so valuable they can't afford to cripple us because that will be one less worker. Instead they just starve us."

The Todts all had big guts, so they were obviously well fed. They also had good shoes and clean bodies. They didn't have much to do except watch us. We did all the work.

There was no bombing during the day, though all day long the sky would be black with American planes. The noise was so loud we covered our ears. To us, the sound was more soul-filling than the finest song. It meant the Americans were winning.

The Americans were flying so low over Munich, Stuttgart, lots of big cities, that we could see their flag insignia. It was like watching bumper-to-bumper traffic, so many planes passed over us. Our site was too small a target to bother with.

I couldn't hear a single cough of antiaircraft fire, nor could I hear the sounds of any kind of dogfight between planes. I guessed that the German air force had been largely eliminated, and the Germans were in very deep trouble indeed.

"We'd like to pray to God we can survive this and talk about what those bastards, murderers, and sadists did to us. They're getting paid back," is what most of us said to each other daily.

We fantasized about what the German cities would look like after being bombed. But the sadist Todt would crack his pole around our shoulders and we'd have to go back to work. I worked under him for three months, but I kept dreaming my dream.

Most days we would stop work about 5:00 P.M., when the Germans would feed us a thin soup and a piece of bread. Then we'd be allowed to sleep.

Occasionally, as we were cleaning up the Munich station, one of the guards would toss a piece of bread into a group of us, then expect us to all dive for it and tear at it as starving animals would. He wasn't disappointed. Every one of us ran for that small piece of bread, knocking people out of our way, falling down and getting up, using up our precious energy. The guards would just point and laugh. This was their idea of sport.

"We would be better off being a dog or a rat. At least we could crawl behind something and hide so nobody could hurt us," I told some of the men working with me at the station.

As the bombs kept raining on Germany, we took that as our satisfaction. We could see when the Allied planes returned, they had not even the smallest bullet holes in them. That meant they were meeting no resistance.

Every night, the prisoners talked to each other. Covered by darkness, we communicated more honestly.

"All we've seen for six years was worth every minute," I'd whisper. "To see them running for their lives. For every plane flying back, there's another one heading for Germany. There is a God in heaven, and He's getting His revenge. So are we. So are we."

Chapter 21

Sabotage and Glue

We had a big problem right in our own ranks: Ben the Shoemaker. Ben was seven feet tall, with muscles rippling like a bag of snakes.

Ben was a bully, always screaming and yelling at the rest of us. He had a voice like an angry elephant's, and his yelling was so loud it bounced off walls. Ben attacked people. He pushed them, hard, with the back of his hand, and they went flying across the room.

The way he acted was typical of our situation. People became animals, and the bigger and stronger prisoners beat up and harassed the smaller ones.

His yelling consisted largely of cursing, such as bellowing, "You stupid son of a bitch." If some of the guys were moving too slowly because they were starving, he screamed at them to move. If he felt he didn't have enough room lying down, he'd threaten people until they moved into someone else's precious space just to give his huge body more room. He was a big guy, and we were little guys. When the Germans served soup, he was the first to get it by pushing everybody else aside.

There was a hot plate in the middle of the barracks which he always used. The Germans paid him to mend their shoes, and they usually paid in potatoes and carrots as well as bread.

The rest of the guys could barely walk, they were so weak. Some of them couldn't even lift their heads, so Ben made them lie down and stay away from the barracks hot plate, just to be a bully. We were too weak and tired to fight him.

"This bastard is no better than the Germans," I told one of the prisoners. "He is big. He finds small and weak people and then beats the hell out of them. The Germans have a big army and they find small and weak countries and then beat the hell out of them. At heart, this guy's a real Nazi."

One day, I heard Ben screaming so loudly everyone was running from him. He was seated on one of the long planks that served as our beds. His screaming was particularly shrill. I was just entering the barracks, and I was so angry and disgusted with his bullying, I just snapped. I ran the length of the barracks, leaped onto him before he could get up and grabbed him by the head. My Russian partisan training took over. I grabbed him by the throat, then sank my thumbs into his windpipe. He started turning blue.

"It's going to stop today," I yelled at him. "There's going to be peace here. If you start yelling at people again, if you push them, I'm going to do this again and again until you stop."

His face got purple, his eyes bugged out, and he foamed at the mouth, but he wouldn't give in.

"If you're not going to stop this, I'm going to do this to you again. It's going to stop today. Enough, dammit, enough," I screamed at him, grinding my thumbs even harder into his windpipe.

After about three minutes, I let go of his throat. I didn't want to hurt him severely, just to scare him. Ben coughed and spluttered and tried massaging his sore windpipe. I discovered I'd been holding my own breath.

"OK, OK, I won't do it anymore," he croaked, his voice still hoarse, his shoulders hunched.

"You had better put that thought into action. Shape up or I'll do that again," I yelled at him.

After that, Ben was a decent human being. He didn't yell, didn't shove his way to the head of the line. He bothered nobody, and nobody bothered him.

Now, people respected me even more. They kept thanking me for putting Ben in his place, but I just nodded. I couldn't tell anyone I'd learned those tricks from the partisans. I simply had used their training and picked the right place and time, and it worked.

I tried to keep up morale. I kept telling the boys that the war might be near the end, that maybe a miracle could happen. I kept on preaching to them, no matter how bad things looked. Even the *Kapos* and the foremen respected me.

I never shouted, never swore at them. I gave them respect, even though they didn't deserve it, and I got respect in return.

Their respect didn't feed me, though. I had to do that for myself. I was always looking for dead birds which I could clean and put on the hot plate. I would even climb tree when I saw a bird's nest and get the eggs. Of course, I was always picking through the garbage. When I was picked to peel potatoes in the kitchen, I would fill my pockets and pants with fat peelings.

Others weren't so lucky. Of the thousand or so men in our camp, about ten died each day from beatings, starvation, or sickness caused by exposure to the snow, cold, and ice. The only oppression we didn't have here was Mengele's selections. Here, we had only natural selection at work. As a result of the climate and the hard work of carrying cement bags up steep hills, the mind and body of many prisoners just collapsed, hollowed out by the harsh conditions. The bodies were thrown into a wagon and carted off.

Food was still our biggest problem. One of our major complaints was the soup. It was barely more than water. It had no meat, no potatoes, nothing more than a little beef flavoring. Ladling out the soup was supposed to be a plum job, but everybody who had it was accused of favoring someone. One day, in the midst of the usual bickering about the soup, one person yelled out, "I'd let Joe Rosenblum do it. He's fair."

The rest of the group turned to me.

"OK, Joe, you do it, and we'll see what happens."

So I did it, and I gave everybody else so much soup there wasn't enough left for me. I could only wipe my fingers on the side of the soup kettle, then lick the droplets off my fingers.

For three nights, I ladled the soup for two hundred people from a battered fifteen-gallon kettle. Each night, I did it with such a generous hand there was nothing left for me. I was flattered, but this honor could end up starving me to death. I resigned the job.

I yelled out to the entire barracks: "Boys, now are you happy? I gave everybody else all the soup. There's nothing else there. There just isn't enough to go around. I resign."

Somebody else took over, but nobody argued with him. I had proved there wasn't enough soup to give everybody a hearty portion.

The best way I found to get food was to steal it from the Todt engineers. They all brought their own little sacks of food. I'd find one, snatch something out, then get a few quick bites before I was discovered. They'd beat me, but so what? I had endured that before. They didn't have guns, and they weren't allowed to beat us so much that we couldn't work, so what did I care?

Still, there was no getting out of my job lugging cement. We had to carry the bags uphill to a series of underground tunnels. When we carried the bags from the train into one of the tunnels, there were no guards, just the engineers from Organisation Todt watching us. Nobody was worried about our escaping. There was nowhere to run, because we were in the middle of Germany.

The tunnels had been bomb shelters. Now the Nazis had moved munitions factories in there.

"They still think they're going to win the war," I muttered to myself. "They don't give a damn which of us they take down with them."

We had to carry the cement bags all the way into the back of the tunnel, about 250 feet. In the coolness, hundreds of us would walk along the cement pathways in an unsteady line, until we arrived at a large opening filled with cement mixers, lights, ladders, and people climbing all over, as though it were an ant farm.

We would dump the bag on a pile next to the cement mixer, then turn around and go back down the path, out into the bitter cold climate. Then we climbed down the hill, picked up a bag, and started back. The bags were a heavy load even for someone healthy and well fed. For someone who was weak from hunger, cold, and beatings, the load was staggering. We each carried about thirty bags a day. I was used to such work, because I had loaded goods in my father's warehouse. The trick was to put the load atop my right shoulder, where I balanced it with my stronger hand and arm. As a result, my right shoulder became much more muscular than my left.

If any prisoner was so drained that he fell over from the weight of the bag and couldn't walk, large and belligerent foremen beat him with a thick stick. Under the crunch and rain of blows, he would stagger to his feet, pick up the bag, and then unsteadily begin the journey again. Quite a few prisoners, however, couldn't get up. Because they couldn't work anymore, they were beaten to death.

For the living, perhaps the worst part of the job was that cement droppings accumulated on the neck and back. The sacks weren't airproof, and little sprays of powder would fly out occasionally. The rain, snow, and sweat dampened them and made them cake on our bodies, because cement dries fast. We had no water to wash with, so the little stringy pieces of cement kept accumulating. There was a chemical in it which made the strings burn like fire on human flesh. After about four months, my neck and back were almost gray with cement.

The winds still whipped around us, almost picking us up and carrying us away. Early in the morning, the temperature felt as though it were forty degrees below zero. When we were working, we shook out the empty cement bags. We washed them with rain or snow, then put them into our lightweight jacket and shoes as insulation.

The pain from the burning cement globules collecting on my back and neck was gradually getting worse. All the water available was used to mix cement. If the foreman and Todts weren't looking, I would scoop up some of the water to drink, but there was no time for washing. The fiery pain was so intense I felt I would die.

One day I was carrying some tools back to the tool shed after work was over. Near the camp there was a fountain, though I never figured out why it was there. Geyser-like water gushed six feet high, then turned into craggy blocks of ice in the circular tub surrounding the fountain itself.

I stared. Dusk was gathering strength, and I shivered a little. I continued staring at the fountain and listened to its gushing water. I could feel cement burning into my neck and back. Suddenly, without thinking, I yanked off my thin jacket and shirt.

Whatever is going to happen, will happen, I thought. *I can't go on like this. If I don't wash off this cement, I'll die.*

I jumped into the fountain and started scrubbing the cement with the icy water, which felt like stabbing knives as it hit my skin. I rubbed and rubbed, and after I softened up the cement I plucked little pieces off my skin.

I drew a crowd of twenty Germans going home from work. "Take a look at what that guy is doing. My God," one of them yelled out. I could see their bulging eyes and hanging jaws, but I didn't care. They all had fur-lined jackets and boots, plus warm sweaters, and here I was with a thin, ragged jacket and my shirt off.

Several of the Germans watching me were so astonished they made the Sign of the Cross in front of themselves while my skin turned a bright cherry.

My God, I thought. *These Germans think of me as less than a human being, less than an animal. But here they are, invoking their own God because of me. In itself, that's a miracle. God must be protecting me. He must want my dream to happen.*

I almost chanted this thought to myself several times as I scrubbed off the cement. As cold as the water and weather were, I was numb. After a couple of minutes, my red skin was plucked clean of cement, so I stepped out of the fountain and dried off with my jacket. I still wore my pants, shoes, and socks.

After I had finished, one of the German Todt guards who had crossed himself stepped forward and said, in a low and shaky voice, what they all had been thinking.

"My God, man. How can you wash up in this weather? It's freezing, the water is freezing, you must be freezing. How can you do this?"

"I can't go on feeling the cement eating up my body. I had to get it off me or die," I told him in German.

He looked at me with a mixture of respect and wonder, handed me a piece of bread, then walked away. I took the tools back to the tool shed, though all the while I could hear the din of people murmuring to each other, "My God, how can he do that?"

The next day I was walking past the fountain again, and the Todt who asked me how I could do that crazy stunt was waiting for me, a small bundle in his hand. It was a couple of old shirts. They were stained and wrinkled, and they had holes, but they also had long sleeves.

"Put them on," he said thrusting them toward me.

"*Danke schön*," I said, and slipped one onto my thin body.

I smiled. I felt I was due for a little break after so many years of starvation and cold, but there wasn't much time to gloat over my new wardrobe. My life and the life of every other prisoner there were in constant danger. Our shuttle trip between the camp and the Munich station continued almost every night while the Allies dropped bombs on the streets of Munich and nearby cities.

On the way to the station, huddled together with the other stinking bodies to keep warm, I also felt warmed by revenge.

"God, God, you're so good to us," I said to myself. "You're destroying them, you're playing their death song, and you're letting us listen to your music. Let them feel our pain. Let them feel our pain."

Then we would make the Munich station tidy for the next day's load of Germans trying to escape the inevitable. When we arrived, rubble and concrete littered the station's floor, thrown there by the percussive effects of the bombs. Each night there was a little more rubble after the bombers paid a visit.

The Germans still left no garbage to slip into our clothing, not even a dead dog to slice open. I was thrilled every night to see how badly the Germans were being battered. On the way back, I could just imagine the Germans, with gaunt faces, sunken eyes, holding small sacks of food and each other, worrying over whether their homes would be taken and they would be killed.

"Just as my family and my people did on the death trains. Let them feel what it was like. Let them know just the slightest bit of how we suffered," I told the other prisoners almost every time we rode back from the cleanup.

We were all fairly feeble ourselves. We had lasted through six years of war, enduring cold, near-starvation diets, beatings, and all the pain the Germans could inflict on us. We were rapidly losing our will to live.

For me, there was some comfort. Hana, one of the boys I had saved, was still with me asking me for help. I had known him for a long time. The partisans had taught me how to take care of myself. Hana, however, had been ripped out of his home at the age of sixteen, and he knew nothing of such things. He was religious, tall, and not very muscular. As always, the Russian prisoners, among others, tried to bully the rest of us. They knew better than to try that abuse with me, but Hana was a different matter. One day he was waiting in line for a little bit of soup. Suddenly, two Russian boys stormed in and yanked several people out of line, including Hana. I wasn't about to put up with that.

I stood right in front of them, even though they were two inches taller. They were very skinny, but they were bullies.

"Get out," I said, pushing them so hard they fell over. The foreman came running. He had been with me in Birkenau.

"What happened, Joe?"

"I pushed them. They fell over. They were trying to kick this man," I said, pointing at Hana. "Look at this boy. He can't fight these bullies."

The foreman looked darkly at the Russians. "Is this what happened?" he asked, a bitter edge to his voice.

The Russians cringed and hung their heads. They knew everybody had seen what they'd done. "Yes, yes, we did that," one of them whispered.

Then the foreman yelled at the Russians: "Hey, get your butt out of here. You came last. That guy was here first. Go to the back of the line, and if you don't get soup, too damned bad."

The Russians backed away and let Hana back in line. Because more people had come in the meantime, they had to go back even farther in the line than if they'd just taken their rightful places. They were lucky. They eventually did get soup.

After it was all over and I was back in line to get my soup, the man ladling out the thin, meager liquid looked at me strangely.

"Why do you fight for him? You've got your own ass to worry about," he asked, while pouring a little extra soup into my battered metal bowl.

"Look at my friend. He's going to die if he doesn't get some soup. These guys were going to get his soup. This place is first come, first served. They came in last. To hell with them."

All the time I was talking, the soup guy was nodding.

"You're doing the right thing. If he's your friend, you should fight for him."

I thought, *You have to fight for a friend, especially in here. Enemies are all around us. Friends are too hard to find not to keep them alive when you can.*

Sometimes, though, it was every man for himself. The foreman who ran our lives still had a vicious streak. One day he was late for work. We were supposed to use shovels and picks to clean up cement and dirt from the factory construction. Of course, the tools were locked up in storage. We waited about an hour.

Given a choice, we would have gone back to the barracks and gone to bed or broken into the storage locker ourselves and started working. Either move would have gotten us into big trouble.

So we sat down, sprawled out, and tried to catch some sleep while we were waiting. Suddenly we heard a huge roar. The foreman was drunkenly swaying in front of us, screaming.

"Pigs, Jewish swine. You bastards just sit around here not working. Why the hell aren't you doing your work? Go to work."

Worse, he had a shovel and was swinging it at us. He was six foot three, in his late twenties, with a bad temper. He just kept swinging the shovel handle.

261

One swipe laid open the side of a prisoner's face. It was a good thing we had lots of piles of cement bags lying around to protect ourselves. Everyone ran for his life. The shovel blade occasionally caught a glint of sunlight as the SS kept swinging.

Of a work party of perhaps fifty, seven were cut open. Some were hit in the head, and the fingers of some others were gashed. Some he kicked in the butt, others he punched in the face. We were so weak we just fell over. Then he'd kick and beat us more.

He kept going in a drunken frenzy for about ninety minutes. Finally, he quieted down, and we all started carrying the bags.

In the larger war, the Battle of the Bulge had been launched on December 16 and would last for nine days. I knew about it; we all knew about it, because now we were getting our information straight from the Germans. When we cleaned up the Munich station, we saw German newspapers lying all over the place. We would put them in our shoes, or we would use them to wipe our rear ends.

Sometimes we'd find tobacco in the newspapers, so we would hide it in our pockets and take the papers back to camp. When nobody was looking, many of us rolled up parts of the paper and some tobacco into a cigarette, then smoked it. Not me. Whatever tobacco I found I gave to my friends.

Before we would use the papers for any other purpose, however, we would read them. Quite a few of us could read German because most of us spoke Yiddish and Polish, which are related to the German language. We hungrily devoured every scrap of information. We'd usually read the papers on our half-hour lunch break. When the guards asked us what we were doing with their papers, we'd say we were putting them into our shoes. That they understood.

When I first read about the Battle of the Bulge, I felt my bladder quiver and my pores sweat. I was afraid the Germans might win. They sure were getting cocky.

"We're going to make it," I heard them say to each other. "We have new weapons, and we're going to take the world." That's also what the newspapers were saying. The guards were strutting arrogantly.

We, however, were feeling the heavy hand of fear suffocating what little hope we had. Now we could only cross our fingers that the Allied planes would do their job.

Those aircraft now swarmed over us by the thousands, blackening the sky from 7:30 in the morning until dark. So thick were their numbers that we couldn't see the sky, and that was why for the most part we worked in a kind of twilight. But for us, that darkness was the light of hope. At night, our short sleep often was disturbed by the faint tremors of British bombing. However, knowing the Germans were being killed warmed us even in winter's chill.

The next day, the German newspapers proclaimed that the Russians were raping German daughters and wives and urged the Germans to fight back. According to the papers, the Russians were vicious to the Germans. I was reading German newspapers, of course, so I had to consider just how much of it was propaganda.

"Still, I hope every word is true," I told Frank. "I hope the Russians are doing to the Germans every bit of what I read there."

Others were far less hopeful.

"The Allies are losing the war. We're all dead men. The only hope we have is the Russian front," Frank would say.

One night when we were cleaning up the station, we found a newspaper story which electrified us all: Dresden had been firebombed in February 1945, and 100,000 had been injured.

I could feel myself become warm inside, just visualizing a German city being consumed by fire. The whispered conversations among the rest of the prisoners showed they felt the same. All of us were still tired, hungry, and cold. This news gave us a shot of life.

"It gives us hope. It gives us hope. It feels beautiful," most of them said.

The Germans, however, were not about to give us a better chance to live. The amount of food we were getting was next to nothing. We had started out with a loaf of bread for four people, which meant a little piece of bread and some watery soup for dinner, with flavored hot water for breakfast and lunch. Now the loaf of bread we were getting was for five people, and the soup was even more watery. We kept working as hard as we could. Those of us whose strength gave out simply died. Day after day, people would just fall over and pass out from starvation. Every morning we awakened to find a few of us had died during the night.

I continued looking for any kind of food I could find. Birds' nests still were my favorite, both for the eggs and for the birds. I'd break the bird's neck, then pluck off the feathers and cook it in the little barracks oven, which was also our wood-burning stove. Of course, I always shared with my friends.

One day a guard called my name and that of two others. I was astonished. After all these years of addressing us by our numbers, the Germans were finally calling us by our names. Something was changing. The two others were elderly Lithuanian Jews. The three of us walked to the guard, who looked at us hard:

"You're a mechanic?" he asked sternly.

The other two, who were sheet metal workers, just nodded their heads. I wasn't a mechanic, and I was sure they knew it. I still didn't have the faintest idea what this was about. But I could sense that maybe there was more to this than just a job reassignment.

"I'm not a mechanic, but I'm good with my hands and I worked on a farm where I had to fix things all the time," I said.

Under ordinary circumstances, I wouldn't have been so honest, but something wasn't kosher here. These guys really were mechanics, so I knew I'd be found out right away. I sensed there was more to this, and I should tell the truth. I thought the guard knew who I was, but I didn't know who he was.

The guard took us to a munitions factory a half-mile away. A slender man in his early twenties waited for us there. We were still in the little camps surrounding Dachau. The man looked at us and said, in both Polish and German, "You're going to work in a factory. It's a lot cleaner than where you were. In here, they make antiaircraft shells. You know what you have to do."

He looked at all of us meaningfully and stared hard at me in particular. If we had any doubts about what he meant, he cleared them away immediately.

"They're making the antiaircraft shells that shoot down planes. It would be better if the planes weren't shot down," he said. "You have to figure out how to do whatever you can do to shorten the war, and that means doing whatever you can. Every little bit helps."

He escorted us into the factory and waved farewell, saying, "Do whatever they tell you to do."

I looked around at my new job assignment. There were foreigners from many countries, Czechoslovakia, the Ukraine, others. They were not prisoners, and their round cheeks and normal-sized bodies said they were getting enough to eat. More starvation was ahead, but I still was gleeful.

"The underground has found me. Even in this godforsaken place, the underground has found me," I said to myself, rejoicing inside. I suddenly felt protected, the way I felt in Birkenau.

It felt strange to look back at Birkenau as a safe haven. There, I had the security of knowing the underground was looking out for my best interests. After I left Birkenau, I had not seen Max, or Mengele's secretary, or Father. There was nobody to look after my life except me, and I felt lonely. Now, I knew I had been found, and I felt good.

I now lived in Dachau's Camp Number One. Some things weren't much of an improvement. The barracks were the same, the food no better. What was an improvement was working inside instead of outside. There were numerous work-benches where people built antiaircraft shells, and the three of us worked at the same table.

The process was actually pretty simple. First, four-by-eight-foot metal sheets were cut into twelve-by-eight-inch pieces. Then the metal was formed into shell casings. I had an idea: we'd have our own assembly line. I used the jigsaw to cut the metal and the other two prisoners then formed the metal into the casing. After that, they glued paper inside the casing, then took the casing to the next table.

Work was the easy part. The hard part was finding food to eat. We all envied the foreigners, who had volunteered to work in Germany. They all got big bowls of soup, too much to eat for one meal, especially because they had their lunch with them.

Our stomachs growled just thinking about that soup. I tried eating the glue we used inside the casing for five or six days. It burned in my stomach, which knotted up and then made me vomit. All three of us tried this glue diet, and we all got sick.

We had to find another way to get food. I had an idea. The foreigners probably wanted to take that extra soup home, but they had no buckets to do it with. We would make their buckets. Using some metal I held back from the casing assembly line, I made up a small bucket the size of two fists and offered it to one of the foreigners just before he was about to leave.

"Want to buy it so you can take soup home?" I asked.

He looked closely at it. "Yeah, yeah, sure. I'll give you a piece of bread and some of the soup," he said.

Jackpot. I made a bucket a day, trading it for a little bit of soup and a piece of bread. I shared my food with the two Lithuanians. We figured out a way to make a lot of buckets. Each metal sheet made seven to eight antiaircraft shells. We would make perhaps three, then cut up the remaining metal for soup buckets. We hid what we were doing by cutting up the leftover metal into very small pieces, so the missing amount wouldn't be detected.

We also cut up a number of sheets into pieces so small they couldn't be made into shells. The Lithuanians didn't know I was connected with the underground, but they knew what we were doing was sabotage. We all knew we were taking a chance, but the war was nearly over. If we kept making soup buckets, maybe we could outlast the Germans. So widespread was the belief the war was about to end that the factory owners only showed up about an hour a week. The foremen didn't care. When we could feel tremors from a bombing run, we would run outside to look.

At least there was something to see in the April weather. For us, bombing runs were like small holidays. There were thousands and thousands of planes, and the sky kept getting darker.

Even though the working conditions were better, we still were malnourished. We were getting two meals a day, mostly a thin soup. Usually there was abandoned food all over the place: soup, bread, a little meat. The civilian workers left it behind because they'd had enough to eat. We weren't allowed to have it, of course.

After about thirty days of our making our little soup buckets, one of the guards walked up behind the Lithuanians and grabbed one by the shoulders.

"What are you doing? What are you making?" he screamed.

The Lithuanians shrugged their shoulders. They didn't speak German, so the guard came to me. I answered honestly.

"We were starving, so we sold about thirty little buckets to get some food. Every little bit helps."

The guard stared at me long and hard, then walked away. The three of us were called into the office. We were met by a nicely dressed man who owned the factory and the manager, who was a woman. They sat us down in small chairs. The owner looked at us in a surprisingly kindly way.

"Look," he said. "Don't do this sabotage. If they find out you're making fewer shells than you're supposed to, you're dead."

"But we're hungry," I said. "We've been hungry for six years and this is the hungriest we've ever been. We've got to eat."

"I know. You look skinny. But the soldiers will shoot you without blinking," the owner said, with some compassion. "This is sabotage and you'll be killed for it. We're letting you off this time because we feel sorry for you. Look, the end of the war is only weeks away. You've managed to make it through years of abuse. Why get killed so close to the end?"

"Ja, ja, they'll kill you," the manager echoed.

Fortunately, they didn't know I'd also cut up and discarded several metal sheets a day. After we left the office, the Lithuanians looked at me. They wanted to know what had happened. I told them quickly in the little bit of Lithuanian I had come to know that the Germans knew about the lunch buckets.

"They will shoot us if we make any more buckets," I told them.

The Lithuanians almost cried. That little bit of extra food had made us all feel stronger. Actually, we didn't have much choice: we had run out of metal to make the buckets.

A few days later, in mid-April, guards told us to line up.

"*Raus, raus, raus*, you scum, *raus*, now," they yelled at us.

The weather actually was pleasant. The temperature was about forty degrees and partly sunny. We were lined up the usual five abreast and marched out from our camp. Our small band joined marching groups from another camp, and then another. Soon we were all marching on the Autobahn, perhaps fifteen thousand strong. We marched for a couple of days, with no food and no water.

We had to stay in formation and march very smartly, or we'd be kicked. Some men fainted and were rolled to the side of the road. They were probably shot. Generally, though, the first few days weren't so bad. People still had a little bit of energy, and the warm weather made us feel better. We didn't know where we were going, but the road signs said we were headed toward Munich.

"We're heading to Dachau, Joe," Frank told me. Dachau and Munich were in the same direction, about thirty miles away.

"How do you know?"

"One of the guys overheard the Germans talking," whispered Frank out of the corner of his mouth.

When the march ended at a large sign which said _Dachau_, our stomachs were gnawing in hunger. We had all heard of Dachau, the notorious death camp, in our small satellite camps. We had no idea what awaited us there. And if we had known, we would have been terrified down to the marrow of our bones.

Chapter 22

Death
on the
March

Dachau was an impressive sight, with a six-foot fence of wood and concertina wire around it. I had been through a lot of camps by now, but I never expected Dachau to be the last one. It was almost as notorious as Birkenau.

"The war is closing in on the Germans. We're going to be gassed. They'll want their revenge," I whispered to Hana as we marched toward the mouth of the camp.

The weather was chilly, about thirty-five degrees, and that seemed fitting. The other prisoners murmured among themselves the thoughts I had just expressed.

"The war's coming to an end. They want to get rid of us. They just need a crematorium and a big space to bury us," one of the men in front of me said. "They just want to do it in their usual way: neat and orderly."

When we marched into Dachau, we were all shocked. Instead of being the usual model of Aryan organization, the entire camp was in disarray. Thousands of other prisoners had been taken in before us. They were wandering around aimlessly or sitting in small ragged clusters.

We arrived late in the afternoon. Like everyone else, we didn't know where to go or what to do. Thousands of prisoners came marching in even after our group arrived. Dachau's satellite camps were being emptied, and people were running around trying to figure out what to do. The first order of business was finding a place to sleep. When we pounded on the barracks doors, nobody let us in. The prisoners who had arrived in time to grab a bunk weren't about to surrender theirs.

Prisoners coming in after we did had the same problems. They had been marching for several days with no food or water, then just let loose. It was like never-ending herds of cattle being led into the slaughterhouse holding pens.

There was one improvement in our situation. The Germans had cleaned out the clothing warehouses and dumped all the garments near the mouth of the camp. Through the years that Dachau had been open, tens of thousands of prisoners had gone through and left behind mountains of clothing.

The bundles were neatly packed and reinforced with wire or rope, a typical German method. The piles were stacked in several ten-foot-high lumpy mounds. We welcomed a chance to change into anything else. The clothing we'd been wearing had rotted away from the rain, the beatings, our sweat, and the abrasions of the cement bags. What remained was simply cloth strips held together by threads, with thin ribbons of our flesh showing through.

The piles kept dwindling as people stole clothing from them after dark. After night cloaked our own efforts, Frank, I, and many others dove toward the piles and pulled out jackets, sweaters, long-sleeved shirts, whatever we could find. There was so much clothing, we almost looked like little kids playing in the grownups' closet. After grabbing new clothing, Frank and I and several other prisoners slept on the ground in the center of camp, bundling together so our body heat kept us warm.

Prisoners were still dying. The Germans continued to stack corpses neatly right outside the barracks. Most of the bodies were gaunt-faced and even a little bloated, typical signs of starvation. Nobody was committing suicide, however.

"Maybe a miracle will happen. Maybe the Germans will give up before we die. Maybe we can survive," I preached at people.

What gave us the most hope was feeling the bombing tremors at night, and, deliciously, sometimes even during the day. Hearing those bombs explode was almost like listening to a lullaby.

Conditions were wretched. Those prisoners who had previously been in the camp had their routine and their bunks. Those of us not so fortunate slept outside. It was April, but the cold had yet to leave this part of Germany and the rain hit like ice pellets.

The disarray worsened. We were running wild. We didn't know where to go, what to do, or how to eat. We had to scrounge all over the camp, but very few of us punched each other over scraps. Most of us were old-timers and knew better than to waste precious energy fighting.

All of us looked around, and we were unsettled.

"What are they going to do with us, Joe?" Frank asked, a despairing look I hadn't seen before settling on his face. "There are so many of us, it would take them weeks just to gas us."

I just shook my head. I had no idea.

The Germans seemed as confused as we were. Every couple of hours the air raid sirens would shriek, and the Germans would run for cover. We saw them jump into cars and trucks. In a chorus of tire squeals and dust clouds, they'd head for somewhere else, only to return when the all-clear signal sounded. We were too weak to escape. This kind of disarray was proof that their discipline had broken down.

To me, this was just another camp. We were strangers here. If they had wanted to keep us working, they would have kept us in the small camps. Even though I had been there only a few days, the place was stuffed with so many people, I didn't think they could squeeze in a pin, let alone another human body.

We were all down to skeleton and flesh. Every part of my ribs showed through my skin. I saw in a pane of glass that my eyes had dulled. I was worried. I knew I had to get food and shelter or I would die.

Things began to change quickly on our last days in Dachau. The public address system, long silent, suddenly crackled. Human breath exploded into the microphone, as someone blew into it to make sure it worked.

"We're going to hand out cans of meat," the tinny, anonymous voice said in German. "Line up just inside the gate."

Suddenly the thousands of listless bodies erupted into action and swarmed to the designated area. Fearful the Germans would run out of food, prisoners pushed and shoved to get a place in line, but only a little. Nobody had the strength to do more.

Frank and I were almost the first to get our tins, because we deliberately stayed close to the gate. In my experience, that was where the Germans handed things out. After we got our meat, Frank and I walked a distance away. I leaned over and whispered in his ear.

"I've got an idea. Everything's a mess. Let's change clothes so they won't recognize us and get another can of meat apiece. We'll go separately."

Frank nodded, and I handed my can to him. Letting someone else hold your food was the ultimate sign of trust in these circumstances. I took off my sweater and Frank wrapped the cans in it. I went through the line. The cans were in big boxes next to the guardhouse. The Germans never looked us in the face, so when one of the guards noted my presence, he just handed me another can, and waved me on. I walked back toward Frank.

"It's your turn," I whispered.

Frank handed me the cans and went back in line to be handed his second portion. It took a few hours, but he got it. Then he returned, and we ran into a shadowed corner behind some German vehicles. We peeled back the top on one of the cans, and the smell almost made our stomachs cramp, it was so good.

We ate the horsemeat immediately. We used our whole hands and stuffed it into our faces. Our faces were smeared with fat after we were through, but we were too hungry to care. Besides, having the meat was dangerous because somebody might grab it from us. At least it now was safe in our stomachs.

After tearing through the first can, we slept on top of the other three tins so they wouldn't be stolen. Before dark the next day, we went off in a corner again and ate a second can. Again, we slept on top of the remainder.

The next day I turned to Frank and said, "We have to eat the rest of this meat. If we don't, somebody will steal it from us. This way, we'll make sure we've used it ourselves."

We did.

We didn't know what was going to happen, and I was pretty sure the Germans didn't know, either. The day after we finished our last two cans, the public address system again burst out an order: "Line up. Line up," and that was it. Nothing else. Not even a good-bye.

We started marching in midmorning in a single column several miles long. The first couple of days we made good time, though we had no idea where we were going.

I looked around. We were marching briskly, considering our malnourished condition. I almost laughed at the guards. They were all in their fifties. Though they all wore uniforms, they clearly were not the pick of German manhood. The gray hair, pot bellies, and slouching almost made me wish for Birkenau. At least there the Germans had trim and toned bodies, and they commanded respect. If my own situation hadn't been so desperate, I would have pitied the guards.

However, they still had rifles. They also had backpacks with a spare shirt and pants in them. Two days after the march began, seven wagons materialized, confiscated from nearby families. The wagons were supposed to be drawn by horses, but I knew from my time in the *Leichenkommandos* what would happen. The Germans grabbed a dozen prisoners and thrust them toward the wagons. "Let's go. Let's move," the guards ordered, then threw their backpacks into the wagons.

There was a rope in the middle of the space where the horses usually were, and the men were positioned in equal numbers on each side of the rope. A couple more were lined up across the back of the wagon to push. Those prisoners peeked into the wagons; that is how we came to know that each of the seven held the guards' personal belongings, such as shoes, underwear, razor blades, a shaving kit.

"Pull," one of the guards commanded those prisoners in front of the wagon, and they did.

We kept marching, with no food, no water, for several more days. Men were dropping by the hundreds near the side of the road in pitiful lumps, there to be shot whenever a German guard took the time to bother.

Those prisoners who pulled the wagons were exhausted quickly, and that condition could be deadly. I figured out that if we got up while the others were still asleep and moved away from the wagons, the Germans wouldn't pick us for wagon duty.

Several days later, we began to understand where we were headed. We could see distant mountains, and we knew we were aiming for the Swiss border. We couldn't figure out why they were taking us there. As we marched higher and higher, the air was thinning. The highway was a skinny fifteen to twenty feet wide. I looked over the edge and saw a long drop down. As we marched farther up the mountains, we started seeing snow patches, then more and more snow, with snow banks two feet high.

We were so weak we didn't know the difference between being sick and not being sick. We had to sleep in the snow with no blankets. More people were dying, either falling over in their tracks or not getting up the next day. Those who couldn't keep marching were hit in the back by a German rifle butt and ordered to keep moving. If that didn't work, they were left by the side of the road to be shot.

The war was right on top of us. All night long, while we were sprawled out on the snow, we could hear the heavy artillery's BOOM, BOOM, BOOM, BOOM, and the rattle of rifle fire. I figured the Germans were retreating to Switzerland, but I couldn't imagine why they were taking us with them. Throughout our sleepless night, we could hear wagons and horses retreating, and bullets started whistling past our heads.

We were numb. We didn't know what to think or feel. We just couldn't figure out what they were going to do with us.

If they're going to kill us, let them do it now, I screamed in my mind.

The guards were tired. They were angry that they had to push us to keep moving and that we were so weak. They clubbed us constantly with their rifle butts.

The road we were on ran between two mountains. Germans were trying to retreat down the mountainside next to the eastern side of the road. The Americans and British were trying to advance along the mountain flanking the western side. Anyone on the highway itself was sandwiched between the two warring armies.

Sometimes at night a hot piece of shrapnel came slicing through, shearing off a head or an arm. The only sign would be a muffled scream. In the morning, the bodies of the dead were left where they fell. The injured were left to bleed to death.

We didn't know what would happen to us from one moment to the next, and we had no time or energy for pity or compassion. We were cold, wet, miserable, and tired. Hunger bored into our souls.

Almost all the shooting and bombing were at night. When we got up in the mornings, the guards instantly started smashing rifle butts into us, screaming, "Let's move," in German. The ones who couldn't move were left behind.

"I wish we had electric wires, so we could just throw ourselves on them," Frank muttered one day. I didn't argue. In fact, I felt so defeated, I was thinking the same thing.

We passed through farm villages every couple of miles. We saw chickens and pigs running around the yard making noises. Our stomachs made noises, too, as we dreamed of what kind of cooked dishes each of those animals could become.

We had to figure out how to feed ourselves in spite of the guards, or we would perish. I watched the guards and their movements. I also peered at the farmyards' chickens, and pigs, as well as the garbage left for them to eat.

That night, I told Frank I had a plan.

"Listen, if we're fast on our feet, we can feed ourselves while those German bastards aren't looking. All we need are a little coordination and some hand signals."

"Damn, Joe, nothing's been that easy since we ended up in these goddamned camps. As for food, the Germans would just as soon see us starve," Frank said.

Then, while darkness hid us, I told him my plan. I'd noticed the guards marched backward for two to three minutes to keep an eye on prisoners behind them. Then they'd march face forward, eying prisoners in front of them.

"As soon as the guards have their backs turned toward us," I told Frank, "you or I can run off the road and into one of the barnyards. We'll scoop into our pockets whatever garbage has been left for the pigs or chickens."

Frank looked at me with wonder.

"But Joe. How do we know when to get back?"

"You got to figure the guards will go through a cycle of facing our group again before they turn the other way. Whichever of us is still marching will hold up his hand and pump it up and down twice when the guards have their backs turned again. Whoever is in the barnyard will run back into line. Then we'll share the food with our friends. Whoever was still marching that time will dive into the barnyard next time, using the same system."

The reason we could bring off this plan was that the marching slowed whenever we reached a village. That day, we marched through many villages, and we succeeded in grabbing food almost every time.

It took a certain timing. We only did it when we were marching, because the Germans would shoot us in a second if they saw us. We also looked closely to make sure nobody was standing outside the farmhouse. Frank and I were fast. We also shared the booty with the other marchers, who were too weak to do it themselves.

I also had a second plan for stealing food, this time from the German soldiers. We were going to die anyway, so why not?

Trucks carried in the guards' food every day, dropping off sacks in the morning after breakfast. The food sacks were put into the back of every wagon holding the guards' possessions. Of course the Jews were pulling each wagon, and some were pushing from the back. The Germans now were marching us even during part of the night.

I stole a spoon and sharpened it on various rocks during the next few days. During the day, we still foraged for food at the farmhouses. We were near the end of our strength. While we were marching, I filled Frank in on the rest of my plan.

"Frank, when it's dark, you and I will push one of the wagons. We'll slit the food sack with the spoon edge, eat the food, then throw the sack into a ditch so they won't be able to trace where it went. They won't be able to see what we're doing."

Frank smiled the biggest smile I had seen from him in months. It worked. The first night we positioned ourselves so that we pushed one of the wagons at night. We knew which bag had the food because we could smell the salami. Frank slit the food bag, and we started eating as we pushed. We kept eating and eating. We slipped the rest of the food into our shirts and pants, then threw the bag away.

Later, after we'd stopped pushing and were lying down for the night, we shared our food with our friends.

"Where did you get this food?" they would ask, with a gasp.

"Don't ask questions. Just eat, eat, eat," we'd tell them. They grabbed the food and stuffed it into their faces.

The next night we felt bolder after having pulled off our little trick, so we slit open two food bags in a wagon. The line crookedly stretched out for eight or ten miles, so nobody was watching the wagons very closely.

As I tossed each bag into the ditch, I thought: *Let the German bastards feel what it's like to go hungry. Let them feel their bodies get colder and colder because they can't fight off the chill. Let them feel wet and cold, just as we do and have for several years.*

In the morning, when the guards went to get their food just before dawn, the sounds we heard were so funny we could barely keep our lips closed. Our stomachs ached from working so hard to contain our belly laughs. The guards ran from one wagon to another, looking for their food supplies. Of course we'd already eaten them. They screamed at each other: "Dumbkopf. Dumbkopf. You've forgotten which wagon you put the food in? Now we're not going to get anything to eat." The other guards shrugged and threw up their hands. We giggled, quietly.

Frank and I did this trick three times. We didn't want to overdo it. Meanwhile, the bombing was getting worse. At night we could hear "Kerwump, kerwump,

kerwump," as the bombs landed and exploded. Every morning when I got up, I noticed the rapidly thinning ranks of the guards. They were deserting in droves.

We didn't have that luxury. We were getting rail-thin and so weak our marching line became increasingly strung out. Every morning, more people had died. With gusty winds, pellet-hard rain, and a thin coating of snow covering everything, we were miserable.

"They still don't know where they're taking us, so they just might shoot us all," I whispered to Frank.

Sometimes we slept by the side of the road, sometimes in the forest. It was too cold and wet to actually sleep, so we just shivered. When we got up in the morning, there were always hundreds of corpses sprawled there, mouths open. The Germans didn't have to shoot us. Hunger and exhaustion did the job for them.

We had started with about 120,000 people, and we were down to about 80,000. The line was stretching out even farther because people were slowing down, they were running out of strength. The weather was getting worse, with lots of rain mixed with snow. The remaining guards wielded their rifle butts mercilessly.

When I looked down at the rest of the marchers, some of them were so far behind they resembled pinpricks on the landscape. Many of us were still living. That isn't what the Germans wanted. I spoke what the others were thinking:

"Look, just because we have survived so far doesn't mean the Germans will keep us alive. The closer we get to Switzerland, the likelier it is they'll gun us all down as revenge for losing the war, then run across the border."

Everyone who heard me nodded his head. It was inconceivable that the Germans would let us live.

We had been on this march for nearly ten days. As bad as the days were, the nights were more fearful when we heard the Americans and French bombing and shooting. I knew who was bombing because I could hear the guards talking.

"We're surrounded. We don't know where we're going or what we're doing. We don't know what the hell we're going to do with all these Jews. We just have to keep going toward the border," the guards said, never saying why.

The piercing whistle of heavy artillery over our heads now was close to nonstop at night.

"Let's press ourselves as close to the ground as possible in the ditches," I whispered to our group. "If you have to scoop out some snow so you can lie even flatter, then do it. It might save your life for another night."

After about the twelfth day, the killing got even worse. The Germans marched us to a place where a mountain stood next to a highway. The mountain was covered with snow, and the snow was piling up in thick, fluffy mounds, making passage almost impossible, so the retreating German army congregated where we were.

They had wagons drawn by huge Belgian horses and they were stopping there for the night. They had food, of course. We didn't see their wagons coming then, because this was evening. When the guards stopped us that night, they barked: "Lie low. Lie low. We're going to stay here." They didn't tell us why we were stopping and they didn't hold a meeting to ask our opinions.

Chapter 23

Freedom
for
What?

We found the deepest ditches we could, then lay as flat as possible. We also entwined ourselves together to exchange body heat. About dusk we could hear artillery starting again.

All night we were lying in the ditches. We were too scared even to put our heads up to see what was happening, but we could hear the artillery's nonstop "Kerwump, kerwump." We didn't sleep. We barely dared to breathe.

When we got up and looked down the road, we saw hundreds of the Belgian horses lying in the snow, blood pools forming around them, their eyes clouded over or shot out. Body parts had been blown off, and blood was streaming everywhere.

When I saw that sight, I told the others to cut off pieces of the horses' flesh. Frank and I used our sharpened spoon. The horsemeat seemed to be a good idea, but our bodies couldn't digest it. I needed the sustenance, but the meat was too rubbery, too hard, too thick. We couldn't chew it enough to swallow it.

We kept marching. Every five or ten miles, we would see a sign saying we were so many kilometers from the Swiss border. The guards would call out, "Faster, faster," and crack somebody with a rifle butt. Even though they knew they were losing the war and they were surrounded, even then, they still treated us as scum.

The next night, there were far fewer of us, and a number of guards had disappeared as well. We were crippled, miserable, hungry, sick. We looked like our worst nightmares. There were still thousands and thousands of us left. However, it was clear that another week of this would kill us all.

This night we all slept in the woods, next to the riverbanks, wherever we could find a spot that was low, protected, or both. The "BOOM, BOOM, BOOM" of the artillery shells exploded right over our heads, preceded by the piercing whistle announcing their arrival. The noise, a constant companion, assaulted our ears repeatedly. We could smell smoke, a really pungent, charred smell, while fire lit the night.

"It's almost over," I told Frank. "Even if it goes on for another couple of days, we're all dead."

My legs were getting wobbly from exhaustion. I couldn't sleep. I would just begin to doze off when the screaming of the artillery shells would pierce the night, seemingly right above our heads. In the midst of the shells whistling and the wind carrying the battle noises, I was terrified.

When we started marching the next day, the landscape was littered with so many dead horses and people that we had to toss them to the side in order to pass by. There were more and more human and animal corpses every day. We couldn't stop. We had to keep going and leave them behind.

As night fell and the whistling sounds and explosions of artillery shells cranked up again, the Germans did something highly unusual. The old guards escorted us to a barn near the road, and I could see other groups being escorted to other nearby barns.

The guards pushed us in, then turned us loose to climb up the bales of hay to find a place to rest. Of course, we had no food. The guards' lantern flickered in the middle of the barn floor.

We all were drained of energy and clammy wet from the cold and rain. Our stomachs cried out for food, but everything else inside us was exhausted. Our bodies chose to attend to the exhaustion. We all tumbled into the sweet-smelling hay. The deep snores and wheezing I heard told me all the others were asleep. I listened to the guards chatting with each other while the ropelike smell of their cigarettes assaulted my nostrils.

I fell asleep around midnight. I dreamed of being liberated, of the Germans' disappearing and the Americans' taking care of me and all the other walking skeletons we had become. I dreamed, and I hoped.

Probably not more than two hours later, I woke up. Judging by the wheezing and snoring, I was the only one awake. I heard the grinding and bouncing of armored cars, of tanks, of people talking.

I ran outside the barn. The night was inky black. I didn't see the guards, who had disappeared from the barn floor. I heard talking, but not the guttural accents of the Germans. I knew a little English, and I'd heard it quite a few times. The language I heard now sounded more melodious than German. I saw tanks which seemed the size of houses. I hadn't seen any German tanks that size.

I walked toward the sounds, which were perhaps twenty-five feet away, not even trying to conceal myself. I figured even if it were the Germans, I had nothing to lose. I was cold and wet, and I didn't care anymore. But I also felt in my gut that it was somebody else.

It was the Americans.

As soon as I stepped out onto the highway, the soldiers covered their eyes and cried out, "Oh my God, oh my God." They kept marching, but they had food in their pockets and bags, and they held it out to me, pleading, "Here, take it; put it into your pockets."

They produced food from everywhere, cookies, candies, food rations. I saw a big army with healthy soldiers dressed to fight. Prisoners started dribbling out of the barns—first in ones and twos, then threes and fours, and then huge swarms of frail and hobbling human beings. They limped over to the Americans.

"Americans, Americans, Americans. We're liberated. My God, we're liberated," they screamed.

We all started kissing each other and jumping up and down, the closest to a full-fledged jig our weakened bodies would allow us.

The big tanks kept rolling and the soldiers kept marching, but they filled our pockets with food, most of which we didn't know how to eat. I didn't care. I ate everything they gave me.

"If I die, I die," I called out.

I could hear prisoners shouting to other prisoners. Their voices were feeble and raspy; even so, they were all screaming and crying.

The passing soldiers were heaping things on us: shirts, jackets, cigarettes. The Americans had military police circling so we wouldn't be shot. There were still plenty of German soldiers around who'd like nothing more than to eliminate one more Jew before the war ended.

I knew the date was May 1, 1945, exactly two years after Yudel, I, and what had remained of my family had been taken to Majdanek. I knew the date because we had nothing else to dwell on except what day it was. I felt ready to cry, but I didn't have the strength to do it.

I was bewildered. I looked around at the other prisoners, all yelling and screaming and crying for happiness. As I bit into some crackers and cookies, I felt the burden of the death of my family, the people I had known who had been killed. As I looked around again, I could tell some of us were going to get to be human beings again. Others wouldn't make it. After six years, I could now say this was the end of it.

"But where will I go?" I asked myself. "Where will I go?"

Frank had run into some of his *landsmen*. We were looking for friends. We were free to look around and see who was still there, so we started running around a little bit, but the army kept on moving.

Dusk was descending, and the soldiers were handing us tins of meat. Suddenly a tall man with wide shoulders and black curly hair stepped toward me. He had a band around his arm which said *MP*.

"Don't eat this stuff; you'll get sick," he yelled, trying to use gestures to cover his mouth and to turn his head away and throw up to show us we shouldn't eat it. Our stomachs were so shriveled we couldn't digest much food. Even so, I was hungry and I ate anyhow.

"I'm a Jewish man," he said, looking directly at me. "Can you speak German? Do you understand me? Can you speak German?"

"You bet I can," I replied, in German. This man wasn't Josef Mengele. I could proudly say I spoke the language.

"Wait. Keep marching and keep your eyes on me. I'm going to make a few runs, and then I'll be back."

We began to march toward the next city, while the American soldiers were marching the other way. We were feeling so good, nothing short of a bullet would have stopped us from getting there. The MP yelled and shouted and suddenly an armored vehicle and a tank opened up a space, and the MP and his Jeep had a place in the line of march.

"Tell about six or seven of them to jump in," he yelled at me. "I'll take you to a farm in the nearest village."

A Jeep wasn't designed to hold that many people, but we didn't care. Our feet didn't have to hurt anymore.

My whole body was full of joy at being free. Our favorite sergeant stopped his Jeep at a place where the army was making pancakes. All of us jumped out of the Jeep, grabbed a pancake, then jumped back in. On the way, the sergeant explained he was a German Jew whose family had left the Fatherland when he was sixteen in 1938. He went to America and attended high school, then joined the American army.

"You don't gotta worry about a German Jew like me," he said, smiling and nodding in case we didn't understand his German. "I have a gun. A very big gun."

He certainly did. It was as big as my head. He was a tall man who kept saying, "These German people are animals for what they did to you. How can they commit such butchery?"

It was dawn. After about a half-hour, we were nearing some farms. In one of them, the lights were on and the smell of bacon, eggs, sausage, and hot rolls curled into our noses. Our MP pulled the Jeep onto the farmhouse road.

He jumped out and knocked on the door. When nobody answered, he kicked the door so hard it splintered slightly. The door opened a crack, and a nose and a pair of wide and frightened eyes peered out.

The MP stroked his enormous gun and said, in German, to the peering eyes, "Shower them and clothe them. Don't give them any fatty foods, just toast and oatmeal. No heavy food. Shave them, and give them a haircut. Give them some clothes. I will come back later and make sure you've done what I told you to do, and if you haven't, we'll kick you out of the house and let them have it."

"*Jawohl, Mein Herr,*" the eyes said.

Then the MP motioned to us to get out of the Jeep. The family was cowering in the corner when we walked in but got very busy putting breakfast in front of us. There were a mother, a father, and a fifteen-year-old boy whose blond locks and blue eyes were the model of Aryan looks. They served us farina, cereal, and toast on small plates. We'd already eaten the pancakes, so we weren't very hungry.

I was about to dive in with both hands, but I noticed the silverware next to my plate. Suddenly I remembered back to what seemed like a lifetime ago, my parents teaching me to use a knife, fork, and spoon. I stopped myself and picked up the spoon to eat. My grip was uncertain, but I knew my mother would approve. The others at the table copied my moves, and we ate the way civilized human beings do once again.

It was an uncomfortable time for everybody in the house. The family clearly was afraid and kept saying to us, "We're not so bad. We're good people. We're not Nazis."

We were bewildered. For two years we had been spat upon, beaten, shot, and starved for being what the Germans considered a pestilence. It had only been a few hours since we had been promoted to human beings again, worthy of respect, attention, and consideration. It was a difficult transition to make, to feel fully entitled to such small things as having a decent meal.

We ate small tidbits of the food they offered us. Small as the portions may have seemed to the Germans, that quantity of food in one meal had been served only to guards. For prisoners, it would have been designed to serve fifty people. We also knew too much food could make us sick. Nibbling was all we could manage.

Our next step was a shower. Most of us hadn't washed our hair in a couple of years. Personally, I think my last time was when the guards were testing the showers for the gas chamber we had just built.

While we were all waiting our turn, the husband waved to his living room and said, "Sit wherever you want." His squeaky voice betrayed his attempt at being hospitable. With several Jews in his house and his country's army defeated, no doubt he was afraid his family would be evicted from the farm and perhaps his wife would be raped. We all collapsed into a couple of sofas, and the family tried to act as though they were entertaining invited guests.

We had lots of emotions. We wondered what the Americans were going to do with us. Most of us were sick or weak. We had no idea where we would go in this strange country.

They made animals out of us. Now we're seeing the end of it, I wearily thought. I wasn't thinking about our reluctant hosts. I had no sympathy for the Germans. I just knew I was tired and weak.

When my turn came, I entered the bathroom. It was fairly primitive. There was a shower which was actually a barrel, with hot water pouring in from a pipe connected to the wall. There were also a toilet and an iron bathtub. I chose the shower. The hot water hitting my skin hurt because it had been so long since I had felt anything like it.

Washing my hair was first, because my scalp itched from all those years of accumulated grease and dirt. I felt clots of oily dirt and dandruff fall away, and my scalp could breathe once more.

We had to learn all over again how to wash ourselves the way human beings do. We each had been given a washcloth, a bar of soap, and a towel. I took a while to remember how to use them, but as the grime on my body began to slough off in clumps, I grew more accustomed to the feeling of the towel and washcloth.

After we showered, the family gave us clothing. Everything they had was huge on our wasted bodies. We could probably have worn children's sizes by that time. I could have wound the jacket I was given around myself three times. No matter how big the clothing was, it was clean, and that was a lot more than I could say for the filthy rags we'd been wearing.

We stayed there for a couple of days. We slept on couches, and one of us got to sleep in a bed that an older son had used before he left home. To us, this was luxury. The house was heated with a potbellied stove. We listened to the family's radio as the war's end was announced.

"The Fatherland is finished," the announcer said, his voice nearly breaking.

The family nodded.

"We blame Hitler. We're not Nazis, we're farmers," the father said, in a voice that almost pleaded for us to exonerate them.

We were silent.

These bastards made themselves fat and rich during the war, I thought, feeling a bitter taste down in my throat. *When the Nazis were in power, I bet all of them were yelling 'Heil Hitler' as loudly as anybody else. They ate and slept well, and they went on about their lives. Now their army has lost, and they want to think that they're just good human beings. Well, not with my help; not with the help of anybody in this room.*

The family was very friendly to us. They had to be. The MP showed up every day to see how we were being treated, and he'd always bark at them in German: "You're a cursed nation. A cursed nation. How can you do this to people who never fought a war with you?"

The family would all shrink back at his words. One day the father answered for all of them.

"We didn't do this. It was the SS, the Gestapo. It was Hitler and Goering. It wasn't us."

The sergeant's face reddened with anger.

"No, it's not right, what you did to innocent people. My family lived in Germany for generations. My family and other Jews built your country, built your houses and your cities. I'm an American Jew now. No more *deutsch*, and I'm proud of it."

He moved forward menacingly. The father manfully stepped in front of his wife and son, but all the sergeant wanted to do was yell.

"It wasn't right what you did to these people! You took away their future, their lives, their families, their homes, and their businesses!"

The parents tried to curse Hitler and tell the sergeant what good people they were. Our MP made it plain he didn't believe a bit of it.

For four consecutive mornings our MP took us to a kitchen and told the cook to make us pancakes and coffee. On the fifth day, he came to pick us up. We thought of him as a guardian angel. We hadn't had so much hope for years.

He drove us to a spot where a large and boatlike truck was standing. It was an amphibious vehicle, though we didn't know it. We thanked the sergeant by shaking his hand and hugging him, with tears in our eyes.

The truck soon coughed into action, and the driver went on a route to several different farms, picking up about thirty people. Then he crossed a river, and we looked in amazement at the water lapping the fenders as we drove to the opposite riverbank. After about a half-hour, we pulled up to a building five stories high, brick, and four hundred feet wide.

"You'll like this place," the driver told us. "It used to be a school for the SS and Gestapo. Here's where the murderers were taught to murder, the torturers were taught to torture. Now it's going to do something useful—making the victims of the Third Reich whole again."

When we got inside, we could see just how cavernous the place was. It was one huge building, with a lobby the size of the largest room I had ever seen. Hanging from the painted ceiling was a chandelier which must have been thirty feet high.

There were no mattresses, of course, nor covers or pillows. We all slept on the floor. We were used to bad sleeping conditions, and this place was like a palace to us. There were thousands of people there. A couple of days later, we were all brought blankets. We had heat, and we had food. It was three meals a day, basic food: milk, farina. Dinner was hamburgers and white bread. To us, white bread was like cake.

About my third day there, each of us was examined by a team of doctors. I was beginning to feel alive again. We had a quiet routine. We had three meals, we washed our clothes, we showered, and mostly we just gathered strength.

A week after I first arrived, there was a huge yelling and shouting and cursing in the lobby. I went running to see what it was about. With so many people in this place, there was always noise, but people didn't yell and scream at each other. We were mending. We were grateful to be alive. Who had time to yell and be miserable with our fellow sufferers?

When I ran to the lobby, there was a clot of people. I was the first one to arrive at the scene, but people soon poured in from all directions. About a dozen people surrounded a man they were kicking and beating. They spit on him, yelling, "You're a traitor. You hurt us. It was bad enough the Germans wouldn't give us food. You had to help them so you'd save yourself."

One man bellowed, "You had your way. Now you've got to pay," followed by a kick into the man's ribs, producing an audible crunching.

Others joined the chorus, screaming, "Gangster, murderer, you don't deserve to live. You're going to die here. We're going to stay alive, but you won't live to see it."

I was astonished. I knew traitors were among us, but this man must have done something horrible. I saw that most of the man's captors were Lithuanian Jews, people I had met by this time. Somebody whispered to me that the man's name was Rudy. He was a German Jew who had been a *Kapo*, and he had whipped, beaten, and even killed thousands of Lithuanian, Estonian, and Latvian Jews.

"He was the one who chased us and beat a lot of people to death, and he's a Jew," the voice said.

Rudy had come from one of the Dachau satellite camps, but he couldn't get a job there as a *Kapo*. Guys who had been in the other camp with him had spotted him. One of them told me what Rudy had done.

Rudy himself was perhaps twenty-five years old. He was five feet, ten inches, skinny, with brown hair. He looked harmless enough, but by the time they had taken him into the lobby, he was bruised and bleeding. Blood was running in streaks all over his forehead. Suddenly I recognized him from Camp 11 as a man who made fun of me and others. I could feel the anger of the original group amplified by the crowds jamming the lobby.

"You don't deserve to live. If we let you live, it's an insult to our people. Many of them are dead, and they're crying out for us to take revenge," one person yelled.

The prisoner was cringing, covering up his head with his forearm so they wouldn't kick him in the face, squatting so they wouldn't kick him in the groin, just as all of us used to do when the Nazis beat us.

"I did what they told me to do, nothing else," the prisoner shouted. He was whining now, and pleading, "I want to live. I'll change. I didn't mean to hurt so many people. Let me live, and I'll run away from here. You'll never see me again."

Suddenly someone appeared with a big coil of rope which had a noose already fashioned at one end. He whirled the other end around his head, then threw it upward at the big chandelier. The rope wrapped around it, leaving the noose suspended about ten feet off the floor.

The man was lifted up by numerous hands, and the noose dropped over his head and around his neck. He was screaming, shouting, begging. His pleas only produced more anger.

"Why should you live when you helped so many to die?" one man called out.

They all had a point, but I just couldn't watch. I'd had enough of seeing dead people. _I don't want to hear or to see whatever they've got to do, or know anything about their doing it_, I screamed inside my mind.

I walked away from the lobby to a hallway and took a walk to the other side of the building. When I returned, I saw people carrying out Rudy's corpse. I knew the terrified look on his face would be stamped in my mind forever.

Sooner or later, Hitler would have killed him anyway, I thought.

Most of the rest of my stay there was peaceful. Army doctors gave us physicals. Quite a few of the liberated prisoners died because they were so sick and weak. Frank was still there, but he wanted to leave because he had somewhere to go.

He was from Czechoslovakia and Hungary, and there were a lot of Czechs and Hungarians there. He stayed with them, and he found girls he knew from home. He spent more and more time with them, less and less with me. Sooner or later, we had to break up. We lived in different worlds. I tried to find some Polish _landsmen_, but there weren't many.

I was there for about ten days. The officials told us this was a place for a short stay, but they would help us as much as they could. If we wanted someplace to stay longer, we could go to one of Hitler's work camps, where we could have access to doctors, bedding, and food. Or we could go into the cities such as Stuttgart or Munich. The Germans were being forced to take us into their houses, and we would get a ration card and food from German stores.

About two weeks later, I heard a lot of survivors were heading to Munich. I wanted to go, too. We were told about a place there where we could locate a camp or find places to take us in.

"Go make a new life," one of the officials said to me.

Standing outside the gate, a chill ran through me. I realized I had nowhere to go.

I have no money, no job, no life to go back to, I thought. *What am I going to do? Why me? I was born at a bad time. I'm like a branch which has fallen off a tree.*

Still, I wanted to get to wherever I was going. But as I passed through the gates, I stopped, and I started to cry.

"Where will I go?" I called out. "Who is there? Who am I? I have no friends, no relatives, no home, no country. What kind of life do I have to go back to?"

My only answer was the wind.

Epilogue

Shortly after I was liberated in May 1945, I started to work for the U.S. Army in Munich. I had approached the army about working for them, and I was told that if I wanted to help the cook at 4:00 A.M., they could find a place for me to sleep and I could eat there, too. From there, I helped the army locate German weapons outside small towns. I could speak German, and so I would accompany the U.S. soldiers and translate for them, asking the local Germans to help them find German military weapons which had been stashed in various places around the countryside.

In exchange for that help, I and five or six other Polish Jews and Gentiles were allowed to march and drill with the soldiers, to make us physically fit. We had heard several rumors. One was that the American Army was soon to be sent to the Pacific to fight Japan. Another was that some Polish soldiers had taken up arms for the British. We hoped that the U.S. Army's letting us sleep in their barracks, work in their kitchen, and march with their soldiers, meant that they would take us to Japan with them, allowing us to become American soldiers and achieve American citizenship—if we survived the war.

I had to earn my keep, though. I spent three months washing potatoes, mopping floors, and doing whatever else required doing in the army kitchen. While I was there, Abe Blady, one of the men I saved by getting him a job on the ramp, found me. I was thrilled to see him. At least I'd have one friend from my old life.

In July, I asked the army for permission to go back to my hometown, Miedzyrzec, in Poland. I was about 650 miles from there, and I sorely wanted to see what had become of my city and my people. Abe went with me.

I took the trip largely sprawled on the roofs of Russian freight trains. Usually I was on top of the locomotive. There were many Russians and their girlfriends taking some legs of the same trip I was. The trains carried tanks and other armored vehicles, so we all piled on top of the train cars, then spread-eagled so we wouldn't fall off. The trains accelerated in a shower of black smoke and soot.

The trip from Munich to Nuremberg took a day and a half. Then Abe and I straddled another locomotive, which arrived near the Polish border. Finally, we arrived at my hometown in the middle of the night, on the back of yet another train.

We had heard other Jews were still around. The night was chilly, and we wound up in what had been part of the ghetto. We heard clucking and discovered a chicken coop. Because it was so cold, Abe and I climbed in to sleep with the chickens. Even though there were plenty of feathers and chicken dung droppings, the chickens' bodies were warm insulation against the chill.

In the morning, we went out to look for Jews. We headed straight for the marketplace, or what was left of it. We figured that if there would by any kind of central gathering place, that would be it. The last time I'd seen the marketplace was when I was being loaded onto the train for Majdanek. Now, there was a pitifully small band of people, perhaps two hundred, living near there.

I saw two of the barrel makers who had been with me when Lazar saved us from execution. They were living in a nice place. Amazingly, I spotted Jacob Wilder; Jacob had remarried. He was liberated six months before we were, but he was in bad shape. A few weeks before I arrived, he had been cleaning a gun which, though he didn't know it, was loaded. The gun went off and made a hole right above his top lip. The bullet was still lodged in his head.

Jacob and I hugged, talked, and cried. We were emotionally shaky, because we'd both heard that Polish Fascists still were roaming the countryside killing Jews. That night, I slept at the house of the two barrel makers. As soon as my head sank onto the pillow, it hit a metal object. Under the pillow I found a submachine gun.

"As soon as they knock on the door, start shooting. Otherwise they'll kill you," the barrel makers told me. Later, they told me they had submachine guns under their pillows, too.

The next day, I went looking for the grave of my brother Hymie. When I arrived at the cemetery, I almost clutched my heart. I saw row upon row of mass graves, with little signs, maybe twenty inches long and ten inches high, sunk into each trench. Each sign told only what year the bodies had been buried, nothing more.

I looked and looked at the now-peaceful earth, but I couldn't figure out where Hymie was. I gave up in despair, then walked back to the marketplace. Our town officially had perhaps sixteen thousand people before the war. I looked around at the pitifully small number living there now. A little less than half the current residents were Jews whom Germans had uprooted from elsewhere and dumped into our town to die. The rest, maybe 120, were all that remained of the thriving town we had been before the war.

I had only a ten-day pass, and soon it was time to return to the army. Jacob begged me to stay.

"Joe, we're family. We're so few here. It's so late. Wait here, we'll go to Germany. I've got a small piece of property to sell. When I do, we'll go," he told me, his eyes pleading.

The barrel makers, too, implored me to stay, but I spurned them all. I had family in America, and I wasn't about to stay in this pitiful wreck of a place.

"I promised the army I'd return. I have to go back. I've got an obligation. I'm not screwing it up. I've got a chance to go to the United States," I told them. I truly wanted to get to America.

"They'll take you anytime," Jacob said.

"No, it's now or never," I replied.

Jacob and I hugged, tears streaming down our faces, flashes of those long, cold nights in the bunkers he had built running through our minds. I thought of my mother, my father, my brothers and sister, Yudel, and Yudel's daughters and their children. Jacob and I trembled at the memories. Then we stopped hugging and said good-bye. Abe and I left.

I heard a couple of years later that Jacob moved out of Poland to Austria to escape the anti-Semites. A few years after that, he died from an infection caused by the bullet in his head.

Abe and I hopped a train to a German border town. We were going into a restaurant when two Polish army MPs stopped us.

"Where are you going? Who are you?" they demanded. Then they threatened to conscript us into the Polish army. We saw a nearby train slowing, so we ran several blocks and jumped on it. We could see the bewildered Polish MPs looking around for us as the train accelerated and we were away.

Then we arrived in Czechoslovakia, where a middle-aged guard threatened to jail us and take us to court. I whispered to Abe that we would split up. Abe would run to the train station and I would have the guard chase me. The plan worked exactly as I thought it would. I ran, the guard got winded, I doubled back, and Abe and I hopped another train.

We soon arrived back at the base, and I again began training with the Americans, hoping they would take me with them to Japan.

Then, suddenly, the war was over.

What will I do now? I thought.

I was back in the same spot as I was when I was liberated. I had no job, no family, no home, no money, no future. I certainly didn't want to stay in Germany for the rest of my life. I hated every inch of it. Even today, I feel that, for the most part, the Germans are a country of murderers, and even the young people now cannot escape from the responsibilities of what their people tried to do to humanity.

I decided I could go to Israel or America. I applied for America because my uncle in Detroit would be my sponsor, and I had several other relatives there. I was told it would be a couple of years before my name turned up on the list. In the meantime, I had to survive.

My uncle strengthened my hope by sending packages and letters and built up my morale all the time I was there. Still, I needed to find a job. I got one with a Munich Jewish relief center which worked under the United Nations. I was a driver, delivering food to refugee camps. I also was required to go to school to learn how to be a mechanic. Once I completed the course, I officially worked for the UN as a mechanic.

The pay wasn't much, and I needed to supplement it. Ironically, I ended up doing a lot of odd jobs for Germans. What could I do? I had to make a living. As much as I detested them, I had to do work for the Germans in order to pay my bills. To my astonishment, some of them turned out to be fairly nice people. I made friends with one. He had been a soldier; his father had been a Nazi. The son took over his father's business—as a former Nazi, the father was somehow barred from owning businesses—and I did a lot of jobs for the son, including delivery work, cement mixing, and all kinds of repairs. I was struck by the irony of my having a friendly relationship with the son of a Nazi. Still, the son was a decent person, and I had to survive.

I kept asking people whether they knew anyone from Miedzyrzec. I found Elke, a woman I had known there living in a camp about forty miles away. I took her some food and cigarettes from the PX, along with chickens and turkey. We married in June 1947. Though I didn't know it at the time, getting married was to set back my American plans by a couple of years because I had to reapply for admission so my application would include Elke. I didn't begrudge the extra years, because I was alone and I was lonely and depressed. She brightened my life.

In the meantime, I also made friends with a German policeman in Munich. I bought PX cigarettes for him. In exchange, his wife, whose name I don't remember, helped us. She was a real estate agent and found Elke and myself a studio apartment. It was only about 450 square feet, but it was more than a lot of other people had in that overpopulated city. The next year, the fight for Israel was on, and she helped me find apartments for people I met who had been shot up in that war. I knew people who were missing arms, legs, and sometimes even the will to live.

Two years later, in January 1949, I got the letter I'd been hoping for. My uncle told me he'd received word that we could now leave for America. We had accumulated almost nothing, knowing full well we'd be departing for the United States. All we took was a few pieces of clothing, like most of the other refugees.

We climbed aboard a crowded boat and crossed the ocean in eight days. We were on the *Ernie Pyle*, which ordinarily was a liner for American officers. There weren't any officers going back and forth, so Jewish refugees were its cargo instead.

We landed in New York City, then traveled all night by train to reach Detroit, where my uncle and the rest of my family met us. My uncle had lined up an apartment with cheap rent.

For a year, I did odd jobs. I painted, welded, and worked in a donut shop. Then I found a full-time job as a house painter. Eighteen months later I was the company foreman. Eighteen months after that, I started my own painting company. We had two children. Sid was born in in 1951 and Marla in 1957.

Eventually, I had seventy-two people working for me and was designated the best painting contractor in Detroit by the municipal and state agencies, as well as the labor unions. I hired people nobody else would hire: refugees who couldn't speak English and people who'd been productive workers but who had been injured on the job.

I painted and built houses for many years. In the late 1970s, Elke contracted crippling arthritis. It was a bad time in Detroit. Most kinds of work were drying up, so not many people were building or buying houses. It was a good time to move.

The doctors said Elke needed a warm climate away from the glacial winds of Detroit. We moved to Florida in 1981. I couldn't sit still, of course, so I started another painting company and had more than seventy employees. I mentioned to people only a few things about my past under the Nazis: working for Mengele and building Birkenau. I also would say a few things about my family and my city and how they were wiped out. A professor I knew kept nudging me to write my story. Another friend who loves listening to Holocaust stories urged me, too.

I still didn't talk much about my experiences to most people. Even Elke and my children didn't know most of it. Then I started to think. I decided I no longer had the the luxury of time. I wasn't an old man, but I was in my late sixties. Finally, I decided I'd do it: I was going to write my book. The professor worked with me for a while, but then he became ill.

I was ill, too. I didn't want to relive these memories. I didn't want to talk about them. But I also wanted to get this project over with. Once you start a project like that, you just want to get it out of your system and out of your mind.

Elke, Sid, and Marla, though they didn't know most of the details, still pressed me to finish. They didn't ask me for the specifics, and I still didn't tell them. I especially didn't want to tell my children, who I felt might be damaged severely by knowing the horrible things I had seen. I have only one photograph showing most of the members of my family, but I've only shown it briefly to my children. Every time I talked about the now-dead relatives, my children would get upset. Then I'd get upset. It was just too painful.

"You'd be too upset. Better I don't start," I would tell them.

When I finished the proposal for this book, I showed it to Elke, Sid, and Marla. Sid couldn't stand to read it. I remember when he was eight years old and came home one day from school wailing, "Why don't I have grandparents like all the other kids?" All I could tell him then was, "Someday you'll know." Maybe someday he will read the whole story. For now, it is too painful for him.

My daughter, on the other hand, read every word of the proposal. Then she called and yelled at me for not telling her what I had been through.

"Why didn't you tell me? Why? Why?" she screamed.

My answer was simple and practical.

"I have nightmares. Why should you?"

Still, she wants to know. Someday soon I will show her the whole book, not just the proposal.

Once I completed the manuscript, I gave it to Elke. She started reading and she was speechless. Then she asked lots of questions. Then she cried, and cried, and cried.

She'd had no idea of what I'd been through. Her father had worked in the leather factory, the only factory left open in my town. Even though she was Jewish, she had eaten fairly well and hadn't been touched by most of the harshness. All I could tell her was that I'd had the worst of luck to go through what I went through, and I'd had the best of luck to survive.

About halfway through reading the manuscript, she had wanted to stop. She was upset to the point of paralysis after reading about Mengele's operating on me and the pus pouring out of my wounds. "You have to do it. You have to keep reading," I quietly told her.

After she had read it all, after she had asked her questions and cried her tears, she said, "If I'd known what it was about, if I'd known it was this tough, maybe I wouldn't have read it at all."

I could see it in her eyes. I could see the pain she felt for all the hunger and torture I had endured.

Two pieces of unfinished business remain. One is with the Zbanski family. Two sisters of the three brothers are still alive and now live in my old city of Miedzyrzec.

One of them recently called me. "We have something here for you, but we can't send it through the mails," she said.

I knew my mother had given the Zbanskis our family valuables for safekeeping all those years ago. I went to Poland to see her and the other members of the family. I knew that if they actually had my mother's jewels, I probably would break into tears. Even if they didn't, just seeing several generations of the family who sheltered me from the Nazis would be enough to make me cry. I knew I would be glad to see them, and that I would be overwhelmed at the sight of them.

I visited Poland, accompanied by my friend Mark Schwartz, to see the Zbankis and revisit some of the death camps where I lived. I had made such a trip right after the war and another five years ago, but they were brief. This time, I went for nearly two weeks. I was thrilled at the idea of seeing the Zbanskis again. I had a jumble of feelings about seeing Majdanek and Auschwitz-Birkenau. I felt guilt, hate, triumph, and bitterness, and many more emotions as well.

I have been in touch with many of the Zbanski family over the years, sending them money when there seemed to be a need. They had, after all, saved my life. I owe the family more than I could ever repay, and I sent them as much as I could.

Most of the family had died. Kazimier, the daughter the grandmother had wanted me to marry, had married someone else and was still living nearby. Marian, her brother, still lives on the farm, though it's not much of a farm anymore. He sold all the livestock and now has only six pigs remaining. The walls of the buildings are weatherbeaten and worn, and many of them lean slightly because they are in such disrepair. So is the rest of it: barn doors are off their hinges, old boards are piled up everywhere, the barn is crumbling, and pieces of machinery sit on the ground in silence.

I learned something that made me sad and yet happy at the same time. The farm family next door to the Zbanskis, the ones who had been gunned down by the Germans for allowing an escaped Russian prisoner to work on their farm, was finally at peace. I had heard that the bodies of the three dead family members had been buried at the farm, which had been abandoned since the executions. Two daughters who had not been home at the time the Germans struck were the only ones left alive. Only a few weeks before I arrived, fifty years after the death of the rest of their family, the two daughters had the bodies exhumed and moved across the road, where they had created their own cemetery: just the three graves, and three large crosses surrounded by baskets of flowers, nothing more.

By the time I arrived, the flowers had all wilted, and only a few petals remained. I thought about how close I had come to being killed along with them. Had I arrived a minute earlier, my grave would have been in that lonely, desolate spot as well, and there would be no parties for me, and hardly anybody would care who I was.

But, fifty-five years later, I was alive and among friends. Marian threw a small party for me, along with his son. Just the two of them, Mark and I, and the driver we'd hired to take us where we needed to go. Kazimier had two parties for me. Her husband is a very well-known architect and engineer, and they are doing well. Her first party was a whiskey-and-buffet affair, to which she invited her own three children and her grandchildren. The second party was a really big bash, to which she invited the whole family and some friends, including a man who is a goodwill ambassador between Poland and Israel. He gave me the name of a man in Israel to see.

The party had lots of drink, food, noise, and toasts. It made me feel welcome in a land where I no longer live. The Zbanskis are my Polish family now. I have no one else there.

I don't even have a hometown. The Miedzyrzec I knew is gone, most of it destroyed in one way or another. Now, much of it has been rebuilt. Our driver took us over all over town. We saw the streets, the shops, and I saw only one building I recognized: the post office where a German postmaster hid us for three days. The irony of my being there washed over me. If not for that German's sheltering me and the other kids, I would not be alive to see how little of the old Miedzyrzec remains. I shivered when I was there. People have no idea that the post office is a monument to the courage of one sympathetic German and the children he hid in the attic. The woods where I hid with the Russian partisans is still there, but much of it has been cut down. What remains is filled with wild pigs, and I didn't dare go in.

As for whatever the Zbanski family was holding for me, I could not find out. Kazimier's sister is the one who called me, and she was ill all during the time I was there. She has no phone, and I didn't feel right imposing myself on a sick person. Kazimier has said she will look into it, and I will have to wait until I hear from her. I tried giving her money to pay for the party she threw for me, but she refused. "Thank God, we are doing well enough," she told me.

When I visited Majdanek, I saw the crematorium and I saw the barracks, lots of barracks. I went to the gauntlet area, where I and the others were forced to run many, many yards while our bodies were being pierced by the points on nail-studded sticks. A wave of memories struck me harder than any of the nails ever had. I remembered the cries, the screams, the beatings, and the blood. It makes me sick to my stomach to see Majdanek, and I wish it would all be destroyed. But it has to be kept standing so the new generation can see it. Otherwise, they might never believe that such a horror could actually exist. I stood in front of my old barracks, Number 46. Its drab and ugly boards seem largely intact, and a small blue padlock keeps the doors closed to visitors. It's just as well. I didn't want to look inside.

Visiting Auschwitz-Birkenau, however, was bittersweet. People saw the tattooed number on my forearm and stopped to ask me questions. They wanted me to talk to the priests, the groups, all the schoolchildren who had congregated there that day. I did my best to oblige a little, but I had my personal business to take care of. Though most of the barracks have been destroyed, a few remain. One of them is Number 8, my old barracks. I stared at its boards. Some are very new, inserted into the structure when the old boards had rotted away. But many of the old boards remain, dark, dirty, dingy, stripped of luster and of dignity, just as we were.

Inside was my old bunk, sitting on top of floorboards that had so much space between them you could get your foot caught if you weren't careful. Mine was a middle bunk, and I put my arm up on it to rest. The bittersweet feeling rose in my throat. I felt bitter because of what I went through. I felt sweet because I'm still here, and I am somebody.

I wish I could have my mother and father here. They wanted me to make something of myself. I wish they were here to see me now. But they're not, and I feel sad and depressed that they and almost all my brothers and sisters are gone. Only Sara survived. But I still have my wife, my children, and my grandchildren. Life has been good to me, I thought.

Oddly, perhaps the most repulsive part of being there was seeing the toilets. The dinginess, the struggle to keep myself clean with the smallest chips of soap and used razor blades, even when the Germans were doing their best to make us feel like animals, all those pictures came back to me.

How can life be so ugly, and where I live, life is so beautiful? I was nobody here. I felt as though I wasn't even 10 percent of a human being there. And now, I have businesses, a wife, children, grandchildren. I am loved and I am somebody, I thought.

Then Mark and I flew to Israel. There, I went to find the person whom the goodwill ambassador between Poland and Israel had told me to see. He is Dr. Shmuel Krakowski, former director and now senior adviser to the Yad Vashem Archives, a repository of much Holocaust material. He had written articles about Miedzyrzec, and he questioned me endlessly about details, about when the ramp was built, and when the selections were. Part of our conversation was eerie: The Germans had caught him near the end of the war and shipped him on one of the death trains to the Birkenau ramp at night. I probably helped to unload him.

We enjoyed our discussion, and the next day he called me and said he was sending over two people with recording equipment. "This is the way we have to do it," he said, insisting that I talk for their camera and describe what my life had been like then.

A man and woman came over and unpacked their camera gear. I spent three and a half hours with them, and, I'm almost ashamed to admit, I did break down once. That was when I was recalling how I took my family food from the Zbanski farm during the last two years I worked there. By that time, my family had run out of money, they had run out of clothing to trade, they had run out of most things. Their world was caving in.

Then, when I went home with my sack of food, I saw the look on their faces, which were so pale, so gaunt, so lined with worry and fear. Seeing the sad, pathetic hope that lit up their dull eyes when I gave them those sacks of food made me cringe inside. I took them so little, but it meant so much. Here I was, a teenaged boy, doing what my father couldn't do, doing what my mother couldn't do. I was the member of the household who kept the whole family alive, and it hurt me to see them so helpless, so afraid, and so desperate.

Remembering all of this sadness was what made me break down during the interviews. I sobbed and sobbed. I put my hands over my eyes, then heard myself making animal noises that I had never heard come out of my mouth. But the pain of recalling how thin and pathetic they looked, how I worked so hard to keep them alive, and how the Nazi bastards won in the end, how they killed them all except Sara and me—all those feelings and memories hammering at me cracked open my composure and my sadness and despair came rushing out, freed after all these years.

The next day I left Israel and returned to my home. It had done me a lot of good to go to Poland to see the graves in my hometown and to look for the place where Hymie is buried. It's a *mitzvah*, a good deed, to visit the dead in cemeteries. I feel I did a good deed to go and see all those people who have died and to try to find Hymie's grave.

People often ask me several questions. One is how I survived. I know some of the reasons. When I was in Birkenau and working every day for Mengele, everybody said I was clean and neat. Even Mengele, when he talked with the three doctors who followed him around, said so. Mengele was happy with me because I knew what to do, and he didn't have to tell me twice—and he especially liked my being clean and neat. I also had blond hair and blue eyes, so when he looked at me, Jewish or not, he saw a vision of the master race he hoped to create to rule the world. And when I got sick, the fact that I was in the underground saved me. I know Father arranged for Mengele's operation on me because I saw him leave Mengele's office just before he told me to report to the hospital.

There were a lot of ingredients in my staying alive while others perished: I tried to survive for just another day. I did what I had to do. I'd hide, wash dishes, steal a wheelbarrow and pretend to have a job, whatever it took. I knew I was going to die, but I figured, let me give it a try. I kept telling my friends, "You have plenty of time to die. Now is the time to live. And don't kill yourself. It's against Jewish law to commit suicide. There's always hope."

They told me I was immature and childish, but I am here, and many of them are not. I thank God every day for having lived through it. I figure one escape from death is a coincidence. Two times is a coincidence. But if it happens three times, you have to have a little ingenuity, some luck and some divine intervention on your side. God said, "You try to help yourself and I'll help you. You don't try, I can't help you."

I tried. I know that my being born with blond hair and blue eyes was a stroke of luck. My being clean and neat was simply what my parents taught me. I left a good taste in people's mouth by being nice, by being a gentleman, and by not being greedy. I didn't care so much about myself, but about other people.

Apparently God cared a lot more about me than he did about many others. That's why, when people ask me whether I believe in God after all I've been through, I tell them: "For me, yes. For other people, no." I didn't believe in God before, but now I do—but only for me. I saw too many good people die for no damned good reason to believe God was interested in looking out for them.

Do I feel guilty that I survived? Yes, emphatically yes. It lives with me every day, like a small, evil man whispering inside my mind. The people I saw die were as good as I am; maybe some were better. They tried in their own way to survive and I tried my way. Basically, I had luck, ingenuity and brains, and the heart to make it through. I'm no better or worse than most of the ones who are gone. But I'm here and they're not.

I'm proud of the fact that after I went through the war years I made something of myself. I'm especially proud that when I had a large contracting company, even when times were tough, when the union sent me people who had been permanently injured, or immigrants came to me and said nobody else would hire them, I found a place for them. They had no life, no destiny, but they came into my shop and I made productive people out of them. I gave them a job, social security, a pension, hospitalization. Many of them went on to become doctors, lawyers, and other professional people. One of them is still working for me after thirty-eight years. When men were injured, I collected five dollars from each worker and the workers would labor an extra half hour. I gave all that money to the families of the injured workers.

A lot of people told me that I was too generous, that I was doing what I shouldn't do, that I was a little guy with a big heart. A lot of people said I should be a big guy with a small heart. I don't think so. That's not my nature, and I'm not about to change now.

But there is one more piece of business from more than half a century ago that I must attend to. Simon Fleishbein, the boy who climbed out of the cart filled with the bloody corpses of my brother Hymie and the others who were gunned down at the lumberyard, the boy who played dead but was only wounded, now lives no more than ten miles from me. I see him at Holocaust survivor events every now and again. I know he still has the bullet in him from that night.

Though I have seen Simon many times, I have never told him I was there the day he climbed out of the cart while covered with blood—his own mixed with Hymie's and all the others—and limped away.

299

Someday after this book is published, I will take him a copy. Then we will sit down and I will tell him what I saw. It will be a time when we relive with each other a scene we both wish had never been. It will be a moment that will pierce both our emotions. It is a moment whose coming will thrill me, and that I dread.

About the Authors

JOE ROSENBLUM was born in Miedzyrzec, Poland, a town slowly strangled to death by the Nazis. Though Joe lost most of his family in the Holocaust, he saved numerous other people as well as himself through almost unflagging optimism, luck and ingenuity. He endured three death camps and a death march. After being liberated, Joe worked in Germany for a couple of years before immigrating to the United States, where he has flourished in the building and painting business. Joe remains in contact with several of the people mentioned in this book and continues to run several family businesses.

DAVID KOHN is a freelance writer who has been in the writing business for 25 years. He has worked in various capacities on several books. As a versatile coauthor, ghostwriter and editor, David has worked on book topics ranging from medicine to magic to memoirs.